Guilty Until Proven Innocent

A Practitioner's and Judge's Guide to the Pennsylvania Post-Conviction Relief Act (PCRA)

by J. Andrew Salemme, Esq.

Copyright 2017 J. Andrew Salemme

All rights reserved

Cover Design by Alexis Dean

www.pcralaw.com

License Statement

The text of this publication may not be reproduced or transmitted in any form or by any means, electronic or mechanical, without the prior written permission of the author, except the sample orders, provisions of the criminal rules and statutes and their comments, and insubstantial cited-quoted portions of the content. Purchaser shall not sell or license the content in any manner. Purchaser may distribute insubstantial cited-quoted portions of the content, insofar as it is included within the purchaser's own legal research and related work, otherwise purchaser is prohibited from distributing the content. The information contained herein does not constitute legal advice with respect to a particular set of facts or circumstances and speaks only to the date that research and writing was completed.

Dedication

To Aiden and Zachary, may you always seek to do what is right and just in whatever endeavor you pursue.

Acknowledgements

This work would not have been possible if not for my friends and colleagues. A special thanks to Michael C. Cruny, Esq. for encouraging me to start this book while we were young attorneys working as law clerks so that he would have less research to do on the PCRA matters that flooded into chambers. In all seriousness, however, I thank all of those individuals who took the time to review the first edition of this work and offer much needed edits and suggestions, especially: Maureen Harvey, Esq., Josh Camson, Esq., and Albert Veverka, Esq. Also, thank you to Marissa Bluestine, Esq. for her kind suggestions regarding the original edition of this work.

Further, an enormous debt of gratitude is owed to Judge Mary Jane Bowes whose tutelage allowed me to continually gain invaluable experience and knowledge and helped my writing skills improve daily. I would be remiss in forgetting to mention Wendy Taylor, Esq., and Michael Payne, Esq., who along with Maureen Harvey, Esq. consistently offered important insights into the law all while being willing to lend an ear to my legal rants and challenging my own views.

In addition, I thank those defense attorneys, prosecutors, judges, and *pro se* petitioners who have offered limited praise for earlier efforts, imperfect as those editions were, thereby encouraging me to sharpen and improve this work. Lastly, I continue to thank my beautiful wife for her enduring patience with me as I attempted to refine earlier renditions of this work. I love you Victoria.

Table of Contents

Introduction	12
Brief History	14
Chapter 1: 42 Pa.C.S. § 9542 Scope of the PCRA	16
A. Sole Means of Relief: *Habeas Corpus* and *Coram Nobis*	16
B. Collateral Consequences	21
C. Innocence	36
D. Limitation of Remedies	37
Chapter 2: 42 Pa.C.S. § 9543 Eligibility for Relief	39
A. Eligibility for Relief: Generally	41
B. Cognizability: Previous Litigation and Waiver	42
C. Cognizability: PCRA Relief not Limited to Claims Impacting the Truth-Determining Process	45
Chapter 3: 42 Pa.C.S. § 9543(a)(2)(i) Constitutional Violations	49
Chapter 4: 42 Pa.C.S. § 9543(a)(2)(ii) Ineffective Assistance of Counsel	54
A. ***Strickland/Pierce*** Test	54
B. ***Commonwealth v. Pierce***, 527 A.2d 973 (Pa. 1987) and "Actual Prejudice"	56
C. ***Strickland/Pierce*** and the Ineffectiveness Test on Direct Appeal and PCRA Review	59

Table of Contents

D. Deferring Claims of Ineffective Assistance of Counsel into the PCRA Process	62
E. The *Holmes* Exception	67
F. *Grant* and the Cognizability Problem	73
G. *Grant* and the Elimination of Layered Claims	75
H. *Grant's* Constitutional Implications	76
Chapter 5: 42 Pa.C.S. § 9543(a)(2)(ii) Common Ineffective Assistance of Counsel Issues	81
A. *Per Se* Ineffectiveness Claims	81
B. Layered Claims: *McGill* and *Hall*	90
C. Failure to Call a Witness	93
D. Prosecutorial Misconduct During Argument	96
E. Withdrawal of Guilty Plea	98
F. Discretionary Sentencing	100
G. Mitigation During Death Penalty Phase	103
H. *Batson* Claims	105
I. Failure to File Suppression Motion	108
J. Diminished Capacity or Insanity Defenses	110
K. Conflict of Interest	111
L. *Mills* Claim	112
M. *Simmons* Instruction	114
N. Jury Instruction Ineffectiveness Claims	114
O. Other Common Claims	116

Table of Contents

P. Cumulative Claims	118
Chapter 6: Section 9543(a)(2)(iii) & Section 9543(a)(2)(iv) Plea of Guilty Unlawfully Induced and Governmental Interference	120
A. Pleading Innocence	120
B. Section 9543(a)(2)(iv) and Governmental Interference	121
Chapter 7: Section 9543(a)(2)(vi)-(viii) After-Discovered Evidence, Sentences that Exceed the Lawful Maximum, and Proceedings in a Tribunal without Jurisdiction	123
A. *Brady* Claims	123
B. Non-*Brady* After-Discovered Evidence Claims	126
C. Sentences that Exceed the Lawful Maximum	127
D. Proceedings in a Tribunal without Jurisdiction	129
Chapter 8: Section 9543(b) Prejudicial Delay	132
Chapter 9: Section 9543.1 Post-Conviction DNA Testing	136
Chapter 10: Section 9544 Previous Litigation and Waiver	145
Chapter 11: Section 9545 Jurisdiction and Proceedings	151
A. Original Jurisdiction	153
B. Timeliness and Jurisdiction	154
C. Second or Subsequent Petitions	159
D. Timeliness Exceptions	161
E. New Rule of Law and Retroactive Effect	168
F. Evidentiary Hearing	174

Table of Contents

G. Attorney-Client Privilege	175
Chapter 12: Section 9546 Relief and Order	176
Chapter 13: Pa.R.Crim.P. 900 Scope and Notice in Death Penalty Case	178
Chapter 14: Pa.R.Crim.P. 901 Initiation of Post-Conviction Collateral Proceedings	182
Chapter 15: Pa.R.Crim.P. 902 Content of Petition; Discovery Requests	185
A. Filing an Amended Petition	191
B. *Turner/Finley* No-Merit Letters	194
C. Discovery	200
Chapter 16: Pa.R.Crim.P. 903 Docketing and Assignment	203
Chapter 17: Pa.R.Crim.P. 904 Appointment of Counsel/Right to Counsel	207
A. Appointment of Counsel/Right to Counsel	212
B. Ineffectiveness of PCRA Counsel	217
C. Hybrid Representation and Allegations of PCRA Counsel's Ineffectiveness after the Filing of a Brief on Appeal	238
Chapter 18: Pa.R.Crim.P. 905 Amendment and Withdrawal of Petition	242
A. Leave to Amend	243
B. Amendments and Defective Petitions	246
Chapter 19: Pa.R.Crim.P. 906 Answer to Petition	250
Chapter 20: Pa.R.Crim.P. 907 Disposition Without Hearing (Notice of Intent to Dismiss)	254

Table of Contents

Chapter 21: Pa.R.Crim.P. 908 Hearing	267
Chapter 22: Pa.R.Crim.P. 909 Procedures for Petitions in Death Penalty Cases: Stays of Execution of Sentence; Hearing; Disposition	272
Chapter 23: Pa.R.Crim.P. 910 Final Order	283
Chapter 24: Standard and Scope of Review on Appeal	287
Chapter 25: A Brief Word on Juvenile Matters	289
Chapter 26: Summary & Checklists	292
Chapter 27: Closing Remarks	303

Samples

A. Order Appointing Counsel	306
B. Sample PCRA Questionairre for Client	307
C. Non-Capital Amended PCRA Petition	309
D. Witness Certifications	312
E. *Turner/Finley* No-Merit Letter	315
F. Petition to Withdraw	321
G. Order Allowing Counsel to Withdraw	322
H. Letter to Client about Request to Withdraw before PCRA court	323
I. Letter to Client about Request to Withdraw before Superior Court	324
J. Petition to Withdraw before Superior Court	325
K. Letter to Client	326
L. Pa.R.Crim.P. 907 Notice of Intent to Dismiss Orders/Opinions (3)	328

Table of Contents

M. Final Order	348
N. Notice of Appeal	349
O. Pa.R.A.P. 1925(a) Opinion	350
P. Appellant's Brief	356
Q. Appellee's Brief	374
R. *Turner/Finley* Brief	382

Statutes

PCRA Statute	391
Capital Unitary Review Act (Suspended)	410
Post-Conviction Hearing Act (1966)	417
Law Reviews and Articles	423
Quick Index/Case References	424

About the Author

Mr. Salemme is currently in private practice and works for The Lindsay Law Firm, P.C., which is located in Butler, Pennsylvania. He has represented numerous individuals pursuing PCRA relief, including having served as PCRA conflict counsel in Washington County, Pennsylvania. He previously worked for the Honorable Mary Jane Bowes of the Pennsylvania Superior Court, assisting in the drafting of both unpublished and published decisions. He was the 2007 first place winner of the nationwide National Rifle Association law student writing contest and served as an associate comment editor for the Duquesne Law Review, graduating *cum laude*. He earned a Bachelor of Arts degree in History from Susquehanna University where he played baseball and graduated *magna cum laude*. He enjoys coaching his son Aiden in baseball and soccer. He is a self-taught guitar player (limited in skill) and resides in Pittsburgh, Pennsylvania with his wife, Victoria, and sons, Aiden and Zachary.

Introduction

The original edition of this work was first conceived as I began work as a law clerk at the trial level and began to encounter numerous petitions filed by state prisoners claiming that they should be released from prison because the following documents were unconstitutional: the entire Pennsylvania Constitution, the Pennsylvania Crimes Code, and the Pennsylvania Rules of Criminal Procedure. These writs of *habeas corpus* continually appeared, sometimes handwritten, sometimes typed, along with the more familiar PCRA petition. As I poured through the voluminous cases dealing with post-conviction relief, I began to wonder why so little comprehensive discussion appeared on the subject.

Despite the outstanding work done by Professor Thomas M. Place, I found that a critical look at the Post-Conviction Relief Act in Pennsylvania and the cases interpreting it was still largely lacking. Moreover, as I advanced in my career and began working on the Pennsylvania Superior Court, I noticed that attorneys and even judges were largely unfamiliar with the rules and law applicable to post-conviction practice. This unfamiliarity, and sometimes lack of attention, frequently caused delays and inconsistent decision making. This work is intended not only as a guide to judges, law clerks, and practitioners, but also is designed to offer critical analysis of an area of law that often times remains confounding.

As with many areas of the law, I believe it is imperative to begin with an understanding of the applicable statute and rules of procedure. Accordingly, I have organized this work around both the PCRA statute and the germane rules of criminal procedure. The answers to many of the questions an attorney or judge may have relative to the PCRA process can be answered by simply referring to the pertinent statute and rules. The remainder of the work focuses on the current state of the case law, offers a

Introduction

limited critique of some areas of the law, makes suggestions to practitioners in developing areas of the law, and perhaps will provide the impetus for constructive thought on how to improve the post-conviction process in Pennsylvania.

I have chosen not to utilize endnotes for citations to cases for this work as I hope it will serve as a quick reference guide for those interested in the post-conviction process. I have found that going back and forth from pages to citations can sometimes prove distracting. As such, I have utilized the method of citation employed in legal opinions and I have cited to select cases within the body of the work. In addition, I have refrained from the frequent use of citation shorthand such as *supra* and *id*.

This book, however, should not serve as a replacement for old-fashioned legal research. Rather, it provides a starting point for the necessary research that must be conducted. As most attorneys are aware, a case may turn on the precise facts therein. Reading the applicable law for the intricacies of the case and being able to distinguish the facts from your own case may prove to be the key to your case whether you are a prosecutor or a defense attorney. Similarly, judges and clerks can more carefully analyze a particular matter and be able to analogize and distinguish the law by closely examining applicable cases.

In this version, I have made minor typographical corrections to the 2016 edition, and included updated citations to new cases. I hope the reader will find this edition an improved version of its predecessors as well as a useful practical resource and a catalyst for reasoned debate on a neglected area of the law.

Brief History

The Pennsylvania General Assembly passed the Post-Conviction Relief Act, commonly known as the PCRA, in 1988. The PCRA significantly amended its predecessor, the Post-Conviction Hearing Act, or PCHA. The legislature enacted the PCHA in 1966 in order to create a comprehensive method of collateral review after the Pennsylvania Supreme Court called for action in the area of post-conviction matters. *See **Commonwealth ex rel. Stevens v. Myers***, 213 A.2d 613, 620 (Pa. 1965).

Prior to the enactment of the PCHA, defendants had begun to rely largely on the writ of *habeas corpus* to seek post-conviction relief. In the early part of both the nation and Pennsylvania, a writ of *habeas corpus* could not be used to challenge a conviction or sentence. ***Ex Parte Watkins***, 28 U.S. 193 (1830); Dallin Oaks, *Habeas Corpus in the States 1776-1865*, 32 Chi.L.Rev. 243 (1965); Kent S. Scheidegger, *Habeas Corpus, Relitigation, and the Legislative Power*, 98 Colum.L.Rev. 888, 928-933 (May 1998). Rather, *habeas corpus* was limited to contesting the competency, *i.e.*, jurisdiction of the court. *See **Commonwealth ex rel. Stevens v. Myers***, 213 A.2d 613, 619 n.13 (Pa. 1965).

Accordingly, once a person was convicted, despite any irregularities in the proceedings, *habeas* relief was unavailable. ***See id***. at 627 (Cohen, J., dissenting) ("Throughout the great and long history of the writ of habeas corpus no court has ever held, and many have expressly rejected the proposition, that the writ could issue on behalf of one who was lawfully confined."). The writ was expanded to include claims regarding the legality of a sentence and eventually came to be utilized as a method of seeking other types of post-conviction relief. In response to the increased usage of *habeas corpus* for purposes of collateral review, the legislature crafted the PCHA. The PCHA mandated the appointment of counsel where the petitioner was indigent and requested counsel, ***Commonwealth v. Hoffman***, 232 A.2d 623 (Pa. 1967), and lasted until 1988 when it was replaced by the PCRA.

The PCHA established "a post conviction procedure for providing relief from convictions obtained and sentences imposed without due process of law." 42 Pa.C.S. § 9542 (1988). Unlike the later PCRA statute, it did not state that the purpose of the statute was to provide relief solely for persons convicted of crimes that they did not commit or who are serving an illegal sentence. *See* 42 Pa.C.S. § 9542. Neither the PCHA nor the original PCRA required petitions to be filed within any designated time frame. This permitted petitioners to file petitions numerous years after their convictions. In 1995, in a significant development, the General Assembly amended the PCRA to require petitioners to file their claims within one year of the finality of their judgment of sentence. Shortly thereafter, the Pennsylvania Supreme Court interpreted the one-year time bar to be purely jurisdictional in nature. *See **Commonwealth v. Peterkin***, 722 A.2d 638 (Pa. 1998).

Subsequently, in a groundbreaking decision, the Pennsylvania Supreme Court declared that all ineffective assistance of counsel claims should be deferred until PCRA review. *See **Commonwealth v. Grant***, 813 A.2d 726 (Pa. 2002). That decision, in turn, has been interpreted by later decisions to require ineffectiveness issues to await collateral review. Thus, the PCRA is almost always the exclusive vehicle for relief when a defendant alleges that his counsel rendered inadequate assistance, and has become the primary mechanism for enforcing the Sixth Amendment and Pennsylvania's Article I, § 9 right to effective assistance of counsel.

Chapter 1: 42 Pa.C.S. § 9542
Scope of the PCRA

Section 9542. Scope of subchapter

This subchapter provides for an action by which persons convicted of crimes they did not commit and persons serving illegal sentences may obtain collateral relief. The action established in this subchapter shall be the sole means of obtaining collateral relief and encompasses all other common law and statutory remedies for the same purpose that exist when this subchapter takes effect, including habeas corpus and coram nobis. This subchapter is not intended to limit the availability of remedies in the trial court or on direct appeal from the judgment of sentence, to provide a means for raising issues waived in prior proceedings or to provide relief from collateral consequences of a criminal conviction. Except as specifically provided otherwise, all provisions of this subchapter shall apply to capital and noncapital cases.

<u>Annotated Comments</u>

<u>A. Sole Means of Relief: *Habeas Corpus* and *Coram Nobis*</u>

The PCRA is intended as the sole means of post-conviction relief. 42 Pa.C.S. § 9542; ***Commonwealth v. Haun***, 32 A.3d 697 (Pa. 2011). Accordingly, the statute has subsumed the common law writs of *coram nobis* and *habeas corpus* for purposes of post-conviction relief. ***Commonwealth v. Morris***, 822 A.2d 684, 693 n.2 (Pa. 2003); ***Commonwealth v. Chester***, 733 A.2d 1242 (Pa. 1999); ***Commonwealth v. Ahlborn***, 699 A.2d 718 (Pa. 1997); ***Commonwealth v. Greer***, 866 A.2d 433 (Pa. Super. 2005); ***Commonwealth v. Pagan***, 864 A.2d 1231 (Pa. Super. 2004); ***Commonwealth v. Fiore***, 665 A.2d 1185 (Pa. Super. 1995); *but see **Commonwealth v. Masker***, 34 A.3d 841 (Pa.

Scope of the PCRA

Super. 2011) (*en banc*) (holding that an ineffective assistance of counsel claim related to counsel's performance at an SVP hearing is not cognizable).

Any issue which is cognizable under the PCRA generally must be raised in a timely PCRA petition and cannot be raised in a *habeas corpus* or *coram nobis* petition. *See Commonwealth v. Peterkin*, 722 A.2d 638 (Pa. 1998); *Commonwealth v. Turner*, 80 A.3d 754 (Pa. 2013); *Commonwealth v. Taylor*, 65 A.3d 462 (Pa. Super. 2013); *Commonwealth v. Pagan*, 864 A.2d 1231 (Pa. Super. 2004); *see also Commonwealth v. Deaner*, 779 A.2d 578 (Pa. Super. 2001) (any collateral petition that raises an issue that the PCRA statute could remedy is to be considered a PCRA petition).

It should be noted, however, that while the PCRA statute's plain language states that it subsumes the writ of *coram nobis*, this common law writ has been applied by federal courts to individuals who have completed their sentence. *See United States v. Orocio*, 645 F.3d 630 (3d Cir. 2011), *abrogated by Chaidez v. United States*, 133 S.Ct. 1103 (2013); *Chaidez v. United States*, 655 F.3d 684 (7th Cir. 2011), *affirmed*, 133 S.Ct. 1103 (2013); *Mendoza v. United States*, 774 F.Supp. 2D 791 (E.D. Va. 2011). Under the PCRA statute, one is ineligible for PCRA relief if no longer serving a sentence. The Superior Court, in *Commonwealth v. Pagan*, 864 A.2d 1231 (Pa. Super. 2004), held that if the petitioner could have pursued the action in the PCRA, *coram nobis* will not be applicable. *See also*, *Commonwealth v. Turner*, 80 A.3d 754 (Pa. 2013).

In *Commonwealth v. Turner*, 80 A.3d 754 (Pa. 2013), the Pennsylvania Supreme Court denied an as applied due process challenge to the requirement that a petitioner still be serving a sentence at the time relief is granted. Therein, the petitioner timely filed a PCRA petition. However, her original sentence was only two years probation. Despite her sentence expiring before the completion of PCRA review, the PCRA court afforded relief. The *Turner* Court reversed, finding that the petitioner could have sought review on direct appeal under *Commonwealth v. Bomar,* 826 A.2d 831 (Pa. 2003). It also rejected *coram nobis* as a potential avenue of relief.

Coram nobis could be applicable to challenge a finding of juvenile delinquency where the juvenile was deprived of counsel or adequate process. This is because the PCRA statute does not apply to juvenile delinquents, *In re A.J.*, 829 A.2d 312 (Pa. Super. 2003), and the juvenile would not be challenging a conviction or sentence. Instead, the juvenile would be contesting a finding of delinquency and a dispositional order. Less certain is the possibility that a defendant's contesting of a Megan's Law or SORNA registration matter and the effectiveness of counsel could utilize *coram nobis*. Again, the petitioner would not be challenging his conviction or sentence and the Superior Court has held that complaints regarding the effectiveness of counsel during a sexually violent predator hearing do not fall within the parameters of the PCRA statute. *See Commonwealth v. Masker,* 34 A.3d 841 (Pa. Super. 2011) (*en banc*).

In the situation where a new constitutional rule of law is given retroactive effect after a defendant's sentence has expired, the writ of *coram nobis* could, in theory, be applicable because the issue could not have afforded relief under the PCRA. However, traditionally *coram nobis* has only been applicable to challenge mistakes of fact. *See Commonwealth v. Turner*, 80 A.3d 754 (Pa. 2013); *but see Commonwealth v. Sheehan*, 285 A.2d 465 (Pa. 1971) (PCHA case finding that errors in process, *i.e.*, where defendant was entirely denied right to counsel, could be remedied via *coram nobis*).

Nonetheless, in **Commonwealth v. Descardes**, 101 A.3d 105 (Pa. Super. 2014) (*en banc*), *reversed at*, 136 A.3d 493 (Pa. 2016), the Superior Court found that *coram nobis* could be

Scope of the PCRA

utilized to bring an ineffectiveness claim relative to advice regarding deportation consequences. Therein, the petitioner was no longer serving his sentence and could not file a timely PCRA petition. In addition, at the time he was sentenced, his claim would not have entitled him to relief.

Despite finding *coram nobis* could be invoked, the Superior Court in ***Descardes*** reasoned that the petitioner was not entitled to relief. It did so on the basis that the United States Supreme Court in ***Chaidez v. United States***, 133 S.Ct. 1103 (2013), held that ***Padilla v. Kentucky***, 130 S.Ct. 1473 (2010), did not apply retroactively. A concurring and dissenting opinion by Judge Bowes noted that the majority failed to properly discuss the retroactivity question once it determined that the PCRA did not apply. Specifically, the majority ignored that retroactivity is generally a matter of state law and only the PCRA statute's express time bar provision requires the United States Supreme Court to hold its pertinent decision applied retroactively.

In addition, the secondary opinion argued that the majority confused a petitioner's ineligibility for relief with whether an issue was cognizable. It opined that the petitioner's ineffectiveness claim was cognizable under the PCRA when he could have presented it in a timely PCRA petition, though it would not have entitled him to relief, and that the majority unnecessarily expanded *coram nobis* in derogation of the plain language of the PCRA statute. The concurring and dissenting judges asserted that all constitutional ineffectiveness claims challenging a conviction or sentence fall within the ambit of the PCRA. The secondary opinion cited a string of cases involving deportation claims that were addressed under the PCRA, and disagreed with the majority's creation of bifurcated review.

The Pennsylvania Supreme Court would echo the view of Judge Bowes in reversing the Superior Court ***Descardes*** decision. ***Commonwealth v. Descardes***, 136 A.3d 493 (Pa. 2016).

Scope of the PCRA

Accordingly, it made clear that ineffectiveness claims related to deportation are cognizable under the PCRA and that *coram nobis* cannot be used to escape the eligibility requirement of the PCRA that the petitioner be serving a sentence.

Petitioners most frequently seek to avoid the PCRA's stringent requirements by filing *habeas corpus* motions. These attempts have largely been unsuccessful and claims that the PCRA is unconstitutional, because it unlawfully suspends *habeas corpus*, have been rejected. ***Commonwealth v. Peterkin***, 722 A.2d 638 (Pa. 1998). Further, the fact that the time for filing a PCRA petition has expired does not make the claims that the petitioner could have raised no longer cognizable. Thus, the failure to timely file a petition will not entitle a petitioner to relief via *habeas corpus*. Should a petitioner title his filing as a writ of *habeas corpus* or a writ of *coram nobis*, the court is to treat the petition as a PCRA petition, if the issue is cognizable under the statute. ***Commonwealth v. Taylor***, 65 A.3d 462 (Pa. Super. 2013).

Therefore, the petition must be filed within one year of the completion of the defendant's judgment of sentence. ***Commonwealth v. Peterkin***, 722 A.2d 638 (Pa. 1998). Simply put, a petitioner generally cannot escape the one year time-bar by titling his request for relief as a writ of *habeas corpus* or *coram nobis*. ***Commonwealth v. Taylor***, 65 A.3d 462 (Pa. Super. 2013). Nonetheless, the common law writs have not been entirely eviscerated.

In ***Commonwealth v. West***, 933 A.2d 1034 (Pa. 2007), and ***Commonwealth v. Judge***, 916 A.2d 511 (Pa. 2007), the Pennsylvania Supreme Court determined that certain claims fall outside the ambit of the PCRA. *See also* ***Commonwealth v. Cunningham***, 81 A.3d 1, 18 (Pa. 2016) (Castille, C.J. concurring) *abrogated on other ground by* ***Montgomery v. Louisiana***, 136 S.Ct. 718 (2016). Hence, the common law writs still exist and may be used where the relief requested is not cognizable under the PCRA. For example, the Superior Court in *Joseph v. Glunt*, 96 A.3d 365 (Pa. Super. 2014), held that a petitioner's contesting of his incarceration on the basis that the Pennsylvania Department of Corrections did not have a copy of his commitment order fit within *habeas corpus* and did not come under the umbrella of the PCRA. Similarly, in *Commonwealth v. Heredia*, 97 A.3d 392 (Pa. Super. 2014), the Court held that a challenge to the Department of Corrections calculation of credit for time served was not cognizable under the PCRA. The Superior Court also held in *Commonwealth v. Partee*, 86 A.3d 245 (Pa. Super. 2014), that a challenge to retroactive application of a sexual offender registration statute did not come within the parameters of the PCRA because the petitioner was not contesting his conviction or his sentence, nor was he alleging ineffective assistance of counsel.

In contrast, claims that assert the Pennsylvania Constitution is unconstitutional, the Pennsylvania Crimes Code is unconstitutional, and that the Pennsylvania Rules of Criminal Procedure are unconstitutional fall under the PCRA. See *Commonwealth v. Stultz*, 114 A.3d 865 (Pa. Super. 2015). Thus, a petitioner making these allegations within a writ of *habeas corpus* must still meet the timeliness requirements of the PCRA for the court to address the merit or lack thereof of the issues. *Commonwealth v. Stout*, 978 A.2d 984 (Pa. Super. 2009); *Commonwealth v. Taylor*, 933 A.2d 1035 (Pa. Super. 2007).

B. Collateral Consequences

The statute, by its plain language, is not intended to apply to the collateral consequences of a criminal conviction. 42 Pa.C.S. § 9542; *Commonwealth v. Abraham*, 62 A.3d 343 (Pa. 2012) ("*Abraham II*"). This is consistent with the Pennsylvania Supreme Court's holding in *Commonwealth v. Frometa*, 555 A.2d 92 (Pa. 1989), *abrogated by Padilla v. Kentucky*, 130 S.Ct.

Scope of the PCRA

1473 (2010). The Pennsylvania Supreme Court in *Frometa* overturned a Superior Court decision that held that counsel could be ineffective for failing to advise a client about deportation consequences. *See Commonwealth v. Wellington*, 451 A.2d 223 (Pa. Super. 1982).

The *Frometa* Court held that the failure to advise a client about possible deportation, if he pled guilty, was a collateral consequence of the guilty plea. It then ruled that counsel could not be found ineffective for neglecting to advise his client about those consequences. *Frometa*, however, was expressly overruled by the United States Supreme Court in *Padilla v. Kentucky*, 130 S.Ct. 1473 (2010).

The United States Supreme Court, in *Padilla*, held that a claim that an attorney was ineffective for not informing the defendant he would face deportation if he pled guilty was a meritorious ineffectiveness claim. The Kentucky courts had previously decided the case by maintaining that deportation was a collateral consequence to the defendant's guilty plea and; therefore, Padilla's counsel, as a matter of law, could not be ineffective for failing to advise his client about deporation. In rendering its decision, the High Court declared that the distinction between direct and collateral consequences, when evaluating an ineffective assistance of counsel claim, was a false construct when dealing with deportation. Instead, the Court determined that the proper focus should be on whether the information that counsel was alleged to have provided, or failed to provide, implicated and was intimately connected to the criminal process.

Prior to the *Padilla* decision, *Frometa* had been cited in Pennsylvania cases addressing ineffective assistance of counsel issues through the lens of direct versus collateral consequences. *See Commonwealth v. Lee*, 820 A.2d 1285 (Pa. Super. 2003) (counsel was not ineffective for failing to advise defendant convicted of a sex crime that he had to provide a blood sample).

Scope of the PCRA

Thus, the decision in *Padilla* appeared to throw open the door to renewed analysis of issues that were previously considered collateral consequences of a plea.

Indeed, *Padilla* appears to render a portion of section 9542 unconstitutional when read in combination with the mandate in *Commonwealth v. Grant*, 813 A.2d 726 (Pa. 2002), that all claims of ineffectiveness be deferred to PCRA review, insofar as the statute prohibits relief from ineffective assistance of counsel claims related to the collateral consequences of a criminal conviction. *See Commonwealth v. Masker*, 34 A.3d 841 (Pa. Super. 2011) (*en banc*) (Bowes, J., concurring and dissenting); *but see Commonwealth v. Abraham*, 62 A.3d 343 (Pa. 2012) (collateral consequence claim unrelated to deportation does not entitle defendant to relief).

Since *Grant* has been interpreted to defer ineffective assistance of counsel challenges to collateral review and the scope of the PCRA statute does not encompass collateral consequences, either *Grant* or the statute must yield to the *Padilla* Court's pronouncement with respect to at least deportation issues. *Commonwealth v. Masker*, 34 A.3d 841 (Pa. Super. 2011) (*en banc*) (Bowes, J., concurring and dissenting). *Padilla* did not altogether do away with the direct versus collateral consequences doctrines, but it is uncertain whether the holding in *Padilla* will substantially impact the scope of the PCRA. *See Commonwealth v. Abraham*, 62 A.3d 343 (Pa. 2012) (holding *Padilla's* distinction between direct and collateral consequences does not apply beyond deportation).

The Pennsylvania Superior Court in *Commonwealth v. Abraham*, 996 A.2d 1090 (Pa. Super. 2010) (*"Abraham I"*), reversed by *Abraham II*, 62 A.3d 343 (Pa. 2012), appeared to signal an expansion of the scope of the PCRA statute by discussing *Padilla*. Specifically, in *Abraham I*, the defendant, a retired school employee, pled guilty to a sexually related offense. As a result of his guilty plea, he lost his pension. On collateral appeal, the petitioner asserted that he would not have pled guilty to the particular offense had his counsel informed him that he would lose his pension due to his plea. The PCRA court held that the petitioner was not entitled to relief because the loss of his pension was a collateral consequence of his plea.

The Superior Court reversed and remanded for an evidentiary hearing to determine if the attorney had a reasonable basis for not advising his client that he would lose his pension and whether the petitioner was prejudiced. The court discussed *Padilla* and reasoned that the Pennsylvania statute that caused the defendant to lose his pension was punitive in nature and implicated the criminal process. The court held, alternatively, that the loss of the defendant's pension was a direct consequence of his plea. This aspect of the holding was erroneous based on the longstanding definition attached to direct and collateral consequences. *See Commonwealth v. Wall*, 867 A.2d 578, 582 (Pa. Super. 2005). The *Abraham I* Court offered no analysis of how the loss of the defendant's pension dealt with the length of his imprisonment or a fine, the traditional direct consequences of a conviction.

In addition, the Superior Court, in *Abraham I*, failed to discuss that the majority in *Padilla* specifically tailored its holding to deportation, or that the PCRA statute by its plain language is not intended to pertain to collateral consequences. The panel also did not examine the possible non-retroactive effect of *Padilla*, *i.e.*, that at the time that the defendant in *Abraham* pled guilty, counsel was under no obligation to explain the collateral consequences of the plea.[1]

---

1 *See* discussion of timeliness exception related to new constitutional rights and retroactive effect for a discussion of such repercussions. Ordinarily, a new rule of law is limited in its retroactive application. Further, counsel is not considered ineffective for failing to anticipate a change in the law. *Commonwealth v. Todaro*, 701 A.2d 1343 (Pa.

Further, *Abraham I's* application of *Padilla* to the facts of that case was questionable. First, *Padilla* did not state that the distinction between direct and collateral consequences was inappropriate. Indeed, the Court stated, "whether that distinction is appropriate is a question we need not consider in this case because of the unique nature of deportation." *Padilla*, 130 S.Ct. at 1481. Therefore, it appears evident that *Padilla* was meant to apply to a narrow set of cases related to deportation and issues closely related to the criminal process.

The *Padilla* Court specifically remarked that deportation, "because of its close connection to the criminal process[,]" is "uniquely difficult to classify as either a direct or a collateral consequence." *Padilla*, 130 S.Ct. at 1482. The Court opined that the distinction between a collateral and direct consequence was "ill suited to evaluating a *Strickland* claim concerning the specific risk of deportation." *Id.* Hence, the *Padilla* Court did not altogether abrogate the collateral consequence doctrine for all post-conviction claims.

1997). An "old rule" generally applies retroactively so long as the issue has been preserved. After *Abraham I*, in *Commonwealth v. Garcia*, 23 A.3d 1059 (Pa. Super. 2011), the Superior Court, in determining whether *Padilla* was a new constitutional right for purposes of the timeliness exception, held that *Padilla* was a mere application of the ineffectiveness test announced in *Strickland v. Washington*, 466 U.S. 668 (1984). The *Garcia* Court's analysis did not consider the ramifications of its holding for timely PCRA petitions, *i.e.*, attorneys in Pennsylvania could be found ineffective based on a pronouncement that was not in existence at the time counsel was advising his or her client. Chief Justice Castille in a concurring opinion in *Abraham II* opined that *Padilla* was a new rule that does not apply retroactively. This author concurs in that assessment as did the United States Supreme Court. *Chaidez v. United States*, 133 S.Ct. 1103 (2013); *see also Commonwealth v. Ghisoiu*, 63 A.3d 1272 (Pa. Super. 2013).

Scope of the PCRA

Second, it is not clear that a statute that causes a person to lose his pension because of a criminal conviction gives rise to a duty on the part of a criminal attorney to inform his client that his plea will result in the loss of the defendant's pension. Furthermore, the court's determination that the statute authorizing the loss of a pension following conviction of certain crimes was punitive in nature was questionable in light of previous case law describing punitive measures. For example, Megan's Law requirements regarding sexually violent predator status and registration have consistently been held not to be punitive despite being directly related to a defendant's crime. *Commonwealth v. Williams*, 977 A.2d 1174 (Pa. Super. 2009); *Commonwealth v. Leidig*, 956 A.2d 399 (Pa. 2008); *Commonwealth v. Price*, 876 A.2d 988 (Pa. Super. 2005).

Accordingly, the Pennsylvania Supreme Court granted allowance of appeal in *Abraham I* to address two issues: 1) whether the distinction between direct and collateral consequences is appropriate under *Strickland v. Washington*, 466 U.S. 668 (1984) and; 2) if the distinction is appropriate, whether forfeiture of a pension is a collateral consequence of a defendant's plea. *Commonwealth v. Abraham*, 9 A.3d 1133 (Pa. 2010). In reversing the Superior Court, the Pennsylvania Supreme Court determined that the collateral consequences doctrine still bars claims under the PCRA that are unrelated to deportation, and that the forfeiture of a pension was a collateral consequence of the defendant's plea. *Commonwealth v. Abraham*, 62 A.3d 343 (Pa. 2012).

The majority declined to confront the retroactivity issue, though Chief Justice Castille opined, in a concurring opinion, that *Padilla* was a new rule of law that does not apply retroactively. *See also Chaidez v. United States*, 133 S.Ct. 1103 (2013) (finding *Padilla* announced a new rule but does not apply retroactively). Nonetheless, claims that typically have not afforded relief under the PCRA, such as issues regarding information supplied to the defendant regarding his parole or probation supervision, may require an analysis of whether the criminal process was implicated and whether the issue has an intimate relationship with the criminal process. For example, prior to *Padilla*, counsel could not be deemed ineffective for not advising a defendant that he would not be automatically paroled. *Commonwealth v. Herrold*, 776 A.2d 994 (Pa. Super. 2001).

In light of *Abraham II*, *Padilla's* repercussions on cases that have utilized the collateral consequences doctrine to dismiss post-conviction claims in Pennsylvania appears to be limited to deportation. However, both the concurring and dissenting opinions in *Padilla* recognized the effects that the majority decision could have on claims unrelated to the deportation context. Yet, it appears that counsel's failure to properly advise a client on matters that were previously considered collateral consequences will not entitle a petitioner to PCRA relief, unless counsel provides affirmative misadvice causing an unknowing guilty plea. *See Commonwealth v. Barndt*, 74 A.3d 185 (Pa. Super. 2013).

In *Barndt*, the Superior Court distinguished between failing to provide information about a collateral consequence of a guilty plea and providing affirmative misadvice. Plea counsel for the petitioner in *Barndt* had informed the defendant that he would not lose all of his parole street time in another case by having committed the crime for which he was pleading guilty. The *Barndt* Court did not confront the language of the PCRA statute.

Instead, it distinguished *Abraham II* on the grounds that it involved an omission by counsel, and relied on past precedent that found counsel ineffective for providing incorrect advice it considered related to the collateral consequences of a plea. Specifically, it opined that *Commonwealth v. Hickman*, 799 A.2d 136 (Pa. Super. 2002), pertained to a collateral consequence. Therein, counsel incorrectly advised the defendant that he was eligible for boot camp for the crime for which he pled guilty. ***Accord Commonwealth v. Kersteter***, 877 A.2d 466 (Pa. Super. 2005).

The panel did not discuss the difference between the fact that ***Hickman*** involved the specific sentence the defendant received after pleading guilty and that ***Barndt*** involved parole considerations for a separate crime and sentence. Nor did it consider that boot camp eligibility was related to the nature of the sentence for which the defendant pled guilty, which could be considered a direct consequence of the plea. *See* ***Commonwealth v. Wall***, 867 A.2d 578, 582 (Pa. Super. 2005) (defining direct consequence of plea).

The ***Barndt*** Court further reasoned that advice that a defendant would serve a county sentence rather than a state sentence for the crime that he pled guilty was a collateral consequence of the plea. *See* ***Barndt***, at 196-197 (citing ***Commonwealth v. Rathfon***, 899 A.2d 365 (Pa. Super. 2006)). This finding is also questionable, since a direct consequence is anything pertaining to the length or nature of the sentence the person will serve for the crime at issue. Whether a person serves a county sentence or state sentence relates directly to the sentence that the individual is serving.

Additionally, the ***Barndt*** panel did not discuss the difference between advice directly related to the sentence for the crime the person was pleading guilty too and advice relative to a separate crime and sentence, which was the concern in ***Barndt***. The likely explanation for the ***Barndt*** Court decision is that it was seeking to circumvent the decision in ***Abraham II*** that declined to extend ***Padilla's*** reasoning that information intimately connected to the criminal process is what is essential to analyzing ineffectiveness claims in a guilty plea situation.

In ***Commonwealth v. Masker***, 34 A.3d 841 (Pa. Super. 2011) (*en banc*), the majority also rejected extending ***Padilla's*** rationale to ineffectiveness claims pertaining to counsel's representation during a sexually violent predator ("SVP") hearing, which occurred during the sentencing process. The lead concurring and dissenting opinion ("CO/DO"), with three judges joining and one judge concurring in the result, discussed what it viewed as the constitutionally-problematic approach taken by the majority. The CO/DO concluded that the issue of ineffectiveness of SVP counsel was cognizable under the PCRA statute based on the Pennsylvania Supreme Court's decisions in *Commonwealth v. Grant*, 813 A.2d 726 (Pa. 2002), and *Commonwealth ex rel. Dadario v. Goldberg*, 773 A.2d 126 (Pa. 2001), and the analysis employed by the *Padilla* Court. It reached this conclusion despite an SVP determination being independent of a conviction or the punishment aspect of a sentence.

The *Masker* majority relied on *Commonwealth v. Price*, 876 A.2d 988 (Pa. Super. 2005), and held that there was no difference between a challenge to the ineffectiveness of SVP counsel and a bald challenge to an SVP determination. From this questionable logic, *see Commonwealth v. Collins*, 888 A.2d 564 (Pa. 2005) (discussing difference between ineffectiveness claims and underlying issue), the majority reasoned that an ineffectiveness challenge during the SVP-sentencing process was not cognizable under the PCRA.

As recognized by the lead CO/DO therein, the majority failed to appreciate the difference between ineffectiveness claims, which were at issue in *Masker*, and *Price* and the other cases cited by the majority, where no ineffectiveness claims were leveled. *See Masker*, 34 A.3d at 849 (Bowes, J., concurring and dissenting) (citing *Price*, 876 A.2d at 994 ("Appellant could have raised this challenge to his SVP classification on direct appeal, but did not.")); *see also Price*, 876 A.2d at 995 ("Appellant presents his claim to us on appeal as if on direct appeal, and without any ineffectiveness of counsel analysis.").

Scope of the PCRA

Contrary to the appellant in *Price*, Masker asserted that SVP/sentencing counsel was ineffective for failing to call an expert witness during his SVP hearing and in neglecting to advise him about his right to remain silent. While the majority was correct that the PCRA statute itself precludes relief on issues that are considered collateral to a plea or conviction, *see* 42 Pa.C.S. § 9542, the PCRA statute's plain language must yield or the interpretation of *Commonwealth v. Grant*, 813 A.2d 726 (Pa. 2002), that precludes ineffectiveness claims from being reviewed on direct review, is rendered unconstitutional.

As the main CO/DO highlighted, "where a challenge relates directly to an ineffective assistance of counsel claim, the issue ordinarily falls within the ambit of the PCRA statute." *Masker*, 34 A.3d at 849 (citing *Commonwealth ex rel. Dadario v. Goldberg*, 773 A.2d 126 (Pa. 2001)). Indeed, it noted that, in *Commonwealth v. Walls*, 993 A.2d 289, 301 (Pa. Super. 2010), the Superior Court previously held an ineffectiveness claim regarding an attorney's representation at an SVP hearing was cognizable under the PCRA statute. In light of *Grant*, defendants generally are foreclosed from raising ineffectiveness claims on direct appeal; therefore, the issue can only be raised in one context: via a PCRA petition.

The Pennsylvania Supreme Court in *Dadario* held that constitutional ineffectiveness claims may be raised in the PCRA regardless of whether the claim is directly related to the guilt or innocence of the defendant. Additionally, the Pennsylvania Supreme Court has consistently construed the PCRA statute broadly, without following a plain language interpretation. *Commonwealth v. Burkett*, 5 A.3d 1260, 1274 (Pa. Super. 2010). In limited circumstances, the Pennsylvania Supreme Court has held that a particular issue that is not cognizable under the PCRA statute may be raised through a writ of *habeas corpus*. *Masker*, 34 A.3d at 850 (Bowes, J., concurring and dissenting) (citing *Commonwealth v. West*, 938 A.2d 1034 (Pa.

2007)); ***Commonwealth v. Judge***, 916 A.2d 511 (Pa. 2007); ***Joseph v. Glunt***, 96 A.3d 365 (Pa. Super. 2014).

According to the ***Masker*** lead CO/DO, while claims that fall outside the purview of the PCRA could be raised via the writ of *habeas corpus*, that writ did not apply to Masker because he was not challenging the current cause of his detention through his ineffectiveness claim and, even if *habeas* did apply, the majority's rationale created a bifurcated system of review.[2]

---

[2] Two judges would have awaited a case in which a petitioner argued the applicability of *habeas corpus* to determine if an SVP defendant could allege ineffectiveness in a *habeas* petition. As noted, this would create a bifurcated system of review, which has expressly and repeatedly been eschewed by the Pennsylvania Supreme Court. These judges appeared to believe a petitioner could be "in custody" based on Megan's Law registration requirements. This view relies on a broad interpretation of being in custody and has consistently been rejected by the federal courts that have considered the issue. *See **Williamson v. Gregoire***, 151 F.3d 1180 (9th Cir. 1997); ***Henry v. Lungen***, 164 F.3d 1240 (9th Cir. 1999); ***McNab v. Kok***, 170 F.3d 1246 (9th Cir. 1999); ***Leslie v. Randle***, 296 F.3d 518 (6th Cir. 2002); ***Davis v. Nassau County***, 524 F.Supp.2d 182 (E.D.N.Y. 2007); ***Hansen v. Marr***, 594 F.Supp.2d 1097 (D.Neb. 2009); ***Clair v. Maynard***, 812 F.Supp.2d 685 (D.Md. 2011).

For example, the author of the secondary CO/DO apparently would have considered whether *any* restraint of liberty places an individual in custody for purposes of a *habeas* petition. This broad interpretation would mean that challenges to all collateral consequences of a criminal conviction could be raised via a *habeas* petition, *i.e.*, the loss of the right to vote, the loss of the ability to possess a firearm, loss of driving privileges, loss of occupational licensing, etc... Pointedly, case law discussing post-conviction *habeas* petitions is limited to challenges related to parole, probation, and sentences of incarceration. Thus, the restraint of liberty aspect of post-conviction *habeas* has consistently been attached to actual detention, though, of course, not necessarily incarceration. In the ***Masker*** case, the petitioner was not

Scope of the PCRA

Simply put, the petitioner's sole means of attacking the effectiveness of his SVP counsel was through the PCRA. The fact that an SVP hearing is considered civil and collateral to a conviction, the CO/DO argued, should not have precluded relief under the PCRA. Indeed, as it recognized, the PCRA itself, much like an SVP hearing, is considered civil and collateral to a conviction, *Pennsylvania v. Finley*, 481 U.S. 551 (1987), but PCRA counsel can, in theory, be held ineffective at a PCRA hearing if the issue is properly raised.

Furthermore, as noted previously, the Supreme Court in *Padilla* "opined that whether a collateral consequence is at issue is not critical to determining an assertion of ineffective assistance of counsel." *Masker*, 34 A.3d at 851 (Bowes, J., concurring and dissenting). Rather, "the crucial inquiry was whether the issue was intimately related to the criminal process." *Masker*, 34 A.3d at 851 (Bowes, J., concurring and dissenting); *but see Commonwealth v. Abraham*, 62 A.3d 343 (Pa. 2012). Undoubtedly, *Padilla* focused on the issue of a guilty plea and deportation, and refused to eliminate the distinction between direct and collateral consequences. However, the *Masker* majority's attempt to distinguish *Padilla* on the grounds that Masker was not challenging his guilty plea failed to acknowledge that, in both *Padilla* and *Masker*, the defendants were asserting constitutional ineffectiveness claims about issues intimately connected to the criminal process. As the lead CO/DO pointed out, the majority:

> misperceived the relevance of *Padilla* by setting forth that an SVP hearing relates to the collateral consequences of a conviction. That an SVP hearing and subsequent SVP determination were collateral to the conviction was not in dispute...However, the fact that

---

detained or in custody because of his SVP status; rather, he was imprisoned based on his convictions, which he was not challenging.

Scope of the PCRA

an SVP hearing and subsequent SVP finding has been considered collateral to a defendant's conviction does not render *Padilla* distinguishable; instead it is precisely what made *Padilla* relevant.

The importance of *Padilla* to the [*Masker*] case is that it directly contradicted the plain language of 42 Pa.C.S. § 9542, which states that the PCRA does not "provide relief from collateral consequences of a criminal conviction." This aspect of the statute can no longer be viewed as sound when *Padilla* and *Grant* are conjoined. Otherwise, as discussed previously, ineffective assistance of counsel claims relating to collateral consequences could not be raised during direct appeal or PCRA review. Simply put, *Padilla* provides that, in at least one instance, relief may be had on an ineffectiveness issue based on a collateral consequence. Concomitantly, *Grant* compels defendants to raise the issue in the PCRA.

Masker, 34 A.3d at 853 (Bowes, J., concurring and dissenting); *but see Commonwealth v. Abraham*, 62 A.3d 343 (Pa. 2012).

While *Padilla* was distinguishable based on its application to the narrow class of deportation cases and because guilty pleas are criminal and not civil, (though the results of an SVP hearing are collateral, sentencing proceedings are criminal and SVP hearings are ordinarily conjoined with the sentencing process), the *Masker* majority did not, as the CO/DO found, recognize that defendants have a statutory right to counsel at an SVP hearing. 42 Pa.C.S. § 9795.4(e)(2). Thus, as in the civil and collateral PCRA process itself, where there is a rule-based right to counsel, *see* Pa.R.Crim.P. 904, Masker had a corresponding statutory right to the effective assistance of counsel during the SVP hearing, which occurred during the sentencing phase of Masker's case.

Scope of the PCRA

Due to *Grant* and case law broadly interpreting the PCRA statute, *i.e.*, ***Commonwealth ex rel. Dadario v. Goldberg***, 773 A.2d 126 (Pa. 2001), and because defendants have a statutory right to counsel at an SVP hearing, and therefore a corresponding right to effective counsel, the lead CO/DO reasoned that the PCRA was the proper means for raising the claim. The CO/DO also contended that SVP counsel was constitutionally mandated because the SVP/sentencing hearing was a critical stage of the criminal proceeding, *i.e.*, sentencing. Additionally, since an SVP hearing may actually determine the appropriate time to file a direct appeal, *see **Commonwealth v. Harris***, 972 A.2d 1196 (Pa. Super. 2009) and ***Commonwealth v. Whanger***, 30 A.3d 1212 (Pa. Super. 2011) (Bowes, J., concurring), there is a convincing argument that there is a constitutional right to counsel during the SVP proceeding. Lastly, there is a considerable originalist argument that Pennsylvania's law of the land constitutional provision, *i.e.*, its due process clause, guarantees a constitutional right to counsel so long as there is a rule based or statutory guarantee of the right to counsel. *See* discussion on Pa.R.Crim.P. 904.

While the *Masker* majority opined that the claim could be raised in another context, it declined to discuss what possible other avenue existed. Its failure to suggest an alternative avenue is no doubt due to the fact, as mentioned previously, that no other mechanism exists without creating a bifurcated system of reviewing ineffectiveness claims. Indeed, the majority decision does not prohibit an ineffectiveness challenge based on counsel's performance during an SVP/sentencing hearing. Instead, it allows SVP defendants to contest counsel's performance during an SVP hearing not only after one-year passes from the finalization of their judgment of sentence, but also permits SVP's to file petitions after they are no longer serving their sentence. For example, a defendant who completes his sentence after ten years may still, in theory, contest his SVP

Scope of the PCRA

status due to counsel's performance at the SVP hearing.

The most appropriate course of action would be for courts to address ineffectiveness issues even if the matter appears to involve a collateral consequence of the conviction so long as that consequence is closely related to the criminal process and would be within the knowledge of a reasonable criminal attorney. To hold otherwise forecloses review of ineffectiveness claims involving a certain class of issues. Certainly, some collateral matters may prove to be as important in advising a client as the direct consequences of the plea. The crucial inquiry should be whether the issue involves information that a criminal attorney is likely to possess and about which he or she is knowledgeable. It is reasonable for a criminal attorney to know that he may call an expert witness during an SVP hearing.[3]

Therefore, although counsel was not ineffective for failing to call an expert in *Masker* because there was no indication that an expert would have testified on his behalf, four judges agreed that an attorney could be ineffective at an SVP hearing, which is usually intertwined with sentencing. Nonetheless, a claim of ineffective assistance of SVP counsel cannot be addressed via the PCRA.

---

3 The *Masker* case is interesting in the collateral consequences field because the petitioner was not challenging his guilty plea, but rather his counsel's actual performance during the SVP-sentencing phase of his case. Actual performance during a sentencing/SVP proceeding is distinguishable from advice concerning collateral consequences of a plea. For example, Masker was not contesting that he should be entitled to withdraw his plea because counsel did not discuss with him the Megan's Law requirements. Such a claim would almost always necessarily fail because the court provides defendants with this information at sentencing.

C. Innocence

The above interpretation is buttressed by the fact that other decisions have ignored the plain language of section 9542 with respect to a second aspect of the scope of the PCRA. Section 9542 also mandates that the PCRA is applicable only to innocent petitioners or those serving an illegal sentence. The Pennsylvania Supreme Court, however, has expanded the statute to afford relief to those alleging certain ineffectiveness claims that do not directly pertain to innocence or an illegal sentence.

In *Commonwealth v. Haun*, 984 A.2d 557 (Pa. Super. 2009) ("*Haun I*"), the Superior Court noted the disconnect between the plain language of the PCRA statute and Pennsylvania Supreme Court precedent. The issue in *Haun I* was whether a petitioner was entitled to the reinstatement of his direct appeal rights where he was expressly found to have admitted his guilt to the crime. The Superior Court, citing several Supreme Court decisions, held that the plain language of section 9542 did not preclude a petitioner from seeking PCRA relief in the nature of a direct appeal, even if he did not proclaim his innocence.

The Supreme Court in *Commonwealth v. Haun*, 32 A.3d 697 (Pa. 2011) ("*Haun II*"), upheld the Superior Court's interpretation of the scope provision of the PCRA statute in order to effectuate a unitary system of collateral review. Therein, the PCRA court held that the scope of the PCRA statute precluded relief to the petitioner because he conceded guilt during his PCRA hearing, his interview for a pre-sentence report, and during a sexually violent predator assessment. According to the PCRA court, the scope of the PCRA statute governed individuals who were wrongly convicted or challenging the legality of their sentence. As noted, the Superior Court reversed, holding that the scope of the PCRA statute did not preclude relief to persons who did not contest guilt. The Supreme Court granted the Commonwealth's allowance of appeal and affirmed the Superior Court.

The Supreme Court highlighted that the PCRA was intended to be the sole means for achieving collateral relief and that a narrow construction of the scope of the statute would create a bifurcated system of review. It reconciled the internal inconsistency of section 9542's "sole means" proviso and innocence-illegality construct by reasoning that the sole means language was last in order of position and "should predominate." *Haun II*, 32 A.3d at 705. Due to the interpretation of *Commonwealth v. Grant*, 813 A.2d 726 (Pa. 2002), as barring ineffectiveness claims on direct appeal, thereby precluding a defendant from being able to raise ineffectiveness claims that do not directly relate to innocence or an illegal sentence, applying a strict interpretation of the scope of the statute renders either the statute or *Grant* unconstitutional.

D. Limitation of Remedies: "This subchapter is not intended to limit the availability of remedies in the trial court or on direct appeal from the judgment of sentence"

Though the PCRA explicitly states that it is not intended to limit remedies in the trial court or on direct appeal, the Pennsylvania Supreme Court's subsequent interpretations of its decision in *Commonwealth v. Grant*, 813 A.2d 726 (Pa. 2002), as precluding raising ineffectiveness claims on direct appeal, does expressly limit the available remedies before the trial court and on direct appeal. Presently, absent an explicit waiver of PCRA review of trial counsel's effectiveness, a trial court is prohibited from addressing ineffectiveness claims in post-sentence motions. *Commonwealth v. Holmes*, 79 A.3d 562 (Pa. 2013). Additionally, appellate courts are precluded from affording relief on ineffectiveness issues on direct appeal. *Id.* At the time of the adoption of both the PCHA and PCRA, both occurring pre-*Grant*, defendants could achieve relief on direct appeal

Scope of the PCRA

based on an ineffectiveness claim. Thus, the interpretation of ***Grant*** to absolutely bar claims of ineffectiveness on direct appeal contradicts the plain language of the PCRA.

Chapter 2: 42 Pa.C.S. § 9543
Eligibility for Relief

Section 9543. Eligibility for relief

(a) General rule.--To be eligible for relief under this subchapter, the petitioner must plead and prove by a preponderance of the evidence all of the following:

(1) That the petitioner has been convicted of a crime under the laws of this Commonwealth and is at the time relief is granted:

(i) currently serving a sentence of imprisonment, probation or parole for the crime;

(ii) awaiting execution of a sentence of death for the crime; or

(iii) serving a sentence which must expire before the person may commence serving the disputed sentence.

(2) That the conviction or sentence resulted from one or more of the following:

(i) A violation of the Constitution of this Commonwealth or the Constitution or laws of the United States which, in the circumstances of the particular case, so undermined the truth-determining process that no reliable adjudication of guilt or innocence could have taken place.

(ii) Ineffective assistance of counsel which, in the circumstances of the particular case, so undermined the truth-determining process that no reliable adjudication of guilt or innocence could have taken place.

(iii) A plea of guilty unlawfully induced where the circumstances make it likely that the inducement caused the

Eligibility for Relief

petitioner to plead guilty and the petitioner is innocent.

(iv) The improper obstruction by government officials of the petitioner's right of appeal where a meritorious appealable issue existed and was properly preserved in the trial court.

(v) Deleted.

(vi) The unavailability at the time of trial of exculpatory evidence that has subsequently become available and would have changed the outcome of the trial if it had been introduced.

(vii) The imposition of a sentence greater than the lawful maximum.

(viii) A proceeding in a tribunal without jurisdiction.

(3) That the allegation of error has not been previously litigated or waived.

<Subsec. (a)(4) is permanently suspended insofar as it references "unitary review" by Pennsylvania Supreme Court Order of Aug. 11, 1997, imd. effective.>

(4) That the failure to litigate the issue prior to or during trial, during unitary review or on direct appeal could not have been the result of any rational, strategic or tactical decision by counsel.

(b) Exception.--Even if the petitioner has met the requirements of subsection (a), the petition shall be dismissed if it appears at any time that, because of delay in filing the petition, the Commonwealth has been prejudiced either in its ability to respond to the petition or in its ability to re-try the petitioner. A petition may be dismissed due to delay in the filing by the petitioner only after a hearing upon a motion to dismiss. This subsection does not apply if the petitioner shows that the petition is based on grounds of which the petitioner could not have discovered by the exercise of reasonable diligence before the delay became prejudicial to the Commonwealth.

(c) Extradition.--If the petitioner's conviction and sentence resulted from a trial conducted in his absence and if the petitioner has fled to a foreign country that refuses to extradite him because a trial in absentia was employed, the petitioner shall be entitled to the grant of a new trial if the refusing country agrees by virtue of this provision to return him and if the petitioner upon such return to this jurisdiction so requests. This subsection shall apply, notwithstanding any other law or judgment to the contrary.

Annotated Comments

A. Eligibility for Relief: Generally

To be eligible for PCRA relief, a petitioner must plead and prove by a preponderance of the evidence that he has been convicted of a crime under the laws of the Commonwealth and is, at the time relief is being sought, serving a sentence of imprisonment, probation, or parole for the crime, or awaiting execution; or serving a sentence which must expire before he can begin serving the sentence being disputed. 42 Pa.C.S. § 9543. Parole eligibility claims do not fall under the parameters of the PCRA. *See Commonwealth v. Camps*, 772 A.2d 70 (Pa. Super. 2001). The statutory areas under which a petitioner can seek relief pertain to jurisdiction (sentence exceeding lawful maximum and tribunal without jurisdiction), constitutional violations, ineffectiveness claims, guilty plea withdrawal, improper obstruction of the right to appeal, and after-discovered evidence.

Direct appeal and PCRA counsel can be held ineffective, although their actions do not directly affect the outcome of the trial. *See generally Commonwealth v. Hackett*, 956 A.2d 978

Eligibility for Relief

(Pa. 2008) (discussing broad effect to be given PCRA statute). A defendant's right to a direct appeal has also been held to be a part of the truth-determining process because it serves as a check on the trial court to determine whether any errors occurred during a trial or guilty plea. *See generally* ***Commonwealth v. Lantzy***, 736 A.2d 564 (Pa. 1999). A petitioner is also required to demonstrate that the issues he raised have not been previously litigated or waived, or that the failure to litigate the issue prior to or during trial, during unitary review (unitary review currently does not exist in Pennsylvania), or on direct appeal could not have been the result of any rational, strategic or tactical decision by counsel. 42 Pa.C.S. § 9543(a)(4).

If the petitioner's sentence has expired, he is not entitled to PCRA relief. ***Commonwealth v. Turner***, 80 A.3d 754 (Pa. 2013); ***Commonwealth v. Ahlborn***, 699 A.2d 718 (Pa. 1997); ***Commonwealth v. Volk***, 138 A.3d 659 (Pa. Super. 2016); ***Commonwealth v. Williams***, 977 A.2d 1174 (Pa. Super. 2009) (finding that a petitioner, after completion of his sentence but while still subject to Megan's Law requirements, was not entitled to PCRA relief); ***Commonwealth v. Matin***, 832 A.2d 1141 (Pa. Super. 2003); ***Commonwealth v. Auchmuty***, 799 A.2d 823 (Pa. Super. 2002); ***Commonwealth v. Hayes***, 596 A.2d 195 (Pa. Super. 1991) (*en banc*). Also, a petitioner is not eligible for relief where the only aspect of his sentence is a fine. ***Commonwealth v. Fisher***, 703 A.2d 714 (Pa. Super. 1997). Similarly, no relief is due when the only component of the sentence remaining is payment of restitution. ***Commonwealth v. James***, 771 A.2d 33 (Pa. Super. 2001).

B. Cognizability: Previous Litigation and Waiver

Before reaching the merits of a claim (assuming the petition is timely), the court must determine if the claim is cognizable under the PCRA, *i.e.*, assuming that the allegations in a petition

Eligibility for Relief

are true and the petitioner suffered prejudice, does the PCRA afford relief. Much of the recent precedent discussing the cognizability of a PCRA claim takes into account the fact that all claims of ineffective assistance of counsel must be deferred to collateral review. *See Commonwealth v. Grant*, 813 A.2d 726 (Pa. 2002). However, the plain language of the PCRA statute does not create eligibility for relief for all claims of ineffective assistance of counsel. *See e.g. Commonwealth v. Masker*, 34 A.3d 841 (Pa. Super. 2011) (*en banc*). Rather, the act narrows the types of claims that a petitioner may bring.

Thus, courts were originally faced with the dilemma of interpreting the language of the statute to determine if a claim was cognizable under the PCRA statute or whether all ineffective assistance of counsel challenges were cognizable. In most instances, the courts eschewed a strict interpretation of the statute and permitted review of ineffectiveness claims that did not fall under the auspices of affecting the reliability of the truth-determining process. *See Commonwealth ex rel. Dadario v. Goldberg*, 773 A.2d 126 (Pa. 2001).

Decisions of both the Pennsylvania Superior Court and the Pennsylvania Supreme Court have, nonetheless, failed to carefully distinguish between whether an issue is not cognizable under the PCRA and whether the issue can no longer be addressed on its merits because it was previously litigated or waived. Because an issue is previously litigated or waived does not mean the underlying issue is non-cognizable and cannot fit within the parameters of the PCRA. Hence, in cases like *Commonwealth v. Smith*, 17 A.3d 873 (Pa. 2011), *Commonwealth v. Paddy*, 15 A.3d 431, 443 (Pa. 2011), *Commonwealth v. Rios*, 920 A.2d 790 (Pa. 2007), *Commonwealth v. Miller*, 746 A.2d 592 (Pa. 2000), *Commonwealth v. Chester*, 733 A.2d 1242 (Pa. 1999), and *Commonwealth v. Hutchins*, 760 A.2d 50 (Pa. Super. 2000), where the courts have stated that a claim which was previously

Eligibility for Relief

litigated is not cognizable under the PCRA, the courts have been less than precise.

This issue is important in the context of *habeas corpus* relief, since issues which truly are not cognizable under the PCRA may be raised in a *habeas corpus* petition outside of the one year time bar. *See **Commonwealth v. Judge**,* 916 A.2d 511 (Pa. 2007); ***Commonwealth v. West**,* 938 A.2d 1034 (Pa. 2007). If one were to take the court's words literally in these cases, the previously litigated issue or, more importantly, a waived issue, *see **Commonwealth v. Tedford**,* 960 A.2d 1, 13 (Pa. 2008), (stating a waived issue is not cognizable pursuant to the PCRA), could be raised in a writ of *habeas corpus,* and a petitioner could be entitled to a review of the issue because the claim was not cognizable under the PCRA.

For example, if on direct appeal a defendant alleged that the trial court erred in not allowing testimony based on the Rape Shield Statute and the issue was decided against the defendant, a petitioner cannot bring the claim again under a writ of *habeas corpus* simply to avoid the previous litigation bar of the PCRA. I also note that, based on the law of the case doctrine, once an issue is decided, it cannot be re-litigated in the PCRA. ***Commonwealth v. Fletcher**,* 986 A.2d 759, 776 n.20 (Pa. 2009). The more appropriate analysis is that the underlying issue is cognizable, but the petitioner is not entitled to relief based on the statutory requirement that claims raised in a post-conviction proceeding not be previously litigated or waived.

Phrased differently, had the challenge not been raised before, the issue could be raised and addressed on its merits in a PCRA petition alleging the ineffectiveness of prior counsel. *See **Commonwealth v. Pagan**,* 864 A.2d 1231 (Pa.Super. 2004) (focus is on claim and whether it could be brought in PCRA petition); *see also **Commonwealth v. Hall**,* 771 A.2d 1232, 1235 (Pa. 2001) ("General Assembly intended that claim that **could**

Eligibility for Relief

be brought under the PCRA **must** be brought under that Act.") (emphases in original); *see also Commonwealth v. Descardes*, 101 A.3d 105 (Pa. Super. 2014) (*en banc*) (Bowes, J., concurring and dissenting); *Commonwealth v. Descardes*, 136 A.3d 493 (Pa. 2016).

In essence, once an issue has been previously determined or waived, the courts are statutorily prohibited from examining the issue. Only where the claim never was eligible for PCRA review can one seek review outside the PCRA. *See Commonwealth v. Turner*, 80 A.3d 754 (Pa. 2013) (citing *Hall*, 771 A.2d at 1236-1237). A more precise definition of cognizability would be that if the claim challenges the petitioner's conviction or sentence, it is cognizable.

C. Cognizability: PCRA Relief not Limited to Claims Impacting the Truth-Determining Process

Generally, PCRA review is limited to petitioners who claim that they were wrongfully convicted or are serving an illegal sentence. 42 Pa.C.S. § 9542; *Commonwealth v. Judge*, 916 A.2d 511 (Pa. 2007); *Commonwealth v. West*, 938 A.2d 1034 (Pa. 2007); *Coady v. Vaughn*, 770 A.2d 287 (Pa. 2001) (Castille, J., concurring); *Commonwealth v. Burkett*, 5 A.3d 1260 (Pa. Super. 2010). Indeed, the specifically-enumerated substantive issues that are reviewable pursuant to the PCRA relate to matters affecting a conviction and sentencing. 42 Pa.C.S. § 9543(a)(2). However, in *Commonwealth v. Hackett*, 956 A.2d 978 (Pa. 2008), the Supreme Court, in discussing the cognizability of a *Batson* claim, noted that the PCRA statute is to be construed broadly, despite the truth-determining process language of the statute. *See also Commonwealth v. Liebel*, 825 A.2d 630 (Pa. 2003); *Commonwealth v. Chester*, 733 A.2d 1242 (Pa. 1999); *Commonwealth v. Burkett*, 5 A.3d 1260 (Pa. Super. 2010).

Eligibility for Relief

Accordingly, claims regarding the mitigation phase of a capital sentence, the failure to file a direct appeal or a petition for allowance of appeal, or ineffectiveness during the plea bargaining process have all been held cognizable claims. *See Commonwealth v. Chester*, 733 A.2d 1242 (Pa. 1999); *Commonwealth v. Lantzy*, 736 A.2d 564 (Pa. 1999); *Commonwealth v. Liebel*, 825 A.2d 630 (Pa. 2003); *Commonwealth ex rel. Dadario v. Goldberg*, 773 A.2d 126 (Pa. 2001).

Nevertheless, the statutory language has given the Superior Court some pause in determining whether a claim couched in language that counsel was ineffective, or a claimed violation of the Constitution of the Commonwealth or the United States Constitution, is cognizable under the PCRA. *See Commonwealth v. Ginglardi*, 758 A.2d 193 (Pa. Super. 2000), *abrogation recognized by Commonwealth v. Prout*, 814 A.2d 693 (Pa. Super. 2003) (*Prout* held that an ineffectiveness claim regarding Rule 1100, the predecessor to Rule 600, is cognizable, recognizing the overruling of *Ginglardi*); *Commonwealth v. Lassen*, 659 A.2d 999 (Pa. Super. 1995) (holding counsel cannot be ineffective at a preliminary hearing because the hearing does not implicate the truth-determining process), *abrogation recognized by Commonwealth v. Stultz*, 114 A.3d 865 (Pa. Super. 2015).

Prior to the Pennsylvania Supreme Court's decision in *Commonwealth ex rel. Dadario v. Goldberg*, 773 A.2d 126 (Pa. 2001), the Superior Court routinely rejected claims because the court assumed that the issue did not implicate the truth-determining process or the reliability of a petitioner's adjudication of guilt. *Commonwealth v. Wolfe*, 580 A.2d 857 (Pa. Super. 1990); *Commonwealth v. Lewis*, 634 A.2d 633 (Pa. Super. 1993); *Commonwealth v. Blackwell*, 647 A.2d 915 (Pa. Super. 1994); *Commonwealth v. Moore*, 653 A.2d 24 (Pa. Super. 1995).

Eligibility for Relief

In light of ***Dadario***, Pennsylvania courts have permitted claims of ineffective assistance of counsel at a sentencing hearing and entertained claims of ineffectiveness at a sexually violent predator hearing. See *Commonwealth v. Walls*, 993 A.2d 289, 301 (Pa. Super. 2010); *see also Commonwealth v. Jones*, 942 A.2d 903 (Pa. Super. 2008); *but see Commonwealth v. Masker*, 34 A.3d 841 (Pa. Super. 2011) (*en banc*) (ineffectiveness challenge pertaining to representation at SVP hearing not cognizable).

The statutory construction problem was exacerbated by the practical adoption of Justice Castille's concurring opinion in *Commonwealth v. Grant*, 813 A.2d 726 (Pa. 2002), which prevents defendants from raising ineffectiveness claims that do not neatly fall within the parameters of the PCRA statute on direct appeal. The clearest solution to the statutory construction dilemma is, of course, to amend the statute to encompass all ineffective assistance of counsel challenges. As it currently stands, the Pennsylvania Supreme Court has determined that only in rare and unique instances does a post-conviction claim not fall within the ambit of the PCRA.

In *Commonwealth v. Judge*, 916 A.2d 511 (Pa. 2007), the Court held that an allegation that Canada violated the petitioner's rights under the International Covenant for Civil and Political Rights, by extraditing him, was not a cognizable claim under the PCRA. Similarly, in *Commonwealth v. West*, 938 A.2d 1034 (Pa. 2007), the Court determined that a substantive due process claim challenging the validity of recommitting the petitioner to prison after a nine year delay, in which the defendant had mistakenly been free on appeal bond, did not come within the parameters of the PCRA. *But see Commonwealth v. Burkett*, 5 A.3d 1260 (Pa. Super. 2010) (holding a due process claim challenging a sixteen year delay in disposing of PCRA petition was a cognizable claim under the statute).

Eligibility for Relief

In sum, if a claim is expressed in terms of ineffective assistance of counsel, the language of the PCRA relative to the truth-determining process and an adjudication of guilt does not serve as a bar to the claim. The critical issue is whether counsel rendered deficient performance and whether that performance caused the defendant to suffer actual prejudice. Hence, the viability of cases handed down by the Superior Court which find a claim non-cognizable should be viewed with caution.

Chapter 3: 42 Pa.C.S. § 9543(a)(2)(i)
Constitutional Violations

(a) General rule.--To be eligible for relief under this subchapter, the petitioner must plead and prove by a preponderance of the evidence all of the following:

....

(2) That the conviction or sentence resulted from one or more of the following:

(i) A violation of the Constitution of this Commonwealth or the Constitution or laws of the United States which, in the circumstances of the particular case, so undermined the truth-determining process that no reliable adjudication of guilt or innocence could have taken place.

Annotated Comments

Section 9543(a)(2)(i) is infrequently utilized as a means of affording or arguing for relief under the PCRA. Although petitioners routinely invoke the section, invariably their argument will be focused on section 9543(a)(2)(ii), relating to ineffective assistance of counsel. Thus, case law discussing and analyzing section 9543(a)(2)(i) is sparse. This, of course, is logical since ordinarily a violation of either the federal or Pennsylvania constitutions will be waived if it is not raised at the first opportunity. Hence, the challenge must usually be leveled as an ineffectiveness claim.

Legality of sentencing issues cannot be waived; therefore, double jeopardy issues, *Apprendi* violations, and *Alleyne* claims may be raised under this section without setting them forth under the ineffectiveness rubric. *Commonwealth v. Brown*, 872 A.2d 1139 (Pa. 2005); *but see Commonwealth v. Ousley*, 21 A.3d 1238, 1242 (Pa. Super. 2011) (holding in one sentence, with no analysis of long-standing precedent, that a legality of sentence claim not raised in a PCRA petition was waived). This statement in *Ousley* is in conflict with every other published decision to discuss legality of sentencing. *See* **Commonwealth v. Springer**, 961 A.2d 1262, 1264 n.3 (Pa. Super. 2008); **Commonwealth v. Robinson**, 931 A.2d 15 (Pa. Super. 2007) (*en banc*); **Commonwealth v. Quinlan**, 639 A.2d 1235 (Pa. Super. 1994); **Commonwealth v. Roach**, 453 A.2d 1001 (Pa. Super. 1983) (PCHA decision); **Commonwealth v. Staples**, 471 A.2d 847, 849-850 (Pa. Super. 1984); **Commonwealth v. Fahy**, 737 A.2d 214, 223 (Pa. 1999).

Under the PCHA, the Supreme Court announced a new constitutional rule regarding illegal sentences in the double jeopardy context. *See* **Commonwealth v. Tarver**, 426 A.2d 569 (Pa. 1981). In a subsequent PCHA case, it declined to apply the rule retroactively to any other collateral review petitioners. **Commonwealth v. Gillespie**, 516 A.2d 1180 (Pa. 1986) (OAJC). The PCHA statute expressly covered double jeopardy claims and afforded an avenue of relief based on "[t]he abridgment in any other way of any right guaranteed by the constitution or laws of this State or the constitution or laws of the United States, including a right that was not recognized as existing at the time of the trial if the constitution requires retrospective application of that right." 1966, January 25, P.L. (1965) 1580, no. 554, § 3(c)(12), effective March 1, 1966. (I note that retroactivity is not generally a constitutional matter, although a constitutional ruling given retroactive effect by the United States Supreme Court merges the federal constitutional question with retroactivity). *See* ***Montgomery v. Louisiana***, 136 S.Ct. 718 (2016).

Of course, if an individual has been sentenced and a new constitutional rule rendering that sentence unlawful is decided during the pendency of the person's direct appeal, applying the new ruling during PCRA review is not an improper retroactive application of the new constitutional pronouncement. ***Commonwealth v. Ruiz***, 131 A.3d 54 (Pa. Super. 2015) (defendant sentenced twelve days after ***Alleyne*** entitled to sentencing relief in timely PCRA matter). This is because new constitutional rules apply on direct appeal and a person sentenced illegally based on the constitutional rule should have been afforded relief on direct appeal even if the issue was not raised. ***Commonwealth v. Ferguson***, 107 A.3d 206 (Pa. Super. 2015). Failure on the part of counsel to raise the ***Alleyne*** issue, where the person was sentenced after ***Alleyne*** or was on direct appeal when ***Alleyne*** was decided, is ineffective assistance.

In ***Commonwealth v. Bretz***, 830 A.2d 1273 (Pa. Super. 2003), the Superior Court held that a claim that the defendant was not represented by counsel, because his attorney was on inactive status at the time of his conviction, was cognizable under section 9543(a)(2)(i). There is no violation where counsel is on inactive status for a technical reason such as failure to pay dues. ***Bretz***, 830 A.2d 1273; ***but see Commonwealth v. Grant***, 992 A.2d 152 (Pa. Super. 2010) (finding entitlement to relief where the attorney representing the defendant was not licensed to practice law due to substantive disciplinary actions).

Due process violations that could not be discovered at an earlier time, *i.e.*, a ***Brady v. Maryland***, 373 U.S. 83 (1963) violation, can fall within this section. *See* ***Commonwealth v. Simmons***, 804 A.2d 625 (Pa. 2001) (OAJC); ***Commonwealth v. Galloway***, 640 A.2d 454 (Pa. Super. 1994) (affording relief on a ***Brady*** claim based on Commonwealth's failure to inform the defendant that a witness's recollection was hypnotically refreshed). Further, deprivation of a defendant's right to counsel comes within the purview of this section. ***Commonwealth v. Smith***, 717 A.2d 1032 (Pa. Super. 1998) (remanding for evidentiary hearing to determine if defendant was denied his right to counsel). Indeed, any constitutional issue that cannot be waived can fall under section 9543(a)(2)(i).

Constitutional Violations

An Eighth Amendment cruel and unusual punishment claim and its state constitutional equivalent would appear to fall within the confines of this section as they are typically unwaivable. However, in *Commonwealth v. Robinson*, 82 A.3d 998 (Pa. 2013), the Supreme Court held that it is improper to seek a new Eighth Amendment rule via the PCRA. *See also Commonwealth v. Fears*, 86 A.3d 795 (Pa. 2014). Two justices in *Robinson* did not fully subscribe to this rationale and even the author of the majority, Chief Justice Castille, acknowledged that there could potentially be exceptions for derivative state constitutional claims under Article I, § 13, based on a United States Supreme Court decision altering Eighth Amendment jurisprudence. *See Commonwealth v. Cunningham*, 81 A.3d 1 (Pa. 2013) (Castille, C.J., concurring) *abrogated on other ground by Montgomery v. Louisiana*, 136 S.Ct. 718 (2016); *but see Robinson*, 82 A.3d at 1021 n.12.

The High Court's interpretation relative to "novel" Eighth Amendment claims is problematic for a number of reasons. First, the General Assembly expressly created the PCRA statute to govern illegal sentencing claims. *See* 42 Pa.C.S § 9542 ("This subchapter provides for an action by which persons convicted of crimes they did not commit and persons serving illegal sentences may obtain collateral relief."). In addition, the Supreme Court's interpretation creates bifurcated review for Eighth Amendment claims, which is at odds with the statute. *See id.* ("The action established in this subchapter shall be the sole means of obtaining collateral relief").

Moreover, section 9543(a)(2)(i), which the High Court did not discuss in *Robinson*, plainly evinces an intent to include Eighth Amendment issues. The PCHA also allowed for arguments seeking new constitutional rights to be advanced. The legislature presumably was aware that Eighth Amendment law is based on an evolving standards of decency test. It makes little logical sense to allow defendants to continually challenge the death

Constitutional Violations

penalty or mandatory sentences of life imprisonment without parole outside the PCRA. The more appropriate analysis is that such claims are cognizable but do not generally afford relief absent a holding by the United States Supreme Court. ***Cf. Commonwealth v. Chester***, 733 A.2d 1242 (Pa. 1999).

The Pennsylvania Supreme Court has reached its conclusion regarding novel Eighth Amendment issues based in part on the retroactivity timeliness provision. Notably, nothing in that section expressly prohibits the Pennsylvania Supreme Court from announcing a new rule via a timely PCRA petition. For example, the retroactivity provision does not read that the Pennsylvania Supreme Court can only announce a new rule during direct appeal. Although petitioners raising novel Eighth Amendment claims are seeking a new pronouncement, they are still asserting that their sentence was illegal when imposed. This is identical to defendant's proceeding on direct appeal. In both instances, no case law has held in favor of the rule sought, and the difference in timing is mostly inconsequential.

Indeed, at the time the retroactivity time provision was added to the PCRA, the legislature passed the Capital Unitary Review Act ("CURA"). CURA melded direct and collateral review for capital defendants, and also contained a retroactivity time provision. There is little difference in permitting novel Eighth Amendment claims during unitary review and a timely PCRA petition.

Pointedly, the retroactivity time provision of the PCRA would be an odd manner to eliminate Eighth Amendment challenges from the purview of the PCRA. This is not to say that constitutional claims that the death penalty is unconstitutional should necessarily succeed in the PCRA, only that these claims can be raised and addressed thereunder.

Chapter 4: 42 Pa.C.S. § 9543(a)(2)(ii)
Ineffective Assistance of Counsel

Section 9543. Eligibility for relief

(a) General rule.--To be eligible for relief under this subchapter, the petitioner must plead and prove by a preponderance of the evidence all of the following:

. . . .

(2) That the conviction or sentence resulted from one or more of the following:

. . . .

(ii) Ineffective assistance of counsel which, in the circumstances of the particular case, so undermined the truth-determining process that no reliable adjudication of guilt or innocence could have taken place.

Annotated Comments

A. *Strickland/Pierce* Test

The test for ineffective assistance of counsel in Pennsylvania is commonly referred to as the *Pierce* test based on the Pennsylvania Supreme Court decision that purported to adopt the United States Supreme Court's holding in *Strickland v. Washington*, 466 U.S. 668 (1984). *See Commonwealth v. Pierce*, 527 A.2d 973 (Pa. 1987). Virtually every PCRA decision since *Pierce* discusses this test. The cases that cite the test are too numerous to list; thus, I have only cited to several cases which give a good general overview of the ineffective assistance of counsel requirements.

To properly assert ineffective assistance of counsel, a petitioner must plead and prove that the underlying issue has arguable

Ineffective Assistance of Counsel

merit; counsel's actions or inaction lacked an objective reasonable basis; and actual prejudice resulted from counsel's act or failure to act. *Commonwealth v. Tedford*, 960 A.2d 1 (Pa. 2008) (citing *Commonwealth v. Pierce*, 527 A.2d 973, 975 (Pa. 1987)). Notably, the *Strickland* test is generally viewed as two prongs whereas the Pennsylvania articulation of the *Strickland* standard is broken down into three prongs. Counsel is presumed effective and will only be deemed ineffective if the petitioner demonstrates that counsel's performance was deficient and he was prejudiced by that deficient performance. *Commonwealth v. Daniels*, 963 A.2d 409, 419 (Pa. 2009). If a petitioner fails to plead or meet any elements of the above cited test his claim must fail. *Commonwealth v. Steele*, 961 A.2d 786 (Pa. 2008); *Commonwealth v. Sneed*, 899 A.2d 1067 (Pa. 2006), *abrogated on other grounds by Commonwealth v. Jones*, 951 A.2d 294 (Pa. 2008); *Commonwealth v. Basemore*, 744 A.2d 717 (Pa. 2000); *Commonwealth v. Paolello*, 665 A.2d 439 (Pa. 1995).

A claim has arguable merit if the facts upon which the claim are based, if taken as true, could afford relief. *Commonwealth v. Stewart*, 84 A.3d 701 (Pa. Super. 2013) (*en banc*); *see also Commonwealth v. Jones*, 876 A.2d 380, 385 (Pa. 2005) ("if a petitioner raises allegations, which, even if accepted as true, do not establish the underlying claim..., he or she will have failed to establish the arguable merit prong related to the claim"). Where the record refutes the alleged facts upon which the claim is premised, then the issue will be without arguable merit. "Whether 'facts rise to the level of arguable merit is a legal determination.'" *Stewart*, 84 A.3d at 707 (quoting *Commonwealth v. Saranchak*, 866 A.2d 292, 304 n.14 (Pa. 2005)).

"The test for deciding whether counsel had a reasonable basis for his action or inaction is whether no competent counsel would have chosen that particular course of action, or, the alternative, not chosen, offered a significantly greater potential for success." ***Stewart***, 84 A.3d at 707 (citing ***Commonwealth v. Colavita***, 993 A.2d 874 (Pa. 2010)). Counsel acts reasonably if his actions had some reasonable basis to effectuate his client's interest. ***Commonwealth v. Miller***, 987 A.2d 638 (Pa. 2009); ***Commonwealth v. Ogrod***, 839 A.2d 294 (Pa. 2003). The court is not to employ a hindsight analysis and compare counsel's actions with other action he could have taken. ***Commonwealth v. Miller***, 987 A.2d 638 (Pa. 2009). Ordinarily, an evidentiary hearing is necessary to determine whether counsel had a reasonable basis for his action or inaction. ***Commonwealth v. Colavita***, 993 A.2d 874 (Pa. 2010); *see also* ***Commonwealth v. McGill***, 832 A.2d 1014 (Pa. 2003); ***Commonwealth v. Reyes-Rodriguez***, 111 A.3d 775 (Pa. Super. 2015) (*en banc*).

Actual prejudice is established if there is a reasonable probability that, but for counsel's errors, the result of the proceeding would have been different. ***Commonwealth v. Steele***, 961 A.2d 786, 797 (Pa. 2008). A reasonable probability "is a probability sufficient to undermine confidence in the outcome." ***Commonwealth v. Rathfon***, 899 A.2d 365, 370 (Pa. Super. 2006). In order to succeed on an ineffectiveness claim, a petitioner must develop argument on each prong of the ***Pierce*** test. Boilerplate statements that counsel's actions had no reasonable basis and that the defendant suffered actual prejudice will not afford relief. ***Commonwealth v. Steele***, 961 A.2d 786 (Pa. 2008); ***Commonwealth v. Bond***, 819 A.2d 33 (Pa. 2002) (boilerplate claim that all counsel were ineffective was insufficient).

B. Commonwealth v. Pierce, 527 A.2d 973 (Pa. 1987) and "Actual Prejudice"

Prior to the decision in ***Pierce***, the ineffectiveness test in Pennsylvania was outlined in ***Commonwealth ex rel. Washington v. Maroney***, 235 A.2d 349 (Pa. 1967). In ***Pierce***, the Pennsylvania Supreme Court determined that ***Maroney*** implicitly recognized that a defendant was only entitled to relief on an ineffectiveness claim if he demonstrated that counsel's ineffectiveness resulted in actual prejudice, which it reasoned was outcome determinative. Thus, the Court in *Pierce* viewed the standard in *Maroney* as identical to the test that the Supreme Court set forth in *Strickland v. Washington*, 466 U.S. 668 (1984). The precise issue in *Pierce* was whether a determination that counsel's actions had no reasonable basis was *per se* prejudicial to the defendant.

The defendant in *Pierce* argued that *Maroney* did not require a showing of actual prejudice and that Pennsylvania should not adopt the *Strickland* test. According to the defendant in *Pierce*, once a defendant demonstrated that counsel had no reasonable basis to act or not act, prejudice was presumed and he was entitled to relief. The Pennsylvania Supreme Court rejected this argument. While this is no longer an issue in Pennsylvania, I have included this discussion because the argument that was rejected by the majority in *Pierce*, and discussed at length by Justice Zappala in dissent, is enlightening. Moreover, it will provide counsel, petitioners, and judges, a better overview of what is required for a person to be entitled to relief under the current PCRA statute. *See also Pierce*, 527 A.2d 973 (Nix, J., concurring) (discussing view that *Strickland* and *Maroney* standards are different).

The argument set forth by the defendant in *Pierce* was that if counsel had no reasonable basis for acting or failing to act he prejudiced the defendant since he compromised his client's constitutional right to effective representation. In his dissent, Justice Zappala recognized that *Maroney* required a showing of prejudice. However, he reasoned that if there was no reasonable basis to support trial counsel's decision, then counsel's decision was inherently prejudicial to the defendant.

According to Justice Zappala, the majority opinion incorrectly concluded that counsel could be ineffective and a petitioner would not be entitled to relief as a result of that ineffectiveness because the defendant was not prejudiced. Justice Zappala further opined that ineffective assistance of counsel could never be harmless. This view was the logical extension of his position that where counsel had no reasonable basis to act or not act the client was prejudiced.

Accordingly, the majority and Justice Zappala had a fundamental disagreement over the definition of "ineffective assistance of counsel." Justice Zappala asserted that ineffective assistance of counsel was prejudicial, while the majority appeared to find that counsel could be ineffective but a defendant not suffer actual prejudice. While the distinction may appear semantic at first blush, there is a critical distinction. *See Pierce*, 527 A.2d 973 (Nix, J., concurring); *see also Commonwealth v. Garvin*, 485 A.2d 36 (Pa. Super. 1984) (Spaeth, P.J., concurring). Under Justice Zappala's view, relief would be easier to obtain because overwhelming evidence could not be used to dismiss the claim. Indeed, Justice Zappala believed that the *Strickland/Pierce* test unfairly burdened a defendant by requiring that he show that counsel's actions substantially contributed to his conviction.

In light of the current PCRA statute, which is essentially a codification of *Strickland*, the *Pierce* standard is closer in line to allowing overwhelming evidence to overcome counsel's actions that may have resulted in some prejudice to the defendant. Perhaps Justice Zappala would have argued that no reliable adjudication can occur when counsel's actions or failure to act has no reasonable basis; nevertheless, a petitioner must demonstrate actual prejudice to be entitled to relief. Thus, even if trial counsel commits an error that error may be considered not to have contributed to the verdict.

If the attorney's error is determined not to have contributed to the verdict then no actual prejudice can be found. It is important to note that, in the context of a PCRA proceeding, the burden rests on the defendant. In contrast, in deciding whether an error was harmless the burden belongs with the Commonwealth. Hence, there is a critical difference between a harmless error analysis and determining whether counsel was ineffective. ***Commonwealth v. Howard***, 645 A.2d 1300, 1307 (Pa. 1994). Of course, if an error is harmless, counsel cannot be deemed ineffective. ***Commonwealth v. Barnett***, 121 A.3d 534 (Pa. Super. 2015).

C. *Strickland/Pierce* and the Ineffectiveness Test on Direct Appeal and PCRA Review

In ***Commonwealth v. Kimball***, 724 A.2d 326 (Pa. 1999), the Pennsylvania Supreme Court addressed the issue of whether claims of ineffective assistance of counsel were to be evaluated utilizing the same standard during both the direct appeal process and during a PCRA proceeding. The majority determined that courts should review ineffectiveness claims with the identical standard regardless of whether the claim was raised on direct appeal or in the context of a PCRA matter. The majority adopted the view expressed by Justice Cappy in his dissenting opinion in ***Commonwealth v. Buehl***, 658 A.2d 771 (Pa. 1995) (plurality).

Justice Cappy, in ***Buehl***, reasoned that the ***Strickland*** standard was strikingly similar to the language contained in the PCRA statute and that to utilize a more stringent standard would give rise to possible violations of a defendant's Sixth Amendment right to effective trial counsel. The ***Kimball*** Court also recognized that the ***Strickland*** test encompassed more than a strict prejudice analysis and additionally focused on the fundamental fairness of the proceeding. The United States Supreme Court has held that where the ineffectiveness did not undermine the fairness of the proceeding, even if the outcome of the proceeding would have been different, counsel would not be considered constitutionally ineffective. *Lockhart v. Fretwell*, 506 U.S. 364 (1993); *but see Missouri v. Frye*, 132 S.Ct. 1399 (2012); *Lafler v. Cooper*, 132 S.Ct. 1376 (2012). Since the Pennsylvania Supreme Court previously concluded that the *Strickland* test was identical to *Pierce*, the *Kimball* Court held that the outcome determinative prejudice aspect of the *Pierce* test was so intertwined with the fundamental fairness discussion contained within *Strickland* that the two could not be separated.

Justice Castille concurred and dissented in *Kimball*, opining that the *Strickland/Pierce* test was different than the standard of ineffectiveness to be employed during the PCRA. He contended that the truth-determining language was more stringent and required more than a finding that there was a reasonable probability that the outcome would have been affected. According to Justice Castille, the question was whether the reliability of the process was undermined. His analysis in this respect was well-reasoned, and highlighted that the decision in *Pierce*, though purportedly adopting *Strickland*, actually set forth a less stringent test.

Nevertheless, he misapprehended Justice Cappy's view in *Buehl* that applying differing standards implicated the Sixth Amendment right to effective trial counsel. Justice Castille asserted that there is no constitutional right to counsel during a PCRA. However, Justice Cappy's concern was not with PCRA counsel's effectiveness, but the enforcement mechanism for the Sixth Amendment right to effective trial counsel as outlined by *Strickland*. Importantly, *Strickland* itself was a collateral review case that indicated that there was no rational reason to distinguish between addressing ineffectiveness on direct appeal or in a collateral proceeding.

Hence, Justice Castille's position relative to the right to counsel during a PCRA was a *non-sequitur*. The issue was whether

Ineffective Assistance of Counsel

applying different standards would result in the PCRA statute itself being a violation of the Sixth Amendment because it created a standard incompatible with Supreme Court precedent. As Justice Cappy highlighted in *Buehl*, the language of the PCRA substantially tracked *Strickland* insofar as that decision stated, "The benchmark for judging any claim of ineffectiveness must be whether counsel's conduct so undermined the proper functioning of the adversarial process that the trial cannot be relied on as having produced a just result." *Buehl*, 658 A.2d at 784 (citing *Strickland v. Washington*, 466 U.S. at 686-687). The legislature also likely had in mind Justice Flaherty's dissenting opinion in *Commonwealth v. Watlington*, 420 A.2d 431, 437 (Pa. 1980), wherein he stated, "I would limit collateral review to claims (1) constituting a denial of due process or fundamental fairness that (2) significantly implicate the truth determining process."

Thus, *Kimball* correctly recognized that the *Strickland* standard is identical to the PCRA statute, but erroneously held that the fundamental fairness portion of *Strickland* is identical to the outcome determination prejudice test also posited in *Strickland*. This error, however, was based on its view that *Pierce* correctly stated that Pennsylvania's ineffectiveness test was identical to *Strickland*. The proper resolution would have been to hold that ineffectiveness claims during direct and PCRA review should be governed by the identical standard set forth in *Strickland* and that *Pierce's* analysis was incomplete because it concluded that a finding of prejudice was purely outcome determinative.[4]

---

4 Typically, the fundamental fairness of a proceeding can be questioned where counsel's actions or inaction would lead to a reasonable probability that the outcome would be different. It is the rare case where the outcome would be different but the fairness of the proceeding would not be undermined. *But see Missouri v. Frye*, 132 S.Ct. 1399 (2012); *Lafler v. Cooper*, 132 S.Ct. 1376 (2012) (both decisions focusing on outcome determinative process over

D. Deferring Claims of Ineffective Assistance of Counsel into the PCRA process

Subsequent to the decision in *Commonwealth v. Kimball*, 724 A.2d 326 (Pa. 1999), the Pennsylvania Supreme Court handed down its seminal decision in *Commonwealth v. Grant*, 813 A.2d 726 (Pa. 2002), which determined that all claims of trial counsel ineffectiveness should be deferred until collateral review. Accordingly, ineffective assistance of counsel issues rarely are addressed on direct appeal.[5]

Kimball helped pave the way for the decision in *Grant*. Had *Kimball* been decided differently, the decision in *Grant* likely would have been more difficult to reach because the appellate courts would have been utilizing differing standards to examine an ineffectiveness claim based on when the defendant raised the issues. The High Court's expanding of the scope of the PCRA in *Commonwealth ex rel. Dadario v. Goldberg*, 773 A.2d 126 (Pa. 2001), to include all constitutional ineffectiveness claims regardless of whether the claim was directly related to the "truth determining process," further cleared the path for the decision in *Grant*. Without *Dadario*, certain ineffectiveness claims may only have been able to be raised on direct appeal, *i.e.*, those that did not involve issues pertaining to jurisdiction, trial, or a guilty plea.

The decision in *Grant* did not involve a PCRA petition. Rather, it involved an appeal from a Superior Court decision that did not remand the defendant's case to the trial court for an evidentiary

---

fundamental fairness aspect of *Strickland*).

5 The Superior Court has held that allegations of appellate counsel's ineffectiveness alleged by that same attorney on direct appeal, where counsel failed to include a meritorious issue in his Pa.R.A.P. 1925(b) concise statement, may be addressed on direct review. *Commonwealth v. West*, 883 A.2d 654 (Pa. Super. 2005); *Commonwealth Marts*, 889 A.2d 608, 612 n.4 (Pa. Super. 2005).

Ineffective Assistance of Counsel

hearing on his claims of prosecutorial misconduct and trial counsel ineffectiveness. Both the defendant and the Commonwealth argued that the practice delineated in *Commonwealth v. Hubbard*, 372 A.2d 687 (Pa. 1977), that claims of ineffectiveness must be raised at the earliest stage in the proceedings at which the alleged ineffective attorney is no longer representing the defendant, should be followed.[6]

The defendant contended that the Superior Court erred in not remanding the case to the trial court to permit him to develop his claims. The *Grant* Court noted that the rule crafted by *Hubbard* was in conflict with traditional rules of appellate procedure, which barred the raising of a claim for the first time on appeal. The Court added that the *Hubbard* rule frequently prevented a trial court from issuing an opinion on the ineffectiveness issue, resulted in the appellate courts acting as fact-finders, and gave attorneys little time to raise the claims. It also found that due to the *Hubbard* decision, layered claims of ineffective assistance of counsel frequently arose.

In light of these considerations, and finding that other jurisdictions relegated most ineffectiveness claims to collateral review, the Pennsylvania Supreme Court held that issues involving ineffective assistance of trial/plea counsel *should* be deferred until collateral review. Justice Castille penned a concurring opinion reasoning that the Court did not go far enough and that the *Grant* deferral rule should be mandatory in all future cases that were not then pending on appeal. His view has substantially become the law.

---

6 The Pennsylvania Attorney General's Office also filed an *amicus* brief arguing in favor of retaining the *Hubbard* rule. Not a single party to the case argued in favor of the decision. Indeed, the Supreme Court *sua sponte* requested the parties to brief the issue and then disregarded their arguments.

Ineffective Assistance of Counsel

The Court explained that the new rule offered defendants the "best avenue to effect his Sixth Amendment right to counsel." *Grant*, 813 A.2d at 738. In this respect, *Grant* does permit the trial court/PCRA court to address any issues of ineffectiveness in the first instance and helps to lessen the oft-confusing layering of ineffective assistance of counsel claims. In addition, *Grant* allows counsel an appropriate amount of time to investigate possible extra-record claims and does not force new counsel to raise an ineffectiveness issue within ten days of sentencing in a post-sentence motion.

Prior to *Grant*, if new counsel was hired after sentencing he had a short time to investigate and review the record for possible ineffectiveness claims, which also had to include non-record claims. Further, when new counsel was hired for an appeal after the filing of a notice of appeal and Pa.R.A.P. 1925(b) concise statement, new counsel was required to raise any issues of trial counsel's ineffectiveness on appeal, but the trial court was not provided an opportunity to address the claim unless the appellate court remanded the case for a hearing. Hence, the exception to *Grant* provided for by *Commonwealth v. Bomar*, 826 A.2d 831 (Pa. 2003), permitted ineffectiveness claims to be reviewed on direct appeal if an evidentiary hearing was held on the issues and a trial court opinion was prepared addressing each of those issues.

Bomar was limited by the Superme Court in *Commonwealth v. Holmes*, 79 A.3d 562 (Pa. 2013). Pursuant to *Holmes*, a defendant can only raise ineffectiveness claims on direct appeal if he waives his right to PCRA review and establishes either good cause or exceptional circumstances. Nonetheless, *Grant's* purported attempt to rectify the lack of a complete record on appeal, and the improper casting of the appellate courts as a fact-finder by deferring all ineffective assistance of counsel issues until PCRA review, took the proverbial sledge hammer to a problem that merely required a tack hammer.

Ineffective Assistance of Counsel

The decision in ***Commonwealth v. Hubbard***, 372 A.2d 687 (Pa. 1977), which ***Grant*** overturned, specifically provided that claims not raised in a post-trial motion were waived. At the time ***Hubbard*** was decided, all issues were required to be preserved in a post-trial motion. ***Hubbard***, 372 A.2d at 696 n.8. Thus, if counsel did raise the issue, a record was developed below and the appellate court was not rendered a fact-finder on appeal. Only in the instance where new counsel was retained after post-verdict motions were filed (or supposed to be filed) did the problem arise, since the raising of an issue in a Pa.R.A.P. 1925(b) statement does not allow for the trial court to conduct any fact-finding.

Of course, if the issue was raised in a 1925(b) statement and required additional fact-finding, the appellate court could simply retain jurisdiction and remand for the appropriate hearing. *See **Hubbard***, 372 A.2d at 696. If the appellate court did not require additional fact-finding, it could resolve the issue. *Id*.; *see also id*. at 703 (Roberts, J., dissenting). Indeed, Justice Saylor, in his concurring opinion in ***Grant***, wrote that the majority neglected to mention that ***Hubbard*** provided for remand, which resolved the problematic issues that the majority assigned to the ***Hubbard*** rule, *i.e.*, "the tension between the rule against raising matters for the first time on direct appeal," and the difficulty with appellate courts acting as a fact-finder. ***Commonwealth v. Grant***, 813 A.2d 726, 739 (Pa. 2002) (Saylor, J., concurring).

The ***Grant*** majority also declined to address that, prior to ***Hubbard***, defendants did not waive extra-record claims of ineffectiveness by failing to raise them in a post-verdict motion. *See **Commonwealth v. Dancer***, 331 A.2d 435 (Pa. 1975); *see also **Commonwealth v. Ly***, 989 A.2d 2 (Pa. 2010) (Saylor, J., dissenting) (discussing ***Dancer***, ***Grant***, and ***Hubbard***). Therefore, the ***Grant*** majority, rather than simply return to the more flexible pre-***Hubbard*** era case law, fundamentally altered Pennsylvania law.

Ineffective Assistance of Counsel

Moreover, at the time the legislature passed the PCRA statute, the law permitting the raising of ineffectiveness claims on direct appeal was settled. The legislature did not intend to alter this practice and crafted the language of the scope of the PCRA accordingly. *See* 42 Pa.C.S. § 9542 ("This subchapter is not intended to limit the availability of remedies in the trial court or on direct appeal from the judgment of sentence").

As a result of *Grant*, the long standing principle that defendants must raise issues at the first opportunity or suffer waiver was abdicated with relation to claims of ineffective assistance of counsel. Counsel now must raise any issues of trial counsel's ineffectiveness on collateral appeal, unless the defendant waives his right to PCRA review of trial counsel's effectiveness, the trial court specifically holds a hearing on all of the ineffectiveness challenges, and authors a 1925(a) opinion addressing each of the claims. *See Commonwealth v. Holmes*, 79 A.3d 562 (Pa. 2013); *see also Commonwealth v. Montalvo*, 986 A.2d 84 (Pa. 2009); *Commonwealth v. Wright*, 961 A.2d 119 (Pa. 2008).

Accordingly, the interpretation of *Grant* requiring defendants to defer ineffectiveness issues to the PCRA makes certain claims more difficult to prove because of the passage of time. *See Commonwealth ex rel. Harbold v. Myers*, 207 A.2d 805, 810 (Pa. 1965) ("It is needless to dwell on the desirability of prompt review and of the difficulties presented by delayed review, difficulties which, among other things, affect both the ability to conduct satisfactorily a comprehensive habeas corpus hearing and the ability to proceed effectively with a new trial if one is required."); *Commonwealth ex rel. Stevens v. Myers*, 213 A.2d 613, 621 (Pa. 1965) ("habeas corpus hearings may be rendered progressively more difficult with the passage of time.").

E. The *Holmes* Exception

The ramifications of *Grant* proved problematic in light of the exception crafted by the Pennsylvania Supreme Court in *Commonwealth v. Bomar*, 826 A.2d 831 (Pa. 2003). In *Bomar*, the jury convicted the defendant of a vicious rape and murder. Following his conviction and sentencing, he filed a post-sentence motion that made numerous allegations of ineffective assistance of counsel. The trial court held hearings on the motions and authored an opinion addressing the issues.

Although the Pennsylvania Supreme Court authored *Bomar* after the *Grant* decision, *Grant* had yet to be decided when the defendant briefed his case. The Court, although clearly afforded an opportunity to do so, neglected to limit its exception to *Grant* to cases that occurred prior to the *Grant* decision. Thus, the *Bomar* Court held that where a defendant raises ineffectiveness claims before the trial court and the trial court creates a record and addresses those issues, an appellate court may address those claims on direct appeal. In cases where defendant's raised ineffective assistance claims on direct appeal under the *Bomar* exception, any new ineffectiveness issues raised under the PCRA must be layered. *Commonwealth v. Robinson*, 82 A.3d 998, 1005-1006 (Pa. 2013); *Commonwealth v. Chmiel*, 30 A.3d 1111, 1128 (Pa. 2011); *Commonwealth v. Sileo*, 32 A.3d 753 (Pa. Super. 2011) (*en banc*).

After *Bomar*, certain members of the court, most notably Chief Justice Castille, continuously attempted to reign in the applicability of its holding. In *Commonwealth v. Liston*, 977 A.2d 1089 (Pa. 2009), the scope and applicability of *Bomar* was discussed at length. *Liston* involved an appeal from a Superior Court decision which reinstated the defendant's right to a direct appeal *nunc pro tunc* based on trial counsel's failure to file a direct appeal. In *Liston*, the defendant filed a timely *pro se* PCRA petition asserting numerous ineffective assistance of

Ineffective Assistance of Counsel

counsel issues, among them was a claim that trial counsel neglected to file a notice of appeal. The PCRA court held an evidentiary hearing on all of the issues, but only addressed the petitioner's assertion that counsel failed to file a direct appeal. It found that the petitioner was entitled to the reinstatement of his direct appeal rights.

The petitioner then filed his direct appeal, which included issues of ineffective assistance of counsel. The Superior Court held that the ineffectiveness claims could not be reviewed on direct appeal, but, citing to ***Bomar***, held that whenever a PCRA court reinstates a defendant's right to a direct appeal it must also permit the defendant to file post-sentence motions. This would then provide the trial court with an opportunity to hold an evidentiary hearing and address any issues of ineffective assistance of counsel. In reversing, the Pennsylvania Supreme Court found that the Superior Court erred by, in effect, determining that the failure to file post-sentence motions was *per se* ineffective assistance of counsel and not requiring the petitioner to demonstrate actual prejudice.

The Court also reasoned that the application of ***Bomar*** in the manner proscribed by the Superior Court granted some defendants an extra chance at challenging their conviction by affording them two separate collateral attacks relative to ineffectiveness claims. Chief Justice Castille, in a concurring opinion, urged that ***Bomar*** be limited to its precise facts, *i.e.*, applicable only to pre-***Grant*** cases. According to the Chief Justice, unless the defendant expressly waived his right to PCRA review, all issues of ineffective assistance of counsel must be deferred until the petitioner filed a PCRA petition. *See also* ***Commonwealth v. Wright***, 961 A.2d 119 (Pa. 2008). Chief Justice Castille reasoned that this would guarantee only one round of challenges to ineffectiveness issues by melding PCRA review and direct review. In his view, this would speed up the PCRA process without providing two opportunities to attack the

Ineffective Assistance of Counsel

effectiveness of trial counsel.

He further opined that the continuing application of ***Bomar*** increased "the potential for abuse, breeds illogical and unfair results by arbitrarily allowing one class of defendants a second round of collateral review, and fosters the requirement that defendants raise 'layered' claims of ineffectiveness for purposes of collateral review." ***Liston***, 977 A.2d at 1099. Indeed, the Chief Justice remarked that is was "difficult to see how it could ever be fair to allow some, but not all, ...defendants an extra round of attack." ***Id***.[7] In sum, the Chief Justice argued that courts should never review ineffectiveness issues on post-verdict motions unless the defendant waived his right to PCRA review.

Chief Justice Castille's view was conclusively adopted in ***Commonwealth v. Holmes***, 79 A.3d 562 (Pa. 2013). Therein, the Supreme Court limited ***Bomar*** to pre-***Grant*** cases. It added that defendants could only raise ineffectiveness claims on direct appeal if they waived their right to PCRA review and either made a showing of exceptional circumstances or good cause. The ***Holmes*** Court described exceptional circumstances as situations where trial counsel's ineffectiveness was apparent from the record and immediate consideration of the claim would serve the interests of justice. It also reasoned that good cause could be shown in situations where the defendant received a short sentence or a probationary sentence. Indeed, Justice Saylor authored a concurring opinion opining that in cases involving short sentences that good cause would always be shown. Similarly, Justice Baer reasoned that defendants would be ill-advised to waive PCRA review unless a short sentence situation

---

7 In reality, the defendant was given a single direct appeal and a single PCRA with one opportunity to litigate an issue. If the defendant raised the issue on direct appeal it was previously litigated, if not, then the issue is addressed during collateral review—the same ineffectiveness issue is not addressed twice.

existed.

Justices Eakin and Todd concurred with the majority decision, but each wrote separately disagreeing with the waiver parameters expressed by the majority. Justice McAffery joined each of their respective opinions. Justice Eakin would not have found that under the good cause exception a defendant had to waive all future PCRA claims. Rather, he contended that only those issues that the defendant raised on direct appeal would be waived for purposes of collateral review.

Justice Todd, in her concurring opinion, reached a similar conclusion. In her view, if a defendant raised ineffectiveness claims on direct appeal under the good cause exception, only those ineffectiveness claims and any derivative ineffectiveness issues should be considered waived. Thus, defendants would be precluded from layering the claims in a subsequent PCRA petition.

The *Holmes* majority also held that, in the instance where a defendant waives PCRA review, the PCRA statutory provision for the filing of a timely petition is to be disregarded. Instead of a defendant having one-year from the finality of his judgment of sentence, the period "spent litigating collateral issues on unitary review must count toward the one year within which a PCRA petition must be filed." *Holmes*, 79 A.3d at 579. Accordingly, almost any PCRA petition filed thereafter would have to allege one of the timeliness exceptions and be filed within sixty days of when the new claim could have been presented.

In support of this paradigm, it noted that the legislature in the suspended Capital Unitary Review Act ("CURA") adopted a similar framework. The *Holmes* Court ignored that since the legislature adopted CURA at the same time it passed the timeliness amendments to the PCRA statute, and *Commonwealth v. Hubbard*, 372 A.2d 687 (Pa. 1977), was the governing precedent, that it did not intend for defendants who

Ineffective Assistance of Counsel

raised ineffectiveness claims during direct appeal to be subject to CURA-like timeliness provisions. Rather, petitioners would still have one year from completion of their direct appeal to file a timely PCRA petition, but would be subject to the waiver and previously litigated sections of the statute.

Prior to *Holmes*, the Superior Court, relying on *Commonwealth v. Liston*, 977 A.2d 1089 (Pa. 2009), and similar pronouncements made in *Commonwealth v. Wright*, 961 A.2d 119 (Pa. 2008) (*Wright* was a three to one decision), and in concurring opinions in *Commonwealth v. Montalvo*, 986 A.2d 84 (Pa. 2009) (Castille, J., concurring), and *Commonwealth v. Rega*, 933 A.2d 997 (Pa. 2007) (Castille J., concurring), held that a defendant must waive his right to PCRA review before a trial court holds an evidentiary hearing addressing claims of trial counsel's ineffectiveness for direct appeal. *Commonwealth. v. Barnett*, 25 A.3d 371 (Pa. Super. 2011) (*en banc*), *vacated*, 84 A.3d 1060 (Pa. 2014).[8] In neither *Barnett* nor subsequent cases published immediately thereafter, *see Commonwealth v. Quel*, 27 A.3d 1033 (Pa. Super. 2011), did the Superior Court remand for a waiver colloquy hearing.

The better procedure in cases like *Barnett* and *Quel*, where the trial court previously held an evidentiary hearing and addressed the ineffectiveness claims, would have been a limited remand. On remand, the court would have given the defendant a colloquy to ascertain whether the individual knowingly, intelligently, and voluntarily was waiving his or her statutory right to PCRA review of trial counsel ineffectiveness claims.[9]

---

8 The decision in *Commonwealth v. Barnett*, 25 A.3d 371 (Pa. Super. 2011) (*en banc*), was vacated in light of *Commonwealth v. Holmes*, 79 A.3d 562 (Pa. 2013). Had the *Barnett* Court remanded, the vacatur would have been unnecessary.

9 A suggested colloquy could consist, in part, of the following.

> Do you understand that for this Court and the

Ineffective Assistance of Counsel

Such a remand would not have run afoul of ***Commonwealth v. Grant***, 813 A.2d 726 (Pa. 2002), and its command that appellate courts refrain from acting as fact finders, as the issues would have been raised and addressed below. The colloquy would inform the defendant that claims of trial or plea counsel's ineffectiveness are ordinarily deferred until collateral review, *i.e.*, a PCRA proceeding. Only if the defendant waived his or her right to pursue claims of trial/plea counsel's effectiveness during PCRA review would the appellate courts be permitted to review

> appellate courts to determine your claims of trial/plea counsel's ineffectiveness you must waive your statutory right to PCRA review of those claims?
>
> By waiving your right to PCRA review you are foregoing a PCRA petition on other grounds, including appellate counsel's effectiveness, unless you establish a timeliness exception. Do you understand?
>
> You understand that all claims of trial (plea/suppression) counsel's ineffectiveness will be barred from PCRA review nor will you be able to raise ineffectiveness claims relative to direct appeal counsel, absent constructive denial of counsel?
>
> Do you understand that the time period for filing a PCRA petition begins to run once you elect to pursue unitary review, *i.e.*, raising ineffectiveness claims on direct appeal?
>
> Do you understand that any PCRA petition will be considered a serial petition?
>
> With the foregoing in mind, are you knowingly, intelligently, and voluntarily relinquishing your statutory right to PCRA review of ineffectiveness of trial counsel claims?

See also *Commonwealth v. Baker*, 72 A.3d 652 (Pa. Super. 2013) (discussing additional requirements of a waiver colloquy).

ineffectiveness claims on direct appeal. Where the defendant had not yet appealed and was attempting to allege ineffectiveness of trial counsel before filing his direct appeal, the court would be required to explain that it cannot consider those claims without a proper waiver.

In ***Commonwealth v. Baker***, 72 A.3d 652 (Pa. Super. 2013), the Superior Court suggested defendants complete a written colloquy as well. The panel also opined that a defendant be made aware of the PCRA eligibility requirements, the right to counsel on first time petitions, the type of issues that can be raised during PCRA review, and that the PCRA is generally the sole means of achieving collateral relief.

A concurring and dissenting opinion ("CO/DO") in ***Barnett*** expressed some concern relative to the manner in which the court is to proceed with a waiver colloquy. For example, the CO/DO took issue with whether the waiver would apply to PCRA review of appellate counsel's effectiveness. Similarly, the CO/DO was concerned with whether a defendant has to waive all issues, irrespective of ineffectiveness claims. In this respect, jurisdictional issues and legality of sentence claims cannot be waived and can be raised by the court *sua sponte*. The Supreme Court in ***Commonwealth v. Holmes***, 79 A.3d 562 (Pa. 2013), without apparently considering such non-ineffectiveness claims, ruled that all PCRA issues must be waived. This seems logically impossible since jurisdictional issues and claims involving sentences that exceed the statutory maximum cannot be waived. Of course, Justices Eakin, McAffery, and Todd would not have applied an across the board waiver requirement.

F. *Grant* and the Cognizability Problem

By funneling all ineffectiveness claims to collateral review, the Pennsylvania Supreme Court failed to consider that the PCRA statute was not intended to direct all claims of ineffective assistance of counsel into the collateral review paradigm. As a result of the decision in *Grant*, claims of ineffective assistance of counsel that do not necessarily implicate the reliability of an adjudication of guilt must be reviewed via the PCRA, although not actually cognizable under a plain reading of the statute. Phrased differently, *Grant* has prevented certain types of ineffective assistance of counsel issues from being addressed on direct review, forcing them to be raised in the ill-fitting PCRA context, thereby torturing the statutory interpretation of the statute.

As noted previously, the Supreme Court attempted to rectify this situation before *Grant* and paved the way for the *Grant* decision in *Commonwealth ex rel. Dadario v. Goldberg*, 773 A.2d 126 (Pa. 2001), by stating that any constitutional claim of ineffectiveness is cognizable under the statute. For example, prior to *Dadario* and *Grant*, claims regarding ineffective assistance of counsel and the discretionary aspects of sentencing were not considered cognizable under the PCRA. See *Commonwealth v. Blackwell*, 647 A.2d 915 (Pa. Super. 1994); *Commonwealth v. Lewis*, 634 A.2d 633 (Pa. Super. 1993).

Subsequent to those decisions, the Superior Court has reviewed claims involving the discretionary aspects of a sentence if set forth under the ineffectiveness rubric. See *Commonwealth v. Scassera*, 965 A.2d 247 (Pa. Super. 2009) (finding ineffectiveness discretionary aspect claim meritorious during PCRA review); *Commonwealth v. Lawrence*, 960 A.2d 473 (Pa. Super. 2008) (ineffectiveness discretionary claim was cognizable under PCRA); *Commonwealth v. Watson*, 835 A.2d 786 (Pa. Super. 2003) (ineffectiveness claim is cognizable); *cf. Commonwealth v. Wrecks*, 934 A.2d 1287 (Pa. Super. 2007) (stating pure discretionary sentencing claim was not cognizable under PCRA without distinguishing between ineffectiveness issues); *Commonwealth v. Friend*, 896 A.2d 607 (Pa. Super. 2006), *abrogated in part on other grounds by Commonwealth v. Pitts*, 981 A.2d 875 (Pa. 2009) (same).

G. *Grant* and the Elimination of Layered Claims

Before the decision in *Grant*, in order to avoid waiver, layered claims of ineffectiveness became necessary. For example, prior to *Grant*, if trial counsel did not raise an issue and new counsel on appeal did not raise that issue under the rubric of ineffective assistance of counsel, a defendant would have to layer the claim on collateral appeal. Hence, PCRA counsel would have to allege that both prior counsel were ineffective. If, however, trial counsel did properly preserve an issue and direct appeal counsel did not raise the issue on appeal, only the ineffectiveness of direct appeal counsel was necessary. After *Grant*, direct appeal counsel could not be ineffective for failing to raise trial counsel's ineffectiveness, but could be ineffective if they did not raise an issue (unrelated to ineffectiveness) that trial counsel had preserved.

The *Grant* Court's attempt to eradicate layered claims was largely unnecessary insofar as the courts are concerned. Addressing a layered claim of ineffective assistance of counsel is far from difficult, though properly raising and arguing such claims can be confusing, especially where numerous attorneys were involved. The court usually must only determine if the first level of counsel alleged to have been ineffective (in most instances trial counsel) was ineffective. If the first attorney was not ineffective, then no subsequent attorney could be ineffective and the petitioner cannot establish arguable merit on the layered claim.

Concomitantly, if the original attorney was ineffective the defendant has proved that he suffered prejudice that would have likely led to a different outcome and all other counsel was ineffective in failing to raise the issue, unless they had a reasonable basis for not addressing the claim. *See Commonwealth v. Reyes*, 870 A.2d 888 (Pa. 2005) (stating that establishing all three claims of trial counsel ineffectiveness on a layered claim of ineffectiveness only establishes the arguable merit prong of the test for subsequent counsel). Importantly, counsel still must properly layer the claim and present argument on each of the prongs of the ineffectiveness test relative to his successor attorneys.

H. *Grant's* Constitutional Implications

There has been no reported case cogently addressing whether *Grant's* requirements violate either due process, equal protection, or a defendant's Sixth Amendment right to effective counsel for defendants serving sentences that will expire before the PCRA process can be instituted. In this latter respect, the decision in *Grant* rendered claims of ineffectiveness moot where a court gave the defendant a short sentence since the appellate process takes approximately one year to complete and a person is not entitled to PCRA relief if he is not serving a sentence. The Superior Court attempted to craft a solution to this constitutional dilemma by creating a short sentence exception to *Grant*; however, the Pennsylvania Supreme Court initially rejected that attempt in *Commonwealth v. O'Berg*, 880 A.2d 597 (Pa. 2005).

The *O'Berg* decision allowed for the deprivation of the Sixth Amendment right to effective trial counsel so long as the sentence imposed, even if for a felony, was short. Indeed, a short probationary sentence that resulted from ineffective assistance of counsel could quickly turn into a lengthy prison sentence based even on technical violations of probation. Certainly, the decision to foreclose PCRA relief for those no longer serving a sentence made sense when defendants could raise ineffectiveness claims on direct appeal.

Additionally, while *Grant* recognized federal and state case law that *preferred* to defer ineffectiveness claims to collateral review, those cases cited by the *Grant* Court did not categorically remove all such claims from direct review.

Ineffective Assistance of Counsel

Pointedly, the cases actually allowed for such review in certain circumstances. Notably, although the United States Supreme Court in *Massero v. U.S.*, 538 U.S. 500 (2003), concluded similarly to *Grant* that deferring ineffectiveness claims to collateral review is more efficient than requiring defendants to raise the issue during direct review, it, like the actual majority opinion in *Grant*, did not mandate such a procedure.

In an attempt to fashion a more economical way of reviewing ineffectiveness claims, the practical adoption of Justice Castille's concurrence in *Grant* saddled defendants and prosecutors with the task of dealing with multiple appeals which could, in limited instances, be better handled in one appeal, at an earlier time, and when a defendant has a clear constitutional right to counsel. The Supreme Court largely rectified the constitutional problems with the *O'Berg* decision in *Commonwealth v. Holmes*, 79 A.3d 562 (Pa. 2013). The *Holmes* Court expressly set forth that a defendant could establish good cause to raise ineffectiveness claims on direct appeal if he received a short sentence.

Pre-*Holmes*, in the event that a defendant actually had a meritorious issue regarding ineffective assistance of counsel, he still had to serve his sentence despite an infirm conviction until the completion of his direct appeal. (Indeed, the defendant in *Grant* achieved federal *habeas* relief in 2013 based on ineffective assistance of trial counsel, over a decade after he attempted to raise and address the issue). Thus, prior to *Commonwealth v. Holmes*, 79 A.3d 562 (Pa. 2013), it was sometimes advisable for a defendant to forego his direct appeal and immediately file a PCRA if **all** of his claims rested on ineffectiveness of trial counsel and he hoped to achieve relief. *Holmes*, 79 A.3d at 580 ("in cases where the only viable issues are collateral, and the sentence is of sufficient length that the defendant will likely satisfy the PCRA custody requirement, the defendant always has the option of proceeding immediately to

Ineffective Assistance of Counsel

PCRA review"); *see also Commonwealth v. Turner*, 80 A.3d 754 (Pa. 2013); *but see Commonwealth v. Berry*, 877 A.2d 479 (Pa. Super. 2005) (*en banc*) (failing to file a direct appeal results in waiver of non-ineffectiveness claims); *Commonwealth v. Walls*, 993 A.2d 289 (Pa. Super. 2010) (same).

In light of *Holmes*, a defendant may choose to waive his right to PCRA review and assert in his post-sentence motion that the court should hold a full evidentiary hearing on any claims of ineffectiveness so that the claim can be raised on direct appeal since he is serving a short sentence that will render him unable to seek relief via the PCRA. *See Commonwealth v. Holmes*, 79 A.3d 562 (Pa. 2013); *see also Commonwealth v. Moore*, 978 A.2d 988 (Pa. Super. 2009) (remanding for filing of post-trial motions and *Bomar* hearing where the appellant was serving a sentence for contempt of Protection From Abuse orders, which cannot exceed six months); *compare Commonwealth v. Reigel*, 75 A.3d 1284 (Pa. Super. 2013) (holding that a defendant on direct appeal, in a case involving summary offenses, could not raise claims of ineffectiveness during that appeal despite the PCRA not being available due to his sentence being only a fine).

Arguments in support of *Grant* based on the statutory language of the PCRA also grossly missed the mark precisely because the statute was passed based on *Hubbard*-era law. The legislature could not have made a conscientious choice "that direct review provides sufficient due process for relatively minor infractions, no matter how grave a defaulted constitutional violation may have occurred." *Commonwealth v. O'Berg*, 880 A.2d at 603 (Castille, J., concurring).

In addition, the language of the scope of the PCRA statute, related to the PCRA being the sole means of achieving collateral relief, is actually a reflection that defendants were no longer to utilize common law writs after direct appeal to raise ineffectiveness and other collateral claims, not that such issues could not be raised on direct appeal. Further, the sole means language of the statute precedes the portion of section 9542 that reads, "This subchapter is not intended to limit the availability of remedies in the trial court or on direct appeal from the judgment of sentence[.]" It is established law that a later proviso in the same statute predominates where there is a conflict in the language and the language was passed at the same time. *Commonwealth v. Haun*, 32 A.3d 697 (Pa. 2011).

Therefore, the language of the PCRA statute does not support mandating that all claims of ineffectiveness be deferred until PCRA review. Rather, it evinces the sound policy of precluding usage of common law writs to raise claims that can be raised in the PCRA. Moreover, the legislature in crafting the waiver portion of the statute contemplated that defendants could waive ineffective assistance of counsel claims by not raising them on direct appeal. 42 Pa.C.S. § 9544(b) ("an issue is waived if the petitioner could have raised it but failed to do so before trial, at trial, during unitary review, on appeal or in a prior state postconviction proceeding."). Hence, the *Grant* decision actually flouts several portions of the PCRA statute.

Grant also proves to be constitutionally problematic in light of the United States Supreme Court's decision in *Padilla v. Kentucky*, 130 S.Ct. 1473 (2010), finding that advice regarding deportation, which is considered to relate to the collateral consequences of an adjudication of guilt, could result in an ineffectiveness finding. This is because the PCRA statute directly bars relief for collateral consequences. *See* 42 Pa.C.S. § 9542. Since *Grant* has been interpreted to compel defendants to raise all ineffectiveness issues during PCRA review, either the language of the PCRA statute must yield or *Grant's* requirement that all ineffectiveness claims be deferred to collateral review unconstitutionally deprives petitioners of an opportunity to challenge ineffectiveness issues related to the collateral consequences of their adjudication of guilt and sentencing. *See*

Commonwealth v. Masker, 34 A.3d 841 (Pa. Super. 2011) (Bowes, J., concurring and dissenting).

It should also be noted that while the United States Supreme Court has held that there is no Sixth Amendment right or due process right to counsel during collateral review, *Pennsylvania v. Finley*, 481 U.S. 551 (1987); *Coleman v. Thompson*, 501 U.S. 722 (1991), the High Court has not foreclosed the possibility that there is a constitutional right to counsel on a first time state collateral proceeding where that proceeding is the first opportunity the defendant will have to raise a particular issue, *i.e.*, ineffective assistance of counsel. *Coleman v. Thompson*, 501 U.S. 722, 754-757 (1991); *see also id.* at 773-774 (Blackmun, J., dissenting with whom Justice Marshall and Justice Stevens joined); *Commonwealth v. Figueroa*, 29 A.3d 1177 (Pa. Super. 2011); *Martinez v. Ryan*, 132 S.Ct. 1309 (2012).

Thus, it appears that in states like Pennsylvania, where claims of ineffective assistance of counsel can generally only be raised during collateral review, the United States Supreme Court would recognize a constitutional right to counsel for purposes of the initial trial level PCRA proceeding. *But see Commonwealth v. Holmes*, 79 A.3d 562 (Pa. 2013). Hence, although not yet announced, in light of *Grant* and *Coleman*, petitioners could argue that they not only have a rule-based right to counsel and therefore a rule-based right to effective counsel, but possibly a federal and state constitutional right to counsel during their first PCRA process at the PCRA court level. *See* discussion in Chapter 17 on Pa.R.Crim.P. 904; *but see Commonwealth v. Smith*, 121 A.3d 1049 (Pa. Super. 2015).

Chapter 5: 42 Pa.C.S. § 9543(a)(2)(ii)
Common Ineffective Assistance Issues

Annotated Comments

By far the most frequently presented issues during PCRA review are those of ineffective assistance of counsel. Indeed, as discussed in the previous chapter, in light of the Pennsylvania Supreme Court's decision in *Commonwealth v. Grant*, 813 A.2d 726 (Pa. 2002), claims of ineffectiveness must be deferred until PCRA proceedings, unless one waives the right to such review. *Commonwealth v. Holmes*, 79 A.3d 562 (Pa. 2013). This chapter offers a brief synopsis of claims that routinely appear in PCRA petitions.

A. *Per Se* Ineffectiveness Claims

Certain claims do not require a petitioner to demonstrate actual prejudice. *See U.S. v. Cronic*, 466 U.S. 648 (1984). In these rare instances, the court will presume prejudice. For example, the failure to protect a defendant's direct appeal rights, *i.e.*, the failure to file a notice of appeal when directed to do so is *per se* ineffectiveness and requires the PCRA court to reinstate a defendant's right to appeal *nunc pro tunc*. ***Commonwealth v. Lantzy***, 736 A.2d 564 (Pa. 1999); *compare **Commonwealth v. Pulanco***, 954 A.2d 639 (Pa. Super. 2008) (defendant not entitled to reinstatement of direct appeal based on allegation of inadequate Pa.R.A.P. 1925(b) statement).

It should be pointed out that even if the defendant did not ask counsel to file a direct appeal, counsel may be held ineffective for failing to adequately consult with his client about his right to appeal. In this instance, however, the petitioner must establish the three-prong ineffectiveness test. *See **Commonwealth v. Markowitz***, 32 A.3d 706 (Pa. Super. 2011); ***Commonwealth v. Carter***, 21 A.3d 680 (Pa. Super. 2011); ***Commonwealth v. Touw***,

781 A.2d 1250 (Pa. Super. 2001); *Roe v. Flores-Ortega*, 528 U.S. 470 (2000). Similarly, counsel may be held ineffective for failing to consult with his client about the ability to file a petition for allowance of appeal. Again, counsel is not *per se* ineffective in this scenario. *See Commonwealth v. Gadsden*, 832 A.2d 1082 (Pa. Super. 2003).

In *Commonwealth v. Lantzy*, 736 A.2d 564 (Pa. 1999), the High Court determined that a direct appeal implicates the truth determining process and deprivation of a direct appeal, although not involving the adjudication at trial or a guilty plea, was cognizable under the PCRA. *Lantzy*, 736 A.2d at 568, 571. A request for *nunc pro tunc* relief must be asserted in a PCRA petition. *Commonwealth v. Eller*, 807 A.2d 838 (Pa. 2002); *Commonwealth v. Hall*, 771 A.2d 1232 (Pa. 2001). The request, therefore, must be asserted within one year of the final judgment of sentence or the court has no jurisdiction to afford relief. *Commonwealth v. Robinson*, 837 A.2d 1157 (Pa. 2003); *Commonwealth v. Geer*, 936 A.2d 1075 (Pa. Super. 2007); *Commonwealth v. Fairiror*, 809 A.2d 396 (Pa. Super. 2002).

This may prove problematic in the situation where the defendant believes he filed a timely notice of appeal but is mistaken. Such a scenario is not far-fetched. Where a defendant is represented by counsel but files a *pro se* post-sentence motion, the *pro se* motion will not toll the thirty day period for filing an appeal since the filing is a nullity, *see Commonwealth v. Nischan*, 928 A.2d 349, 355 (Pa. Super. 2007), even if the trial court addresses the motion.[10] The direct appeal may then be quashed as untimely

---

10 A trial court is under no obligation to respond to a *pro se* filing where the petitioner is represented by counsel. *See Commonwealth v. Pursell*, 724 A.2d 293 (Pa. 1999); *Commonwealth v. Ellis*, 626 A.2d 1137 (Pa. 1993); *Commonwealth v. Colson*, 490 A.2d 811 (Pa. 1985) *abrogated on other grounds by Commonwealth v. Burke*, 781 A.2d 1136 (Pa. 2001). Further, the Comments to Pa.R.Crim.P. 720 and Pa.R.Crim.P. 576, when read together, indicate that no deadline is

and the run date for the one year jurisdictional time bar will not have been tolled. ***See Commonwealth v. Brown***, 943 A.2d 264 (Pa. 2008).

If the appellate court takes more than one year to quash the case then the defendant will have lost his opportunity to file a timely petition. In addition, since a PCRA petition is ordinarily dismissed if it is filed while a direct appeal is pending, the defendant may not be able to preserve his ability to file a timely PCRA petition. ***See Commonwealth v. Seay***, 814 A.2d 1240 (Pa. Super. 2003); ***Commonwealth v. Leslie***, 757 A.2d 984 (Pa. Super. 2000); ***Commonwealth v. O'Neil***, 573 A.2d 1112 (Pa. Super. 1990). Counsel is therefore advised to file a PCRA petition and request that the court stay the proceedings rather than dismiss the petition if it appears that there is a possibility that the defendant's direct appeal will be quashed.

Once the court determines that counsel has failed to file a requested direct appeal, the petitioner is entitled to the reinstatement of his direct appeal rights. ***Compare Commonwealth v. Markowitz***, 32 A.3d 706 (Pa. Super. 2011) and ***Commonwealth v. Donaghy***, 33 A.3d 12 (Pa. Super. 2011). However, the court should ordinarily not reach the merits of any additional claims raised in the petition. ***Commonwealth v. Bronaugh***, 670 A.2d 147 (Pa. Super. 1995); ***Commonwealth v. Hoyman***, 561 A.2d 756 (Pa. Super. 1989). In ***Commonwealth v. Harris***, 114 A.3d 1 (Pa. Super. 2015), the Superior Court held that the lower court erred in addressing the merits of the petitioner's trial counsel ineffectiveness claims and granting him a new trial after it determined that he was entitled to the

---

triggered by the filing of a *pro se* motion when the individual is represented by counsel. A *pro se* filing will be considered where the person is represented by counsel where counsel files a ***Turner/Finley*** no-merit letter and the court issues a notice of intent to dismiss but counsel has not yet been permitted to withdraw. ***See Commonwealth v. Pitts***, 981 A.2d 875 (Pa. 2009).

Common Ineffective Assistance Issues

reinstatement of his direct appeal rights

Should the defendant fail to garner relief from his *nunc pro tunc* direct appeal, he may file a subsequent PCRA petition. That petition will be considered a first PCRA petition and does not fall under the *Commonwealth v. Lawson*, 549 A.2d 107 (Pa. 1988) standard that requires a petitioner to establish a miscarriage of justice. *Commonwealth v. Figueroa*, 29 A.3d 1177 (Pa. Super. 2011); *Commonwealth v. Fowler*, 930 A.2d 586 (Pa. Super. 2007); *Commonwealth v. O'Bidos*, 849 A.2d 243 (Pa. Super. 2004); *Commonwealth v. Karanicolas*, 836 A.2d 940 (Pa. Super. 2003).

Where the petitioner alleges that trial counsel failed to file a direct appeal, the PCRA court must hold an evidentiary hearing on the issue, so long as the defendant timely filed his petition. A petitioner seeking reinstatement of his direct appeal rights still bears the burden of proving by a preponderance of the evidence that he requested counsel to file a direct appeal. *Commonwealth v. Touw*, 781 A.2d 1250 (Pa. Super. 2001) (the failure of trial counsel to meet with defendant or consult with defendant about filing an appeal is not *per se* ineffectiveness, as petitioner must still show he was prejudiced); *Roe v. Flores-Ortega*, 528 U.S. 470 (2000); *Commonwealth v. Harmon*, 738 A.2d 1023 (Pa. Super. 1999). Where the PCRA court reinstates a petitioner's direct appeal rights, the Commonwealth must challenge that order within thirty days. *Commonwealth v. Walter*, 119 A.3d 255 (Pa. 2015). Failing to contest the reinstatement order within thirty days precludes the Commonwealth from arguing that the subsequent appeal is untimely or an appellate court from raising the issue *sua sponte*. *Walter*, 119 A.3d at 260 n.5.

Unlike failing to file a direct appeal, neglecting to file a post-sentence motion is not *per se* ineffectiveness. *Commonwealth v. Liston*, 977 A.2d 1089 (Pa. 2009); *Commonwealth v. Reaves*, 923 A.2d 1119 (Pa. 2007); *Commonwealth v. Fransen*, 986

A.2d 154 (Pa. Super. 2009); *but see Commonwealth v. Corley*, 31 A.3d 293 (Pa. Super. 2011) (where defendant was completely denied counsel after his conviction, reinstatement of post-sentence motion rights is appropriate). Hence, where counsel simultaneously seeks the reinstatement of post-sentence motion rights *nunc pro tunc*, via his PCRA petition, the petitioner must establish the three-prong ineffectiveness test. *Commonwealth v. Liston*, 977 A.2d 1089 (Pa. 2009); *Commonwealth v. Reaves*, 923 A.2d 1119 (Pa. 2007); *Commonwealth v. Fransen*, 986 A.2d 154 (Pa. Super. 2009).

Where a defendant has already filed a PCRA petition and did not appeal from its dismissal, the reinstatement of his PCRA appellate rights is treated as a serial PCRA petition. *Commonwealth v. Fairiror*, 809 A.2d 396 (Pa. Super. 2002). Furthermore, it is virtually impossible for a petitioner to file a PCRA petition seeking reinstatement of his PCRA appellate rights within one year of the completion of direct review, unless he files his PCRA immediately after his direct appeal concludes and the PCRA court made a decision relatively quickly. *Commonwealth v. Fairiror*, 809 A.2d 396 (Pa. Super. 2002). Thus, a PCRA petition seeking reinstatement of the right to appeal the dismissal of a previous PCRA petition will almost never entitle the petitioner to relief because it will be untimely. *But see Commonwealth v. Bennett*, 930 A.2d 1264 (Pa. 2007) (finding that counsel's abandonment can be a newly-discovered fact for purposes of timeliness exception); *see also Commonwealth v. Blackwell*, 936 A.2d 497 (Pa. Super. 2007).

An assertion that appellate counsel failed to file a petition for allowance of appeal is cognizable under the PCRA and, if the claim is brought within the appropriate time frame, requires an evidentiary hearing to determine if appellate counsel and the petitioner discussed filing the petition. *Commonwealth v. Liebel*, 825 A.2d 630 (Pa. 2003); *Commonwealth v. Cooke*, 852 A.2d 340 (Pa. Super. 2004); *Commonwealth v. Ellison*, 851

A.2d 977 (Pa. Super. 2004); ***Commonwealth v. Gadsden***, 832 A.2d 1082 (Pa. Super. 2003).

In ***Commonwealth v. Liebel***, 825 A.2d 630 (Pa. 2003), the Supreme Court held that counsel's failure to file a requested petition for allowance of appeal was a cognizable claim. It further opined that counsel's failure to file a requested petition for allowance of appeal, where counsel informed his client that he would do so, left the petitioner without counsel.

In a footnote, it stated that the petitioner still must establish the three-prong ineffectiveness test before the PCRA court. ***Commonwealth v. Liebel***, 825 A.2d 630, 636 n.11 (Pa. 2003). Subsequent decisions have held that prejudice is presumed. *See* ***Commonwealth v. Reed***, 971 A.2d 1216 (Pa. 2009); ***Commonwealth v. Reaves***, 923 A.2d 1119 (Pa. 2007); ***Commonwealth v. Ellison***, 851 A.2d 977 (Pa. Super. 2004). This is because the ***Liebel*** Court held that the petitioner was not required to show that the Supreme Court would have granted the petition in order to establish prejudice. If a petitioner requested the appeal, then the PCRA court must determine if counsel's failure to file the petition was justified. ***Commonwealth v. Ellison***, 851 A.2d 977 (Pa. Super. 2004).

The petitioner does not need to establish his innocence for reinstatement of his appeal rights. ***Commonwealth v. Ellison***, 851 A.2d 977 (Pa. Super. 2004). However, in ***Ellison***, the court did hold that, in order for counsel to be *per se* ineffective, the petitioner must not only show that he asked his attorney to file a petition for allowance of appeal but that the claims were not completely frivolous. ***Ellison***, 851 A.2d at 981; *see also* ***Commonwealth v. Liebel***, 825 A.2d at 635. Relying on ***Ellison***, the Superior Court in ***Commonwealth v. Rigg***, 84 A.3d 1080 (Pa. Super. 2014), held that appellate counsel was not *per se* ineffective for declining to seek allowance of appeal where the defendant's sole challenge was a discretionary aspects of sentencing claim. The ***Rigg*** Court reasoned that because the Pennsylvania Supreme Court did not have jurisdiction to review the merits of the discretionary sentencing matter, prejudice would not be presumed.

In ***Commonwealth v. Bath***, 907 A.2d 619 (Pa. Super. 2006), the Superior Court differentiated between the situation where a client asks his attorney to file a petition for allowance of appeal and the failure of counsel to consult with his client about filing a discretionary appeal. In the latter instance, it concluded that counsel is not *per se* ineffective, but a petitioner could establish counsel was ineffective if a duty to consult arose and the attorney neglected to adequately consult with his client.

The failure of counsel to file an amended petition on behalf of his or her client has been held to be *per se* ineffectiveness and requires the appellate court to remand to the PCRA court to permit counsel the opportunity to file the appropriate petition. ***Commonwealth v. Powell***, 787 A.2d 1017 (Pa. Super. 2001); ***Commonwealth v. Priovolos***, 746 A.2d 621 (Pa. Super. 2000); ***Commonwealth v. Davis***, 526 A.2d 440 (Pa. Super. 1987); ***Commonwealth v. Irons***, 385 A.2d 1004 (Pa. Super. 1978); *see also* ***Commonwealth v. Tedford***, 781 A.2d 1167 (Pa. 2001); ***Commonwealth v. Burkett***, 5 A.3d 1260 (Pa. Super. 2010) (collecting cases); ***Commonwealth v. Lasky***, 934 A.2d 120 (Pa. Super. 2007); ***Commonwealth v. Perez***, 799 A.2d 848 (Pa. Super. 2002) (counsel must be appointed on first time petition).

This can be the situation even where evidentiary hearings have been held and appointed counsel filed memorandum in support of the defendant's PCRA petition. ***Commonwealth v. Davis***, 526 A.2d 440 (Pa. Super. 1987); ***but see Commonwealth v. Murray***, 836 A.2d 956 (Pa. Super. 2003), *abrogated on other grounds by* ***Commonwealth v. Robinson***, 970 A.2d 455 (Pa. Super. 2009) (*en banc*). Whenever counsel files a memorandum or brief the appellate courts should treat it as the amended PCRA petition. It

Common Ineffective Assistance Issues

is a waste of judicial resources to remand for the filing of an amended petition where an evidentiary hearing has been held developing the issues and counsel filed a document arguing in favor of the petitioner's issues.

Neglecting to file an appellate brief is *per se* ineffective assistance. *See Commonwealth v. Bennett*, 930 A.2d 1264 (Pa. 2007) (finding counsel's failure to file appellate brief could constitute newly-discovered fact for timeliness exception). However, the filing of a deficient brief is not *per se* ineffective assistance of counsel. *Commonwealth v. Reed*, 971 A.2d 1216 (Pa. 2009). Yet, where a counseled brief is filed but results in the appellate court being unable to reach the merits of any of the issues due to its insufficiencies, counsel has rendered *per se* ineffective assistance. *See Commonwealth v. Rosado*, __ A.3d __ (Pa. 2016) (filed November 22, 2016); *Commonwealth v. Fink*, 24 A.3d 426 (Pa. Super. 2011); *Commonwealth v. Johnson*, 889 A.2d 620 (Pa. Super. 2005); *Commonwealth v. Franklin*, 823 A.2d 906 (Pa. Super. 2003); *Commonwealth v. Hernandez*, 755 A.2d 1 (Pa. Super. 2000); *but see Commonwealth v. Mikell*, 968 A.2d 779 (Pa. Super. 2009) (defendant is not entitled to reinstatement of his direct appeal rights where counsel perfects the appeal but does not raise certain issues).

Failing to file or improperly filing and serving a Pa.R.A.P. 1925(b) concise statement for purposes of direct appeal is *per se* ineffectiveness, and will require a remand for counsel to file the appropriate concise statement. ***Commonwealth v. Halley***, 870 A.2d 795 (Pa. 2005). *But see Commonwealth v. Hill*, 16 A.3d 484, 495 n.14 (Pa. 2011) ("We note, however, that the amendment speaks of remand only in 'criminal cases.' Technically, the PCRA is civil in nature.... Moreover, according to the Note to the amended Rule [1925(b)], amended subsection (c)(3) is intended to codify the procedure the Superior Court devised in *Commonwealth v. West*, *supra*, which was neither a

Rule 1925(b) case nor a PCRA appeal.");[11] ***Commonwealth v. Pulanco***, 954 A.2d 639 (Pa. Super. 2008) (filing of Pa.R.A.P. 1925(b) statement that preserves some but not all claims does not entitle defendant to reinstatement of direct appeal rights).

The Superior Court has also held that the untimely filing of a Pa.R.A.P. 1925(b) statement is ineffective assistance of counsel. ***Commonwealth v. Burton***, 973 A.2d 428 (Pa. Super. 2009). The untimely filing or failure to file a Pa.R.A.P. 1925(b) statement does not ordinarily require PCRA relief because the appellate courts will remand to the trial court during the direct appeal process. In ***Commonwealth v. Lane***, 81 A.3d 974 (Pa Super. 2013), a remand did not occur during the earlier direct appeal. The ***Lane*** Court found counsel *per se* ineffective for filing an untimely Pa.R.A.P. 1925(b) statement and reinstated the defendants appeal rights, although on direct appeal an *en banc* panel of the Superior Court considered a legality of sentence issue.

Failing to meet with a capital defendant face-to-face prior to trial, though held not to be *per se* ineffective, did result in a successful ineffectiveness claim without the Supreme Court analyzing whether there was a reasonable probability that the outcome of the trial would have been different. ***Commonwealth v. Brooks***, 839 A.2d 245 (Pa. 2003); ***see also id.*** (Castille, J., concurring); ***Commonwealth v. Perry***, 644 A.2d 705 (Pa. 1994) (capital counsel ineffective under ***Strickland/Pierce*** for failing to interview client, use investigator, and not being aware that client was facing death penalty); ***but see Commonwealth v. Elliott***, 80 A.3d 415 (Pa. 2013); ***Commonwealth v. Breakiron***, 729 A.2d 1088, 1093 (Pa. 1999) ("The length of time that trial counsel spends with defendant does not, by itself, imply the extent of trial counsel's preparation for trial."); ***Commonwealth***

---

11 Failing to file a Pa.R.A.P. 1925(b) statement during a PCRA proceeding will result in waiver.

Common Ineffective Assistance Issues

v. Poindexter, 646 A.2d 1211 (Pa. Super. 1994) (same); ***Commonwealth v. Johnson***, 51 A.3d 237 (Pa. Super. 2012) (*en banc*).

Agreeing to a stipulated non-jury trial is not *per se* ineffective assistance. ***Commonwealth v. Brown***, 18 A.3d 1147 (Pa. Super. 2011). In addition, neglecting to life qualify a capital jury is not *per se* ineffective assistance of counsel. ***Commonwealth v. Carson***, 913 A.2d 220 (Pa. 2006); ***Commonwealth v. Bond***, 819 A.2d 33 (Pa. 2002); ***Commonwealth v. Rollins***, 738 A.2d 435 (Pa. 1999). Further, the Supreme Court will not presume prejudice where a defendant waives his right to a jury trial where no oral colloquy is given. ***Commonwealth v. Mallory***, 941 A.2d 686 (Pa. 2008). Where counsel is not licensed to practice as a result of a suspension at the time of trial, the Superior Court has determined that the defendant was constructively without counsel. ***Commonwealth v. Grant***, 992 A.2d 152 (Pa. Super. 2010). In sum, only where there is constructive or actual abandonment of counsel that entirely deprives a defendant of representation will the courts deem counsel *per se* ineffective. ***See U.S. v. Cronic***, 466 U.S. 648 (1984).

B. Layered Claims: *McGill* and *Hall*

Before the decision in ***Commonwealth v. Grant***, 813 A.2d 726 (Pa. 2002), whenever a petitioner had different counsel at trial and on direct appeal it was often necessary to frame issues which were not raised at trial or on direct appeal by layering the claims. ***Commonwealth v. McGill***, 832 A.2d 1014 (Pa. 2003); ***Commonwealth v. Hall***, 872 A.2d 1177 (Pa. 2005). A layered claim argues that all prior counsel were ineffective in failing to raise the underlying issue. *McGill*, 832 A.2d 1014. In order to properly layer the claim, the petitioner must go through the three-prong ineffectiveness test for each counsel he alleges was ineffective. ***Commonwealth v. Reyes***, 870 A.2d 888 (Pa. 2005).

Common Ineffective Assistance Issues

In the context of alleging PCRA counsel ineffectiveness, the claim must also be layered. Thus, the petitioner would have to go through the three-prong test for PCRA counsel, perhaps direct appeal counsel, and trial counsel. *See Commonwealth v. Morales*, 701 A.2d 516 (Pa. 1997); *Commonwealth v. Ligons*, 971 A.2d 1125 (Pa. 2009) (plurality); *but see Commonwealth v. Pitts*, 981 A.2d 875 (Pa. 2009) (holding that claims of ineffective assistance of PCRA counsel cannot be raised for first time on appeal); *Commonwealth v. Henkel*, 90 A.3d 16 (Pa.Super. 2014) (*en banc*) (collecting Pennsylvania Supreme Court cases and holding the same).

If the underlying issue was trial counsel's ineffectiveness, and the case occurred after the 2002 decision in *Grant*, then direct appeal counsel cannot be found ineffective for failing to raise trial counsel's ineffectiveness on direct appeal. On the other hand, if trial counsel raised an issue at trial or in a post-sentence motion and direct appeal counsel failed to raise that issue, then the issue is waived unless counsel alleges direct appeal counsel was ineffective. This claim, however, is not a layered claim of ineffectiveness.

Where a petitioner properly develops his layered record-based claim related to trial counsel, but fails to develop his claim with respect to his later counsel and he was not placed on notice of this deficiency, he was formerly entitled to a remand to the PCRA court in cases that were pending prior to the decision in *McGill*. Of course, where the petitioner is unable to meet all three prongs of the ineffectiveness test relative to trial counsel, there is no need for remand and the petitioner's issue must fail. *Commonwealth v. McGill*, 832 A.2d 1014 (Pa. 2003); *Commonwealth v. Daniels*, 963 A.2d 409 (Pa. 2009); *Commonwealth v. Washington*, 880 A.2d 536 (Pa. 2005); *Commonwealth v. Williams*, 863 A.2d 505 (Pa. 2004).

In addition, whenever a defendant filed a petition before *McGill* but filed an appellate brief after *McGill* and the ineffectiveness issue was an extra-record claim, the courts will look through the appellate ineffectiveness issues and address trial counsel's effectiveness without remanding for an evidentiary hearing. *Commonwealth v. Walker*, 36 A.3d 1 (Pa. 2011); *Commonwealth v. Keaton*, 45 A.3d 1050 (Pa. 2012). In this respect, the *Walker* Court stated, "we now conclude that the better practice is not to reject claims of [direct] appellate counsel's ineffectiveness on the grounds of inadequate development in the appellate brief [on PCRA appeal] if the deficiencies in the brief mirror those in the PCRA pleadings, unless the PCRA court invoked these deficiencies as the basis for its decision and afforded an opportunity to amend." *Walker*, 36 A.3d at 8-9. In the event that a defendant raised ineffective assistance claims on direct appeal, any new ineffectiveness issues presented during PCRA review must be layered. *Commonwealth v. Robinson*, 82 A.3d 998, 1005-1006 (Pa. 2013); *Commonwealth v. Chmiel*, 30 A.3d 1111, 1128 (Pa. 2011); *Commonwealth v. Sileo*, 32 A.3d 753 (Pa. Super. 2011) (*en banc*).

Successfully asserting that trial counsel (or direct appeal counsel) was ineffective, however, only proves the arguable merit portion of subsequent counsel's ineffectiveness. *Commonwealth v. Reyes*, 870 A.2d 888 (Pa. 2005). Accordingly, a petitioner must still plead and prove the remaining prongs of the *Pierce* ineffectiveness test. *Reyes*, 870 A.2d 888. Nonetheless, if a petitioner can establish actual prejudice resulted from trial counsel's actions or inactions, only if subsequent counsel had a reasonable basis for not leveling the issue can the claim fail.

One, however, would be hard pressed to find a reasonable basis for not asserting an issue that resulted in actual prejudice at the trial level. Petitioners and counsel are strongly advised to read

Commonwealth v. McGill, 832 A.2d 1014 (Pa. 2003), if they need to layer claims, since it provides an excellent roadmap for the proper layering procedure in Pennsylvania. For further discussion of layered claims see also ***Commonwealth v. Walker***, 36 A.3d 1 (Pa. 2011).

C. Failure to Call a Witness

To establish that counsel was ineffective for failing to call a witness, the defendant must establish: (i) the witness existed; (ii) the witness was available to testify; (iii) counsel knew of, or should have known of, the existence of the witness; (iv) the witness was willing to testify; and (v) the absence of the testimony was so prejudicial as to have denied the defendant a fair trial. ***Commonwealth v. Washington***, 927 A.2d 586 (Pa. 2007); ***Commonwealth v. Hall***, 872 A.2d 1177 (Pa. 2005). Prejudice results when the absence of the testimony denied the petitioner a fair trial.

This test pertains equally to expert witness testimony. ***Commonwealth v. Chmiel***, 30 A.3d 1111 (Pa. 2011); ***Commonwealth v. Cox***, 983 A.2d 666, 692 (Pa. 2009) (counsel was not ineffective for failing to call a medical, forensic or scientific expert to evaluate expert testimony presented by the Commonwealth); ***Commonwealth v. Wright***, 961 A.2d 119, 150-151 (Pa. 2008); ***Commonwealth v. Collins***, 957 A.2d 237 (Pa. 2008) (failure to call defense expert was not ineffective where counsel could effectively cross-examine the Commonwealth's expert witness); ***Commonwealth v. Begley***, 780 A.2d 605 (Pa. 2001) (discussing ineffectiveness claim regarding qualifying an expert witness); ***Commonwealth v. Copenhefer***, 719 A.2d 242 (Pa. 1998); ***Commonwealth v. Williams***, 640 A.2d 1251 (Pa. 1994) (counsel was not ineffective for neglecting to call an expert where counsel was able to effectively cross-examine the prosecution's expert witness and elicit beneficial testimony); ***Commonwealth v.***

Common Ineffective Assistance Issues

Walls, 993 A.2d 289 (Pa. Super. 2010); *Commonwealth v. Masker*, 34 A.3d 841 (Pa. Super. 2011) (*en banc*) (Bowes, J., concurring and dissenting).

Appointed PCRA counsel may secure funding for the appointment of an expert through the PCRA court if such testimony is necessary to establish relief. *Commonwealth v. Jarosz*, __ A.3d __ (Pa. Super. 2016) (filed December 13, 2016). However, that decision is discretionary. *Jarosz, supra*; *see also Commonwealth v. Reid*, 99 A.3d 470, 505 (Pa. 2014).

Failure to call a witness is not *per se* ineffectiveness since it implicates matters of trial strategy. *Commonwealth v. Washington*, 927 A.2d 586 (Pa. 2007). The failure to call a witness is distinct from neglecting to interview or investigate a witness. *Commonwealth v. Stewart*, 84 A.3d 701 (Pa. Super. 2013) (*en banc*); *Commonwealth v. Dennis*, 950 A.2d 945, 960 (Pa. 2008); *see also Commonwealth v. Mabie*, 359 A.2d 369 (Pa. 1976); *Commonwealth v. Perry*, 644 A.2d 705 (Pa. 1994). PCRA counsel should raise the failure to interview or investigate a witness, when applicable, in addition to asserting the failure to call the witness.

A petitioner cannot successfully allege ineffectiveness on the part of counsel for failing to call additional witnesses when the defendant is given a colloquy and acknowledges that he agreed with trial counsel's decision not to present those witnesses. *Commonwealth v. Paddy*, 800 A.2d 294 (Pa. 2002); *see also Commonwealth v. Pander*, 100 A.3d 626 (Pa. Super. 2014) (*en banc*). Where counsel did not call an alibi witness, but that witness's testimony was cumulative of other testimony, counsel was not held ineffective on direct appeal in *Commonwealth v. McKendrick*, 514 A.2d 144 (Pa. Super. 1986), and *Commonwealth v. Olivencia*, 402 A.2d 519 (Pa. Super. 1979).

However, in *Dennis*, 950 A.2d 945, the Court declined to consider potential alibi testimony cumulative where the person who did testify as to the alibi was the defendant's father. Where a court colloquies a defendant on his decision to forego presenting his alibi defense, he cannot successfully allege trial counsel was ineffective for not presenting the defense. ***Commonwealth v. Rios***, 920 A.2d 790 (Pa. 2007). In ***Commonwealth v. Johnson***, 139 A.3d 1257 (Pa. 2016), the Supreme Court remanded for an evidentiary hearing on the petitioner's claim that counsel was ineffective in failing to investigate, discover and present alibi witnesses.

Defendants generally cannot successfully claim ineffective assistance of counsel on the basis that counsel did not call the defendant to testify where the court colloquies the defendant on his decision not to testify. ***Commonwealth v. Peay***, 806 A.2d 22 (Pa. Super. 2002); ***Commonwealth v. Lawson***, 762 A.2d 753 (Pa. Super. 2000); ***Commonwealth v. Schultz***, 707 A.2d 513 (Pa. Super. 1997); *but see* ***Commonwealth v. Nieves***, 746 A.2d 1102 (Pa. 2000) (finding counsel ineffective on direct appeal despite the court conducting a colloquy regarding the defendant's right to testify); ***Commonwealth v. Walker***, 110 A.3d 1000 (Pa. Super. 2015).

In ***Commonwealth v. Walker***, 110 A.3d 1000 (Pa. Super. 2015), a divided Superior Court panel remanded for a hearing on a claim that counsel was ineffective for not calling his client as a witness. The *Walker* Court held that the petitioner was not required to prove that the outcome of the trial likely would have been altered. Instead, it ruled that actual prejudice can be shown if the defendant would have testified but for counsel's erroneous advice. This decision relied on precedent involving the waiver of the right to trial by jury. Unlike the decision to waive a jury trial, the decision not to testify has no effect on the very structure of the trial proceeding. The more appropriate analogy is to other failure to call witness claims. In these cases, the actual prejudice analysis requires the testimony to have likely led to a different outcome.

Declining to present character witnesses is not ineffective assistance if the Commonwealth could have cross-examined the witnesses about knowledge of the defendant's conduct which bears on the character trait at issue. *Commonwealth v. Fulton*, 830 A.2d 567 (Pa. 2003); *Commonwealth v. Peterkin*, 513 A.2d 373 (Pa. 1986); *see also Commonwealth v. Morales*, 701 A.2d 516 (Pa. 1997) (declining to use character witnesses is not ineffective where the witness can be questioned about prior bad acts). However, character evidence itself may be sufficient to acquit a defendant; thus, the failure to put on character witnesses may be ineffective assistance of counsel if counsel has no reasonable basis for not calling the witness. *See Commonwealth v. Hull*, 982 A.2d 1020 (Pa. Super. 2009) (finding counsel ineffective in a sexual assault case for not calling character witnesses); *Commonwealth v. Weiss*, 606 A.2d 439 (Pa. 1992).

For further discussion on failing to call a witness, see also *Commonwealth v. Hall*, 701 A.2d 190 (Pa. 1997) and *Commonwealth v. Carbone*, 707 A.2d 1145 (Pa. Super. 1998) (trial counsel held ineffective in murder trial where female defendant claimed self-defense and counsel did not call witness who had encountered the victim and had to use a gun to keep the victim from pursuing her); *Commonwealth v. Matias*, 63 A.3d 807 (Pa. Super. 2013) (*en banc*); *Commonwealth v. Johnson*, 815 A.2d 563 (Pa. 2002).

D. Prosecutorial Misconduct During Argument

Where the allegation is that the prosecutor committed misconduct during trial, and counsel did not object, the claim must be argued as an ineffective assistance of counsel claim. The Pennsylvania Supreme Court in *Commonwealth v. Tedford*, 960 A.2d 1 (Pa. 2008), has clearly outlined what a defendant must prove to successfully raise an ineffectiveness claim for failure to object to a prosecutor's comments.

The Court in *Tedford* stated, "ineffectiveness claims stemming from a failure to object to a prosecutor's conduct may succeed when the petitioner demonstrates that the prosecutor's actions violated a constitutionally or statutorily protected right, such as the Fifth Amendment privilege against compulsory self-incrimination or the Sixth Amendment right to a fair trial, or a constitutional interest such as due process." *Tedford*, 960 A.2d at 29. Additionally, the prosecutorial misconduct must be of sufficient significance to result in the denial of the defendant's right to a fair trial. A prosecutor's comments will only be reversible error when the comments effect is to unavoidably prejudice the jury, "forming in their minds a fixed bias and hostility toward the defendant such that they could not weigh the evidence objectively and render a fair verdict." *Tedford*, 960 A.2d at 33.

If a prosecutor's comments "are based on the evidence or proper inferences therefrom, or represent mere oratorical flair," they are not objectionable. *Tedford*, 960 A.2d at 33. Furthermore, during the penalty phase, where the presumption of innocence is no longer applicable, the prosecutor is permitted even greater latitude in presenting argument. ***Commonwealth v. Travaglia***, 661 A.2d 352, 365 (Pa. 1995). Challenges to prosecutorial comments also are evaluated in the context in which they are made. *Id*.

Pennsylvania case law is clear that a prosecutor is allowed to argue the appropriateness of the death penalty. ***Commonwealth v. Tedford***, 960 A.2d 1 (Pa. 2008). While a prosecutor should refrain from couching his point as a personal belief, ***Commonwealth v. Rollins***, 738 A.2d 435 (Pa. 1999), a prosecutor does not engage in misconduct that rises to the level of reversible error when he argues for the appropriateness of the death penalty. Counsel could properly determine a comment did not require an objection if the jury is instructed that a prosecutor's comments are not evidence. *See Tedford*, 960 A.2d

1. In addition, a prosecutor is allowed to fairly respond to arguments made by defense counsel. ***Commonwealth v. Abu-Jamal***, 720 A.2d 79 (Pa. 1998).

E. Withdrawal of Guilty Plea (See Also Section on Guilty Plea Withdrawal Claims)

A defendant may withdraw a guilty plea if ineffective assistance of counsel caused the defendant to enter an involuntary plea. ***Commonwealth v. Rathfon***, 899 A.2d 365 (Pa. Super. 2006); ***Commonwealth v. Kersteter***, 877 A.2d 466 (Pa. Super. 2003); ***Commonwealth v. Lynch***, 820 A.2d 728 (Pa. Super. 2003); ***Commonwealth v. Barbosa***, 819 A.2d 81 (Pa. Super. 2003); ***Commonwealth v. Hickman***, 799 A.2d 136 (Pa. Super. 2002). The voluntariness of a plea will depend upon whether counsel's advice was within the range of competence demanded of attorneys in a criminal case. ***Commonwealth v. Rathfon***, 899 A.2d 365 (Pa. Super. 2006). For example, if counsel fails to or erroneously informs the defendant of his maximum possible sentence he may be ineffective. ***Commonwealth v. Barbosa***, 819 A.2d 81 (Pa. Super. 2003). The defendant must set forth the claim under the three-prong test outlined in ***Pierce***.

To demonstrate that a defendant was prejudiced in the context of entering a guilty plea, the defendant ordinarily must show that it is reasonably probable that he would not have pled guilty and would have gone to trial (or accepted a different plea offer) but for counsel's advice or lack of advice. ***Commonwealth v. Rathfon***, 899 A.2d 365 (Pa. Super. 2006); see also ***Commonwealth v. Mallory***, 941 A.2d 686 (Pa. 2008) (discussing ***Hill v. Lockhart***, 474 U.S. 52 (1985), which found that the prejudice requirement when a defendant pleads guilty is whether there is a reasonable probability that the outcome of the plea hearing would be different).

Generally, a defendant is bound by statements made under oath during his guilty plea and cannot withdraw his plea based on different after-the-fact representations. ***Commonwealth v. Turetsky***, 925 A.2d 876 (Pa. Super. 2007); ***Commonwealth v. D'Collanfield***, 805 A.2d 1244 (Pa. Super. 2003); ***Commonwealth v. Pollard***, 832 A.2d 517 (Pa. Super. 2003); *but see* ***Commonwealth v. Strader***, 396 A.2d 697 (Pa. Super. 1978); ***Commonwealth v. Henderson***, 444 A.2d 720 (Pa. Super. 1982); ***Commonwealth v. Farnwalt***, 429 A.2d 664 (Pa. Super. 1981); ***Commonwealth v. McCall***, 406 A.2d 1077 (Pa. Super. 1979) (PCHA cases directing courts to hold evidentiary hearings as to whether counsel's misrepresentations caused an invalid plea despite admissions in colloquies that plea was not induced by any promises).

A conviction based on a guilty plea can be withdrawn if it was the result of an involuntary pretrial confession. ***Commonwealth v. Vealey***, 581 A.2d 217 (Pa. Super. 1990). The petitioner must show the confession was involuntary, the guilty plea was primarily motivated by the confession, and the petitioner was incompetently advised by counsel to plead guilty. ***Vealey***, 581 A.2d 217. A conviction based on a guilty plea is not the result of a pretrial confession or any evidence held by the Commonwealth, but on the defendant's open court admission of guilt. ***Vealey***, 581 A.2d 217. Therefore, an involuntary confession does not automatically entitle a petitioner to relief; rather, the confession must be the primary reason for the guilty plea. ***Vealey***, 581 A.2d 217. A defendant also may withdraw a guilty plea based on ineffectiveness if counsel failed to relay a plea offer and prejudice is established. ***Commonwealth v. Korb***, 617 A.2d 715 (Pa. Super. 1992); ***Commonwealth v. Copeland***, 554 A.2d 54 (Pa. Super. 1988); ***Lafler v. Cooper***, 132 S.Ct. 1376 (2012); ***Missouri v. Frye***, 132 S.Ct. 1399 (2012).

Counsel may be found ineffective for failing to advise his or her client regarding deportation consequences prior to the plea. ***Padilla v. Kentucky***, 130 S.Ct. 1473 (2010). However, counsel will not be ineffective for informing his client that his conviction may result in deportation instead of instructing his client that he will be deported. *Commonwealth v. Escobar*, 70 A.3d 838 (Pa. Super. 2013); *Commonwealth v. McDermitt*, 66 A.3d 810 (Pa. Super. 2013); *Commonwealth v. Wah*, 42 A.3d 335 (Pa. Super. 2012); *see also Commonwealth v. Ghisoiu*, 63 A.3d 1272 (Pa. Super. 2013).

In *Commonwealth v. Lippert*, 85 A.3d 1095 (Pa. Super. 2014), the court held that the petitioner was entitled to an evidentiary hearing on his claim that counsel misinformed him regarding the registration requirements for his sex offense. It declined to rule that because sex offender registration is a collateral consequence of a plea that counsel's alleged misadvice could not result in ineffective assistance. *See also Commonwealth v. Barndt*, 74 A.3d 185 (Pa. Super. 2013) (affirmative misadvice about alleged collateral consequence was ineffective assistance of counsel).

Plea counsel was also held ineffective in *Commonwealth v. Melendez-Negron*, 123 A.3d 1087 (Pa. Super. 2015), for not advising his client that the mandatory sentencing statute that the Commonwealth invoked was no longer constitutionally sound pursuant to *Alleyne v. United States*, 133 S.Ct. 2151 (2013). Importantly, *Alleyne* had been decided prior to the defendant's plea and the Superior Court had recognized that the mandatory statute at issue was unconstitutional before the entry of the plea.

F. Discretionary Sentencing

In *Commonwealth v. Wrecks*, 934 A.2d 1287 (Pa. Super. 2007) ("*Wrecks II*"), the Superior Court held that a pure discretionary aspect of sentencing claim, *i.e.*, one that did not allege ineffective assistance of counsel, was not cognizable under the PCRA. Therefore, the trial court therein did not err in treating a post-sentence motion as untimely rather than as a PCRA petition. The *Wrecks II* Court relied upon a footnote in *Commonwealth v. Friend*, 896 A.2d 607 (Pa. Super. 2006), *abrogated in part on other grounds by Commonwealth v. Pitts*,

981 A.2d 875 (Pa. 2009), in support of its position. *Friend*, however, cited to *Commonwealth v. Blackwell*, 647 A.2d 915 (Pa. Super. 1994), which in turn referenced *Commonwealth v. Lewis*, 634 A.2d 633 (Pa. Super. 1993).

Lewis was a decision that utilized the truth-determining language of the PCRA to conclude that the issue did not fall within the parameters of the PCRA, a rationale expressly disapproved of by the Pennsylvania Supreme Court in *Commonwealth v. ex rel. Dadario v. Goldberg*, 773 A.2d 126 (Pa. 2001). Furthermore, *Blackwell* itself found that an ineffectiveness claim regarding the discretionary aspects of sentencing was non-cognizable.

However, in *Commonwealth v. Jones*, 942 A.2d 903 (Pa. Super. 2008), the Superior Court properly addressed a claim of ineffectiveness that asserted counsel failed to raise a claim regarding the discretionary aspects of a sentence, although the court ultimately held that counsel was not ineffective. Similarly, in *Commonwealth v. Scassera*, 965 A.2d 247 (Pa. Super. 2009), the court found meritorious an ineffectiveness claim regarding the discretionary aspects of sentencing. Further, in *Commonwealth v. Lawrence*, 960 A.2d 473 (Pa. Super. 2008), the Superior Court specifically held that an ineffectiveness issue with respect to the discretionary aspects of sentencing was cognizable. *See also Commonwealth v. Hernandez*, 755 A.2d 1 (Pa. Super. 2000).

Finally, in *Commonwealth v. Liston*, 977 A.2d 1089, 1095 n.9 (Pa. 2009), the Supreme Court, in a footnote (and in *dicta*), stated that claims that involve ineffectiveness of counsel and the discretionary aspects of sentencing could be raised during collateral review. Accordingly, *Blackwell* is no longer good law for the position that a discretionary aspect of sentencing claim argued under the rubric of ineffective assistance of counsel is not cognizable. *Commonwealth v. Taylor*, 65 A.3d 462 (Pa.

Super. 2013).

It should also be noted that the decision in **Wrecks II** conflicts with other Superior Court decisions. **Wrecks II** involved a patently untimely post-sentence motion filed *pro se* while the defendant was not represented by counsel. Ordinarily, post-sentence motions filed after finality of judgment of sentence are to be treated as a PCRA petition. **Commonwealth v. Taylor**, 65 A.3d 462 (Pa. Super. 2013); **Commonwealth v. Jackson**, 30 A.3d 516 (Pa. Super. 2011); **Commonwealth v. Fowler**, 930 A.2d 586 (Pa. Super. 2007); **Commonwealth v. Evans**, 866 A.2d 442 (Pa. Super. 2005); **Commonwealth v. Guthrie**, 749 A.2d 502 (Pa. Super. 2000).

The trial court, however, treated the motion as an ordinary untimely post-sentence motion and dismissed the motion. On appeal, counsel filed an *Anders* brief. The **Wrecks II** Court held that, because the defendant raised a bald discretionary aspect of sentencing claim in his *pro se* motion, the issue was not cognizable under the PCRA and it affirmed. This ignored that in both **Commonwealth v. Evans**, 866 A.2d 442 (Pa. Super. 2005), and **Commonwealth v. Guthrie**, 749 A.2d 502 (Pa. Super. 2000), the Superior Court opined that the issues raised therein were properly considered discretionary sentencing issues and treated the motions as PCRA petitions. **Commonwealth v. Taylor**, 65 A.3d 462 (Pa. Super. 2013).

Moreover, counsel was not appointed prior to the appeal. Therefore, the defendant was never afforded an opportunity to amend his motion to include his claim under the rubric of ineffective assistance of counsel. In **Commonwealth v. Kutnyak**, 781 A.2d 1259 (Pa. Super. 2001), the court held that a petitioner "is entitled to counsel to represent him despite any apparent untimeliness of the petition or the **apparent non-cognizability** of the claims presented." (emphasis added). Hence, under then-existing precedent, counsel should have been appointed after the filing of the *pro se* motion and directed to file an amended petition or ***Turner/Finley*** no-merit letter. ***See also Commonwealth v. Evans***, 866 A.2d 442 (Pa. Super. 2005); *cf.* ***Commonwealth v. Fowler***, 930 A.2d 586 (Pa. Super. 2007).[12]

In sum, a bald discretionary aspect of sentencing claim will fail because the issue is waived as it should have been raised at sentencing or in a post-sentence motion and on any direct appeal. However, setting forth the claim as one of ineffectiveness will overcome this waiver and permit review. PCRA courts should permit defendants to amend a defective petition if the claim is not raised as an ineffectiveness claim.

G. Mitigation During Death Penalty Phase

The Pennsylvania Supreme Court has consistently recognized that a defendant has the right to effective assistance of counsel during the penalty phase of capital sentencing. ***Commonwealth v. Chester***, 733 A.2d 1242 (Pa. 1999) (finding that the penalty phase of a capital case involves the truth determining process). The fact that the PCRA statute also affords relief for sentences that exceed the lawful maximum indicates that the statute encompasses capital-sentencing issues. Indeed, the issue for which the Pennsylvania Supreme Court most often grants PCRA relief is a claim of ineffective assistance of counsel during the sentencing phase of a capital case; specifically, counsel's failure to investigate or present mitigation evidence.

"Counsel has a duty to undertake reasonable investigations or to make reasonable decisions that render particular investigations unnecessary." ***Commonwealth v. Basemore***, 744 A.2d 717, 735

---

12 The ***Anders*** brief in ***Wrecks II*** addressed a legality of sentence question, which falls within the parameters of the PCRA statute, *see **Commonwealth v. Hockenberry***, 689 A.2d 283 (Pa. Super. 1997) (*en banc*), although the *pro se* motion raised only discretionary sentencing claims.

(Pa. 2000). The reasonableness of an attorney's investigative decisions can depend critically upon information that a client relates to counsel. ***Commonwealth v. Gribble***, 863 A.2d 455 (Pa. 2004). In a capital case, defense counsel has a duty to conduct a thorough investigation of the defendant's background in order to prepare and present mitigation evidence at a capital defendant's sentencing hearing. ***Gribble***, 865 A.2d at 475 (citing ***Williams v. Taylor***, 529 U.S. 362 (2000)).

Where there is no notice to counsel of mitigating evidence, he will not be found to be ineffective for failing to find or present the evidence. ***Basemore***, 744 A.2d 717. Additionally, "strategic choices made after less than complete investigation are reasonable precisely to the extent that reasonable professional judgments support the limitations on investigation." ***Gribble***, 863 A.2d at 476, (citing ***Wiggins v. Smith***, 539 U.S. 510, 528 (2003)). If witnesses whom counsel "is faulted for failing to have interviewed and presented at the penalty phase are the sort of witnesses whose existence should have been readily apparent or discoverable to any counsel who conducted a reasonable investigation," then counsel may be ineffective. ***Gribble***, 863 A.2d at 476.

In determining whether the failure to present mitigation evidence was ineffective assistance of counsel, the court must compare the evidence presented during the penalty phase to the evidence and argument that could have been presented based on information counsel had or could have had if he or she conducted a proper investigation. ***Commonwealth v. Williams***, 732 A.2d 1167 (Pa. 1999); ***Basemore***, 744 A.2d 717; ***Commonwealth v. Bond***, 819 A.2d 33 (Pa. 2002). The focus of the court is on whether the investigation conducted by counsel in relation to his decision not to introduce certain mitigating evidence was reasonable. ***Commonwealth v. Sneed***, 899 A.2d 1067 (Pa. 2006). In addition, in considering mitigation evidence, the court is to weigh the mitigating circumstances qualitatively and not quantitatively. ***Commonwealth v. Tharp***, 101 A.3d 736 (Pa. 2014). Accordingly, a determination by the jury that the catch-all mitigator applied but was outweighed by the aggravating factors does not automatically preclude a finding of ineffectiveness. ***Commonwealth v. Treiber***, 121 A.3d 435 (Pa. 2014)

For more information on mitigation claims see ***Commonwealth v. Lesko***, 15 A.3d 345 (Pa. 2011); ***Commonwealth v. Martin***, 5 A.3d 177 (Pa. 2010); ***Commonwealth v. Rios***, 920 A.2d 790 (Pa. 2007); ***Commonwealth v. Gorby***, 909 A.2d 775 (Pa. 2006); ***Commonwealth v. Malloy***, 856 A.2d 767 (Pa. 2004); ***Commonwealth v. Miller***, 746 A.2d 592 (Pa. 2000); ***Commonwealth v. Rollins***, 738 A.2d 435 (Pa. 1999); ***Commonwealth v. Hall***, 701 A.2d 190 (Pa. 1997).

H. *Batson* Claims

A ***Batson*** challenge is one where a petitioner alleges that the Commonwealth used its peremptory strikes in a discriminatory manner, usually to strike members of a certain race from the jury. However, ***Batson*** claims can be maintained based on gender. Ordinarily, a record must be established at trial by properly objecting to the alleged improper strikes. However, in the PCRA context, the petitioner will usually be alleging that trial counsel failed to raise the ***Batson*** issue during *voir dire*. See ***Commonwealth v. Basemore***, 744 A.2d 717 (Pa. 2000); ***Commonwealth v. Smith***, 17 A.3d 873 (Pa. 2011).

Where trial counsel did not develop a record during *voir dire*, the PCRA petitioner has the burden of showing actual discrimination and must establish a record of the race or gender of the persons struck by the Commonwealth, those struck by the defendant, the race or gender of the entire panel, and the race or gender of those selected to the jury. These requirements are generally referred to as the ***Spence*** requirements based on ***Commonwealth v. Spence***, 627 A.2d 1176 (Pa. 1993).

Spence was criticized by the Third Circuit Court of Appeals in ***Holloway v. Horn***, 355 F.3d 707 (3d Cir. 2004), however, it has not been overturned by the Pennsylvania Supreme Court or the United States Supreme Court. The criticism centered around the belief that the requirements place an undue burden on a defendant to establish a violation of his constitutional rights. However, the Third Circuit did not address the ***Spence*** requirements in the context of when no ***Batson*** claim was raised at trial. As the Pennsylvania Supreme Court in ***Commonwealth v. Basemore***, 744 A.2d 717, 729 (Pa. 2000), stated:

> Absent a timely objection and preservation of a trial record, there will most often be no proof of the race of venirepersons; the prosecutor will have had no reason to provide race-neutral explanations; the trial judge will have had no evidence to weigh or occasion to make an assessment; and, ultimately, there will be nothing available to review on appeal.

In the context of a PCRA matter, however, the ***Spence*** requirements are problematic for petitioners. First, discovery is only allowed in a non-capital case upon a showing of exceptional circumstances and in capital cases after the party demonstrates good cause. Where trial counsel did not develop a record, the petitioner bears the burden of combing through the record and determining the race or gender of the *voir dire* panel, the jurors who were struck, and the race or gender of those actually selected to the jury. Sometimes it will be necessary for the defendant to request information from the Commonwealth in order to establish this record, yet in a non-capital case, he must show exceptional circumstances to be entitled to this discovery. Moreover, the Commonwealth is not required to turn over all of the information it has regarding the race of the jury panel, those stricken, and the race of the final jury panel members. ***Commonwealth v. Uderra***, 862 A.2d 74 (Pa. 2004).

Common Ineffective Assistance Issues

Uderra presents issues for defendants with respect to ineffective assistance *Batson* claims in several respects, most notably its statement that a *Batson* proffer must have support from the record. The Court in *Uderra* held that the proffer, a transcript of a training video explaining the practice of the Philadelphia District Attorney's Office regarding peremptory strikes, excerpts from the *voir dire* transcript, references to portions of the record, and voter registration records was insufficient to meet the *Spence* requirements. As discussed above, the *Spence* requirements are virtually impossible to meet in the context of a PCRA petition where no objection was raised during *voir dire*.

The Pennsylvania Supreme Court, perhaps recognizing the difficulties inherent in meeting the *Spence* requirements, went on to indicate in *Uderra* that because the court did not afford the petitioner an evidentiary hearing it would look to the proffer to see if it was believed would it establish actual, purposeful discrimination, and require a remand for an evidentiary hearing. The Court found that the proffer, which alleged four of five Hispanic venirepersons were stricken from the jury panel, (the defendant was Hispanic) did not, if believed, establish actual, purposeful, discrimination. Such reasoning, largely conclusory in nature, ignored that if four of five Hispanics were stricken from the jury, that alone if believed could potentially establish discrimination.

The most problematic aspect of *Uderra* for defendants is that it requires support from the record to demonstrate that the proffer was adequate, but the purpose of the evidentiary hearing would have been to develop the record based on the proffer. The proffer itself should not require support in the record, (it, of course, should comply with Pa.R.Crim.P. 902 and 42 Pa.C.S. § 9545(D)(1)), to determine if an evidentiary hearing is required. This is because the typical *Batson* claim raised in a PCRA petition will not ordinarily have support in the record precisely because the allegation is that counsel did not object during *voir dire* and neglected to make the necessary record.

Further, the purpose of the evidentiary hearing would be to develop the record for purposes of the ***Batson*** claim. Nonetheless, a defendant and his counsel must be careful to supply the appropriate information and or make the appropriate requests to meet the ***Spence*** requirements when raising a ***Batson*** issue. See *Commonwealth v. Jones*, 951 A.2d 294 (Pa. 2008). For more discussion on ***Batson*** issues see *Commonwealth v. Reid*, 99 A.3d 427 (Pa. 2014); *Commonwealth v. Hanible*, 30 A.3d 426 (Pa. 2011); *Commonwealth v. Smith*, 17 A.3d 873 (Pa. 2011); *Commonwealth v. Williams*, 980 A.2d 510 (Pa. 2009); *Commonwealth v. Ligons*, 971 A.2d 1125 (Pa. 2009); *Commonwealth v. Clark*, 961 A.2d 80 (Pa. 2008); *Commonwealth v. Cook*, 952 A.2d 594 (Pa. 2008); *Commonwealth v. Hackett*, 956 A.2d 978 (Pa. 2008); *Commonwealth v. Perrin*, 947 A.2d 1284 (Pa. Super. 2008); *Commonwealth v. Bond*, 819 A.2d 33 (Pa. 2002).

I. Failure to File Suppression Motion

The failure to file a suppression motion may be ineffective assistance of counsel. *Commonwealth v. Arch*, 654 A.2d 1141 (Pa. Super. 1995);[13] *Commonwealth v. Nelson*, 574 A.2d 1107 (Pa. Super. 1990); *Commonwealth v. Boyer*, 962 A.2d 1213 (Pa. Super. 2008). Additionally, even if counsel does file a suppression motion, but does not include a meritorious ground for suppression in that motion, he may be found ineffective. *Commonwealth v. Kilgore*, 719 A.2d 754 (Pa. Super. 1998) (the failure to argue a violation of the Pennsylvania Constitution relative to warrantless search of a vehicle was ineffective). If

---

13 The ***Arch*** decision occurred on direct appeal. The defendant therein was sentenced to five to twelve months probation. This demonstrates the importance of allowing defendant's to raise ineffectiveness issues on direct appeal.

counsel advises a petitioner to plead guilty but a suppression motion could have resulted in the suppression of evidence of the petitioner's guilt then a petitioner will be permitted to withdraw his guilty plea. ***Commonwealth v. Nelson***, 574 A.2d 1107 (Pa. Super. 1990).

In ***Commonwealth v. Harris***, 972 A.2d 1196 (Pa. Super. 2009), the Superior Court held that the failure to file a suppression motion, where the petitioner alleged he requested an attorney prior to his confession but was not afforded a lawyer before giving a statement, was not ineffective assistance because the petitioner reinitiated the conversation with the police and subsequently waived his ***Miranda*** rights.

However, in ***Commonwealth v. Boyer***, 962 A.2d 1213 (Pa. Super. 2008), the court found that counsel was ineffective for not filing a suppression motion. There, the defendant asserted that he requested an attorney when questioned by police but the police questioned him without an attorney. According to the ***Boyer*** Court, where the court determines that the failure to file a suppression motion results in actual prejudice it does not strictly address the merits of the suppression issue and the trial court is not required to suppress the evidence at issue. Rather, the court must conduct a suppression hearing to determine if it should suppress the evidence. ***See also Commonwealth v. Arch***, 654 A.2d 1141 (Pa. Super. 1995).

The Pennsylvania Supreme Court vacated a Superior Court decision finding counsel ineffective for failing to seek suppression of a defendant's inculpatory post-polygraph statement. ***Commonwealth v. Hill***, 104 A.3d 1220 (Pa. 2014). There, trial counsel waived ***Miranda*** before the polygraph test. After the polygraph test, police questioned the defendant. The Superior Court held that counsel's pre-polygraph ***Miranda*** waiver did not encompass the post-polygraph interview and that trial counsel had no reasonable basis for not seeking to suppress statements made during the latter interview.

In vacating, the *Hill* Court opined that the Superior Court failed to analyze the issue under then-prevailing law. It further faulted the Superior Court for not closely examining the trial evidence in conducting its prejudice analysis. Ultimately, the High Court remanded to the Superior Court for additional consideration. Thus, it did not foreclose that trial counsel was ineffective.

The Supreme Court determined that trial counsel was not ineffective in not contesting a warrantless entry and search of the defendant's home in *Commonwealth v. Davido*, 106 A.3d 611 (Pa. 2014). Police therein were responding to a report of a domestic assault. The *Davido* Court declined to recognize a *per se* rule permitting police to enter a residence when alerted to possible domestic violence, but agreed with the PCRA court that the totality of the circumstances warranted police in believing an emergency situation justified their entry. It thus affirmed the PCRA court's finding of probable cause and exigent circumstances.

Additional discussion on ineffective assistance of counsel and suppression issues can be found in *Commonwealth v. Franklin*, 990 A.2d 795 (Pa. Super. 2010), and *Commonwealth v. Vealey*, 581 A.2d 217 (Pa. Super. 1990).

J. Diminished Capacity or Insanity Defenses

A diminished capacity/voluntary intoxication defense is a limited defense that does not exculpate the defendant from criminal liability but rather negates the element of criminal intent. *Commonwealth v. Williams*, 980 A.2d 510, 527 (Pa. 2009). In essence, a diminished capacity defense admits that the person has committed a wrong but did not possess the required state of mind to be convicted of the crime for which he or she is charged. Therefore, an attorney cannot be found ineffective if the client maintains his innocence. *Commonwealth v.*

Hutchinson, 25 A.3d 277 (Pa. 2011); ***Commonwealth v. Smith***, 17 A.3d 873 (Pa. 2011); ***Commonwealth v. Johnson***, 815 A.2d 563 (Pa. 2002) (seeking acquittal rather than pursuing a diminished capacity defense is not ineffective assistance of counsel). Similarly, counsel will not be held ineffective for neglecting to pursue an insanity defense where the defendant's theory at trial is that he did not commit the criminal act. ***Commonwealth v. Smith***, 17 A.3d 873 (Pa. 2011).

K. Conflict of Interest

An attorney owes a client a duty to avoid conflicts of interest. ***Commonwealth v. Tedford***, 960 A.2d 1 (Pa. 2008). An actual conflict exists when the interests of a client and another client to whom counsel has obligations, "diverge with respect to a material factual or legal issue or to a course of action." *Tedford*, 960 A.2d at 54. "A defendant cannot prevail on a conflict of interest claim absent a showing of actual prejudice." ***Commonwealth v. Small***, 980 A.2d 549, 562 (Pa. 2009). To establish prejudice, a client must demonstrate counsel actively represented conflicting interests and the actual conflict adversely affected counsel's performance. *Small*, 980 A.2d 549. A defendant is not necessarily prejudiced by the fact that counsel represented a Commonwealth witness at a prior time. ***Commonwealth v. Hawkins***, 787 A.2d 292 (Pa. 2001). A conflict of interest also may exist where the district attorney representing the Commonwealth at the PCRA hearing represented the defendant before trial. ***Commonwealth v. Townsend***, 850 A.2d 741 (Pa. Super. 2004). For further discussion on conflict of interest claims see ***Commonwealth v. Williams***, 980 A.2d 510 (Pa. 2009) and ***Commonwealth v. Collins***, 957 A.2d 237 (Pa. 2008).

L. *Mills* Claim

In *Mills v. Maryland*, 486 U.S. 367 (1988), the Supreme Court held that, during the sentencing phase of a capital case, a jury cannot be precluded from considering any relevant mitigating circumstances. It then concluded that a jury instruction that could reasonably be read to require the jury to unanimously find mitigating circumstances violated the federal constitution. Subsequently, in *Beard v. Banks*, 542 U.S. 406 (2004), the High Court found that the *Mills* decision was a new rule of law that was not entitled to retroactive affect.

Accordingly, defendants whose final judgment occurred before June 6, 1988, the date of the *Mills* decision, were not entitled to the benefit of the *Mills* holding. In *Commonwealth v. Cox*, 863 A.2d 536 (Pa. 2004), and *Commonwealth v. Duffey*, 889 A.2d 56 (Pa. 2005), the Pennsylvania Supreme Court concluded that *Mills* did not apply to cases where the jury instructions were given before the *Mills* decision even if the case was pending on appeal at the time the Supreme Court decided *Mills*. The *Cox* and *Duffey* Court's rightly noted that counsel cannot be held to be ineffective for failing to anticipate a change in the law; hence, the failure to object to the instruction would not be ineffective. In addition, the failure to object waived the future *Mills* claim. *See also Commonwealth v. Ly*, 980 A.2d 61 (Pa. 2009); *Commonwealth v. Steele*, 961 A.2d 786 (Pa. 2008).

The Pennsylvania Supreme Court has also held that the pre-*Mills* Pennsylvania standard instruction did not imply a requirement that the jury find mitigating circumstances unanimously. Therefore, in Pennsylvania, the claim would fail on its merits. *Commonwealth v. Breakiron*, 729 A.2d 1088 (Pa. 1999). The Third Circuit Court of Appeals has concluded to the contrary, holding that it is an unreasonable application of *Mills* to hold that the Pennsylvania standard jury instruction in pre-*Mills* cases does not violate the rule set forth in *Mills*. *See Frey v. Fulcomer*, 132 F.3d 916 (3d Cir. 1997); *Abu-Jamal v. Secretary, Pennsylvania Dept. of Corrections*, 643 F.3d 370 (3d Cir. 2010); *see also Steele v. Beard*, 830 F.Supp.2d 49 (W.D. Pa. 2011); *but see Duffey v. Beard*, 2011 WL 4401681 (M.D. Pa. 2011).

The Third Circuit has also reached the conclusion that defendants whose jury instructions occurred before the *Mills* decision, which announced a new constitutional rule of law, are entitled to application of *Mills* so long as their direct appeal was not decided until after the *Mills* case. Further, the Third Circuit has declined to find that counsel's failure to raise an objection to the instruction is an independent state grounds precluding the federal courts from reaching the merits of the issue during federal *habeas* review. The rationale for this latter proposition is that Pennsylvania formerly applied what is known as the relaxed waiver doctrine. This doctrine permitted the Pennsylvania Supreme Court, within its discretion, to reach significant issues of record that were waived before the trial court in capital cases. The Pennsylvania Supreme Court abrogated the relaxed waiver doctrine during PCRA review in *Commonwealth v. Albrecht*, 720 A.2d 693 (Pa. 1998).

Under the relaxed waiver doctrine, the Pennsylvania Supreme Court did not *sua sponte* raise and address *Mills* issues. Moreover, the federal court's application, in effect, gives the *Mills* decision retroactive effect since at the time of the trial the jury instructions were entirely proper. *See Commonwealth v. Ly*, 980 A.2d 61 (Pa. 2009); *Commonwealth v. Cox*, 863 A.2d 536 (Castille, J., concurring). Currently, the jury instructions and jury verdict slip in capital cases are clear that the jury need not unanimously find a mitigating circumstance; thus, no *Mills* claims can occur. A *Mills* claim for cases in which the jury instructions occurred before June 6, 1988, also will fail in the Pennsylvania courts, but can succeed in the lower federal courts.

M. *Simmons* Instruction

A ***Simmons*** instruction informs the jury during the capital sentencing phase of a trial that a life sentence means life without the possibility of parole and derives from the United States Supreme Court decision in ***Simmons v. South Carolina***, 512 U.S. 154 (1994) (plurality). In Pennsylvania, prior to the ***Simmons*** decision, such an instruction was actually not permitted. ***Commonwealth v. Williams***, 732 A.2d 1167 (Pa. 1999). Counsel will not be held ineffective for failing to anticipate this change in the law, ***Commonwealth v. Ly***, 980 A.2d 61 (Pa. 2009), and ***Simmons*** does not apply retroactively. ***Commonwealth v. Rollins***, 738 A.2d 435 (Pa. 1999). The instruction is only necessary when the prosecution argues the future dangerousness of a defendant. ***Commonwealth v. Williams***, 732 A.2d 1167 (Pa. 1999); *see also* ***Commonwealth v. Lesko***, 15 A.3d 345 (Pa. 2011); ***Commonwealth v. Watkins***, 108 A.3d 692, 727-730 (Pa. 2014).

N. Jury Instruction Ineffectiveness Claims

A court looks to the jury instructions as a whole in deciding if an instruction is deficient. ***Commonwealth v. Cook***, 952 A.2d 594 (Pa. 2008). The failure to request a no-adverse inference jury instruction presents a claim of arguable merit. ***Commonwealth v. Howard***, 645 A.2d 1300 (Pa. 1994). The no adverse inference jury instruction requires the court to instruct the jury that a defendant's silence at trial cannot be used to infer the defendant is guilty. A defendant still, of course, must establish prejudice on the issue. *See* ***Commonwealth v. Collins***, 687 A.2d 1112 (Pa. 1996) (OAJC); ***Commonwealth v. Perez***, 103 A.3d 344 (Pa. Super. 2014). Counsel will not be found ineffective for declining to pursue a jury instruction requiring a jury to determine the applicability of the sentencing guidelines deadly weapon enhancement based on ***Apprendi v. New Jersey***, 530 U.S. 466 (2000), since ***Apprendi*** and its progeny do not apply to

Pennsylvania's sentencing guidelines. ***Commonwealth v. Lowery***, 784 A.2d 795 (Pa. Super. 2001).

A courts usage of the word "refrain" in its jury instruction on reasonable doubt is not error; therefore, counsel cannot be ineffective for declining to object to the instruction. ***Commonwealth v. Uderra***, 862 A.2d 74 (Pa. 2004); ***Commonwealth v. Sattazahn***, 952 A.2d 640 (Pa. 2008). Similarly, a reasonable doubt jury instruction that utilizes the term "restrain" does not violate the law and counsel will not be held ineffective for not lodging an objection. ***Commonwealth v. Rios***, 920 A.2d 790 (Pa. 2007); ***Commonwealth v. Carson***, 913 A.2d 220 (Pa. 2006).

In ***Commonwealth v. Brady***, 741 A.2d 758 (Pa. Super. 1999), the Superior Court found that trial counsel was ineffective in failing to object to or request a limiting instruction after the trial court improperly admitted hearsay evidence of a co-defendant's statement as substantive evidence against the defendant. *See also **Commonwealth v. Billa***, 555 A.2d 835 (Pa. 1989) (counsel held ineffective for not seeking a limiting instruction); ***but see Commonwealth v. Miller***, 481 A.2d 1221 (Pa. Super. 1984) (where counsel chooses to refuse a curative instruction based on a legitimate tactical reason, *i.e.*, the prejudicial reference was brief and counsel did not want to highlight the issue he will not be found ineffective); ***compare also Commonwealth v. Hutchinson***, 25 A.3d 277 (Pa. 2011). Failure to request an alibi jury instruction where witnesses testify as to an alibi was determined to be ineffective assistance in ***Commonwealth v. Mikell***, 729 A.2d 566 (Pa. 1999). ***But see Commonwealth v. Sileo***, 32 A.3d 753 (Pa. Super. 2011) (*en banc*). Counsel was not deemed ineffective in ***Commonwealth v. Bennett***, 57 A.3d 1185 (Pa. 2012), for failing to object to an accomplice and conspiracy liability instruction in a first-degree murder case.

In ***Commonwealth v. Reyes-Rodriguez***, 111 A.3d 775 (Pa. Super. 2015) (*en banc*), the Superior Court determined that the petitioner failed to prove ineffectiveness where counsel did not request a jury instruction that character testimony alone may raise a reasonable doubt as to the defendant's guilt. Therein, PCRA counsel failed to question trial counsel regarding his decision not to seek such an instruction and otherwise neglected to create a record on the issue during the PCRA evidentiary hearing.

O. Other Common Claims

Appellate counsel will not be held ineffective for not addressing all potentially meritorious issues on direct appeal, unless there was no reasonable basis for his actions and there is a reasonable probability that the result of the direct appeal would have been affected. ***Commonwealth v. Showers***, 782 A.2d 1010 (Pa. Super. 2001). It should be noted that the defendant in ***Showers*** was eventually granted a new trial by the federal courts based on a layered claim of ineffectiveness. The Third Circuit in ***Showers v. Beard***, 635 F.3d 625 (3d Cir. 2011), upheld the lower federal court determination that appellate counsel was ineffective in not raising trial counsel's ineffectiveness for not calling an expert witness to testify.

Declining to object to an expert witness's testimony that invades the jury's credibility determining function and bolsters the credibility of a victim can be ineffective assistance. ***Commonwealth v. Balodis***, 747 A.2d 341 (Pa. 2000). Courts will not find an attorney ineffective for declining to question a witness about inconsistencies in his testimony if it would enable the witness to clarify his testimony. ***Commonwealth v. Greene***, 702 A.2d 547 (Pa. Super. 1997). Similarly, counsel is not ineffective for failing to impeach a witness based on a minor inconsistency between his preliminary hearing and trial testimony. ***Commonwealth v. Baez***, 720 A.2d 711, 733-34 (Pa.

1998).

Neglecting to impeach a prosecution eyewitness regarding bias was held to constitute ineffectiveness in *Commonwealth v. Murphy*, 591 A.2d 278 (Pa. 1991). Counsel was also held ineffective for not objecting to the subject matter jurisdiction of the court where it took action more than thirty days after it issued its final order. *Commonwealth v. Butler*, 566 A.2d 1209 (Pa. Super. 1989). I add that subject matter jurisdiction can be raised at any time during a timely PCRA, therefore, the claim need not be set forth under the ineffectiveness test. *See Commonwealth v. Quinlan*, 639 A.2d 1235 (Pa. Super. 1994) (asserting that trial court was without jurisdiction to modify a defendant's sentence more than thirty days after entry of the judgment of sentence).

Failure to invoke the spousal privilege, where the privilege is applicable, is a claim of arguable merit. *Commonwealth v. Savage*, 695 A.2d 820 (Pa. Super. 1997); *see also Commonwealth v. Hancharik*, 633 A.2d 1074 (Pa. 1993). Where counsel did not introduce a police report via the business record hearsay exception, which demonstrated that the victim's testimony during trial was inconsistent with the information in the police report, the Superior Court, on direct appeal, held counsel ineffective. *Commonwealth v. Shaffer*, 763 A.2d 411 (Pa. Super. 2000).

Additionally, failing to object to cross-examination of a character witness presents a claim of arguable merit where counsel does not object to a prosecutor's questioning of the witness regarding the defendant's prior conviction for which he has not been sentenced. *Commonwealth v. Ross*, 856 A.2d 93 (Pa. Super. 2004) (I note that *Ross* addressed an ineffectiveness claim on direct review based on the "short sentence" rule); *see also Commonwealth v. Morgan*, 739 A.2d 1033 (Pa. 1999) (holding that a character witness cannot be questioned regarding a defendant's prior arrests); ***Commonwealth v. Yeager***, 461 A.2d 281 (Pa. Super. 1983); Pa.R.E. 405(a). Counsel may be found ineffective for failing to object to the improper cross-examination of a defense witness regarding the defense witness's prior arrests. ***Commonwealth v. Doswell***, 621 A.2d 104 (Pa. 1993) (plurality).

In ***Commonwealth v. Pander***, 100 A.3d 626 (Pa. Super. 2014) (*en banc*), the court rejected an ineffectiveness claim based on counsel's failure to request a jury instruction based on ***Commonwealth v. Kloiber***, 106 A.2d 820 (Pa. 1954), relative to identification testimony. There, the trial court had issued a modified ***Kloiber*** instruction. Similarly, the Pennsylvania Supreme Court rejected a ***Kloiber*** ineffectiveness challenge in ***Commonwealth v. Reid***, 99 A.3d 427 (Pa. 2014), and ***Commonwealth v. Reid***, 99 A.3d 470 (Pa. 2014), as well as ***Commonwealth v. Johnson***, 139 A.3d 1257 (Pa. 2016).

P. Cumulative Claims

Pennsylvania state appellate courts have consistently rejected the idea that cumulative claims can lead to post-conviction relief if the claims have no arguable merit. The courts have maintained that if a petitioner is not entitled to relief on one claim then no amount of claims added up entitle him to relief. ***Commonwealth v. Cox***, 983 A.2d 666 (Pa. 2009); ***Commonwealth v. Steele***, 961 A.2d 786 (Pa. 2008); ***Commonwealth v. Washington***, 927 A.2d 586 (Pa. 2007). Nonetheless, the Pennsylvania Supreme Court has expressed that while cumulative claims will not be considered where the issues have no arguable merit, issues that are dismissed based on a lack of prejudice will be considered together. *See* ***Commonwealth v. Johnson***, 966 A.2d 523 (Pa. 2009); ***Commonwealth v. Spotz***, 18 A.3d 244 (Pa. 2011).

This rationale is sound in light of the actual prejudice element of the ineffective assistance of counsel test. As a practical matter, a

Common Ineffective Assistance Issues

trial attorney's cumulative mistakes are much more likely to result in prejudice to the defendant than a singular mistake. Simply put, the more mistakes counsel makes that have arguable merit, the more likely that no reliable adjudication of guilt or innocence could have taken place.

Further, the PCRA statute does not specifically state that cumulative claims cannot be grounds for relief. Accordingly, cumulative claims of arguable merit can provide a possible basis for PCRA relief. Nevertheless, both PCRA courts and the Superior Court generally are precluded from granting relief based upon a cumulative error assertion. A cumulative error claim can succeed during federal *habeas* review in the Third Circuit; and, therefore, should be forwarded in certain instances so as to preserve the claim for federal review.

Chapter 6: 42 Pa.C.S. § 9543(a)(2)(iii) & 9543(a)(2)(iv)

Plea of Guilty Unlawfully Induced/Governmental Interference

(2) That the conviction or sentence resulted from one or more of the following:

. . . .

(iii) A plea of guilty unlawfully induced where the circumstances make it likely that the inducement caused the petitioner to plead guilty and the petitioner is innocent.

(iv) The improper obstruction by government officials of the petitioner's right of appeal where a meritorious appealable issue existed and was properly preserved in the trial court.

Annotated Comments

A. Pleading Innocence

A petitioner who claims that ineffective assistance of counsel caused him to plead guilty need not plead that he is innocent. However, where the petitioner brings his claim under section 9543(a)(2)(ii), relating to his guilty plea being unlawfully induced, a petitioner must plead and prove by a preponderance of the evidence that he is innocent. ***Commonwealth v. Moore***, 653 A.2d 24 (Pa. Super. 1995); ***Commonwealth v. Laszczynski***, 715 A.2d 1185 (Pa. Super. 1998) (It should be noted that ***Laszczynski's*** analysis regarding the truth-determining process is no longer valid).

In ***Commonwealth v. Lynch***, 820 A.2d 728 (Pa. Super. 2003), the Superior Court found that where a guilty plea is entered because of advice of counsel, and counsel's advice was below the range of competence demanded of counsel, a petitioner is entitled to withdraw his plea. *See also **Commonwealth v. Hickman**,* 799 A.2d 136 (Pa. Super. 2002); ***Commonwealth v. Kersteter**,* 877 A.2d 466 (Pa. Super. 2003). Since a petitioner need not demonstrate innocence in the context of an ineffective assistance claim regarding a guilty plea, counsel is strongly advised to file any claims regarding a guilty plea under the ineffective assistance of counsel rubric rather than bring the claim under 42 Pa.C.S. § 9543(a)(2)(ii).

To withdraw a plea on the grounds that the plea was unlawfully induced, the defendant must prove that the plea was the result of manifest injustice. ***Commonwealth v. Holbrook**,* 629 A.2d 154 (Pa. Super. 1993); ***Commonwealth v. Bedell**,* 954 A.2d 1209 (Pa. Super. 2008). To demonstrate a manifest injustice, the defendant must show that the plea was involuntary or was entered without knowledge of the charges. ***Commonwealth v. Fluharty**,* 632 A.2d 312 (Pa. Super. 1993); ***Commonwealth v. Bedell**,* 954 A.2d 1209 (Pa. Super. 2008). As stated in ***Fluharty**,* 632 A.2d at 314, a determination as to the validity of a guilty plea is "made by examining the totality of the circumstances surrounding the entry of the plea." (citations omitted). Defects in a plea colloquy will not result in an invalid plea where "the circumstances surrounding the entry of the plea disclose that the defendant had a full understanding of the nature and consequences of his plea and that he knowingly and voluntarily decided to enter the plea." ***Fluharty**,* 632 A.2d at 314.

B. Section 9543(a)(2)(iv) and Governmental Interference

Unlike issues surrounding ineffective assistance of counsel, where case law is voluminous, claims regarding governmental interference with the right to appeal have not been significantly litigated. Thus, the case law dealing with the issue is sparse. Indeed, most cases that discuss governmental interference do so in the context of a timeliness exception and not a claim under section 9543(a)(2)(iv). In *Commonwealth v. Hanes*, 579 A.2d 920 (Pa. Super. 1990), the Superior Court did analyze an issue raised under section 9543(a)(2)(iv). Therein, the district attorney allegedly encouraged the defendant to forego his right of appeal. The court determined that the defendant was not entitled to relief under this subsection.

Chapter 7: 42 Pa.C.S. § 9543(a)(2)(vi)-(viii)
After-Discovered Evidence, Sentences that Exceed the Lawful Maximum, and Proceeding in a Tribunal without Jurisdiction

Section 9543(a)(2)(vi)-(viii)

(2) That the conviction or sentence resulted from one or more of the following:

. . . .

(vi) The unavailability at the time of trial of exculpatory evidence that has subsequently become available and would have changed the outcome of the trial if it had been introduced.

(vii) The imposition of a sentence greater than the lawful maximum.

(viii) A proceeding in a tribunal without jurisdiction.

Annotated Comments

A. *Brady* Claims

In ***Brady v. Maryland***, 373 U.S. 83 (1963), the United States Supreme Court held that prosecutorial suppression of evidence that is material to guilt or punishment violates due process. A *Brady* claim is specifically cognizable under the PCRA. 42 Pa. C.S. § 9543(a)(2)(vi). ***Commonwealth v. Simpson***, 66 A.3d 253, 264 n.16 (Pa. 2013).

> A *Brady* violation consists of three elements: (1) suppression by the prosecution (2) of evidence, whether exculpatory or impeaching, favorable to the defendant, (3) to the prejudice of the defendant. No violation occurs if the evidence at issue is available to

the defense from non-governmental sources. More importantly, a ***Brady*** violation only exists when the evidence is material to guilt or punishment, *i.e.*, when 'there is a reasonable probability that, had the evidence been disclosed to the defense, the result of the proceeding would have been different.'

Commonwealth v. Tedford, 960 A.2d 1, 30 (Pa. 2008) (citations omitted). Evidence is material where it affects the credibility of a witness. ***Commonwealth v. Ly***, 980 A.2d 61 (Pa. 2009). However, evidence is not to be considered exculpatory merely because a petitioner alleges the evidence is exculpatory. ***Commonwealth v. Lambert***, 884 A.2d 848 (Pa. 2005). A ***Brady*** claim, unlike a non-***Brady*** after-discovered evidence issue, can succeed if the after-discovered evidence would have been used solely to impeach a witness. ***Commonwealth v. Galloway***, 640 A.2d 454 (Pa. Super. 1994).

The prosecution's ***Brady*** obligations extend through all phases of the case including PCRA proceedings. ***Commonwealth v. Williams***, 732 A.2d 1167, 1175-1176 (Pa. 1999). "The burden of proof is on the defendant to establish that the Commonwealth withheld evidence. A prosecutor is not required to deliver his entire file to defense counsel, nor is a prosecutor's duty to disclose such that it would provide a defendant with a right to discovery." ***Commonwealth v. Burkett***, 5 A.3d 1260, 1268 (Pa. Super. 2010).

Additionally, "the mere possibility that an item of undisclosed information might have helped the defense or might have affected the outcome of the trial does not establish materiality in the constitutional sense." ***Burkett***, 5 A.3d at 1268 (citing ***Commonwealth v. Miller***, 987 A.2d 638 (Pa 2009)). Further, "In determining the materiality of alleged withheld evidence the court must view the evidence in relation to the record as a whole. In addition, where there are multiple allegations of ***Brady*** violations, the court must consider the total effect of the alleged ***Brady*** violations." ***Burkett***, 5 A.3d at 1268.

The Commonwealth does not violate ***Brady*** by not turning over a complete and detailed report of all police investigatory work on a case, nor is it required to disclose possible defense theories to the defendant. ***Commonwealth v. Appel***, 689 A.2d 891, 907 (Pa. 1997); *see also **Commonwealth v. Lambert***, 884 A.2d 848 (Pa. 2005). Failure to disclose a pre-sentence investigation of a witness was held not to constitute a violation of ***Brady*** in ***Commonwealth v. Miller***, 987 A.2d 638 (Pa. 2009). A ***Brady*** issue cannot succeed, absent an allegation of ineffectiveness, where trial counsel was aware of the ***Brady*** material and did not raise the issue. ***See Commonwealth v. Simpson***, 66 A.3d 253, 268 n.20 (Pa. 2013). Concomitantly, counsel cannot be ineffective for failing to raise a meritless ***Brady*** claim. ***Id***. at 268.

"[A] witnesses assumption that he will benefit from cooperating in the prosecution of the defendant, without more, is insufficient to establish that an agreement existed, and does not trigger ***Brady*** disclosure requirements." ***Commonwealth v. Busanet***, 54 A.3d 35, 49 (Pa. 2012). Where no agreement exists between the Commonwealth and a witness, there can be no ***Brady*** violation for not disclosing a non-existent deal. ***Commonwealth v. Koehler***, 36 A.3d 121 (Pa. 2012). Similarly, where the Commonwealth does not have a duty to disclose evidence, the ***Brady*** claim is meritless. ***Busanet***, 54 A.3d at 49. There is generally no entitlement to PCRA relief for a ***Brady*** violation where the evidence is cumulative of other evidence, or the ***Brady*** material is equally available to the defendant. ***Commonwealth v. Simpson***, 66 A.3d 253, 264 (Pa. 2013).

After-Discovered Evidence, Sentences that Exceed the Lawful Maximum, and Proceeding in a Tribunal without Jurisdiction

For more discussion on ***Brady*** claims see ***Commonwealth v. Lesko***, 15 A.3d 345, 367-373 (Pa. 2011); ***Commonwealth v. Paddy***, 15 A.3d 431, 450-454 (Pa. 2011); ***Commonwealth v. Johnson***, 815 A.2d 563, 572-574 (Pa. 2002); ***Commonwealth v. Breakiron***, 781 A.2d 94 (Pa. 2001); ***Commonwealth v. Galloway***, 640 A.2d 454 (Pa. Super. 1994).

B. Non-Brady After-Discovered Evidence Claims

In order to obtain relief based on a non-***Brady*** after-discovered evidence claim, a petitioner must establish that the evidence has been discovered after trial and it could not have been obtained at or prior to trial through reasonable diligence; the evidence is not cumulative; and is not being used solely to impeach the credibility of a witness. ***Commonwealth v. Pagan***, 950 A.2d 270 (Pa. 2008); ***Commonwealth v. Washington***, 927 A.2d 586 (Pa. 2007); *but see **Commonwealth v. Choice***, 830 A.2d 1005 (Pa. Super. 2003) (Klein, J., dissenting) (opining that the last prong is over-broad and inapplicable where impeachment evidence can alter the verdict); ***Commonwealth v. Perrin***, 59 A.3d 663 (Pa. Super. 2013) (Wecht, J., concurring); ***Commonwealth v. Foreman***, 55 A.3d 532 (Pa. Super. 2012) (Wecht, J., concurring).

Additionally, a petitioner must demonstrate that the evidence would likely compel a different verdict. ***Washington***, 927 A.2d 586; ***Commonwealth v. Fisher***, 870 A.2d 864 (Pa. 2005); ***Commonwealth v. Fiore***, 780 A.2d 704 (Pa. Super. 2001). In the absence of a plausible explanation for a defendant's inability to discover the evidence at or during trial, evidence obtained following trial is not after-discovered evidence. ***Commonwealth v. Padillas***, 997 A.2d 356, 364 (Pa. Super. 2010).

A determination of whether after-discovered evidence is cumulative of additional evidence elicited at trial depends on the strength of the evidence supporting the conviction. ***Padillas***, 997

A.2d at 364. Also, in deciding whether the new evidence would likely compel a different verdict, the PCRA court should examine the overall strength of the evidence introduced at trial, the motive of those offering the new evidence, and the integrity of the after-discovered evidence. *Padillas*, 997 A.2d at 365. It should, however, be noted that *Padillas* concluded that a confession by another person would have been used solely for impeachment purposes. This aspect of *Padillas* is less than sound since a confession can be used as substantive evidence.

Frequently, after-discovered evidence claims arise in the context of recantation evidence, which is considered highly unreliable especially when the recantation involves an admission of perjury. *Commonwealth v. D'Amato*, 856 A.2d 806 (Pa. 2004). Nonetheless, recantation may be grounds for an evidentiary hearing. *D'Amato*, 856 A.2d 806. However, a court may, in limited instances, determine that recantation evidence lacks credibility without conducting an evidentiary hearing. *Commonwealth v. Washington*, 927 A.2d 586, 597 (Pa. 2007).

In addressing issues regarding newly-discovered evidence, both the PCRA court and appellate courts are reminded that there are two separate and distinct areas of the PCRA statute that refer to after or newly-discovered evidence. *See* 42 Pa.C.S. § 9543(a)(2)(vi) and § 9545(b)(2). These sections should not be confused and require different analysis. *See Commonwealth v. Lambert*, 884 A.2d 848 (Pa. 2005); *Commonwealth v. Bennett*, 930 A.2d 1264 (Pa. 2007).

C. Section 9543(a)(2)(vii): Sentence that Exceeds the Lawful Maximum

A sentence that exceeds the lawful maximum is an illegal sentence and does not require the issue to be leveled under the ineffectiveness rubric, nor can it be waived. *Commonwealth v. Jones*, 932 A.2d 179 (Pa. Super. 2007). Of course, the issue still

After-Discovered Evidence, Sentences that Exceed the Lawful Maximum, and Proceeding in a Tribunal without Jurisdiction

must be raised in a timely PCRA petition. *Commonwealth v. Fahy*, 737 A.2d 214, 223 (Pa. 1999); *Commonwealth v. Taylor*, 65 A.3d 462 (Pa. Super. 2013); *Commonwealth v. Concordia*, 97 A.3d 366 (Pa. Super. 2014).

In *Commonwealth v. Ousley*, 21 A.3d 1238 (Pa. Super. 2011), the Superior Court summarily concluded that a merger issue was waived because it was not raised before the PCRA court. This decision is an outlier and, as discussed in prior chapters, is in conflict with numerous other decisions. *Commonwealth v. Springer*, 961 A.2d 1262, 1264 n.3 (Pa. Super. 2008); *Commonwealth v. Robinson*, 931 A.2d 15 (Pa. Super. 2007) (*en banc*); *Commonwealth v. Roach*, 453 A.2d 1001 (Pa. Super. 1983); *Commonwealth v. Staples*, 471 A.2d 847, 849-850 (Pa. Super. 1984). Not all illegal sentencing claims involve sentences that exceed the lawful maximum. For example, improper imposition of a mandatory minimum sentence has been construed as an illegal sentence. *See Commonwealth v. Foster*, 17 A.3d 332 (Pa. 2011) (OAJC); *Commonwealth v. Barnes*, __ A.3d __ (Pa. 2016) (filed December 28, 2016). In certain situations, the claim should be set forth under the ineffectiveness test; otherwise, a defendant risks the court concluding that the PCRA statute will not afford relief. Indeed, the only pure sentencing issue that the PCRA statute expressly discusses affording relief for is a sentence that exceeds the lawful maximum.

An Eighth Amendment claim may fall within this section as well as section 9543(a)(2)(i). However, the Pennsylvania Supreme Court has held that novel Eighth Amendment claims are not cognizable under the PCRA. *Commonwealth v. Robinson*, 82 A.3d 998 (Pa. 2013); *Commonwealth v. Fears*, 86 A.3d 795 (Pa. 2014). It has not yet foreclosed bringing derivative state constitutional cruel punishment claims in the PCRA. *Cf. Robinson*, 82 A.3d at 1021 n.12 (noting such claims may be addressed outside the PCRA). The interpretation of the PCRA in this regard is inconsistent with the original meaning of the PCRA. *See* Chapter 3.

D. Section 9543(a)(2)(viii): Proceedings in a Tribunal without Jurisdiction.

All common pleas courts in Pennsylvania have subject matter jurisdiction over criminal matters occurring in Pennsylvania. ***Commonwealth v. Bethea***, 828 A.2d 1066, 1074 (Pa. 2003). In this regard, jurisdiction is not to be confused with venue. *Id*. Subject matter jurisdiction also is not identical to the power or authority of the court to act. ***In re Melograne***, 812 A.2d 1164 (Pa. 2002). Claims related to the court's power to act are waivable, whereas subject matter jurisdiction issues cannot be waived. ***In re Melograne***, 812 A.2d at 1167.

In ***Commonwealth v. Quinlan***, 639 A.2d 1235 (Pa. Super. 1994), although not citing the jurisdiction provision, the panel held that the PCRA court erred in denying the petitioner's claim that the sentencing court was without jurisdiction to correct his original sentence over two years after it was entered. The sentencing court had orally sentenced the petitioner to eleven and one-half to twenty three months incarceration to be followed by five years probation. However, the written sentencing order omitted the probationary sentence. The petitioner completed his jail sentence and his parole expired. Five months later he was arrested for new crimes. The Commonwealth alleged that he violated his probation. The trial court then entered a written order purportedly correcting the original sentence by including the probationary sentence. Subsequently, the court resentenced the petitioner for violating probation. The ***Quinlan*** panel ruled that the trial court was without jurisdiction to amend the petitioner's original sentence and therefore his subsequent sentence was void.

After-Discovered Evidence, Sentences that Exceed the Lawful Maximum, and Proceeding in a Tribunal without Jurisdiction

In *Commonwealth v. Butler*, 566 A.2d 1209 (Pa. Super. 1989), the Superior Court found trial counsel ineffective for not objecting to a trial court's jurisdiction. There, the trial court granted the defendant's motion to dismiss charges based on then Rule 1100, now Rule 600. The Commonwealth filed a motion for reconsideration, which the trial court granted thirty-five days after it had dismissed the case. The *Butler* Court held that the trial court lacked jurisdiction to grant the reconsideration motion more than thirty days after entry of its final order.

The Superior Court in *Commonwealth v. Stultz*, 114 A.3d 865 (Pa. Super. 2015), addressed claims frequently raised by *pro se* petitioners regarding subject matter jurisdiction. The petitioner alleged that because the Pennsylvania Constitution of 1968 did not contain a savings clause all criminal statutory law became void upon its ratification. In addition, he averred that the Pennsylvania General Assembly had no constitutional power to pass criminal law and that the Pennsylvania Supreme Court lacked constitutional authority to promulgate rules of criminal procedure and evidence. Further, he posited that the Crimes Code lacked an enacting clause and was therefore null and void.

The *Stultz* Court noted that the Crimes Code and the Motor Vehicle Code, the latter of which the defendant had violated, were passed after the 1968 Pennsylvania Constitution. Thus, the ratification of the Pennsylvania Constitution could not invalidate that legislation. It further offered a detailed examination of why the lack of savings clause did not abrogate prior laws. The *Stultz* panel also thoroughly discredited the view that the General Assembly could not pass criminal statutes and conclusively established that the Pennsylvania Supreme Court had authority to craft procedural rules. The *Stultz* Court added that both the Crimes Code and Motor Vehicle Code included enacting clauses. It thus rejected all of the petitioner's subject matter jurisdiction claims.

After-Discovered Evidence, Sentences that Exceed the Lawful Maximum, and Proceeding in a Tribunal without Jurisdiction

For a discussion of the argument that the entire current Pennsylvania Constitution is unconstitutional and why that position is legally without merit see the discussion on that issue in the third sample Notice of Intent to Dismiss order in the back of this book.

Chapter 8: 42 Pa.C.S. § 9543(b)
Prejudicial Delay

(b) Exception.--Even if the petitioner has met the requirements of subsection (a), the petition shall be dismissed if it appears at any time that, because of delay in filing the petition, the Commonwealth has been prejudiced either in its ability to respond to the petition or in its ability to re-try the petitioner. A petition may be dismissed due to delay in the filing by the petitioner only after a hearing upon a motion to dismiss. This subsection does not apply if the petitioner shows that the petition is based on grounds of which the petitioner could not have discovered by the exercise of reasonable diligence before the delay became prejudicial to the Commonwealth.

Annotated Comments

Delay in submitting a petition has become a limited concern since the institution of the one-year time-bar and the Pennsylvania Supreme Court's interpretation of the time-bar provision as jurisdictional. Simply put, because petitions must be filed within one-year, it is the rare case where prejudicial delay will occur. Section 9543(b), of course, was made part of the PCRA statute before the time-bar was instituted, when petitions could be filed five, ten, fifteen, twenty years after the petitioner's conviction. Currently, in order for the provision to be utilized, an evidentiary hearing on prejudicial delay must be conducted by the PCRA court.

In ***Commonwealth v. Weatherill***, 24 A.3d 435 (Pa. Super. 2011), the Superior Court determined that prejudicial delay prohibited relief where the defendant timely filed his first *pro se* petition, but counsel did not file an amended petition for another ten years. Since Weatherill had fired his original PCRA counsel, sat idly for six years, and witnesses were deceased, the Court concluded that section 9543(b) applied.[14]

The Court therein relied on *Commonwealth v. Renchenski*, 988 A.2d 699 (Pa. Super. 2010), *affirmed*, 52 A.3d 251 (Pa. 2012). In the Superior Court's *Renchenski* decision, the Court agreed that even a timely petition did not preclude dismissal based on prejudicial delay that ensued after the filing of the original petition. The Superior Court in *Renchenski* made this determination not based on the language of the statute, but instead on a broad-based policy position. The Court found that delay in seeking permission to amend a petition was governed by section 9543(b) because the statute's "purpose is to ensure that the Commonwealth is not prejudiced by a defendant's delay in pursuing his rights under the PCRA." *Commonwealth v. Weatherill*, 24 A.3d 435, 439 (Pa. Super. 2011) (discussing Superior Court holding in *Renchenski*). Indeed, the Superior Court's decision in *Renchenski* assumed that delay in filing a petition pertained to an original petition and not to an amended petition.

However, in *Commonwealth v. Markowitz*, 32 A.3d 706 (Pa. Super. 2011), the Superior Court took a different approach. Therein, the defendant filed his PCRA petition before the passage of the one-year time bar, but approximately thirteen years after he pled guilty to criminal homicide. While his petition was pending, evidence was lost due to a flood. The Commonwealth argued prejudicial delay and the PCRA court agreed after hearing argument on the matter but without conducting an evidentiary hearing. An earlier Superior Court panel, in an unpublished decision, remanded for a hearing based on the plain language of the statute. Following the hearing, the

---

14 The *Weatherill* Court did not explain how the Commonwealth was prejudiced by delay in dealing with the petitioner's merger sentencing claim. However, the Superior Court rejected the merger claim.

Prejudicial Delay

PCRA court dismissed all but one issue based on prejudicial delay. The issue it decided and rejected on the merits was whether the defendant was entitled to reinstatement of his direct appeal rights.

On appeal, the defendant raised only the issue concerning the reinstatement of his appellate rights. The Superior Court determined that section 9543(b) applied to that issue also and affirmed. The Court noted that several witnesses were no longer available, physical evidence had been destroyed by court order, and no record of the testimony from the defendant's degree-of-guilt hearing existed. It concluded both that the delay in filing the original petition and the delay in submitting amended petitions was prejudicial. In discussing this latter issue, it did not rely on the Superior Court's ***Renchenski's*** policy-based argument and instead expressly addressed the language of the statute.

The ***Markowitz*** Court recognized that a PCRA court is only permitted to address an amended petition on first-time PCRA matters and the text of the statute did not limit consideration to delay in submission of an original petition. According to the ***Markowitz*** decision, the statute allows a court to find prejudicial delay at any time if there was a delay in filing a petition, which it considered to include amended petitions since prejudice could arise in the Commonwealth's ability to respond to an amended petition. The Court recognized that prejudicial delay would occur most frequently under the current statute by delays in filing amended petitions since delay in filing an original petition would render it untimely. The Supreme Court in its later ***Renchenski*** decision echoed ***Markowitz***, finding that delay in filing an amended petition can constitute prejudicial delay pursuant to section 9453(b).

Quoting ***Markowitz***, the Supreme Court stated:

Under the current statute, prejudicial delay will most

often result not in the filing of an original petition, but from any subsequently amended petitions. Section 9543(b) provides a mechanism to ensure that counsel and petitioners maintain some level of diligence in pursuing collateral relief both before and after the filing of an original petition.

Renchenski, 52 A.3d 251, 260 (Pa. 2012) (quoting ***Commonwealth v. Markowitz***, 32 A.3d 706, 713 (Pa. Super. 2011)). The Supreme Court in ***Renchenski*** also reiterated the view espoused in the ***Markowitz*** decision that the petition a PCRA court will most often be deciding is an amended petition and that the "any time" language of section 9543(b) reflected a concern for more than the filing of an original petition. *See Renchenski*, 52 A.3d 251, 259-260 (Pa. 2012); *see also Markowitz*, 32 A.3d at 713. In sum, an amended petition may be dismissed if the petitioner does not pursue relief. However, the Supreme Court in ***Renchenski*** also reminded PCRA courts of their duty to adequately manage their docket. Where delay is caused by the court, it is inappropriate to attribute prejudice to the defendant. *See Markowitz*, 32 A.3d at 713 n. 6.

Chapter 9: 42 Pa.C.S. § 9543.1
Post-Conviction DNA Testing

(a) Motion.--

(1) An individual convicted of a criminal offense in a court of this Commonwealth and serving a term of imprisonment or awaiting execution because of a sentence of death may apply by making a written motion to the sentencing court for the performance of forensic DNA testing on specific evidence that is related to the investigation or prosecution that resulted in the judgment of conviction.

(2) The evidence may have been discovered either prior to or after the applicant's conviction. The evidence shall be available for testing as of the date of the motion. If the evidence was discovered prior to the applicant's conviction, the evidence shall not have been subject to the DNA testing requested because the technology for testing was not in existence at the time of the trial or the applicant's counsel did not seek testing at the time of the trial in a case where a verdict was rendered on or before January 1, 1995, or the applicant's counsel sought funds from the court to pay for the testing because his client was indigent and the court refused the request despite the client's indigency.

(b) Notice to the Commonwealth.—

(1) Upon receipt of a motion under subsection (a), the court shall notify the Commonwealth and shall afford the Commonwealth an opportunity to respond to the motion.

(2) Upon receipt of a motion under subsection (a) or notice of the motion, as applicable, the Commonwealth and the court shall take the steps reasonably necessary to ensure that any remaining biological material in the possession of the

Post-Conviction DNA Testing

Commonwealth or the court is preserved pending the completion of the proceedings under this section.

(c) Requirements.--In any motion under subsection (a), under penalty of perjury, the applicant shall:

(1) (i) specify the evidence to be tested;

(ii) state that the applicant consents to provide samples of bodily fluid for use in the DNA testing; and

(iii) acknowledge that the applicant understands that, if the motion is granted, any data obtained from any DNA samples or test results may be entered into law enforcement databases, may be used in the investigation of other crimes and may be used as evidence against the applicant in other cases.

(2) (i) assert the applicant's actual innocence of the offense for which the applicant was convicted; and

(ii) in a capital case:

(A) assert the applicant's actual innocence of the charged or uncharged conduct constituting an aggravating circumstance under section 9711(d) (relating to sentencing procedure for murder of the first degree) if the applicant's exoneration of the conduct would result in vacating a sentence of death; or

(B) assert that the outcome of the DNA testing would establish a mitigating circumstance under section 9711(e)(7) if that mitigating circumstance was presented to the sentencing judge or jury and facts as to that issue were in dispute at the sentencing hearing.

(3) present a prima facie case demonstrating that the:

(i) identity of or the participation in the crime by the

perpetrator was at issue in the proceedings that resulted in the applicant's conviction and sentencing; and

(ii) DNA testing of the specific evidence, assuming exculpatory results, would establish:

(A) the applicant's actual innocence of the offense for which the applicant was convicted;

(B) in a capital case, the applicant's actual innocence of the charged or uncharged conduct constituting an aggravating circumstance under section 9711(d) if the applicant's exoneration of the conduct would result in vacating a sentence of death; or

(C) in a capital case, a mitigating circumstance under section 9711(e)(7) under the circumstances set forth in subsection (c)(1)(iv).

(d) Order.—

(1) Except as provided in paragraph (2), the court shall order the testing requested in a motion under subsection (a) under reasonable conditions designed to preserve the integrity of the evidence and the testing process upon a determination, after review of the record of the applicant's trial, that the:

(i) requirements of subsection (c) have been met;

(ii) evidence to be tested has been subject to a chain of custody sufficient to establish that it has not been altered in any material respect; and

(iii) motion is made in a timely manner and for the purpose of demonstrating the applicant's actual innocence and not to delay the execution of sentence or administration of justice.

(2) The court shall not order the testing requested in a

Post-Conviction DNA Testing

motion under subsection (a) if, after review of the record of the applicant's trial, the court determines that there is no reasonable possibility that the testing would produce exculpatory evidence that:

(i) would establish the applicant's actual innocence of the offense for which the applicant was convicted;

(ii) in a capital case, would establish the applicant's actual innocence of the charged or uncharged conduct constituting an aggravating circumstance under section 9711(d) if the applicant's exoneration of the conduct would result in vacating a sentence of death; or

(iii) in a capital case, would establish a mitigating circumstance under section 9711(e)(7) under the circumstances set forth in subsection (c)(1)(iv).

(e) Testing procedures.—

(1) Any DNA testing ordered under this section shall be conducted by:

(i) a laboratory mutually selected by the Commonwealth and the applicant;

(ii) if the Commonwealth and the applicant are unable to agree on a laboratory, a laboratory selected by the court that ordered the testing; or

(iii) if the applicant is indigent, the testing shall be conducted by the Pennsylvania State Police or, at the Pennsylvania State Police's sole discretion, by a laboratory designated by the Pennsylvania State Police.

(2) The costs of any testing ordered under this section shall be paid:

(i) by the applicant; or

Post-Conviction DNA Testing

(ii) in the case of an applicant who is indigent, by the Commonwealth of Pennsylvania.

(3) Testing conducted by the Pennsylvania State Police shall be carried out in accordance with the protocols and procedures established by the Pennsylvania State Police.

(f) Posttesting procedures.—

(1) After the DNA testing conducted under this section has been completed, the applicant may, pursuant to section 9545(b)(2) (relating to jurisdiction and proceedings), during the 60-day period beginning on the date on which the applicant is notified of the test results, petition to the court for postconviction relief pursuant to section 9543(a)(2)(vi) (relating to eligibility for relief).

(2) Upon receipt of a petition filed under paragraph (1), the court shall consider the petition along with any answer filed by the Commonwealth and shall conduct a hearing thereon.

(3) In any hearing on a petition for postconviction relief filed under paragraph (1), the court shall determine whether the exculpatory evidence resulting from the DNA testing conducted under this section would have changed the outcome of the trial as required by section 9543(a)(2)(vi).

(g) Effect of motion.--The filing of a motion for forensic DNA testing pursuant to subsection (a) shall have the following effect:

(1) The filing of the motion shall constitute the applicant's consent to provide samples of bodily fluid for use in the DNA testing.

(2) The data from any DNA samples or test results obtained as a result of the motion may be entered into law enforcement databases, may be used in the investigation of

Post-Conviction DNA Testing

other crimes and may be used as evidence against the applicant in other cases.

(h) Definitions.--As used in this section, the following words and phrases shall have the meanings given to them in this subsection:

"**Applicant.**" The individual who files a motion under subsection (a).

"**DNA.**" Deoxyribonucleic acid.

Annotated Comments

In 2002, 42 Pa.C.S. § 9543.1 went into effect. The provision allows a petitioner to file a written motion with the court requesting DNA testing on specific evidence related to the investigation or prosecution of his case. The PCRA court may then order DNA testing. This motion is distinct from petitions seeking substantive relief under the PCRA statute. ***Commonwealth v. Gacobano***, 65 A.3d 416 (Pa. Super. 2013); ***Commonwealth v. Perry***, 959 A.2d 932 (Pa. Super. 2008).

To be entitled to DNA testing of specific items in existence, the defendant must establish that the item he seeks to be tested is available at the time he files his petition. ***Commonwealth v. Conway***, 14 A.3d 101 (Pa. Super. 2011). Additionally, the evidence, if discovered prior to the defendant's conviction, must not have been tested either because such technology did not exist, or counsel did not request testing and the verdict occurred before January 1, 1995, or a request was made for testing because the defendant was indigent and the court refused the request. ***Conway***, 14 A.3d 101. The identity of the perpetrator must also have been at issue and the DNA testing establish actual innocence. ***Conway***, 14 A.3d 101; ***Commonwealth v. Heilman***, 867 A.2d 542 (Pa. Super. 2005); ***Commonwealth v. Walsh***, 125 A.3d 1248 (Pa. Super. 2015) (absence of victim's

DNA on hammer used in attack on victim would not have established actual innocence).

In ***In re Payne***, 129 A.3d 546 (Pa. Super 2016) (*en banc*), the Court held that the term actual innocence did not preclude DNA testing where the petitioner had been found guilty of felony murder. The Commonwealth argued that because the DNA testing would not establish that the petitioner was actually innocent, the petitioner was not entitled to testing. The majority applied a federal *habeas* standard for defining actual innocence. The majority's definition was previously espoused in ***Conway***, 14 A.3d 101, and requires the DNA evidence to make it more likely than not that no reasonable juror would have found the defendant guilty. In a stinging dissent, Judge Stabile maintained that the majority improperly re-defined the term "actual innocence" in derogation of the PCRA statute. He interpreted the phrase to mean factual innocence.

Where the verdict occurs after January 1, 1995, and counsel did not seek DNA testing, a petitioner may bring a claim of ineffective assistance of counsel. ***Commonwealth v. Williams***, 899 A.2d 1060 (Pa. 2006) (court remanded to determine if counsel had a reasonable basis for not seeking DNA testing). However, section 9543.1 does not apply to this situation. ***Williams***, 899 A.2d 1060.

A petition requesting DNA testing is not subject to the one-year time bar of the PCRA. ***Commonwealth v. Gacobano***, 65 A.3d 416 (Pa. Super. 2013); ***Commonwealth v. Conway***, 14 A.3d 101 (Pa. Super. 2011); ***Commonwealth v. Brooks***, 875 A.2d 1141 (Pa. Super. 2005). However, a petitioner still must timely seek the DNA testing. ***Commonwealth v. Edmiston***, 65 A.3d 339 (Pa. 2013); ***Commonwealth v. Walsh***, 125 A.3d 1248 (Pa. Super. 2015); 42 Pa.C.S. § 9542.1(d)(1)(iii). In ***Edmiston***, the Court found that the motion was not timely. Therein, Edmiston had indicated during his trial that he was satisfied with the DNA

Post-Conviction DNA Testing

testing that had been performed, did not seek DNA testing during his first PCRA petition, and was aware of the physical evidence he asked to be tested for over twenty years. The timeliness of a DNA motion, however, is not a jurisdictional matter. *In re Payne*, 129 A.3d 546 (Pa. Super. 2015) (*en banc*). Accordingly, the Commonwealth may waive a challenge to the timeliness of the motion by failing to contest it. *But see Payne, supra* (Gantman, P.J., dissenting).

Following DNA testing pursuant to section 9543.1, the petitioner has sixty days from notification of the test results to file his PCRA petition. The PCRA court must then, if the petition is timely filed, conduct a hearing and determine if the evidence would have altered the outcome of the trial. Where the DNA testing has not yet been conducted under the relevant provision, DNA cannot be after-discovered evidence. *Commonwealth v. Baker*, 828 A.2d 1146 (Pa. Super. 2003). However, the PCRA court can clearly order DNA testing before applying the newly-discovered fact timeliness provision of the PCRA. *Commonwealth v. McLaughlin*, 835 A.2d 747 (Pa. Super. 2003).

Additionally, the DNA testing provision itself does not create a timeliness exception; rather, once DNA is obtained, a petitioner may file a PCRA petition alleging newly-discovered evidence in the nature of the DNA test. *Commonwealth v. Weeks*, 831 A.2d 1194 (Pa. Super. 2003). As a practical matter, however, the DNA provision does create a timeliness exception since the petition seeking DNA evidence need not be filed within one year of the completion of direct review from the judgment of sentence. *See Brooks*, 875 A.2d 1141. Rather, a petitioner may seek the DNA testing and, if the court grants the petition, file a PCRA petition within sixty days of receiving the test results. Nevertheless, the Superior Court has treated motions requesting DNA testing as an actual PCRA petition, although these petitions are a precursor to filing a PCRA petition based on newly-discovered evidence.

Commonwealth v. Young, 873 A.2d 720 (Pa. Super. 2005), *abrogated on other ground by **Commonwealth v. Wright**,* 14 A.3d 798 (Pa. 2011).

There is no right to counsel for purposes of filing a DNA motion. ***Commonwealth v. Brooks***, 875 A.2d 1141 (Pa. Super. 2005). A DNA motion cannot raise claims unrelated to DNA testing to avoid the one-year timeliness provision of the PCRA statute. ***Brooks***, 875 A.2d 1141; ***Commonwealth v. Walsh***, 125 A.3d 1248 (Pa. Super. 2015). Further, if a DNA motion is treated as a PCRA petition, the subsequent petition that utilizes DNA as grounds for meeting the timeliness exception provided for in section 9545(b)(2) must be treated as a first time petition. Of course, if a defendant filed a PCRA petition before seeking the DNA evidence, then the subsequent petition, which uses DNA evidence to fall within the timeliness requirements of the PCRA statute, must be treated as a serial petition subject to the miscarriage of justice and/or actual innocence standard.

A person who pleads guilty is not eligible for the PCRA DNA provision. ***Williams v. Erie County District Attorney's Office***, 848 A.2d 967 (Pa. Super. 2004). Nor is a petitioner entitled to DNA testing when there is no evidence to test; however, a voluntary confession does not preclude DNA testing. ***Commonwealth v. Wright***, 14 A.3d 798 (Pa. 2011). When a petitioner is awarded DNA testing the order is final and the Commonwealth can file an immediate appeal. ***Commonwealth v. Scarborough***, 64 A.3d 602 (Pa. 2013).

Chapter 10: 42 Pa.C.S. § 9544
Previous Litigation and Waiver

Section 9544. Previous litigation and waiver

(a) PREVIOUS LITIGATION.-- For purposes of this subchapter, an issue has been previously litigated if:

(1) Deleted.

(2) the highest appellate court in which the petitioner could have had review as a matter of right has ruled on the merits of the issue; or

(3) it has been raised and decided in a proceeding collaterally attacking the conviction or sentence.

(b) ISSUES WAIVED.-- For purposes of this subchapter, an issue is waived if the petitioner could have raised it but failed to do so before trial, at trial, during unitary review, on appeal or in a prior state postconviction proceeding.

Annotated Comments

In order to be eligible for relief under the PCRA, a petitioner must plead and prove by a preponderance of the evidence that the issues raised have not been previously litigated. An issue is previously litigated if "the highest appellate court in which the petitioner could have had review as of right has ruled on the merits of the issue," or if the issue was "raised and decided in a proceeding collaterally attacking the conviction or sentence." 42 Pa.C.S. § 9544; ***Commonwealth v. Rios***, 920 A.2d 790 (Pa. 2007); ***Commonwealth v. Reyes***, 870 A.2d 888 (Pa. 2005); ***Commonwealth v. Bond***, 819 A.2d 33 (Pa. 2002).

Where a PCRA petition has been filed after the completion of a direct appeal, the PCRA court must examine the issues raised on direct appeal to determine if an issue has been previously

Previous Litigation and Waiver

litigated. In ***Commonwealth v. Kindler***, 722 A.2d 143 (Pa. 1998), the Pennsylvania Supreme Court held that the defendant was not entitled to PCRA relief where, during the pendency of his post-verdict motions, he became a fugitive and the trial court held that he failed to preserve any issues for review. After the defendant was captured and the Pennsylvania Supreme Court heard his case, it agreed that his issues were waived. During PCRA review, the High Court determined that the question concerning his post-verdict motion waiver of claims was previously litigated on direct appeal. Additionally, a defendant who becomes a fugitive while his case is on appeal forfeits all of his claims. ***Commonwealth v. Judge***, 797 A.2d 250 (Pa. 2002).

When a prior PCRA proceeding was initiated, any issues raised therein cannot be litigated again. However, a PCRA court is cautioned that an issue is not previously litigated when the petition raises an issue via ineffective assistance of counsel, unless that issue was earlier set forth under the rubric of ineffective assistance of counsel. ***Commonwealth v. Collins***, 888 A.2d 564 (Pa. 2005). For example, if a defendant raises an issue on direct appeal related to a jury instruction and then during PCRA review contends that trial counsel was ineffective for not objecting to the instruction, the latter issue is not previously litigated.

A petitioner cannot advance a new argument in support of an issue which has been previously litigated or waived. ***Commonwealth v. Hutchins***, 760 A.2d 50 (Pa. Super. 2000); ***Commonwealth v. Morales***, 701 A.2d 516 (Pa. 1997); ***Commonwealth v. Marshall***, 812 A.2d 539 (Pa. 2002); ***Commonwealth v. Faulkner***, 735 A.2d 67 (Pa. 1999). Issues raised in a prior federal *habeas* proceeding are previously litigated. ***Commonwealth v. Burkett***, 5 A.3d 1260 (Pa. Super. 2010). Nevertheless, claims that could have been raised in the federal proceeding, which were not, will not result in waiver. 42 Pa.C.S. § 9544(b). The Pennsylvania Supreme Court has declined to find waiver of an ineffectiveness issue where the claim was raised in boilerplate fashion where the PCRA court did not discuss waiver or order amendment of a defective petition. ***Commonwealth v. Simpson***, 66 A.3d 253, 261 (Pa. 2013).

Claims which could have been raised "at trial. . . .on appeal or in a prior state post-conviction proceeding," are waived. 42 Pa.C.S. § 9544(b); ***Commonwealth v. Rios***, 920 A.2d 790 (Pa. 2007); ***Commonwealth v. Bond***, 819 A.2d 33 (Pa. 2002) (failure to raise issue in PCRA petition will result in waiver on appeal); ***Commonwealth v. Wallace***, 724 A.2d 916 (Pa. 1999) (same); ***Commonwealth v. Quaranibal***, 763 A.2d 941 (Pa. Super. 2000) (petitioner waived issue that under the Vienna Convention he was entitled to contact the El Salvadoran consulate at time of arrest). A person is ineligible for relief under the PCRA statute if an issue is waived, unless the "failure to litigate the issue prior to or during trial. . . .or on direct appeal could not have been the result of any rational, strategic or tactical decision by counsel." 42 Pa.C.S. § 9543(4).

Relaxed waiver existed in capital PCRA matters from 1994, *see* ***Commonwealth v. DeHart***, 650 A.2d 38 (Pa. 1994), until the decision in ***Commonwealth v. Albrecht***, 720 A.2d 693 (Pa. 1998). Under the relaxed waiver doctrine, the Pennsylvania Supreme Court had discretionary authority to review a record-based claim during a capital appeal that was not presented at the trial level. Since there is currently no relaxed waiver under the PCRA, ***Albrecht***, 720 A.2d 693, where the claims could have been raised at trial or post-trial and were not, those issues are waived and can only be properly brought forth by alleging that counsel was ineffective in failing to set forth the claim. ***Commonwealth v. Wallace***, 724 A.2d 916 (Pa. 1999).

Also, a PCRA petition is not a substitute for a Pa.R.A.P. 1925(b) statement; therefore, if a Pa.R.A.P. 1925(b) order is entered, the petitioner must raise his issues in his statement or risk waiver. ***Commonwealth v. Butler***, 756 A.2d 55 (Pa. Super. 2000), *affirmed*, 812 A.2d 631 (Pa. 2002). A previously unlitigated issue is not waived when raised under the rubric of ineffective assistance of counsel. ***Commonwealth v. Allen***, 732 A.2d 582 (Pa. 1999); *see also **Commonwealth v. Collins***, 888 A.2d 564 (Pa. 2005).

Issues may be waived where a defendant withdraws his direct appeal on counsel's advice but does not allege the ineffectiveness of counsel for providing that advice. ***Commonwealth v. Hanyon***, 772 A.2d 1033 (Pa. Super. 2001); ***Commonwealth v. McKinney***, 772 A.2d 1023 (Pa. Super. 2001). Notably, in ***McKinney***, the court found that the issues raised were waived when counsel advised the defendant to withdraw his direct appeal and file a PCRA petition alleging trial counsel's ineffectiveness. In light of ***Commonwealth v. Grant***, 813 A.2d 726 (Pa. 2002), which declared that all claims of ineffective assistance of counsel should be deferred until collateral review, such advice would not automatically be ineffective or result in waiver of ineffectiveness claims.

The failure to file a direct appeal has been held to waive non-legality of sentence and non-ineffectiveness claims. ***Commonwealth v. Walls***, 993 A.2d 289 (Pa. Super. 2010); ***Commonwealth v. Berry***, 877 A.2d 479 (Pa. Super. 2005) (*en banc*). Thus, where a defendant has preserved issues that pertain to trial court error he must file a direct appeal or risk losing an opportunity to litigate the issue. Issues that are waived on direct appeal are not previously litigated. ***Commonwealth v. Jones***, 932 A.2d 179 (Pa. Super. 2007).

This author is also compelled to remark on the split in Superior Court authority on the issue of waiver with regard to legality of sentence questions. Prior to 2011, it was well settled that an illegality of sentence issue could be raised *sua sponte* by a court and did not need to be preserved in a PCRA petition. ***Commonwealth v. Staples***, 471 A.2d 847, 849-850 (Pa. Super. 1984) (case decided under PCHA, which found, "despite the fact that appellant has previously filed post-trial motions, a direct appeal to the Supreme Court, two prior PCHA petitions, and an appeal from the first of those petitions to the Supreme Court, the issue now raised involves the illegality of sentence, which is not a waivable issue"); ***Commonwealth v. Thomas***, 484 A.2d 155 (Pa. Super. 1984), *overturned on separate grounds*, 516 A.2d 328 (Pa. 1986); ***Commonwealth v. Rivera***, 10 A.3d 1276 (Pa. Super. 2010) (*sua sponte* raising issue labeling it as legality of sentence and affording relief);[15] *see also* ***Commonwealth v. Fahy***, 737 A.2d 214, 223 (Pa. 1999) ("Although legality of sentence is always subject to review within the PCRA, claims must still first satisfy the PCRA's time limits or one of the exceptions thereto."); ***Commonwealth v. Springer***, 961 A.2d 1262, 1264 n.3 (Pa. Super. 2008); ***Commonwealth v. Jones***, 932 A.2d 179 (Pa. Super. 2007).

Further, the Pennsylvania Supreme Court has held that waiver in the PCRA context applies only "to those claims that are required to be preserved." ***Commonwealth v. Brown***, 872 A.2d 1139, 1154 (Pa. 2005). Legality of sentence issues have never been required to be preserved. However, in ***Commonwealth v. Ousley***, 21 A.3d 1238 (Pa. Super. 2011), the Superior Court, without analysis and in one sentence, held that a legality of

---

15 The ***Rivera*** Court's conclusion that the issue was a legality of sentencing claim is questionable. According to the decision, the petitioner's claim was that he could not be guilty of the offense because he had not committed a crime under the applicable statute. In essence, this was a legal question involving statutory interpretation, not a sentencing issue. The Court opined that if the defendant could not be convicted he could not be sentenced, but this is true in all sufficiency of the evidence claims. Unless one is a capital defendant, a defendant can waive sufficiency of the evidence issues.

sentence merger issue was waived because it was not included within the petitioner's PCRA petition. The ***Ousley*** decision relied on two PCRA decisions that discussed waiver of non-legality of sentence claims, but did not address countervailing precedent. In light of the decision in ***Brown***, attorneys are advised that the ***Ousley*** decision conflicts with the Pennsylvania Supreme Court's holding that the waiver provision of the PCRA statute applies only to issues that can be waived. ***But see Brown***, 872 A.2d at 1167 (Castille, J., dissenting).

In addition to legality of sentence issues and jurisdictional claims, ***see Commonwealth v. Quinlan***, 639 A.2d 1235 (Pa. Super. 1994), issues pertaining to a defendant's competency to stand trial are also non-waivable under the PCRA. ***Commonwealth v. Blakeney***, 108 A.3d 739 (Pa. 2014) (citing ***Brown***, 872 A.2d at 1153).

Chapter 11: 42 Pa.C.S. § 9545
Jurisdiction and Proceedings

NOTICE: Effective immediately, subsecs. (c)(3) and (d)(2) of this section are permanently suspended by Supreme Court Order dated August 11, 1997. It shall retroactively apply to all cases on or after January 1, 1996 in which the death penalty was imposed, and that appointments of counsel shall remain in effect for purposes of challenges under the Post Conviction Relief Act (amended 1995 and by the order of 1997) and under Chapter 1500 (1997 order as amended).

Section 9545. Jurisdiction and proceedings

(a) ORIGINAL JURISDICTION.-- Original jurisdiction over a proceeding under this subchapter shall be in the court of common pleas. No court shall have authority to entertain a request for any form of relief in anticipation of the filing of a petition under this subchapter.

(b) TIME FOR FILING PETITION.--

1) Any petition under this subchapter, including a second or subsequent petition, shall be filed within one year of the date the judgment becomes final, unless the petition alleges and the petitioner proves that:

(i) the failure to raise the claim previously was the result of interference by government officials with the presentation of the claim in violation of the Constitution or laws of this Commonwealth or the Constitution or laws of the United States;

(ii) the facts upon which the claim is predicated were unknown to the petitioner and could not have been ascertained by the exercise of due diligence; or

Jurisdiction and Proceedings

(iii) the right asserted is a constitutional right that was recognized by the Supreme Court of the United States or the Supreme Court of Pennsylvania after the time period provided in this section and has been held by that court to apply retroactively.

2) Any petition invoking an exception provided in paragraph (1) shall be filed within 60 days of the date the claim could have been presented.

3) For purposes of this subchapter, a judgment becomes final at the conclusion of direct review, including discretionary review in the Supreme Court of the United States and the Supreme Court of Pennsylvania, or at the expiration of time for seeking the review.

4) For purposes of this subchapter, "government officials" shall not include defense counsel, whether appointed or retained.

(c) STAY OF EXECUTION.--

(1) No court shall have the authority to issue a stay of execution in any case except as allowed under this subchapter.

(2) Except for first petitions filed under this subchapter by defendants whose sentences have been affirmed on direct appeal by the Supreme Court of Pennsylvania between January 1, 1994, and January 1, 1996, no stay may be issued unless a petition for postconviction relief which meets all the requirements of this subchapter has been filed and is pending and the petitioner makes a strong showing of likelihood of success on the merits. [Suspended by Supreme Court Order dated August 11, 1997.]

(3) If a stay of execution is granted, all limitations periods set forth under sections 9574 (relating to answer to petition),

Jurisdiction and Proceedings

9575 (relating to disposition without evidentiary hearing) and 9576 (relating to evidentiary hearing) shall apply to the litigation of the petition.

(d) EVIDENTIARY HEARING.—

(1) Where a petitioner requests an evidentiary hearing, the petition shall include a signed certification as to each intended witness stating the witness's name, address, date of birth and substance of testimony and shall include any documents material to that witness's testimony. Failure to substantially comply with the requirements of this paragraph shall render the proposed witness's testimony inadmissible.

(2) No discovery, at any stage of proceedings under this subchapter, shall be permitted except upon leave of court with a showing of exceptional circumstances. [Suspended by Supreme Court Order dated August 11, 1997.]

(3) When a claim for relief is based on an allegation of ineffective assistance of counsel as a ground for relief, any privilege concerning counsel's representation as to that issue shall be automatically terminated.

Annotated Comments

A. Original Jurisdiction: 42 Pa.C.S. § 9545(a)

All PCRA matters must begin in the court of common pleas. In *Commonwealth v. Martorano*, 89 A.3d 301 (Pa. Super. 2014), the Superior Court held that the Philadelphia Municipal Court does not have jurisdiction to hear PCRA matters. A petitioner must file his petition with the court in the county in which he was convicted. A court cannot entertain cognizable forms of post-conviction relief, including providing discovery, unless a PCRA petition has been filed. In a similar respect, absent the filing of a *pro se* petition, it is premature to appoint counsel in anticipation of a person filing a petition.

B. Timeliness and Jurisdiction: 42 Pa.C.S. § 9545(b)

In accordance with 42 Pa.C.S. § 9545, any PCRA petition shall be filed within one year of the date the judgment becomes final. 42 Pa.C.S. § 9545(b)(1); *Commonwealth v. Albrecht*, 994 A.2d 1091 (Pa. 2010); *Commonwealth v. Chester*, 895 A.2d 520 (Pa. 2006). Petitioners who were convicted prior to 1995 could file a timely PCRA petition within one year of January 16, 1996; however, the petition must have been the individual's first collateral petition. *Commonwealth v. Crawley*, 739 A.2d 108 (Pa. 1999); *Commonwealth v. Fahy*, 737 A.2d 214 (Pa. 1999); *Commonwealth v. Thomas*, 718 A.2d 326 (Pa. Super. 1998) (*en banc*).[16]

A judgment becomes final at the conclusion of or upon withdrawal of direct review, *see Commonwealth v. Conway*, 706 A.2d 1243 (Pa. Super. 1997), including discretionary review in the United States Supreme Court and the Pennsylvania Supreme Court, or at the expiration of time for seeking such review, 42 Pa.C.S. § 9545(b)(3); *Commonwealth v. Hutchins*, 760 A.2d 50 (Pa. Super. 2000); *Commonwealth v. Owens*, 718 A.2d 330 (Pa. Super. 1998) (one year time-bar did not begin to run until ninety days after Pennsylvania Supreme Court denied

---

16 The Superior Court has properly held that the applicable proviso in the 1995 amendments required a first time petition filed by a petitioner convicted on or before the effective date of the 1995 amendments to be filed by January 16, 1997. *See Commonwealth v. Thomas*, 718 A.2d 326 (Pa. Super. 1998) (*en banc*); *Commonwealth v. Garcia*, 23 A.3d 1059 (Pa. Super. 2011). The Supreme Court in several cases has incorrectly stated that petitioners had until January 17, 1997, to file a timely first time petition. *Commonwealth v. Ly*, 980 A.2d 61 (Pa. 2009); *Commonwealth v. Rollins*, 738 A.2d 435 (Pa. 1999). In *Commonwealth v. Sneed*, 45 A.3d 1096, 1102 n.5 (Pa. 2012), the Supreme Court correctly indicated that the appropriate date is January 16, 1997.

Jurisdiction and Proceedings

petition for allowance of appeal). An attorney should be aware of Pa.R.Crim.P. 720 (post-sentence motions), Pa.R.A.P. 903 (time for appeal), Pa.R.A.P. 1113 (time for petitioning for allowance of appeal), and U.S. Sup. Ct. R. 13 (review for certiorari) for purposes of determining when judgment becomes final.[17]

In *Commonwealth v. Harris*, 972 A.2d 1196 (Pa. Super. 2009), the Superior Court determined that a Commonwealth appeal tolled the completion of the finality of judgment of sentence for purposes of determining when the one year time-bar began to run. Therein, the Commonwealth appealed the determination that Megan's Law, governing sex offenders, was unconstitutional. The Superior Court ruled that a hearing mandated by Megan's Law is part of sentencing and the period for filing a PCRA petition did not begin until after the Supreme Court remanded the case.

In *Commonwealth v. Callahan*, 101 A.3d 118 (Pa. Super. 2014), the petitioner successfully achieved reinstatement of his direct appeal rights *nunc pro tunc*. The PCRA court therein also addressed additional ineffectiveness issues on the merits and found them meritless. **But see Commonwealth v. Bronaugh**, 670 A.2d 147 (Pa. Super. 1995); **Commonwealth v. Hoyman**, 561 A.2d 756 (Pa. Super. 1989). The petitioner elected not to pursue his *nunc pro tunc* direct appeal. Instead, he chose to file an appeal from the PCRA court's denial of his remaining claims. After the completion of that appeal, he filed a serial PCRA petition. The Superior Court ruled that this serial petition was untimely. In doing so, it ruled that the petitioner's judgment of sentence, for purposes of his serial petition, became final thirty days after the PCRA court reinstated his direct appeal rights.

---

17 Before January 1, 1990, defendants had sixty days to file a writ of *certiorari* with the United States Supreme Court. Defendants now have ninety days to seek such review.

Jurisdiction and Proceedings

Since the petitioner did not file his subsequent petition within one year of that date, the petition was untimely.

It also should be noted that where a new sentence is imposed following a revocation hearing, the date of the revocation hearing is used to determine the date of finality of the judgment of sentence relative to any new sentencing issues, *i.e.*, legality of the new sentence and the validity of the hearing. ***Commonwealth v. Cappello***, 823 A.2d 936 (Pa. Super. 2003); ***Commonwealth v. Anderson***, 788 A.2d 1019 (Pa. Super. 2001); *compare* ***Commonwealth v. McKeever***, 947 A.2d 782 (Pa. Super. 2008) (holding that a new sentence does not reset the clock for filing a PCRA for other convictions and sentences).

Insofar as ***McKeever*** can be read as holding that a person cannot file a new timely PCRA petition challenging new sentencing counsel's representation after a previous PCRA decision resulted in a remand for resentencing, such a reading is incorrect. *See* ***Commonwealth v. Lesko***, 15 A.3d 345, 366 (Pa. 2011). Similarly, ***Commonwealth v. Dehart***, 730 A.2d 991, 994 n.2 (Pa. Super. 1999), is incorrect to the extent that it found that re-sentencing will not reset the clock for filing a timely petition as to re-sentencing counsel's representation. *See Lesko*, 15 A.3d 366-368 (Pa. 2011); *Cappello*, 823 A.2d 936; *Anderson*, 788 A.2d 1019. ***Dehart*** also was implicitly overruled by ***Commonwealth v. ex rel. Dadario v. Goldberg***, 773 A.2d 126 (Pa. 2001), insofar as it held, based on the truth-determining language of the PCRA statute, that the PCRA only pertains to a conviction and not sentencing. Of course, an individual contesting new or re-sentencing counsel's representation cannot challenge issues other than sentencing matters.

When a petition is untimely, the PCRA court lacks jurisdiction to reach the merits of the case and must deny the petition. ***Commonwealth v. Albrecht***, 994 A.2d 1091 (Pa. 2010); ***Commonwealth v. Fahy***, 737 A.2d 214 (Pa. 1999);

Commonwealth v. Perrin, 947 A.2d 1284 (Pa. Super. 2008); *Commonwealth v. Wilson*, 824 A.2d 331 (Pa. Super. 2003) (failure to timely file PCRA petition prevents court from addressing merits of appellate counsel's ineffectiveness for not filing a brief). The PCRA court does not, however, lack subject matter jurisdiction to determine jurisdiction in the first instance. *See U.S. v. Shipp*, 203 U.S. 563 (1906). Although it is hornbook law that claims regarding an illegal sentence cannot be waived, when the issue is asserted in a PCRA petition, the petition still must be timely filed or the court is without jurisdiction to reach the issue. *Commonwealth v. Fahy*, 737 A.2d 214 (Pa. 1999); *Commonwealth v. Taylor*, 65 A.3d 462 (Pa. Super. 2013); *Commonwealth v. Slotcavage*, 939 A2d 901 (Pa. Super. 2007); *Commonwealth v. Beck*, 848 A.2d 987 (Pa. Super. 2004).

The interpretation of the one-year time bar as jurisdictional in nature has been criticized by at least two commentators. *See* Thomas M. Place, Claim is Cognizable but the Petition is Untimely: The Pennsylvania Supreme Court's Recent Collateral Relief Decisions, 10 Temp. Pol. Civ. Rts. L. Rev. 49 (2000); Louis M. Natalie, Jr., New Bars in Pennsylvania Capital Post-Conviction Law and Their Implications in Federal Habeas Corpus Review, 73 Temp. L. Rev. 69 (Spring 2000). Their position emphasizes that while it is true that the one-year-time-bar falls under the heading of "Jurisdiction and proceedings[,]" the term jurisdiction is never mentioned in discussing the time requirements.

Rather, the word "jurisdiction" is mentioned in the statute only where the legislature set forth that post-conviction proceedings are to begin in the court of common pleas. Moreover, on the federal level, courts interpreting the federal *habeas* statute, AEDPA, and its similar one-year time bar, have held that the one year provision is a statute of limitations subject to equitable tolling. Nonetheless, the legislature has not amended the statute to reflect that the time bar was intended as a statute of limitations and not a jurisdictional bar.[18]

Since the Pennsylvania Supreme Court has construed the time-bar as jurisdictional, courts must *sua sponte* raise and address the timeliness of a petition. ***Commonwealth v. Yarris***, 731 A.2d 581, 587 (Pa. 1999); ***Commonwealth v. Hawkins***, 953 A.2d 1248 (Pa. 2006) (OAJC). A *pro se* petition is deemed filed pursuant to the prisoner mailbox rule when the petition is mailed or placed in the hands of prison authorities for mailing. ***Commonwealth v. Castro***, 766 A.2d 1259 (Pa. Super. 2001); ***Commonwealth v. Little***, 716 A.2d 1287 (Pa. Super. 1998). A PCRA court has no authority to extend the filing period. ***Commonwealth v. Robinson***, 837 A.2d 1157 (Pa. 2003).

In addition, the PCRA court lacks jurisdiction to determine a PCRA petition if the case is currently on direct appeal, ***Commonwealth v. Leslie***, 757 A.2d 984 (Pa. Super. 2000), or another PCRA petition is pending on appeal. ***Commonwealth v. Lark***, 746 A.2d 585 (Pa. 2000); *see also **Commonwealth v. O'Neil***, 573 A.2d 1112 (Pa. Super. 1990) (quashing appeal from dismissal of *pro se* PCRA where direct appeal was pending). It should be noted that an untimely direct appeal will not toll the filing of a PCRA petition. Hence, if the petitioner files a direct

---

18 The Pennsylvania Supreme Court's rationale for why the one-year time-bar is jurisdictional hardly qualifies as a scholarly discussion of legislative intent and statutory interpretation. The original case to find the time bar was jurisdictional was ***Commonwealth v. Peterkin***, 722 A.2d 638 (Pa. 1998). The High Court engaged in no meaningful analysis on the jurisdictional issue and did not engage in any sort of traditional statutory interpretation. Indeed, for how critically important the matter is, the discussion on whether the legislature originally intended the one-year time bar to be jurisdictional is embarrassing. The most comprehensive discussion of rationale for the time-bar being jurisdictional is contained in a footnote in a concurring decision by Chief Justice Castille, *see **Commonwealth v. Brown***, 943 A.2d 264, 270 n.2 (Pa. 2008), and is extremely limited.

Jurisdiction and Proceedings

appeal which is quashed as untimely, the one year time period runs from when the period of filing a direct appeal ended. ***Commonwealth v. Brown***, 943 A.2d 264 (Pa. 2008). Thus, there are situations where a defendant may need to file a PCRA petition while a direct appeal is pending to preserve the right to file a timely petition. The Pennsylvania Supreme Court has indicated that as applied constitutional challenges to the time bar may be raised. ***Commonwealth v. Brown***, 943 A.2d 264, 268 n.4 (Pa. 2008).

The filing of a federal *habeas* petition seeking federal review does not toll the timeliness requirements. ***Commonwealth v. Whitney***, 817 A.2d 473 (Pa. 2003); ***Commonwealth v. Fahy***, 737 A.2d 214 (Pa. 1999). Also, federal review usually cannot occur until state remedies have been exhausted; however, filing a federal *habeas* petition does not bar the filing of a PCRA petition. ***Commonwealth v. Whitney***, 817 A.2d 473 (Pa. 2003). Therefore, a PCRA petition should be filed before a federal *habeas* petition. A timely PCRA petition tolls the time period for filing a federal petition.

C. Second or Subsequent Petitions

Once a first time PCRA petition is withdrawn, so long as counsel was appointed, a subsequently filed petition must be treated as a second petition. ***Commonwealth v. Rienzi***, 827 A.2d 369 (Pa. 2003). Second or subsequent petitions must be filed within the one-year time bar. No definition of what constitutes a second or subsequent petition is found in either the statute or the rules of procedure. The second or subsequent language of the statute derives from the Supreme Court's decision in ***Commonwealth v. Lawson***, 549 A.2d 107 (Pa. 1988). ***Commonwealth v. Rykard***, 55 A.3d 1177 (Pa. Super. 2012).

The Superior Court in ***Rykard***, 55 A.3d 1177, carefully surveyed the usage of the second or subsequent phraseology in the statute and the criminal procedural rules and concluded that the

Jurisdiction and Proceedings

legislature intended for the language to apply to petitions that result in multiple proceedings and not the raising of new ineffectiveness claims on appeal. According to the *Rykard* Court, "It is evident that the original meaning of the second or subsequent petition language did not include ineffectiveness claims being asserted for the first time on appeal or a response to a notice of dismissal." *Commonwealth v. Rykard*, 55 A.3d at 1189; *compare Commonwealth v. Moore*, 805 A.2d 1212 (Pa. 2002) (Castille, J., concurring and dissenting) (arguing that ineffectiveness claim raised for first time on appeal is a serial petition); *Commonwealth v. Jones*, 815 A.2d 598 (Pa. 2002) (OAJC) (Justice Castille reiterating view from *Moore* decision); *Commonwealth v. Ligons*, 971 A.2d 1125, 1159-1171 (Castille, C.J., concurring).[19]

Indeed, a response to a notice of intent to dismiss is not considered a second or subsequent petition, but is viewed as an objection to the dismissal. *Commonwealth v. Rykard*, 55 A.3d 1177 (Pa. Super. 2012); *Commonwealth v. Derrickson*, 923 A.2d 466 (Pa. Super. 2007); *Commonwealth v. Williams*, 732 A.2d 1167, 1191-1192 (Pa. 1999); *Commonwealth v. Paddy*, 15 A.3d 431, 471 (Pa. 2011); *see also* Pa.R.Crim.P. 907 and Pa.R.Crim.P. 909 (treating amended petition and response to notice of dismissal differently); *Commonwealth v. D'Amato*, 856 A.2d 806, 825 n.19 (Pa. 2004); *compare Commonwealth v. Blackwell*, 936 A.2d 497 (Pa. Super. 2007) (response to notice that seeks to withdraw the current petition and asks for

---

[19] Chief Justice Castille engaged in no meaningful statutory analysis of the original meaning intended by the General Assembly's usage of the term "second or subsequent petition." Rather, he viewed the issue through a post-*Grant* analytical framework. This approach is problematic as a matter of statutory interpretation since *Grant* did not occur until after the second or subsequent language was engrafted onto the statute and should not be considered in determining the original intent of the legislature in crafting the PCRA statute.

Jurisdiction and Proceedings

reinstatement of appellate rights based on governmental interference treated as petition to withdraw and new petition). An amended petition filed during a first-time PCRA proceeding is not considered a serial petition. ***Commonwealth v. Padden***, 783 A.2d 299 (Pa. Super. 2001).

Prior to the adoption of the jurisdictional time bar, the Court in ***Commonwealth v. Lawson***, 549 A.2d 107, 112 (Pa. 1988), held that second or subsequent PCRA petitions "will not be entertained unless a strong *prima facie* showing is offered to demonstrate that a miscarriage of justice may have occurred." *See also **Commonwealth v. Stokes***, 959 A.2d 306 (Pa. 2008); ***Commonwealth v. Allen***, 732 A.2d 582 (Pa. 1999). This standard is met if the petitioner shows that the proceedings resulting in his conviction were so unfair that a miscarriage of justice occurred which no civilized society can tolerate or that the petitioner is innocent of the crime(s) charged. ***Commonwealth v. Carpenter***, 725 A.2d 154 (Pa. 1999); ***Commonwealth v. Morales***, 701 A.2d 516 (Pa. 1997); ***Commonwealth v. Beasley***, 678 A.2d 773 (Pa. 1996); ***Commonwealth v. Szuchon***, 633 A.2d 1098 (Pa. 1993).

The miscarriage of justice and actual innocence standards are separate and distinct. ***Commonwealth v. Beasley***, 967 A.2d 376 (Pa. 2009) (discussing a claim related to the sentencing phase of a trial can be a miscarriage of justice without proving actual innocence). Nonetheless, the already difficult task of seeking relief via collateral review is rendered even more burdensome if the petitioner has filed a previous PCRA petition.

D. Timeliness Exceptions

If the PCRA petition is filed after one year from the completion of direct review or the period of time in which a direct appeal could have been sought, then a petitioner must allege one of three timeliness exceptions for the PCRA court to have jurisdiction and be able to reach the merits of the issue(s) raised.

Jurisdiction and Proceedings

Commonwealth v. Stokes, 959 A.2d 306 (Pa. 2008); *Commonwealth v. Saunders*, 60 A.3d 162 (Pa. Super. 2013). In addition, the defendant must raise the exception within sixty days of the date the claim could be forwarded. *Stokes*, 959 A.2d 306. The exceptions to the timeliness requirements must be explicitly raised in the PCRA court to preserve the issue on appeal. *Commonwealth v. Beasley*, 741 A.2d 1258 (Pa. 1999); *but see Commonwealth v. Wiley*, 966 A.2d 1153 (Pa. Super. 2009); *Commonwealth v. Blackwell*, 936 A.2d 497 (Pa. Super. 2007).

The timeliness exceptions are as follows:

> (i) the failure to raise the claim previously was the result of interference by government officials with the presentation of the claim in violation of the Constitution or laws of this Commonwealth or the Constitution or laws of the United States;

> (ii) the facts upon which the claim is predicated were unknown to the petitioner and could not have been ascertained by the exercise of due diligence; or

> (iii) the right asserted is a constitutional right that was recognized by the Supreme Court of the United States or the Supreme Court of Pennsylvania after the time period provided in this section and has been held by that court to apply retroactively.

> (2) Any petition invoking an exception provided in paragraph (1) shall be filed within 60 days of the date the claim could have been presented.

42 Pa.C.S. § 9545(b).

There is little case law discussing in detail the governmental interference timeliness exception. A *Brady* claim can be considered governmental interference. *Commonwealth v.*

Jurisdiction and Proceedings

Breakiron, 781 A.2d 94 (Pa. 2001); ***Commonwealth v. Beasley***, 741 A.2d 1258 (Pa. 1999); ***Commonwealth v. Williams***, 105 A.3d 1234 (Pa. 2014); ***but see Commonwealth v. Howard***, 788 A.2d 351 (Pa. 2002) (prosecutor's failure to turn over documents is not governmental interference without a specific claim that the defendant was unable to either discover or develop his claim due to governmental interference). The failure on the part of the clerk of courts to file a *pro se* notice of appeal, when a defendant seeks a direct appeal, does not constitute governmental interference for purposes of the timeliness exception, presumably because the defendant should be aware of this information before filing his PCRA petition. *See* ***Commonwealth v. Camps***, 772 A.2d 70 (Pa. Super. 2001). Of course, such a claim could theoretically fall within section 9543(a)(2)(iv). Appointed or private counsel's failure to file an appeal also does not fit within this exception since defense attorneys do not fit within the statute's definition of a government actor. 42 Pa.C.S. § 9545(b)(4).

Pennsylvania courts have held that the denial of access to court documents when no petition is pending before the PCRA court is not governmental interference, ***Commonwealth v. Crider***, 735 A.2d 730 (Pa. Super. 1999), nor can a proper court order be considered governmental interference. ***Commonwealth v. Howard***, 788 A.2d 351 (Pa. 2002). Additionally, confinement in restricted housing while in prison is not governmental interference with a petitioner's right to assert an issue. ***Commonwealth v. Barrett***, 761 A.2d 145 (Pa. Super. 2000).

The second timeliness exception, based on newly-discovered facts, has routinely been misinterpreted. The timeliness exception is not the same as the after-discovered test required for section 9543(a)(2)(vi), although there is case law finding exactly that. *See* ***Commonwealth v. Johnson***, 841 A.2d 136 (Pa. Super. 2003) (conflating the two sections); ***Commonwealth v. Baker***, 828 A.2d 1146 (Pa. Super. 2003); ***Commonwealth v.***

Jurisdiction and Proceedings

Palmer, 814 A.2d 700 (Pa. Super. 2002). The after-discovered evidence test, relative to section 9543, provides that the evidence must not be corroborative or cumulative, cannot be used for impeachment purposes, and is of such a nature and character that a different verdict will likely result. ***Commonwealth v. Washington***, 927 A.2d 586 (Pa. 2007); ***Commonwealth v. Padillas***, 997 A.2d 356 (Pa. Super. 2010). This test requires the court to examine the merits of the issue.

As noted, however, the timeliness exception directly relates to jurisdiction and without jurisdiction the court cannot reach the merits of the claim. In contrast to the after-discovered evidence provision found at section 9543(a)(2)(vi), the timeliness exception, section 9545(b)(2)(ii), only compels that the facts the claim are based on to have been unknown and that the facts could not have been ascertained through the exercise of due diligence. *See **Commonwealth v. Lambert***, 884 A.2d 848 (Pa. 2005); ***Commonwealth v. Bennett***, 930 A.2d 1264 (Pa. 2007); ***Commonwealth v. Stokes***, 959 A.2d 306 (Pa. 2008).

Thus, cases which equate the timeliness exception with the after-discovered evidence test rely on circular logic. This is because the court cannot reach the merits of a case if it does not have jurisdiction and to determine if it has jurisdiction it had to reach the merits of the issue. The proper analysis is to determine whether the claim is based on relevant information that could not have been obtained by due diligence and was raised within sixty days of discovering the information. *See **Bennett***, 930 A.2d 1264; ***Lambert***, 884 A.2d 848.

Where a petitioner becomes aware of newly-discovered evidence while the dismissal of his PCRA petition is pending on appeal, a subsequent PCRA petition must be filed within sixty days of the date of the order which finally resolves the PCRA petition which was pending on appeal. ***Commonwealth v. Lark***, 746 A.2d 585 (Pa. 2000). The failure to provide the date upon which the defendant learned of the newly-discovered evidence pertaining to the timeliness exception will result in dismissal because the PCRA court will be unable to discern if the petition was filed within sixty days of learning the fact. ***Commonwealth v. Vega***, 754 A.2d 714 (Pa. Super. 2000).

The sixty day period is not extended by a request for discretionary review with the United States Supreme Court. ***Commonwealth v. Breakiron***, 781 A.2d 94 (Pa. 2001). A judicial opinion will not be considered a newly-discovered fact. ***Commonwealth v. Watts***, 23 A.3d 980 (Pa. 2011); ***Commonwealth v. Robinson***, 12 A.3d 477 (Pa. Super. 2011). Furthermore, matters that are of public record prior to trial cannot be considered newly-discovered facts. ***Commonwealth v. Chester***, 895 A.2d 520 (Pa. 2006); *but see **Commonwealth v. Bennett***, 930 A.2d 1264 (Pa. 2007).

However, in ***Commonwealth v. Burton***, 121 A.3d 1063 (Pa. Super. 2015) (*en banc*), *allowance of appeal granted*, 134 A.3d 446 (Pa. 2016), the Superior Court held that information that was contained in public court records after the completion of the defendant's trial could be a newly-discovered fact. There, the petitioner had been found guilty of first-degree murder in 1993. In 2013, he received a letter from the Pennsylvania Innocence Project that contained a 2009 motion to expunge filed by Burton's co-defendant, in which the co-defendant stated he killed the victim in Burton's case in self-defense.

Within sixty days of receipt of the letter, Burton filed a serial PCRA petition. The PCRA court dismissed the petition as untimely. On appeal, the Superior Court held that a public record is not precluded from being a newly-discovered fact where the petitioner is *pro se*. The court maintained that *pro se* petitioners, which constitute the overwhelming number of serial petitioners, do not have presumptive access to public records. The majority then, in a reversal of the burden of proof, set forth,

Jurisdiction and Proceedings

"[a]bsent evidence demonstrating Appellant's access to the contents of [his co-defendant's] criminal docket, the public records rule does not apply." *Burton*, 121 A.3d at 1073.

The dissent in *Burton* noted that the majority improperly shifted the burden of pleading and proof and asserted that Burton had not established due diligence in uncovering the information included in the expungment motion. It highlighted that Burton's *pro se* status and the fact that he was incarcerated did not distinguish his case from virtually every other petitioner seeking to come under a timeliness exception. The paradigm created by the majority in *Burton*, to the extent it requires the Commonwealth to prove a *pro se* defendant had access to the information, is in direct opposition to the language of the PCRA statute, which places the burden on the petitioner to show that the fact is both newly-discovered and that he used due diligence in uncovering the information.

The Superior Court decision in *Burton* also gives rise to additional concerns. The decision results in PCRA petitioners being treated differently under the law based on whether they are represented. Thus, a petitioner who is *pro se* is afforded a presumption that he did not have access to a public record, whereas a represented petitioner is not accorded that presumption. Accordingly, petitioners bringing facially untimely petitions are provided a disincentive for retaining an attorney. For example, in *Burton*, the Pennsylvania Innocence Project provided the petitioner with the information triggering his claim. Had the Innocence Project entered an appearance, presumably there would have been no presumption in favor of Burton. This is an illogical distinction.

The more appropriate analysis is to focus on the facts in the public record and whether the record and facts were available prior to or during trial. If the information in the public record or the public record itself was available before or during trial it cannot be a newly-discovered fact. Similarly, where a record becomes public after trial but the facts contained therein were available during or before the trial then the record cannot be a newly-discovered fact. However, where the facts and public record only became available after trial then the inquiry turns to due diligence. In ***Burton***, even assuming the fact that Burton's co-defendant claimed to have killed the victim in self-defense was not available during trial, the petitioner made no showing of due diligence in uncovering the facts or the public record, which should have precluded relief.

A newly-discovered source of previously known information is not newly-discovered evidence. ***Commonwealth v. Marshall***, 947 A.2d 714 (Pa. 2008); *compare **Commonwealth v. Brown***, 141 A.3d 491 (Pa. Super. 2016). The Pennsylvania Supreme Court has also determined that a study on racial discrimination in death penalty cases asserting that the death penalty was utilized in a racially discriminatory manner was not a newly-discovered fact for purposes of the timeliness exception. ***Commonwealth v. Whitney***, 817 A.2d 473 (Pa. 2003). An allegation of structural error, *i.e.*, a constitutional violation that affects the framework within which the trial proceeds, in contrast to an error in the trial process, does not overcome the PCRA time-bar. ***Commonwealth v. Baroni***, 827 A.2d 419 (Pa. 2003).

A claim of mental incompetence can satisfy the newly-discovered fact timeliness provision, *i.e.*, a petitioner who is mentally incompetent during the time period for filing a PCRA petition may possibly file a timely petition within sixty days of becoming competent. ***Commonwealth v. Cruz***, 852 A.2d 287 (Pa. 2004); *compare **Commonwealth v. Haag***, 809 A.2d 271 (Pa. 2002) (incompetent defendant must proceed with PCRA via next friend); ***Commonwealth v. Monaco***, 996 A.2d 1076 (Pa. Super. 2010) (defendant's learning that he had post-traumatic stress disorder was not a newly-discovered fact). The petitioner must establish his incompetence by a preponderance of the evidence. *See **Commonwealth v. Zook**,* 887 A.2d 1218 (Pa. 2005); *see also **Commonwealth v. Wright**,* 78 A.3d 1070 (Pa. 2013).

Importantly, claims of ineffective assistance of counsel do not constitute an exception to the jurisdictional time bar, **Commonwealth v. Gamboa-Taylor**, 753 A.2d 780 (Pa. 2000); **Commonwealth v. Howard**, 788 A.2d 351 (Pa. 2002); **Commonwealth v. Robinson**, 139 A.3d 178 (Pa. 2016); **Commonwealth v. Davis**, 816 A.2d 1129 (Pa. Super. 2003), nor is the failure of counsel to file a direct appeal newly-discovered evidence. **Commonwealth v. Carr**, 768 A.2d 1164 (Pa. Super. 2001); *but see **Commonwealth v. Bennett**,* 930 A.2d 1264 (Pa. 2007) (abandonment by counsel may be a newly-discovered fact for purposes of timeliness exception); **Commonwealth v. Blackwell**, 936 A.2d 497 (Pa. Super. 2007).

E. New Rule of Law Retroactive Effect

The third timeliness exception involves a new constitutional rule of law given retroactive effect. The constitutional rule must have already been recognized as retroactive by the court announcing the new rule. **Commonwealth v. Abdul-Salaam**, 812 A.2d 497 (Pa. 2002); *but see **Commonwealth v. Secreti**,* 134 A.3d 177 (Pa. Super. 2016). In *Secreti*, the Superior Court ruled that a petitioner who filed a PCRA petition within sixty days of *Miller v. Alabama*, 132 S.Ct. 2455 (2012), (holding unconstitutional mandatory life imprisonment without parole sentences for juvenile homicide defendants), was not required to re-file and litigate his entitlement to resentencing based on the United States Supreme Court decision in *Montgomery v. Louisiana*, 136 S.Ct. 718 (2016), which clarified that *Miller* applied retroactively. That is, the *Secreti* Court did not determine that the petition was premature where it was filed prior to the *Montgomery* decision declaring *Miller* retroactive.

Jurisdiction and Proceedings

Only the United States Supreme Court or the Pennsylvania Supreme Court can determine whether a new constitutional right is at issue and is to be afforded retroactive effect for purposes of the timeliness exception. ***Commonwealth v. Copenhefer***, 941 A.2d 646 (Pa. 2007). The United States Supreme Court has indicated that state courts may give retroactive effect to a Supreme Court decision even if it does not. ***Danforth v. Minnesota***, 552 U.S. 264 (2008). This, however, would not afford a state petitioner a timeliness exception. Accordingly, if the Pennsylvania Superior Court were to declare a new constitutional rule, it would have no ramifications for purposes of the PCRA.

The test generally applied to decide whether a new constitutional rule has been announced and held to apply retroactively is extremely amorphous and is based on the plurality decision reached by the United States Supreme Court in ***Teague v. Lane***, 489 U.S. 288 (1989), a federal *habeas* appeal. The ***Teague*** tests discuss both whether a rule is new and if the new rule should apply retroactively. ***Teague*** is not binding on state courts and did not consider whether state courts "can provide remedies for violations of [newly-recognized constitutional] rights in their own postconviction proceedings." ***Danforth v. Minnesota***, 552 U.S. 264, 275 (2008).

However, the Pennsylvania Supreme Court has adopted the tests announced in ***Teague***. ***Commonwealth v. Cunningham***, 81 A.3d 1 (Pa. 2013) (applying ***Teague*** test in a timely petition but suggesting that ***Teague*** retroactivity test may not always be appropriate for state collateral review), *abrogated on other ground by* ***Montgomery v. Louisiana***, 136 S.Ct. 718 (2016); ***Commonwealth v. Bracey***, 986 A.2d 128 (Pa. 2009); ***Commonwealth v. Spotz***, 896 A.2d 1191, 1243-1246 (Pa. 2006); ***Commonwealth v. Hughes***, 865 A.2d 761, 780-782 (Pa. 2004); ***Commonwealth v. Blystone***, 725 A.2d 1197, 1202-1203 (Pa. 1999); *see also* ***Commonwealth v. Riggle***, 119 A.3d 1058 (Pa.

Super. 2015); ***Commonwealth v. Ross***, 140 A.3d 55 (Pa. Super. 2016); ***Commonwealth v. Washington***, 142 A.3d 810 (Pa. 2016).[20]

The Pennsylvania Supreme Court in ***Commonwealth v. Cunningham***, 81 A.3d 1 (Pa. 2013), *abrogated on other ground*, ***Montgomery v. Louisiana***, 136 S.Ct. 718 (2016), a timely PCRA matter, opined that utilization of the *Teague* principles "is subject to potential refinement" and "is not necessarily a natural model for retroactivity jurisprudence as applied at the state level." ***Cunningham***, 81 A.3d at 8. Nonetheless, no decision discussing the PCRA and retroactivity has detailed a differing retroactivity analysis. Under ***Teague***, "a rule is considered 'new' when the result 'was not dictated by precedent existing at the time the defendant's conviction became final.'" ***Bracey***, 986 A.2d 128, 144 (quoting ***Teague***, 489 U.S. at 301); ***Commonwealth v. Riggle***, 119 A.3d 1058 (Pa. Super. 2015).

A further articulation of the ***Teague*** new rule test asks whether the outcome of the alleged new rule case was "susceptible to debate among reasonable minds[,]" ***Butler v. McKellar***, 494 U.S. 407, 415 (1990), and if a court would have felt compelled by existing precedent to find that the law announced in the alleged new rule case was mandated by the Constitution. A rule is not new where it merely applies existing precedent to a new set of facts. ***Commonwealth v. Feliciano***, 69 A.3d 1270 (Pa. Super. 2013) (holding ***Lafler v. Cooper***, 132 S.Ct. 1376 (2012), and ***Missouri v. Frye***, 132 S.Ct. 1399 (2012), pertaining to counsel's duty to inform a client of plea offers, did not announce new constitutional rules); ***Commonwealth v. Wojtaszek***, 951 A.2d 1169 (Pa. Super. 2008) (holding ***Cunningham v. California***, 549 U.S. 270 (2007), was a mere application of

---

[20] The decision in *Teague* was subsequently adopted by a majority of the United States Supreme Court for purposes of federal *habeas* review. *See* **Commonwealth v. Lesko**, 15 A.3d 345, 363 (Pa. 2011).

Jurisdiction and Proceedings

Apprendi v. New Jersey, 530 U.S. 466 (2000), and not a new constitutional right).

In *Commonwealth v. Garcia*, 23 A.3d 1059 (Pa. Super. 2011), the Pennsylvania Superior Court held that *Padilla v. Kentucky*, 130 S.Ct. 1473 (2010), did not announce a new rule because it was dictated by application of *Strickland v. Washington*, 466 U.S. 668 (1984). However, in *Chaidez v. United States*, 133 S.Ct. 1103 (2013), the Supreme Court expressly disagreed with this rationale. The High Court in *Chaidez* held that *Padilla* was a new rule of law that does not apply retroactively. Thus, *Garcia's* rationale is invalid. See also *Commonwealth v. Abraham*, 62 A.3d 343 (Pa. 2012) (Castille, C.J., concurring); *Commonwealth v. Ghisoiu*, 63 A.3d 1272 (Pa. Super. 2013).

Only a very narrow class of cases have been afforded retroactive effect. The Supreme Court has divided new rules into two categories: substantive rules and procedural rules. *Schriro v. Summerlin*, 542 U.S. 348, 351 (2004); *Commonwealth v. Riggle*, 119 A.3d 1058 (Pa. Super. 2015); *Commonwealth v. Moss*, 871 A.2d 853 (Pa. Super. 2005) (finding *Blakely v. Washington*, 542 U.S. 296 (2004), does not apply retroactively). A substantive new rule is one that either narrows the scope of a criminal statute by interpreting its terms, forbids punishment of certain primary conduct, or prohibits a certain category of punishment for a class of defendants because of their status or offense. *Beard v. Banks*, 542 U.S. 406, 417 (2004); *Commonwealth v. Hughes*, 865 A.2d 761 (Pa. 2004); *Commonwealth v. Moss*, 871 A.2d 853 (Pa. Super. 2005). These substantive rules are given retroactive effect.

The United States Supreme Court in *Schriro v. Summerlin*, 542 U.S. 348, also opined that a holding by that Court making a fact essential to punishment is a substantive ruling. *Schriro*, 542 U.S. at 354-55 ("This Court's holding that, **because Arizona** has made a certain fact essential to the death penalty, that fact must be found by a jury, is not the same as **this Court's** making a certain fact essential to the death penalty. The former was a procedural holding; the latter would be substantive.") (emphases in original).[21]

In contrast to substantive rules, procedural rules do not apply retroactively unless they are considered a watershed procedural rule. A procedural rule is considered watershed if it is necessary to prevent an impermissibly large risk of an inaccurate conviction or sentence and also changes the understanding of bedrock procedural elements essential to the fairness and accuracy of the proceeding. *Whorton v. Bockting*, 549 U.S. 406 (2007); *Commonwealth v. Riggle*, 119 A.3d 1058 (Pa. Super. 2015); *Commonwealth v. Washington*, 142 A.3d 810 (Pa. 2016).

The prime, indeed, only example used by the Supreme Court for such a groundbreaking rule is *Gideon v. Wainwright*, 372 U.S. 335 (1963), which requires the appointment of counsel at trial for defendants charged with a felony. No other procedural constitutional rule has ever been held to apply retroactively by the Supreme Court and the Supreme Court has not conclusively held that a watershed procedural rule would apply to defendants pursuing state collateral review. *See Danforth v. Minnesota*, 552 U.S. 264 (2008).

A new constitutional rule must not only be considered retroactive, but the holding must apply to the facts of the petitioner's case. *See Commonwealth v. Cintora*, 69 A.3d 759

---

21 In the 2016 edition of this work, this author discussed *Schriro* in critiquing the Pennsylvania Supreme Court's decision in *Commonwealth v. Cunningham*, 81 A.3d 1 (Pa. 2013) *abrogated by Montgomery v. Louisiana*, 136 S.Ct. 718 (2016), and set forth that *Cunningham* was likely erroneously decided. The United States Supreme Court, in *Montgomery*, adopted a similar view to that expressed by this author.

Jurisdiction and Proceedings

(Pa. Super. 2013) (holding *Miller v. Alabama*, 132 S.Ct. 2455 (2012), does not apply to adult defendants convicted of murder since that decision applied to juveniles). Similarly, it is the holding of a case that is relevant for the timeliness exception and not the rationale of the case. *Commonwealth v. Chambers*, 35 A.3d 34 (Pa. Super. 2011).

In *Commonwealth v. Miller*, 102 A.3d 988 (Pa. Super. 2014), the Superior Court found that *Alleyne v. United States*, 133 S.Ct. 2151 (2013), was not held retroactive by the United Supreme Court, although the decision in *Alleyne* did not apply to the petitioner. *Alleyne* held that mandatory minimum statutes, permitting a court to increase a defendant's sentence based on facts determined by a judge at sentencing by a preponderance of the evidence standard, violated the jury trial right. The decision, however, did not apply to mandatory minimum sentences triggered by prior convictions. The petitioner in *Miller* was sentenced to a mandatory sentence based on his prior convictions. Thus, *Alleyne* could not have served as a timeliness exception for the petitioner. In *Commonwealth v. Riggle*, 119 A.3d 1058 (Pa. Super. 2015), the Superior Court held, in a timely PCRA matter, that *Alleyne* was not retroactive. The Supreme Court adopted the same approach in *Commonwealth v. Washington*, 142 A.3d 810 (Pa. 2016).

Whenever the Pennsylvania Supreme Court or United States Supreme Court announce a new retroactive constitutional rule, the petitioner must raise his claim within sixty days of the decision announcing recognition of that right. *See Commonwealth v. Baldwin*, 789 A.2d 728 (Pa. Super. 2001). An example of a retroactive substantive new rule of law is *Atkins v. Virginia*, 536 U.S. 304 (2002) (ruling that a mentally retarded individual cannot be executed), *see Commonwealth v. Bracey*, 986 A.2d 128 (Pa. 2009); *Commonwealth v. Miller*, 888 A.2d

624, 629 n.5 (Pa. 2005).[22]

F. Evidentiary Hearing: 42 Pa.C.S. § 9545(d)(1)

An evidentiary hearing is required whenever the petition raises an issue of material fact. Counsel must include a signed certification relative to each witness he or she intends to present at the hearing. The certification is not an affidavit and can be signed by the petitioner or the attorney and should delineate the name, address, date of birth, and substance of the testimony that the witness will present. ***Commonwealth v. Pander***, 100 A.3d 626 (Pa. Super. 2014) (*en banc*); ***Commonwealth v. Brown***, 767 A.2d 576 (Pa. Super. 2001). The crucial information is the individual's name and proposed testimony. Where a certification is not provided, the PCRA court may rule the testimony of a witness inadmissible. *See also* discussion contained in the comments after Pa.R.Crim.P. 908.

However, the failure to provide a witness certification is not grounds for summary dismissal absent alerting the petitioner of this defect. ***Commonwealth v. Robinson***, 947 A.2d 710 (Pa. 2008); *see also* ***Commonwealth v. Pander***, 100 A.3d 626 (Pa. Super. 2014) (*en banc*); *compare* ***Commonwealth v. Collins***, 687 A.2d 1112 (Pa. 1996) (OAJC) (failure of petitioner to attach an affidavit or other documents to his petition regarding an allegation that counsel failed to file a direct appeal rendered his claim without merit); ***Commonwealth v. Marshall***, 812 A.2d 539 (Pa. 2002) (court in addressing reasonable basis of trial counsel's action regarding presentation of mental health mitigation evidence found it significant that the defendant did not attach an affidavit from prior counsel). It is important to note that neither the PCRA statute nor the rules of procedure require affidavits. As the Superior Court cogently delineated in ***Brown***,

---

22 Defendants who raise an *Atkins* claim during PCRA review are not entitled to a jury determination of mental retardation during that review. ***Commonwealth v. Bracey***, 986 A.2d 128 (Pa. 2009).

767 A.2d 576, the law only requires witness certifications, which may be authored by an attorney or petitioner and need not be signed by the witness. *See also Commonwealth v. Pander*, 100 A.3d 626 (Pa. Super. 2014) (*en banc*).

However, in *Commonwealth v. McLaurin*, 45 A.3d 1131 (Pa. Super. 2012), the court appeared to find that the failure to provide affidavits was sufficient to reject a failure to call a witness claim. The Superior Court expressly overruled *McLaurin* on this issue in *Pander*. It noted that *McLaurin* was in conflict with *Brown*, 767 A.2d 567, the PCRA statute, and Pa.R.Crim.P. 902(A)(15). Since *McLaurin* relied principally on *Commonwealth v. Khalil*, 806 A.2d 415 (Pa. Super. 2002), a case that did not involve a PCRA petition, the *Pander* Court rejected its analysis in favor of *Brown*.

G. Attorney-Client Privilege: 42 Pa.C.S. § 9545(d)(3)

Upon raising an ineffective assistance of counsel claim, a petitioner waives his attorney-client privilege as to that issue. However, the attorney-client privilege is not entirely eviscerated by a petitioner asserting ineffectiveness claims. In *Commonwealth v. Flor*, 136 A.3d 150 (Pa. 2016), the Commonwealth requested the production of trial counsel's records. PCRA counsel contested that motion both on attorney-client privilege and work product grounds and sought additional time to separate materials in the file that would not be privileged.

When the PCRA court entered a blanket order to turn over the material, counsel took an interlocutory appeal. The Supreme Court ruled that ineffectiveness claims "do not waive attorney-client privilege and work product as to all material counsel may possess[.]" *Flor*, 136 A.3d at 159. Accordingly, it ruled that an issue-specific analysis is required to determine if those doctrines apply and vacated the broad discovery order.

Chapter 12: 42 Pa.C.S. § 9546
Relief and Order

(a) GENERAL RULE.-- If the court rules in favor of the petitioner, it shall order appropriate relief and issue supplementary orders as to rearraignment, retrial, custody, bail, discharge, correction of sentence or other matters that are necessary and proper.

(b) Deleted.

(c) Deleted.

(d) REVIEW OF ORDER IN DEATH PENALTY CASES.-- An order under this subchapter granting the petitioner final relief in a case in which the death penalty has been imposed shall be directly appealable by the Commonwealth to the Supreme Court pursuant to its rules. An order under this subchapter denying a petitioner final relief in a case in which the death penalty has been imposed shall not be reviewable in the Superior Court but shall be reviewable only by petition for allowance of appeal to the Supreme Court.

Annotated Comments

This section is largely self-explanatory. Nonetheless, it should be noted that in the event that relief is granted, the Commonwealth may choose to appeal. Once the Commonwealth appeals, the trial court's ability to rule on bail, discharge, or the correction of a sentence are removed, (except in the case of correcting a sentencing error that is patent on its face), because the trial court no longer has jurisdiction over the matter. *See generally Commonwealth v. Bishop*, 829 A.2d 1170 (Pa. Super. 2003). Prior to the taking of an appeal, the PCRA court may grant bail where there is a compelling reason, *i.e.*,

Relief and Order

where it appears obvious that the petitioner will prevail on the merits. ***Commonwealth v. McMaster***, 730 A.2d 524, 529 n.1 (Pa. Super. 1999); ***Commonwealth v. Bonaparte***, 530 A.2d 1351 (Pa. Super. 1988).

All appeals from death penalty cases are heard by the Pennsylvania Supreme Court. ***See also*** Pa.R.Crim.P. 909; ***Commonwealth v. Bryant***, 780 A.2d 646 (Pa. 2001). However, where a case that originally resulted in the death penalty is remanded for a new penalty phase hearing and a subsequent sentencing hearing does not impose the death penalty, jurisdiction properly lies with the Superior Court. ***Commonwealth v. Rompilla***, 983 A.2d 1207 (Pa. 2009). Further, a denial of relief on a petitioner's guilt phase claims while also awarding relief on a capital sentencing issue is a final order appealable to the Pennsylvania Supreme Court. ***Commonwealth v. Bryant***, 780 A.2d 646 (Pa. 2001).

Chapter 13: Rule 900
Scope; Notice In Death Penalty Cases

(A) The rules in Chapter 9 apply to capital and noncapital cases under the Post Conviction Relief Act, 42 Pa.C.S. §§ 9541-9546, as amended by Act 1995-32 (SS1).

(B) Notice in Death Penalty Cases. In all death penalty cases upon the Supreme Court's affirmance of the judgment of a death sentence, the Prothonotary shall include in the mailing required by Pa.R.A.P. 2521 (Entry of Judgment or Other Order) the following information concerning the Post Conviction Relief Act and the procedures under Chapter 9 of the Rules of Criminal Procedure. "Parties" as used in Pa.R.A.P. 2521 shall include the defendant, the defendant's counsel, and the attorney for the Commonwealth for the purposes of this rule.

(1) A petition for post-conviction collateral relief must be filed within one year of the date the judgment becomes final, except as otherwise provided by statute.

(2) As provided in 42 Pa.C.S. § 9545(b)(3), a judgment becomes final at the conclusion of direct review, which includes discretionary review in the Supreme Court of the United States and the Supreme Court of Pennsylvania, or at the expiration of time for seeking the review.

(3)(a) If the defendant fails to file a petition within the one-year time limit, the action may be barred. See 42 Pa.C.S. § 9545(b).

(b) Any issues that could have been raised in the post-conviction proceeding, but were not, may be waived. See 42 Pa.C.S. § 9544(b).

(4) Pursuant to Rule 904 (Appointment of Counsel; in

Forma Pauperis), the trial judge will appoint new counsel for the purpose of post-conviction collateral review, unless:

(a) the defendant has elected to proceed pro se or waive post-conviction collateral proceedings, and the judge finds, after a colloquy on the record, that the defendant is competent and the defendant's election is knowing, intelligent, and voluntary;

(b) the defendant requests continued representation by original trial counsel or direct appeal counsel, and the judge finds, after a colloquy on the record, that the petitioner's election constitutes a knowing, intelligent, and voluntary waiver of a claim that counsel was ineffective; or

(c) the judge finds, after a colloquy on the record, that the defendant has engaged counsel who has entered, or will promptly enter, an appearance for the collateral review proceedings.

> *Comment*: The 1995 amendments to the Post Conviction Relief Act specifically provide that, "except as specifically provided otherwise, all provisions of this subchapter shall apply to capital and noncapital cases." *See* 42 Pa.C.S. § 9542.
>
> *See* Rule 909 (Procedures for Petitions in Death Penalty Cases: Stays of Execution of Sentence; Hearing; Disposition) concerning requests for, and length of, stays of execution in death penalty cases.
>
> Under the 1995 amendments to the PCRA, a petition for post-conviction relief, including second and subsequent petitions, must be filed "within one year of the date the judgment becomes final," 42 Pa.C.S. § 9545(b)(1), unless one of the statutory exceptions applies, *see* 42 Pa.C.S. § 9545(b)(1)(i)-(iii). Any

petition invoking one of these exceptions must be filed within 60 days of the date the claim could have been presented. *See* 42 Pa.C.S. § 9545(b)(2).

See Rule 904 for the procedures for the appointment of counsel.

Pursuant to paragraph (B), the Supreme Court's Prothonotary must include with the mailing required by Rule of Appellate Procedure 2521 (Entry of Judgment or Other Order) the information set forth in paragraph (B)(1)-(4). Rule 2521 requires, inter alia, on the date a judgment or order is entered, that the prothonotary is to send to all parties by first class mail a copy of any opinion, or judgment, or order.

Note: Rule 1500 adopted August 11, 1997, effective immediately; *Comment* revised July 23, 1999, effective September 1, 1999; renumbered Rule 900 and amended March 1, 2000, effective April 1, 2001; amended March 26, 2002, effective July 1, 2002.

Annotated Comments

Rule 900 largely summarizes the PCRA statute and directs the prothonotary of the Pennsylvania Supreme Court to inform defendants subject to the death penalty of their PCRA rights following completion of direct review. Specifically, the prothonotary must give notice to the defendant, the defendant's lawyer, and the Commonwealth regarding Rule 900(B)(1)-(4). This information sets forth that a PCRA petition must be filed within one-year of the finalization of judgment of sentence and defines when a judgment becomes final.

Interestingly, and giving credence to those who argue that the one year time-bar was not intended to be jurisdictional, the rule states that a petition that is filed after one year from finalization of judgment of sentence "may be barred." Pa.R.Crim.P. 900(B)(3)(a). Seemingly, if the statute reflected a clear jurisdictional time bar then the phrase should state, "would be barred."

The rule further provides that issues that could have been raised in a PCRA petition but were not may be barred. Pa.R.Crim.P. 900(B)(3)(b). This aspect of Rule 900 is slightly different from the statute, which actually states that waived claims cannot afford relief. In addition, Rule 900 defines how a petitioner can elect to proceed *pro se* or continue with counsel who represented him during his direct appeal. Pa.R.Crim.P. 900(4)(a)-(b). In either of these events, Rule 900 mandates that the PCRA court conduct an on-the-record colloquy to ascertain whether the petitioner voluntarily, intelligently, and knowingly is waiving his rule-based right to new counsel. *See* **Commonwealth v. Robinson**, 970 A.2d 455 (Pa. Super. 2009) (*en banc*); **Commonwealth v. Stossel**, 17 A.3d 1286 (Pa. Super. 2011).

Where a defendant does not elect to proceed *pro se* on his first time petition or continue with direct appeal counsel, the court must appoint a new attorney, unless the defendant has hired counsel. Pa.R.Crim.P. 900(B)(4)(c). Where a capital petitioner wishes to withdraw his PCRA petition, the court must conduct a waiver colloquy before granting the request. **Commonwealth v. Bronshtein**, 729 A.2d 1102 (Pa. 1999); *see also* Pa.R.Crim.P. 900(B)(4)(a); *but see* **Commonwealth v. Wright**, 78 A.3d 1070 (Pa. 2013).

Chapter 14: Rule 901
Initiation of Post-Conviction Collateral Proceedings

(A) A petition for post-conviction collateral relief shall be filed within one year of the date the judgment becomes final, except as otherwise provided by statute.

(B) A proceeding for post-conviction collateral relief shall be initiated by filing a petition and 3 copies with the clerk of the court in which the defendant was convicted and sentenced. The petition shall be verified by the defendant.

> *Comment*: The rules in Chapter 9 govern proceedings to obtain relief authorized by the Post Conviction Relief Act, 42 Pa.C.S. §§ 9541 et seq. (hereinafter PCRA).
>
> By statute, a court may not entertain a request for any form of relief in anticipation of the filing of a petition for post-conviction collateral relief. *See* 42 Pa.C.S. § 9545(a). For stays of execution, see 42 Pa.C.S. § 9545(c) and Rule 909(A).
>
> The petition for post-conviction relief under these rules is not intended to be a substitute for or a limitation on the availability of appeal or a post-sentence motion. *See* Pa.Rs.Crim.P. 720 and 811. Rather, the Chapter 9 Rules are intended to require that, in a single proceeding, the defendant must raise and the judge must dispose of all grounds for relief available after conviction and exhaustion of the appellate process, either by affirmance or by the failure to take a timely appeal. Except as provided in Rule 902(E)(2) for death penalty cases, no discovery is permitted at any stage of

the proceedings, except upon leave of the court with a showing of exceptional circumstances. *See* Rule 902(E)(1), which implements 42 Pa.C.S. § 9545(d)(2).

As used in the Chapter 9 Rules, "petition for post-conviction collateral relief" and "petition" are intended to include an amended petition filed pursuant to Rule 905, except where the context indicates otherwise.

Under the 1995 amendments to the PCRA, a petition for post-conviction relief, including second and subsequent petitions, must be filed "within one year of the date the judgment becomes final," 42 Pa.C.S. § 9545(b)(1), unless one of the statutory exceptions applies, see 42 Pa.C.S. § 9545(b)(1)(i)-(iii). Any petition invoking one of these exceptions must be filed within 60 days of the date the claim could have been presented. *See* 42 Pa.C.S. § 9545(b)(2).

The 1995 amendments to the PCRA apply to petitions filed on or after January 16, 1996. A petitioner whose judgment has become final on or before the effective date of the Act is deemed to have filed a timely petition under the Act if the first petition is filed within one year of the effective date of the Act. *See* § 3 of Act 1995-32 (SS1).

For the purposes of the PCRA, a judgment becomes final at the conclusion of direct review, which includes discretionary review in the Supreme Court of the United States and the Supreme Court of Pennsylvania, or at the expiration of time for seeking the review. *See* 42 Pa.C.S. § 9545(b)(3).

Note: Previous Rule 1501 adopted January 24, 1968, effective August 1, 1968; amended November 25, 1968, effective February 3, 1969; amended February 15, 1974, effective immediately; rescinded December 11, 1981, effective June 27, 1982; rescission vacated June 4, 1982; rescinded November 9, 1984, effective January 2, 1985. Former Rule 1501 adopted November 9, 1984, effective January 2, 1985; rescinded February 1, 1989, effective July 1, 1989, and replaced by present Rule 902. Present Rule 1501 adopted February 1, 1989, effective July 1, 1989; amended March 22, 1993, effective January 1, 1994; amended August 11, 1997, effective immediately; *Comment* revised July 23, 1999, effective September 1, 1999; renumbered Rule 901 and amended March 1, 2000, effective April 1, 2001; *Comment* revised June 4, 2004, effective November 1, 2004.

Annotated Comments

Rule 901 delineates the number of copies of the petition a petitioner must file, four, and where the petition should be filed, the clerk of courts in the county the defendant was convicted, as well as the time frame for filing the petition. Pa.R.Crim.P. 901(A)-(B). Further, the rule requires the petitioner to file a verification with his petition. Pa.R.Crim.P. 901(B). The comment to the rule also provides additional information, most of which is contained within the statute or other aspects of the procedural rules. For example, the comment discusses requests for discovery, the one-year time-bar, and the 1995 amendments. The comments indicate that the PCRA is designed to afford a defendant a single proceeding to address all grounds for relief of a conviction and that the term petition includes amended petitions, unless otherwise indicated.

Chapter 15: Rule 902

Content of Petition for Post-Conviction Collateral Relief; Discovery Requests

(A) A petition for post-conviction collateral relief shall bear the caption, number, and court term of the case or cases in which relief is requested and shall contain substantially the following information:

(1) the name of the defendant;

(2) the place where the defendant is confined, or if not confined, the defendant's current address;

(3) the offenses for which the defendant was convicted and sentenced;

(4) the date on which the defendant was sentenced;

(5) whether the defendant was convicted by a jury, by a judge without jury, on a plea of guilty, or on a plea of nolo contendere;

(6) the sentence imposed and whether the defendant is now serving or waiting to serve that sentence;

(7) the name of the judge who presided at trial or plea and imposed sentence;

(8) the court, caption, term, and number of any proceeding (including appeals, prior post-conviction collateral proceedings, and federal court proceedings) instituted by the defendant to obtain relief from conviction or sentence, specifying whether a proceeding is pending or has been completed;

(9) the name of each lawyer who represented the defendant at any time after arrest, and the stage of the case at which

Content of Petition for Post-Conviction Collateral Relief; Discovery Requests

each represented the defendant;

(10) the relief requested;

(11) the grounds for the relief requested;

(12) the facts supporting each such ground that:

(a) appear in the record, and the place in the record where they appear; and

(b) do not appear in the record, and an identification of any affidavits, documents, and other evidence showing such facts;

(13) whether any of the grounds for the relief requested were raised before, and if so, at what stage of the case;

(14) a verification by the defendant that:

(a) the facts set forth in the petition are true and correct to the best of the defendant's personal knowledge or information and belief and that any false statements therein are made subject to the penalties of the Crimes Code, 18 Pa.C.S. § 4904, relating to unsworn falsification to authorities; and

(b) the attorney filing the petition is authorized by the defendant to file the petition on the defendant's behalf;

(15) if applicable, any request for an evidentiary hearing. The request for an evidentiary hearing shall include a signed certification as to each intended witness, stating the witness's name, address, and date of birth, and the substance of the witness's testimony. Any documents material to the witness's testimony shall also be included in the petition; and

(16) if applicable, any request for discovery.

Content of Petition for Post-Conviction Collateral Relief; Discovery Requests

The petition may, but need not, include concise argument or citation and discussion of authorities.

(B) Each ground relied upon in support of the relief requested shall be stated in the petition. Failure to state such a ground in the petition shall preclude the defendant from raising that ground in any proceeding for post-conviction collateral relief.

(C) The defendant shall state in the petition the name and address of the attorney who will represent the defendant in the post-conviction collateral proceeding. If the defendant is unable to afford or otherwise procure counsel, and wants counsel appointed, the defendant shall so state in the petition and shall request the appointment of counsel.

(D) The defendant shall attach to the petition any affidavits, records, documents, or other evidence which show the facts stated in support of the grounds for relief, or the petition shall state why they are not attached.

(E) Requests for Discovery

(1) Except as provided in paragraph (E)(2), no discovery shall be permitted at any stage of the proceedings, except upon leave of court after a showing of exceptional circumstances.

(2) On the first counseled petition in a death penalty case, no discovery shall be permitted at any stage of the proceedings, except upon leave of court after a showing of good cause.

> *Comment*: All privately retained counsel must enter an appearance as provided in Rule 904.
>
> Paragraph (A)(14) was amended in 2002 to require the defendant to include a verification that the attorney is authorized to file the petition.

Content of Petition for Post-Conviction Collateral Relief; Discovery Requests

Pursuant to paragraph (A)(6), the petition should include specific information about the sentence imposed, including whether the defendant is currently serving a sentence of imprisonment or probation for the crime; awaiting execution of a sentence of death for the crime; or serving a sentence which must expire before the defendant may commence serving the disputed sentence; the minimum and maximum terms of the sentence; the amount of fine or restitution, if any; and whether the defendant is released on parole. *See* 42 Pa.C.S. § 9543(a).

Sections 9543(a)(2), (3), and (4) of the Post Conviction Relief Act, 42 Pa.C.S. § 9543(a)(2), (3), and (4), require that to be eligible for relief, the defendant must plead and prove by a preponderance of the evidence all of the following:

"(2) That the conviction or sentence resulted from one or more of the following:

"(i) A violation of the Constitution of this Commonwealth or the Constitution or laws of the United States which, in the circumstances of the particular case, so undermined the truth-determining process that no reliable adjudication of guilt or innocence could have taken place.

"(ii) Ineffective assistance of counsel which, in the circumstances of the particular case, so undermined the truth-determining process that no reliable adjudication of guilt or innocence could have taken place.

"(iii) A plea of guilty unlawfully induced where the circumstances make it likely that the inducement caused the petitioner to plead guilty and the petitioner

Content of Petition for Post-Conviction Collateral Relief; Discovery Requests

is innocent.

"(iv) The improper obstruction by government officials of the petitioner's right of appeal where a meritorious appealable issue existed and was properly preserved in the trial court."

(v) Deleted by statute.

"(vi) The unavailability at the time of trial of exculpatory evidence that has subsequently become available and would have changed the outcome of the trial if it had been introduced.

"(vii) The imposition of a sentence greater than the lawful maximum.

"(viii) A proceeding in a tribunal without jurisdiction.

"(3) That the allegation of error has not been previously litigated or waived.

"(4) That the failure to litigate the issue prior to or during trial ..., or on direct appeal could not have been the result of any rational, strategic or tactical decision by counsel." *See* 42 Pa.C.S. § 9543(a)(2), (3), and (4). (Note: the statutory reference to unitary review in this paragraph is not shown in view of the Court's 1997 suspension of the Capital Unitary Review Act.)"

By statute, a court may not entertain a request for any form of relief in anticipation of the filing of a petition for post-conviction relief. *See* 42 Pa.C.S. § 9545(a). For stays of execution, see 42 Pa.C.S. § 9545(c) and Rule 909(A).

Paragraphs (A)(16) and (E) were added in 1997 to address requests for discovery. Paragraph (A)(16)

Content of Petition for Post-Conviction Collateral Relief; Discovery Requests

requires that a request for discovery be included in the petition, if applicable. Paragraph (E) sets forth the standards for permitting discovery. Under paragraph (E)(1), which applies in all cases except on the first counseled petition in a death penalty case, no discovery is permitted at any stage of the proceedings, except upon leave of the court with a showing of exceptional circumstances. *See* 42 Pa.C.S. § 9545(d)(2). Under paragraph (E)(2), which applies to first counseled petitions in death penalty cases, discovery is permitted only upon leave of court for good cause shown. For purposes of paragraph (E)(2), "first counseled petition" includes petitions on which defendants have elected to proceed pro se pursuant to Rule 904(F)(1)(a).

Second or subsequent petitions will not be entertained unless a strong prima facie showing is offered to demonstrate that a miscarriage of justice may have occurred. *See Commonwealth v. Szuchon*, 633 A.2d 1098, 1099 (Pa. 1993) (citing *Commonwealth v. Lawson*, 549 A.2d 107 (Pa. 1988)). This standard is met if the petitioner can demonstrate either: (1) that the proceedings resulting in the petitioner's conviction were so unfair that a miscarriage of justice occurred which no civilized society can tolerate; or (2) that the petitioner is innocent of the crimes charged. *See Commonwealth v. Szuchon*, 633 A.2d 1098, 1100 (Pa. 1993).

It is expected that a form petition will be prepared incorporating the required contents set forth herein which will be available for distribution to uncounseled defendants. This rule is not intended to require an attorney to use a printed form or any other particular format in preparing a petition or an amended petition

Content of Petition for Post-Conviction Collateral Relief; Discovery Requests

> for post-conviction collateral relief, provided, of course, that the attorney must include in a petition or amended petition substantially all of the information set forth in this rule.
>
> The petition should be typewritten or legibly handwritten.

Note: Previous Rule 1502 adopted January 24, 1968, effective August 1, 1968; rescinded December 11, 1981, effective June 27, 1982; rescission vacated June 4, 1982; rescinded February 1, 1989, effective July 1, 1989, and replaced by present Rules 1503 and 1505. Present Rule 1502 adopted February 1, 1989, effective July 1, 1989; amended August 11, 1997, effective immediately; amended July 23, 1999, effective September 1, 1999; *Comment* revised January 21, 2000, effective July 1, 2000; renumbered Rule 902 and *Comment* revised March 1, 2000, effective April 1, 2001; amended February 26, 2002, effective July 1, 2002; *Comment* revised April 28, 2005, effective August 1, 2005.

Annotated Comments

A. Filing an Amended Petition

Rule 902 is one of the most critical rules of criminal procedure for PCRA petitioners. The rule sets forth the information that must be contained within a petition. Although the practice is not prohibited, counsel is strongly discouraged from merely adopting by incorporation a petitioner's *pro se* PCRA petition. The reason is practical as petitioners are not lawyers and oftentimes are not aware of issues which may or may not have merit. Additionally, most *pro se* petitions do not fully develop claims raised under the ineffectiveness rubric and will be subject to dismissal without a court having to reach the merits. Indeed, it could be ineffective assistance of counsel to incorporate an

Content of Petition for Post-Conviction Collateral Relief; Discovery Requests

issue by reference since it subjects the issue to dismissal without the court reaching the merits. *See Commonwealth v. Williams*, 950 A.2d 294 (Pa. 2008).

Accordingly, counsel must file an amended PCRA petition that develops the issues of merit and avoid advancing a boilerplate adoption of the petitioner's *pro se* claims. PCRA counsel should raise all issues of merit, regardless of whether the issue was raised by a petitioner in his *pro se* petition. If counsel files a petition that does not develop the ineffectiveness test he should file a brief in support of the petition which does properly develop the claim. *See Commonwealth v. Irons*, 385 A.2d 1004, 1006 (Pa. Super. 1978) (reversing upon finding that the record demonstrated that PCHA counsel "did not file an amended petition to clarify the facts and conclusions of law asserted in appellant's petition. . . . failed to file a supporting brief, to make oral argument, or to present evidence to the lower court."); *Commonwealth v. Davis*, 526 A.2d 440 (Pa. Super. 1987).

Understandably, there are times when petitioners insist on raising issues that have been previously litigated or have no merit, and in those instances counsel often feel as though they are forced to raise those issues. Nonetheless, petitioners are not entitled to hybrid representation and counsel should avoid raising meritless issues whenever possible. Of course, if all of the issues lack merit, counsel should file a ***Turner/Finley*** no-merit letter. Where a PCRA court encounters a petition that does not develop the claims in the petition or a brief, the court should require counsel to file a subsequent amended petition.[23]

There is no standard PCRA petition for filing purposes. *See Commonwealth v. Kutnyak*, 781 A.2d 1259 (Pa. Super. 2001);

---

23 Pa.R.Crim.P. 902(16)(A) sets forth that citation to legal authority is not required in a petition. Thus, a brief is necessary if counsel does not provide legal authority for its arguments.

Content of Petition for Post-Conviction Collateral Relief; Discovery Requests

Commonwealth v. Jerman, 762 A.2d 366 (Pa. Super. 2000). If a court dismisses a PCRA petition by issuing a notice of intent to dismiss and the dismissal does not reach the merits of a claim that counsel believes has merit, counsel should, within twenty days, file a response to the dismissal and within that response request an opportunity to amend the petition pursuant to Pa.R.Crim.P. 905. *See* Pa.R.Crim.P. 907.

I note that the purpose of the PCRA statute is to allow the PCRA court to reach the merits of the claims that a petitioner raises in a first time petition. ***See Commonwealth v. Rykard***, 55 A.3d 1177 (Pa. Super. 2012). Hence, unless the claim is waived or previously litigated, or the petition is untimely, the PCRA court should attempt to reach the merits of the issue. If the PCRA court finds that the PCRA petition does not allow it to reach the merits of an issue because the pleading is insufficient, it should provide counsel an opportunity to file an amended petition. Pa.R.Crim.P. 905. Should counsel fail to respond where at least one amended petition has already been filed, the PCRA court may dismiss the petition or appoint different counsel to develop the petitioner's claims. Pa.R.Crim.P. 905(B).

I recommend attorneys file a substantive brief in support of petitions setting forth detailed argument on each issue that has been raised, similar to an appellate brief. A well-reasoned and quality brief greatly aids the PCRA court in deciding a case. As noted previously, clients may demand that counsel raise certain issues which have no merit. Rather than raise those issues, a well-reasoned letter with legal support, similar to a no-merit letter, written to the client explaining why a certain claim lacks merit may be beneficial to both the attorney and the client as it will provide the attorney an opportunity to examine and explore whether an issue is meritless. Clients should also be made aware that raising fewer but meritorious claims is far more beneficial than asserting numerous issues, most of which are frivolous.

Content of Petition for Post-Conviction Collateral Relief; Discovery Requests

B. *Turner/Finley* No-Merit Letters

In both ***Commonwealth v. Turner***, 544 A.2d 927 (Pa. 1988), and ***Commonwealth v. Finley***, 550 A.2d 213 (Pa. Super. 1988) (*en banc*), the appellate courts set forth the method for withdrawal of court-appointed counsel in collateral attacks on criminal convictions. Counsel may file a ***Turner/Finley*** letter before the PCRA court or before the appellate court. The requirements of ***Turner/Finley*** are less stringent than the typical ***Anders/McClendon*** brief required for direct appeals. First, counsel must make an independent review of the record and detail the nature and extent of that review. *See **Turner***, 544 A.2d 927; ***Finley***, 550 A.2d 213. The no-merit letter must list each issue the petitioner wished to raise and have reviewed. *See also **Commonwealth v. Glover***, 738 A.2d 460 (Pa. Super. 1999).

Counsel must explain why the issues are meritless, and provide the petitioner with a copy of the no-merit letter. ***Commonwealth v. Friend***, 896 A.2d 607 (Pa. Super. 2006), *abrogated in part by* ***Commonwealth v. Pitts***, 981 A.2d 875 (Pa. 2009); ***Commonwealth v. Widgins***, 29 A.3d 816 (Pa. Super. 2011). A no-merit letter which does not address each issue raised in the defendant's *pro se* petition is insufficient. Nevertheless, an attorney is not required to conduct an extra-record investigation and address non-record claims that were not submitted in the *pro se* petition. ***Commonwealth v. Porter***, 728 A.2d 890, 894-895 (Pa. 1999). Counsel should, nevertheless, carefully review all relevant information to determine if other meritorious issues exist in the record.

Further, counsel cannot file a ***Turner/Finley*** no-merit letter arguing that the issue is without merit because the petitioner did not set it forth as an ineffectiveness claims since counsel could file an amended petition properly arguing the issue under the ineffectiveness test. *See **Commonwealth v. Jones***, 932 A.2d

179, 182 n.2 (Pa. Super. 2007). When the *Turner/Finley* letter does meet the appropriate requirements, the PCRA court is permitted to allow counsel to withdraw.

Where the no-merit letter is inadequate, the court should direct counsel to either file a compliant *Turner/Finley* letter or an amended petition. The PCRA court or an appellate court must independently review the entire record, not merely the *pro se* petition. Where the court finds an issue that has merit that is not addressed by PCRA counsel or the *pro se* petition, it should not permit counsel to withdraw. *But see Commonwealth v. Doty*, 48 A.3d 451 (Pa. Super. 2012) (permitting counsel to withdraw on appeal after filing an inadequate *Turner/Finley* brief because the petition was untimely); *Commonwealth v. Liebensperger*, 904 A.2d 40 (Pa. Super. 2008) (same).

If the PCRA court does not expressly grant counsel the right to withdraw in its final order disposing of the petition or before, PCRA counsel still must represent the petitioner on appeal if the petitioner wishes to file an appeal. When the PCRA court is completely satisfied with the *Turner/Finley* no-merit letter that has been submitted, counsel should be permitted to withdraw and the court advise the defendant that he may file an appeal *pro se* or hire private counsel. Once the PCRA court grants counsel's petition to withdraw, the petitioner is not entitled to a new attorney for purposes of an appeal. *Commonwealth v. Maple*, 559 A.2d 953 (Pa. Super. 1989).

Although *Commonwealth v. Friend*, 896 A.2d 607 (Pa. Super. 2006), was overturned in part by *Commonwealth v. Pitts*, 981 A.2d 875 (Pa. 2009), counsel still is required to serve upon his client a statement informing the defendant that he may proceed *pro se* or hire private counsel if counsel is permitted to withdraw pursuant to *Turner/Finley*. *See Commonwealth v. Widgins*, 29 A.3d 816 (Pa. Super. 2011) (counsel in *Widgins* was not

Content of Petition for Post-Conviction Collateral Relief; Discovery Requests

attempting to comply with *Turner/Finley*, having incorrectly followed the *Anders* procedures). These requirements were not delineated in either *Turner* or *Finley*. Yet, in order to respond to a court's notice of intent to dismiss, based on a *Turner/Finley* no-merit letter, the defendant must have a copy of the no-merit letter to adequately articulate why he believes it was inadequate and/or PCRA counsel was ineffective. *See Commonwealth v. Pitts*, 981 A.2d 875 (Pa. 2009).

The PCRA court should be careful to ensure that the *Turner/Finley* no-merit letter addresses each of the issues raised in the *pro se* PCRA petition. If the court allows counsel to withdraw and the *Turner/Finley* letter was inadequate, a petitioner may allege on appeal that the court improperly granted the withdrawal. However, the issue must be raised as an error by the PCRA court and not as an ineffectiveness claim, unless the petitioner alleges PCRA counsel's ineffectiveness in the petitioner's response to the court's notice of intent to dismiss, since such ineffectiveness claims cannot be raised for the first time on appeal. *See Commonwealth v. Pitts*, 981 A.2d 875 (Pa. 2009); *Commonwealth v. Henkel*, 90 A.3d 16 (Pa. Super. 2014) (*en banc*) (collecting Pennsylvania Supreme Court cases concluding that claims of PCRA counsel ineffectiveness cannot be raised for the first time on appeal absent recognition of a constitutional right to collateral review counsel before the PCRA court); *Commonwealth v. Ford*, 44 A.3d 1190 (Pa. Super. 2012) (same).

Counsel cannot argue during an evidentiary hearing on a first time petition that his client's issues have no-merit, even if he has filed a no-merit letter. *Commonwealth v. Willis*, 29 A.3d 393 (Pa. Super. 2011) (remand for new PCRA proceeding where counsel submitted but did not properly file a *Turner/Finley* no-merit letter and argued against client at the hearing). This may put counsel in a difficult position if the court schedules a

Content of Petition for Post-Conviction Collateral Relief; Discovery Requests

hearing without addressing the *Turner/Finley* no-merit letter and petition to withdraw. Indeed, a PCRA court should not schedule an evidentiary hearing when a *Turner/Finley* no-merit letter has been filed without first analyzing the no-merit letter. *Willis*, 29 A.3d 393.

In *Willis*, counsel submitted, but did not properly file, a no-merit letter and petition to withdraw. The PCRA court failed to rule on counsel's motion and held an evidentiary hearing. The *Willis* Court held that even if counsel believes the issues a petitioner seeks to raise have no-merit, he cannot argue, at a hearing, the lack of merit in those issues or question witnesses to support that view. Logically, the decision can be read to compel counsel to argue meritless issues.

During an appeal, PCRA counsel may file a *Turner/Finley* brief with the appellate court. PCRA counsel need not file an *Anders* brief on appeal. Indeed, *Anders* formerly required that an attorney not advocate against the appellant, while *Turner/Finley* requires counsel to expressly explain why the issues are meritless. However, in 2009, the Pennsylvania Supreme Court altered the *Anders* requirements to require counsel explain why the issues on appeal are frivolous. *See Commonwealth v. Santiago*, 978 A.2d 349 (Pa. 2009). Therefore, the difference between an *Anders* brief and a *Turner/Finley* no-merit letter have been blurred.

When the *Turner/Finley* no-merit letter addresses each of the issues raised in the petitioner's *pro se* petition and explains why the issues lack merit and the appellate court, after review of the record, agrees that the issues lack merit and no other meritorious issues appear of record, PCRA counsel will be permitted to withdraw and the appeal dismissed. However, if PCRA counsel files a *Turner/Finley* brief on appeal, the appellant has the right to file a brief advocating on his own behalf. *See*

Content of Petition for Post-Conviction Collateral Relief; Discovery Requests

Commonwealth v. Friend, 896 A.2d 607, 615 fn.12 (Pa. Super. 2006), *abrogated in part by* ***Commonwealth v. Pitts***, 981 A.2d 875 (Pa. 2009) (citing *Commonwealth v. Baney*, 860 A.2d 127 (Pa. Super. 2004)); *Commonwealth v. Dukeman*, 605 A.2d 418 (Pa. Super. 1992) (addressing *pro se* brief after counsel filed petition to withdraw). Counsel should advise his client that the petitioner may proceed *pro se* or hire private counsel before the Superior Court permits him to withdraw when following ***Turner/Finley*** on appeal.

In ***Commonwealth v. Baney***, 860 A.2d 127 (Pa. Super. 2004), one judge on the three judge panel concluded that when counsel files an ***Anders*** brief, the appellant is effectively without counsel and the court must review any *pro se* brief filed by the appellant. The court in ***Friend*** ostensibly extended this rationale to PCRA appeals. The rationale of the opinion in ***Baney*** appears sound at first blush in the PCRA context because when PCRA counsel files a no-merit letter he is expressly arguing against the position of the petitioner.

Also, once the ***Turner/Finley*** no-merit letter has been filed it has consistently been held that the PCRA petitioner is effectively without counsel. ***Commonwealth v. Karanicolas***, 836 A.2d 940 (Pa. Super. 2003). Thus, if the appellate court were not to consider a brief filed by the petitioner after counsel filed a ***Turner/Finley*** no-merit letter, it would in effect deny the petitioner his ability to argue on his own behalf, rendering the right of that person to proceed *pro se* meaningless. ***Baney***, however, is logically inapplicable in the PCRA context based on the case law interpreting ***Turner/Finley*** for the following reasons.

When the ***Turner/Finley*** no-merit letter is inadequate the appellate court will not reach the merits of the issues but will require counsel to either file an advocate's brief or a no-merit

Content of Petition for Post-Conviction Collateral Relief; Discovery Requests

letter which meets the requirements of *Turner/Finley*. Since the court will not analyze a *pro se* brief where counsel files an insufficient *Turner/Finley* no-merit letter, this, in effect, renders the ability of the petitioner to successfully proceed *pro se* impossible because if the *Turner/Finley* letter is proper then the court will dismiss the appeal.

Unlike **Baney**, which citing to ***Commonwealth v. Hernandez***, 783 A.2d 784 (Pa. Super. 2001), found that *Anders* required review of claims that were otherwise waived, claims that are not raised below in the PCRA context are waived; thus, a petitioner cannot raise claims in his *pro se* brief that were not raised in a **proper** *Turner/Finley* no-merit letter. This is so because a proper *Turner/Finley* letter addresses all issues raised by the petitioner and any issue that cannot be waived, such as an illegal sentencing claim.

On the other hand, if the issue was raised before the PCRA court but not addressed in the appellate *Turner/Finley* no-merit letter, then the *Turner/Finley* no-merit letter is inadequate and requires remand, unless review of the record reveals that the petition is untimely. *See **Commonwealth v. Doty***, 48 A.3d 451 (Pa. Super. 2012); ***Commonwealth v. Liebensperger***, 904 A.2d 40 (Pa. Super. 2008).[24]

---

24 A question as to waiver may arise if a legality of sentence question was not preserved before the PCRA court but exists on the record. Where the issue pertains to a sentence that exceeds the lawful maximum or another legality of sentence claim it should not be considered waived and *Turner/Finley* counsel on appeal should not be permitted to withdraw without addressing the issue. There is, however, a single case, finding waiver in the PCRA context where a merger legality of sentence question was not presented to the PCRA court. ***Commonwealth v. Ousley***, 21 A.3d 1238 (Pa. Super. 2011). As discussed previously in this work, *Ousley* is in conflict with numerous other decisions. At the same time, failure to preserve a legality of

Content of Petition for Post-Conviction Collateral Relief; Discovery Requests

Simply put, it appears that based on the appellate court's handling of *Turner/Finley* no-merit letters, once a *Turner/Finley* letter is filed on appeal, the court will not afford relief based on a *pro se* brief. *Commonwealth v. Dukeman*, 605 A.2d 418 (Pa. Super. 1992) (finding *Turner/Finley* no-merit letter sufficient and addressing a *pro se* brief and concluding that petitioner was not entitled to relief).

C. Discovery

Discovery is limited in PCRA proceedings. Pursuant to the rules, a request for discovery is to be filed along with the first counseled petition. Pa.R.Crim.P. 902(A)(16). In non-capital cases, a defendant must show that there are "exceptional circumstances" to be entitled to discovery. Pa.R.Crim.P. 902(E)(1). In a capital case, a defendant is entitled to discovery if he makes a showing of "good cause." Pa.R.Crim.P. 902(E)(2); *Commonwealth v. Williams*, 86 A.3d 771 (Pa. 2014).

Both the terms "exceptional circumstances" and "good cause" are amorphous and neither are defined within the rules or statute and must be evaluated on a case-by-case basis. A court's decision to grant or deny discovery is analyzed by the appellate courts under an abuse of discretion standard. *Commonwealth v. Hanible*, 30 A.3d 426 (Pa. 2011); *Commonwealth v. Miller*, 987 A.2d 638 (Pa. 2009); *Commonwealth v. Williams*, 732 A.2d 1167 (Pa. 1999); *Commonwealth v. Ly*, 980 A.2d 61 (Pa. 2009); *Commonwealth v. Abu-Jamal*, 720 A.2d 79 (Pa. 1998). No discovery will be granted in anticipation of the filing of a PCRA petition; thus, if a petitioner, following his conviction, requests

---

sentence issue that is based on a new constitutional rule that was not retroactively applied should not afford relief in cases that were final before that decision since the court would, in effect, be applying the law retroactively. *See Commonwealth v. Riggle*, 119 A.3d 1058 (Pa. Super. 2015).

discovery for purposes of determining whether or not to file a PCRA, the court cannot grant the petitioner's request. *Commonwealth v. Martin*, 705 A.2d 1337 (Pa. Super. 1998).

Moreover, a petitioner is not entitled to discovery to prove the merits of a claim where the petition is untimely. *Commonwealth v. Dennis*, 859 A.2d 1270 (Pa. 2004); *see also Commonwealth v. Tilley*, 780 A.2d 649 (Pa. 2001). With respect to a *Brady* issue, *i.e.*, allegations that the Commonwealth withheld exculpatory evidence, the Commonwealth is not required to turn over its entire file. *Commonwealth v. Ly*, 980 A.2d 61 (Pa. 2009); *Commonwealth v. Appel*, 689 A.2d 891 (Pa. 1997) (Commonwealth does not violate *Brady* by failing to turn over detailed report of all police investigatory work).

In *Commonwealth v. Williams*, 86 A.3d 771 (Pa. 2014), the Pennsylvania Supreme Court reversed a court's discovery order in a capital PCRA proceeding. The *Williams* Court found that the discovery order implicated attorney work product and ruled that it had jurisdiction to hear the appeal based on the collateral order doctrine. The petitioner had requested the prosecutor's notes relative to meetings and discussions with several witnesses who testified against the petitioner. According to the petitioner, discovery of these alleged notes would enable him to show a *Brady* violation. The High Court ruled that a *Brady* violation allegation does not alone establish good cause.

Further, the Pennsylvania Supreme Court has ruled that, relative to *Batson* claims, the Commonwealth is not required to supply a petitioner with discovery pertaining to the claim where no *Batson* objection was leveled. *Commonwealth v. Jones*, 951 A.2d 294 (Pa. 2008). This decision severely hamstrings a petitioner's ability to develop the required record for review of a *Batson* ineffectiveness claim. For more discussion on discovery see *Commonwealth v. Carson*, 913 A.2d 220 (Pa. 2006);

Content of Petition for Post-Conviction Collateral Relief; Discovery Requests

Commonwealth v. Collins, 957 A.2d 237 (Pa. 2008); ***Commonwealth v. Frey***, 41 A.3d 605 (Pa. Super. 2012) (Bowes, J., dissenting).

Chapter 16: Rule 903
Docketing and Assignment

(A) Upon receipt of a petition for post-conviction collateral relief, the clerk of courts promptly shall time stamp the petition with the date of receipt and make a docket entry, at the same term and number as the underlying conviction and sentence, reflecting the date of receipt, and promptly shall place the petition in the criminal case file. The clerk shall transmit the petition and the criminal case file to the trial judge, if available, or to the administrative judge, if the trial judge is not available. If the defendant's confinement is by virtue of multiple indictments or informations and sentences, the case shall be docketed to the same term and number as the indictment or information upon which the first unexpired term was imposed, but the court may take judicial notice of all proceedings related to the multiple indictments or informations.

(B) When the petition is filed and the docket entry is made, the clerk shall transmit a copy of the petition to the attorney for the Commonwealth.

(C) The trial judge, if available, shall proceed with and dispose of the petition in accordance with these rules, unless the judge determines, in the interests of justice, that he or she should be disqualified.

(D) When the trial judge is unavailable or disqualified, the administrative judge promptly shall assign and transmit the petition and the record to another judge, who shall proceed with and dispose of the petition in accordance with these rules.

> *Comment*: As used in this rule, "trial judge" is intended to include the judge who accepted a plea of guilty or

Docketing and Assignment

nolo contendere.

The transmittal of the petition to the attorney for the Commonwealth does not require a response unless one is ordered by the judge as provided in these rules, or required by Rule 906(E).

Although most references to indictments and indicting grand juries were deleted from these rules in 1993 since the indicting grand jury has been abolished in all counties, see Pa.Const. art I, § 10 and 42 Pa.C.S. § 8931(b), the reference was retained in paragraph (A) of this rule because there may be some cases still pending that were instituted under the former indicting grand jury rules prior to the abolition of the indicting grand jury in 1993. These references to "indictment" do not apply in the context of an indicting grand jury convened pursuant to the new indicting grand jury procedures adopted in 2012 in which an information would be filed after a grand jury indicts a defendant. *See* Rules 103 and 556.11.

If a defendant in a death penalty case files a petition before the trial judge has made a determination concerning the appointment of counsel as required by Rule 904(G), after making the docket entry and placing the petition in the criminal case file, the clerk promptly must forward a copy of the petition to the trial judge for that determination.

Note: Previous Rule 1503 adopted January 24, 1968, effective August 1, 1968; rescinded December 11, 1981, effective June 27, 1982; rescission vacated June 4, 1982; rescinded February 1, 1989, effective July 1, 1989, and replaced by present Rule 1504. Present Rule 1503 adopted February 1, 1989, effective July 1, 1989; amended June 19, 1996, effective July 1, 1996; amended August 11, 1997, effective immediately; *Comment* revised

January 21, 2000, effective July 1, 2000; renumbered Rule 903 and *Comment* revised March 1, 2000, effective April 1, 2001; amended March 3, 2004, effective July 1, 2004; *Comment* revised June 21, 2012, effective in 180 days [December 18, 2012]. (bracket in original).

Annotated Comments

A PCRA petition should ordinarily be decided by the judge who presided over the defendant's trial or guilty plea. Pa.R.Crim.P. 903(C). In limited instances, a petitioner may request that the PCRA judge recuse himself or herself. A judge may also *sua sponte* recuse himself. Pa.R.Crim.P. 903(C). A request for recusal must ordinarily be made at the earliest opportunity, *i.e.*, when the petitioner files his PCRA petition or counsel files a petition or first amended petition. **See Commonwealth v. Miller**, 987 A.2d 638 (Pa. 2009). Failure to request recusal at the earliest opportunity will result in the PCRA court beginning the sometimes arduous task of combing through the applicable record to determine whether a hearing is appropriate, as the rules require that the court immediately review the record upon receipt of a petition. Thus, neglecting to request a recusal in the first counseled PCRA petition should be held to be a waiver of the recusal issue. **See Commonwealth v. Stafford**, 749 A.2d 489 (Pa. Super. 2000).

In deciding whether to recuse for purposes of a PCRA proceeding the court goes through the normal analysis of determining whether recusal is appropriate. **Commonwealth v. Miller**, 987 A.2d 638 (Pa. 2009). Accordingly, the judge must first make a conscientious determination of his ability to assess the case free of personal bias or interest in the outcome, and then consider whether his continued involvement in the case creates an appearance of impropriety and/or would tend to undermine public confidence in the judiciary. **Commonwealth v. Abu-Jamal**, 720 A.2d 79 (Pa. 1998); **Commonwealth v.**

Birdsong, 24 A.3d 319 (Pa. 2011).

In ***Commonwealth v. Travaglia***, 661 A.2d 352 (Pa. 1995), the Pennsylvania Supreme Court upheld a PCRA judge's decision not to recuse himself, despite the judge having made public statements following the defendant's trial that if any defendant was deserving of the death penalty it was the defendant in that case. Oftentimes the request for recusal will come as a result of the trial judge's statements made during sentencing. Simply because a judge gives certain reasons for imposing a sentence should not be grounds for recusal; otherwise, every judge who has sentenced a defendant would be subject to having to recuse himself in that petitioner's PCRA proceeding.

Chapter 17: Rule 904

Appointment of Counsel/Right to Counsel

(A) Counsel for defendant shall file a written entry of appearance with the clerk of courts promptly after being retained, and serve a copy on the attorney for the Commonwealth.

(1) If a firm name is entered, the name of an individual lawyer shall be designated as being responsible for the conduct of the case.

(2) The entry of appearance shall include the attorney's address, phone number, and attorney ID number.

(B) When counsel is appointed, the filing of the appointment order shall enter the appearance of appointed counsel.

(C) Except as provided in paragraph (H), when an unrepresented defendant satisfies the judge that the defendant is unable to afford or otherwise procure counsel, the judge shall appoint counsel to represent the defendant on the defendant's first petition for post-conviction collateral relief.

(D) On a second or subsequent petition, when an unrepresented defendant satisfies the judge that the defendant is unable to afford or otherwise procure counsel, and an evidentiary hearing is required as provided in Rule 908, the judge shall appoint counsel to represent the defendant.

(E) The judge shall appoint counsel to represent a defendant whenever the interests of justice require it.

(F) When counsel is appointed,

(1) the judge shall enter an order indicating the name,

Appointment of Counsel/Right to Counsel

address, and phone number of the appointed counsel, and the order shall be served on the defendant, the appointed counsel, the previous attorney of record, if any, and the attorney for the Commonwealth pursuant to Rule 114 (Orders and Court Notices: Filing; Service; and Docket Entries); and

(2) the appointment of counsel shall be effective throughout the post-conviction collateral proceedings, including any appeal from disposition of the petition for post-conviction collateral relief.

(G) When a defendant satisfies the judge that the defendant is unable to pay the costs of the post-conviction collateral proceedings, the judge shall order that the defendant be permitted to proceed in forma pauperis.

(H) Appointment of Counsel in Death Penalty Cases.

(1) At the conclusion of direct review in a death penalty case, which includes discretionary review in the Supreme Court of the United States, or at the expiration of time for seeking the review, upon remand of the record, the trial judge shall appoint new counsel for the purpose of post-conviction collateral review, unless:

(a) the defendant has elected to proceed pro se or waive post-conviction collateral proceedings, and the judge finds, after a colloquy on the record, that the defendant is competent and the defendant's election is knowing, intelligent, and voluntary;

(b) the defendant requests continued representation by original trial counsel or direct appeal counsel, and the judge finds, after a colloquy on the record, that the petitioner's election constitutes a knowing, intelligent, and voluntary waiver of a claim that counsel was ineffective; or

Appointment of Counsel/Right to Counsel

(c) the judge finds, after a colloquy on the record, that the defendant has engaged counsel who has entered, or will promptly enter, an appearance for the collateral review proceedings.

(2) When counsel is appointed,

(a) the judge shall enter an order indicating the name, address, and phone number of the appointed counsel, and the order shall be served on the defendant, the appointed counsel, the previous attorney of record, if any, and the attorney for the Commonwealth pursuant to Rule 114 (Orders and Court Notices: Filing; Service; and Docket Entries); and

(b) the appointment of counsel shall be effective throughout the post-conviction collateral proceedings, including any appeal from disposition of the petition for post-conviction collateral relief.

(3) When the defendant satisfies the judge that the defendant is unable to pay the costs of the post-conviction collateral proceedings, the judge shall order that the defendant be permitted to proceed in forma pauperis.

> *Comment:* If a defendant seeks to proceed without an attorney, the court may appoint standby counsel. *See* Rule 121.
>
> Consistent with Pennsylvania post-conviction practice, it is intended that counsel be appointed in every case in which a defendant has filed a petition for post-conviction collateral relief for the first time and is unable to afford counsel or otherwise procure counsel. However, the rule now limits appointment of counsel on second or subsequent petitions so that counsel should be appointed *only* if the judge determines that

Appointment of Counsel/Right to Counsel

an evidentiary hearing is required. Of course, the judge has the discretion to appoint counsel in any case when the interests of justice require it.

Paragraph (B) was added in 2005 to make it clear that the filing of an order appointing counsel to represent a defendant enters the appearance of appointed counsel. Appointed counsel does not have to file a separate entry of appearance.

Paragraphs (F)(1) and (H)(2)(a) require that (1) the judge include in the appointment order the name, address, and phone number of appointed counsel, and (2) the order be served on the defendant, appointed counsel, the previous attorney of record, if any, and the attorney for the Commonwealth pursuant to Rule 114 (Orders and Court Notices: Filing; Service; and Docket Entries).

Pursuant to paragraphs (F)(2) and (H)(2)(b), appointed counsel retains his or her assignment until final judgment, which includes all avenues of appeal through the Supreme Court of Pennsylvania. In making the decision whether to file a petition for allowance of appeal, counsel must (1) consult with his or her client, and (2) review the standards set forth in Pa.R.A.P. 1114 (Considerations Governing Allowance of Appeal) and the note following that rule. If the decision is made to file a petition, counsel must carry through with that decision. *See Commonwealth v. Liebel*, 573 Pa. 375, 825 A.2d 630 (2003). Concerning counsel's obligations as appointed counsel, see *Jones v. Barnes*, 463 U.S. 745 (1983). *See also Commonwealth v. Padden*, 783 A.2d 299 (Pa. Super. 2001).

Paragraph (H) was added in 2000 to provide for the appointment of counsel for the first petition for post-conviction collateral relief in a death penalty case at the conclusion of direct review.

Paragraph (H)(1)(a) recognizes that a defendant may proceed *pro se* if the judge finds the defendant competent, and that the defendant's election is knowing, intelligent, and voluntary. In *Indiana v. Edwards*, 128 S.Ct. 2379, 2388 (2008), the Supreme Court recognized that, when a defendant is not mentally competent to conduct his or her own defense, the U. S. Constitution permits the judge to require the defendant to be represented by counsel.

An attorney may not represent a defendant in a capital case unless the attorney meets the educational and experiential requirements set forth in Rule 801 (Qualifications for Defense Counsel in Capital Cases).

Note: Previous Rule 1504 adopted January 24, 1968, effective August 1, 1968; rescinded December 11, 1981, effective June 27, 1982; rescission vacated June 4, 1982; rescinded February 1, 1989, effective July 1, 1989, and replaced by Rule 1507. Present Rule 1504 adopted February 1, 1989, effective July 1, 1989; amended August 11, 1997, effective immediately; amended January 21, 2000, effective July 1, 2000; renumbered Rule 904 and amended March 1, 2000, effective April 1, 2001; amended February 26, 2002, effective July 1, 2002; *Comment* revised March 12, 2004, effective July 1, 2004; *Comment* revised June 4, 2004, effective November 1, 2004; amended April 28, 2005, effective August 1, 2005; *Comment* revised March 29, 2011, effective May 1, 2011.

Annotated Comments

A. Appointment of Counsel/Right to Counsel

The United States Supreme Court has held that no federal constitutional right to counsel exists for purposes of post-conviction relief. ***Pennsylvania v. Finley***, 481 U.S. 551 (1987); ***Commonwealth v. Christy***, 656 A2d 877 (Pa. 1995); *but see* ***Commonwealth v. Figueroa***, 29 A.3d 1177, 1181 n.6 (Pa. Super. 2011); *see also* ***Coleman v. Thompson***, 501 U.S. 722 (1991) (the United States Supreme Court did not foreclose that there may be a constitutional right to counsel on a first time state collateral proceeding where that proceeding is the first opportunity the defendant will have to raise a particular issue, *i.e.*, ineffective assistance of counsel); ***Martinez v. Ryan***, 132 S.Ct. 1309 (2012) (ineffectiveness of initial state collateral review counsel can serve as cause to overcome federal *habeas* procedural default and permit federal court to review underlying trial counsel ineffectiveness claim); ***Trevino v. Thaler***, 133 S.Ct. 1911 (2013) (same).

While Pennsylvania has delineated that PCRA proceedings are civil, the rules governing PCRA procedure are criminal procedural rules, indicating that the PCRA is criminal in nature. Other states have labeled post-conviction proceedings as civil whereas some states have provided that collateral proceedings are both criminal and civil in nature.

Nonetheless, by rule in Pennsylvania, counsel must be appointed for all first time PCRA petitions. ***Commonwealth v. Tedford***, 781 A.2d 1167 (Pa. 2001); ***Commonwealth v. Duffey***, 713 A.2d 63 (Pa. 1998); ***Commonwealth v. Peterson***, 683 A.2d 908 (Pa. Super. 1996); ***Commonwealth v. Kaufmann***, 592 A.2d 691 (Pa. Super. 1991). This is true regardless of whether the petition appears facially untimely, or to be patently without merit, unless the defendant elects to proceed *pro se*. ***Commonwealth v. Smith***, 818 A.2d 494 (Pa. 2003);

Appointment of Counsel/Right to Counsel

Commonwealth v. Ferguson, 722 A.2d 177 (Pa. Super. 1998); ***Commonwealth v. Kutnyak***, 781 A.2d 1259 (Pa. Super. 2001); ***Commonwealth v. Stossel***, 17 A.3d 1286 (Pa. Super. 2011) (appellate court may *sua sponte* address issue of appointment of counsel and defendant must undergo colloquy before being permitted to proceed *pro se*); **but see *Commonwealth v. Auchmuty***, 799 A.2d 823 (Pa. Super. 2002) (distinguishing the situation where counsel is not appointed on a first time petition where the defendant is no longer serving a sentence and finding harmless error in the failure to appoint counsel); **but see also *Commonwealth v. Ramos***, 14 A.3d 894 (Pa. Super. 2011) (holding that person sentenced to one year of probation in 1987 was entitled to counsel for the filing of his first PCRA petition despite being ineligible for relief).

Ramos is in conflict with ***Auchmuty***. The ***Ramos*** Court did not distinguish between the fact that there are exceptions to the timeliness requirement that counsel could foreseeably discover, thereby providing a rationale for the appointment of counsel, whereas there are no exceptions to when a person is no longer serving a sentence. Further, although the ***Ramos*** Court held that the record was unclear as to whether the defendant was no longer serving his sentence twenty-two years after the sentence expired, a look at the grading of the offense charged and the maximum possible sentence could have resolved that question.

When a court receives a first time non-capital *pro se* PCRA petition its first order of business is to appoint counsel and direct counsel to file either an amended PCRA petition or a ***Turner/Finley*** no-merit letter. ***Commonwealth v. Smith***, 818 A.2d 494 (Pa. 2003); ***Commonwealth v. Guthrie***, 749 A.2d 502 (Pa. Super. 2000). Where counsel is appointed, the appointment serves as the attorney's entry of appearance. Pa.R.Crim.P. 904(B). When counsel is privately retained, he must enter his appearance. Pa.R.Crim.P. 904(A). A petitioner, however, can forfeit his right to PCRA counsel. In ***Commonwealth v. Staton***,

Appointment of Counsel/Right to Counsel

120 A.3d 277 (Pa. 2015), the petitioner brutally assaulted his attorney in the courtroom during the PCRA proceedings. The court permitted counsel to withdraw and denied the petition. The *Staton* Court held that the assault on counsel resulted in Staton's forfeiture of his right to PCRA counsel.

Any petition filed after the defendant's judgment of sentence is final, which requests post-conviction relief, will be treated as a PCRA petition regardless of the title. ***Commonwealth v. Taylor***, 65 A.3d 462 (Pa. Super. 2013); ***Commonwealth v. Fowler***, 930 A.2d 586 (Pa. Super. 2007); ***Commonwealth v. Jackson***, 30 A.3d 516 (Pa. Super. 2011). This includes *habeas corpus* or *coram nobis* petitions or a motion to vacate the sentence. ***Commonwealth v. Evans***, 866 A.2d 442 (Pa. Super. 2005) (*pro se* motion raising discretionary sentencing issue entitled defendant to appointment of counsel under PCRA); ***Commonwealth v. Price***, 876 A.2d 988 (Pa. Super. 2005); ***Commonwealth v. Beck***, 848 A.2d 987 (Pa. Super. 2004); ***Commonwealth v. Johnson***, 803 A.2d 1291 (Pa. Super. 2002); ***Commonwealth v. Lutz***, 788 A.2d 993 (Pa. Super. 2001); ***Commonwealth v. Kutnyak***, 781 A.2d 1259 (Pa. Super. 2001); ***Commonwealth v. Hutchins***, 760 A.2d 50 (Pa. Super. 2000); ***Commonwealth v. Guthrie***, 749 A.2d 502 (Pa. Super. 2000). It does not include a post-sentence motion filed within ten days of sentencing or a motion filed within thirty days from the judgment of sentence, *see* Comment to Pa.R.Crim.P. 901, nor does it include a petition to expunge a record. ***Commonwealth v. Rodland***, 871 A.2d 216, 218 n.3 (Pa. Super. 2005).

Once the court appoints counsel, he is to continue representation throughout the proceedings unless the court grants counsel permission to withdraw. ***Commonwealth v. Quail***, 729 A.2d 571 (Pa. Super. 1999); ***Commonwealth v. Jackson***, 965 A.2d 280 (Pa. Super. 2009). Where counsel is not permitted to withdraw and does not file a brief, the case will be remanded for appointment of new counsel or counsel will be directed to

Appointment of Counsel/Right to Counsel

resume his stewardship. ***Commonwealth v. Quail***, 729 A.2d 571 (Pa. Super. 1999); ***but see Commonwealth v. Glacken***, 32 A.3d 750 (Pa. Super. 2011) (court quashing PCRA appeal where counsel had not withdrawn and did not file a brief).[25]

If the PCRA court did not authorize counsel's withdrawal and is aware that a petitioner is appealing his first time PCRA matter *pro se*, it must notify counsel of record and inform counsel that he must continue his representation. ***Commonwealth v. Quail***, 729 A.2d 571 (Pa. Super. 1999). When counsel files a no-merit letter before the PCRA court and the petition is dismissed, but the PCRA court does not expressly grant counsel's request to withdraw, counsel need not file an ***Anders*** brief. Rather, counsel should file an appropriate ***Turner/Finley*** no-merit letter on appeal requesting permission to withdraw. ***Commonwealth v. Karanicolas***, 836 A.2d 940 (Pa. Super. 2003).

Counsel must either file an amended petition or prepare a no-merit letter, helping a petitioner with a *pro se* petition is insufficient. ***Commonwealth v. Duffey***, 713 A.2d 63 (Pa. 1998); ***Commonwealth v. Perez***, 799 A.2d 848 (Pa. Super. 2002) (remanding even though counsel filed an amended petition but did not address untimeliness of petition). An amended petition is not untimely when submitted after the running of the one-year time-bar where the *pro se* petition was timely filed, nor is an amended petition considered a second or subsequent petition. ***Commonwealth v. Padden***, 783 A.2d 299 (Pa. Super. 2001).

Additionally, where the court dismisses a first time PCRA petition where counsel was not appointed or did not file an amended petition, a second petition will relate back to the first

---

[25] The procedure in ***Glacken*** should be disfavored compared to that used in ***Quail*** since ***Glacken*** elongates the PCRA process by requiring a subsequent petition to be filed alleging ineffective assistance of appellate counsel. *See **Commonwealth v. Bennett***, 930 A.2d 1264, 1274 n.12 (Pa. 2007).

pro se petition. ***Commonwealth v. Tedford***, 781 A.2d 1167 (Pa. 2001); ***see also Commonwealth v. Wiley***, 966 A.2d 1153 (Pa. Super. 2009) (Superior Court remanding where second petition, though untimely on its face, revealed that the defendant was chronically underrepresented during his first petition and no amended petition was filed in original PCRA proceeding).

The filing of a deficient brief can result in remand for appointment of new counsel. ***Commonwealth v. Kenney***, 732 A.2d 1161 (Pa. 1999). Where counsel files a ***Turner/Finley*** letter on appeal which is inadequate, the petitioner is considered uncounseled. ***Commonwealth v. Karanicolas***, 836 A.2d 940 (Pa. Super. 2003). Hence, even if the petitioner files his own brief after counsel files a ***Turner/Finley*** no-merit letter, and the ***Turner/Finley*** letter is insufficient, the court will remand for the filing of a proper ***Turner/Finley*** no-merit letter or advocate's brief.

A first-time PCRA petitioner may be permitted to proceed *pro se* before the PCRA court or on appeal. However, he must be given a colloquy on the issue so that the waiver of counsel is knowing, intelligent, and voluntary. ***Commonwealth v. Robinson***, 970 A.2d 455 (Pa. Super. 2009) (*en banc*); ***Commonwealth v. Stossel***, 17 A.3d 1286 (Pa. Super. 2011) (selection of box indicating that petitioner does not want counsel on standardized pre-printed PCRA petition insufficient); ***see also Commonwealth v. Grazier***, 713 A.2d 81 (Pa. 1998); ***but see Commonwealth v. Staton***, 12 A.3d 277 (Pa. 2010) (discussing but not concluding whether defendants have a right to proceed *pro se* on appeal). A petitioner cannot claim his own ineffectiveness. ***Commonwealth v. Blakeney***, 108 A.3d 739 (Pa. 2014); ***Commonwealth v. Martin***, 5 A.3d 177, 183-184 & n.9 (Pa. 2010); ***Commonwealth v. Fletcher***, 986 A.2d 759 (Pa. 2009); ***Commonwealth v. Green***, 709 A.2d 382, 384 (Pa. 1998); ***Commonwealth v. Appel***, 689 A.2d 891 (Pa. 1997).

Appointment of Counsel/Right to Counsel

Therefore, if a defendant represents himself on a first time PCRA petition or a subsequent PCRA matter he cannot layer any claims of ineffective assistance of counsel and will not be due any relief. A defendant, on a second or subsequent petition, is not by rule entitled to counsel unless the judge is satisfied that, "the defendant is unable to afford or otherwise procure counsel, and an evidentiary hearing is required." Pa.R.Crim.P. 904(C); ***Commonwealth v. Jackson***, 965 A.2d 280 (Pa. Super. 2009); ***Commonwealth v. Kubis***, 808 A.2d 196 (Pa. Super. 2002). If an evidentiary hearing is required then counsel must be appointed. ***Commonwealth v. Jackson***, 965 A.2d 280 (Pa. Super. 2009).

B. Ineffectiveness of PCRA counsel

Certain actions on the part of PCRA counsel are considered *per se* ineffective assistance of counsel. Those include the failure to file an appellate brief, ***see Commonwealth v. Bennett***, 930 A.2d 1264 (Pa. 2007), and the failure to file an amended PCRA petition. ***Commonwealth v. Priovolos***, 746 A.2d 621 (Pa. Super. 2000). Where counsel fails to file an amended PCRA petition or a ***Turner/Finley*** no-merit letter, the PCRA court cannot dismiss the PCRA for that reason, ***Commonwealth v. Hampton***, 718 A.2d 1250 (Pa. Super. 1998). The court either must direct counsel to file the petition or remove the attorney and appoint different counsel.

If counsel fails to file an amended petition and the matter is appealed, the appellate courts will remand for the filing of an amended PCRA petition if the issue is properly raised. While the failure to file a Pa.R.A.P. 1925(b) statement in a criminal case is *per se* ineffective assistance of counsel and a case will be remanded for the opportunity of counsel to file the statement, *see* Pa.R.A.P. 1925(c), and ***Commonwealth v. Hopfer***, 965 A.2d 270 (Pa. Super. 2009), where PCRA counsel neglects to file the required statement, the court will find waiver. ***Commonwealth*** *v. Hill*, 16 A.3d 484, 495 n.14 (Pa. 2011) (noting that PCRA is not a criminal proceeding and Pa.R.A.P. 1925(c) may not apply); *see also Commonwealth v. Butler*, 756 A.2d 55 (Pa. Super. 2000), *affirmed*, 812 A.2d 631 (Pa. 2002).

Raising and addressing non-*per se* ineffectiveness of PCRA counsel claims prior to 2009 did not appear to be a hot button issue, although there was some debate on the matter. *Commonwealth v. Moore*, 805 A.2d 1212 (Pa. 2002) (OAJC) (Castille, J., concurring and dissenting) (arguing that it was inappropriate to review a claim of PCRA counsel's effectiveness after a grant of allocator, *i.e.*, during discretionary review); *Commonwealth v. Jones*, 815 A.2d 598 (Pa. 2002) (OAJC). So long as the ineffectiveness claim was raised and a properly layered claim was set forth, an appellate court could reach issues which were raised for the first time on appeal, *i.e.*, PCRA counsel's ineffectiveness. *Commonwealth v. Albrecht*, 720 A.2d 693 (Pa. 1998); *Commonwealth v. Pursell*, 724 A.2d 293 (Pa. 1999); *Commonwealth v. Hall*, 872 A.2d 1177 (Pa. 2005); *Commonwealth v. Albert*, 561 A.2d 736 (Pa. 1989); *Commonwealth v. Lauro*, 819 A.2d 100 (Pa. Super. 2003); *Commonwealth v. Malone*, 823 A.2d 931 (Pa. Super. 2003); *Commonwealth v. Gonzalez*, 858 A.2d 1219, 1222 n.1 (Pa. Super. 2004); *Commonwealth v. Klinger*, 470 A.2d 540 (Pa. Super. 1983).

This was the rule despite the general rule of appellate practice mandating that appellate courts not hear claims raised for the first time on appeal. Indeed, at the time the legislature authored and ratified the PCRA statute, lawyers were not only allowed to raise ineffectiveness claims on direct review, but could raise ineffective assistance of PCHA counsel ineffectiveness for the first time on appeal. *See Commonwealth v. Albert*, 561 A.2d 736 (Pa. 1989); *Commonwealth v. Hill*, 549 A.2d 199 (Pa. Super. 1988); *Commonwealth v. Jones*, 493 A.2d 662, 664 n.2 (Pa. 1985); *Commonwealth v. Klinger*, 470 A.2d 540 (Pa.

Appointment of Counsel/Right to Counsel

Super. 1983); *Commonwealth v. Ramsey*, 446 A.2d 974 (Pa. Super. 1982).

However, a clear division in the Pennsylvania Supreme Court became evident in the case of *Commonwealth v. Ligons*, 971 A.2d 1125 (Pa. 2009), and shortly thereafter in *Commonwealth v. Pitts*, 981 A.2d 875 (Pa. 2009). The differing views were espoused by Chief Justice Castille and Justice Baer; thus, I refer to the approaches respectively as the Castille approach and the Baer approach.[26] For an overview of the debate, *see Commonwealth v. Henkel*, 90 A.3d 16 (Pa. Super. 2014) (*en banc*).

In *Ligons*, Chief Justice Castille revisited his views from his concurring and dissenting opinion in *Commonwealth v. Moore*, 805 A.2d 1212 (Pa. 2002) (OAJC), and his discussion in *Commonwealth v. Jones*, 815 A.2d 598 (Pa. 2002) (OAJC). Joined by Justice McCaffery and Justice Eakin, the Chief Justice urged that allegations of PCRA counsel ineffectiveness not be reviewed on appeal without affording the PCRA court the opportunity to rule on the issues. Justice Baer, (joined by Justice Saylor and Justice Todd), countered by arguing that an appellant's claims of PCRA counsel ineffectiveness, raised for the first time on appeal, should be entertained because it is the only way to afford a PCRA petitioner an opportunity to enforce his rule-based right to effective PCRA counsel. *Ligons*, 971 A.2d at 1140; *Commonwealth v. Henkel*, 90 A.3d 16 (Pa. Super. 2014) (*en banc*); *Commonwealth v. Ford*, 44 A.3d 1190 (Pa. Super. 2012).

Specifically, Justice Baer noted that, under normal circumstances, a PCRA petitioner has no opportunity to claim PCRA counsel's ineffectiveness because it would require a petitioner to challenge PCRA counsel's stewardship during the

---

26 Justice Nigro, prior to leaving the Pennsylvania Supreme Court, was also a strong supporter of the rationale discussed by Justice Baer.

Appointment of Counsel/Right to Counsel

ongoing proceeding before the PCRA court. According to Justice Baer's view, a PCRA petitioner can never demonstrate that he was prejudiced by PCRA counsel's performance, *i.e.*, demonstrate that the outcome of the PCRA proceeding would have been different, because the PCRA proceeding has not yet concluded and no ruling by the PCRA court has been issued.

In support of his opposing view, Chief Justice Castille noted that the decisions relied upon by Justice Baer, ***Commonwealth v. Albrecht***, 720 A.2d 693 (Pa. 1998), ***Commonwealth v. Pursell***, 724 A.2d 293 (Pa. 1999), and ***Commonwealth v. Hall***, 872 A.2d 1177 (Pa. 2005), were decided and/or litigated prior to the Court's determination of ***Commonwealth v. Grant***, 813 A.2d 726 (Pa. 2002). According to Chief Justice Castille, ***Grant*** removed the requirement that ineffective assistance claims be raised at the first opportunity and "the normal appellate review/issue preservation paradigm, and the strictures of the PCRA" are what were left. ***Ligons***, 971 A.2d at 1165-1166; *see also* ***Commonwealth v. Henkel***, 90 A.3d 16 (Pa. Super. 2014) (*en banc*); ***Commonwealth v. Ford***, 44 A.3d 1190 (Pa. Super. 2012). Moreover, Chief Justice Castille opined that Justice Baer's approach created an extra statutory "'as-of-right' ability to litigate a new, unlimited, and essentially serial PCRA petition on PCRA appeal." ***Ligons***, 971 A.3d at 1166; ***Burkett***, 5 A.3d at 1273.

Chief Justice Castille further noted that the PCRA's waiver provision makes no exception for allegations of PCRA counsel ineffectiveness. *See* 42 Pa.C.S. § 9543(a)(3). Section 9544(b) defines waiver as including any issue that the petitioner could have raised but failed to "in a prior state postconviction proceeding." 42 Pa.C.S. § 9544(b). Justice Baer countered by arguing that Chief Justice Castille's approach was flawed for two significant reasons: (1) ***Grant*** did not involve a collateral appeal pursuant to the PCRA, and (2) the decision in ***Commonwealth v. Hall***, 872 A.2d 1177 (Pa. 2005), was decided years after ***Grant*** was handed down.

The debate continued in ***Commonwealth v. Pitts***, 981 A.2d 875 (Pa. 2009), where the majority discussed, in two footnotes, that although Pitts had asserted that his PCRA appeal was the first opportunity he had to challenge PCRA counsel's stewardship because he was no longer represented by PCRA counsel, he could have challenged PCRA counsel's representation after receiving counsel's withdrawal letter and the notice of the PCRA court's intent to dismiss. Since he had failed to do so, the court reasoned that the issue of whether PCRA counsel was ineffective for failing to raise the issue at bar in that case was waived.

Chief Justice Castille, in a concurring opinion, again reiterated the view that no claim of PCRA counsel ineffectiveness could be reviewed by an appellate court when it is raised for the first time on appeal. Rather, according to the Castille view, a petitioner must file a second petition raising PCRA counsel's ineffectiveness and properly layer the claim according to the dictates of ***Commonwealth v. McGill***, 832 A.2d 1014 (Pa. 2003), and be subject to the timeliness requirements of the statute as well as the ***Lawson*** standard for subsequent petitions.

Justice Baer, in his dissenting opinion in ***Pitts***, reiterated his position in ***Ligons*** that such an approach renders it virtually impossible for a petitioner to ever raise a timely claim of PCRA counsel's ineffectiveness, rendering the rule-based right to effective assistance of counsel in a PCRA meaningless. *See* ***Commonwealth v. Albert***, 561 A.2d 736, 738 (Pa. 1989) ("It is axiomatic that the right to counsel includes the concomitant right to effective assistance of counsel. ***Commonwealth ex rel. Washington v. Maroney***, 427 Pa. 599, 235 A.2d 349 (1967). Indeed[,] the right to counsel is meaningless if effective assistance is not guaranteed. Since appellant was entitled to representation by an attorney in his pursuit of this collateral attack, he was entitled to adequate representation of his claims at both the hearing and appellate levels.").

The Baer approach noted that a petitioner has only one year from the conclusion of direct review to file a petition or the PCRA court will have no jurisdiction to reach the merits. He further added that once a petitioner has filed a petition he cannot raise a claim of PCRA counsel ineffectiveness until after the completion of the original PCRA matter, and the filing of one PCRA petition does not toll the time for the filing of a subsequent petition. Recognizing the practicalities of the appeal process, Justice Baer concluded it would be impossible to raise a claim of PCRA counsel's ineffectiveness in a timely fashion in a subsequent PCRA petition.

Each of the arguments have support in the law. As a practical matter, a claim of PCRA counsel ineffectiveness, if not reviewed for the first time on appeal, would result in the claim having to be brought in a serial PCRA petition, which would ensure in almost every instance that the petition would be untimely. Thus, the PCRA court would have no jurisdiction to reach the merits of the claim. Additionally, the petition would be subject to the even more stringent *Lawson* standard applied to serial PCRA petitions.

Justice Baer's observation that claims of PCRA counsel cannot be properly raised during the PCRA proceedings below is cogent precisely because the proceeding has not ended and one cannot demonstrate prejudice until there is a final outcome. ***Commonwealth v. Ford***, 44 A.3d 1190 (Pa. Super. 2012). Furthermore, there is no right to hybrid representation during PCRA review. His next premise, however, that the claim must be raised on appeal or be waived is no longer sound. Chief Justice Castille was accurate in his conclusion that, subsequent to the Pennsylvania Supreme Court's seminal decision in ***Grant***, issues of ineffective assistance of counsel are not waived if they are not asserted at the first opportunity.

While Justice Baer noted that ***Grant*** was not a PCRA case, it directly decided, in direct contradiction of the PCRA statute's waiver provision and its section declaring that it did not limit relief during direct appeal, that issues of ineffectiveness need not be brought at the first opportunity. This, of course, is not to say that a person could allege that counsel during a first time petition was ineffective by raising the issue in a third PCRA petition. Rather, the petitioner would have to assert PCRA counsel ineffectiveness in his second PCRA petition or waive the issue and allege that the petition fell under a timeliness exception.

Chief Justice Castille's view that an issue generally cannot be raised for the first time on appeal is also sound and is long standing law in the Commonwealth. Nevertheless, the Chief Justice's position relative to waiver under the statute and claims of PCRA counsel effectiveness is inaccurate. His position is that the statute makes no waiver exception for claims of PCRA counsel's ineffectiveness. However, in citing to the statute he defeats his own argument. Waiver applies to claims that could have been brought in a prior state collateral attack and on direct appeal. Claims of PCRA counsel's ineffectiveness cannot be brought in the underlying PCRA process, precisely as Justice Baer points out, because the outcome of the proceedings has not ended and one is not entitled to hybrid representation. ***Commonwealth v. Ford***, 44 A.3d 1190 (Pa. Super. 2012).

Moreover, the waiver provision of the PCRA statute provides that an issue is waived if not raised for the first-time on appeal or in a ***prior*** PCRA or *habeas* matter. *See* 42 Pa.C.S. § 9544 ("an issue is waived if the petitioner could have raised it but failed to do so before trial, at trial, during unitary review, **on appeal or in a prior state postconviction proceeding**."). (emphasis added); ***Commonwealth v. Henkel***, 90 A.3d 16 (Pa.

Super. 2014) (*en banc*). Thus, the statute actually supports permitting raising claims of PCRA counsel ineffectiveness for the first time on appeal and that a petitioner does not waive the issue by not raising it in the ongoing post-conviction proceeding.

Following ***Ligons*** and ***Pitts***, the Supreme Court again signaled that it would no longer review claims of PCRA counsel's effectiveness in ***Commonwealth v. Colavita***, 993 A.2d 874 (Pa. 2010). In *Colavita*, the Superior Court granted relief to the petitioner based on a substantive due process violation when the district attorney commented on the petitioner's hiring of an attorney. The Commonwealth appealed, asserting that the Superior Court improperly afforded relief by raising the issue *sua sponte*. The Supreme Court agreed and, in a footnote, without analysis and citing to ***Pitts***, commented that the petitioner's argument that PCRA counsel was ineffective for not properly raising the issue was not before the court and an ineffectiveness claim could not be raised for the first time on appeal.

The ***Colavita*** footnote could possibly be viewed as *dicta* because, as the court stated, the issue was not before the court as a result of its grant of review. ***But see Commonwealth v. Jette***, 23 A.3d 1032 (Pa. 2011) (Castille, C.J., concurring) (opining that the ***Colavita*** footnote was binding precedent); ***Commonwealth v. Robinson***, 139 A.3d 178, 184 n.8 (Pa. 2016) (recognizing binding nature of ***Colavita***); *compare* ***Commonwealth v. Henkel***, 90 A.3d 16 (Pa. Super. 2014) (*en banc*) (Bender, J., dissenting). The Superior Court, after the decision in ***Colavita***, distinguished ***Pitts*** in ***Commonwealth v. Burkett***, 5 A.3d 1260 (Pa. Super. 2010), noting that ***Pitts*** involved a case where the court filed a notice of intent to dismiss.

In *Burkett*, the defendant filed his original petition in 1993, *i.e.*, pre-*Commonwealth v. Grant*, 813 A.2d 726 (Pa. 2002), but due to his various counsels' continued failure to file an appropriate petition he did not receive a hearing for fifteen years and the court did not decide the matter until a year after the hearing, resulting in sixteen years passing from his initial filing.

The PCRA court decision in *Burkett* was rendered before *Pitts* and *Colavita*. On appeal, the appellant made an allegation regarding PCRA counsel's effectiveness, which was not raised below. Noting the *Ligons* plurality and *Pitts* decision, the *Burkett* Court concluded that the defendant could not raise the issue below as he was not afforded a notice of intent to dismiss and was still represented by that attorney. Further, the petitioner's sentence was set to expire and due to the delay in the PCRA court's handling of the matter he would not be able to raise the issue. Accordingly, the court in *Burkett* addressed the issue on its merits, concluding that PCRA counsel was not ineffective.

Subsequently, in *Commonwealth v. Jette*, 23 A.3d 1032 (Pa. 2011), the Supreme Court reiterated that a challenge to PCRA counsel's effectiveness cannot be alleged for the first time on appeal. The *Jette* Court, citing to *Colavita* and *Pitts*, but without discussing the facts of *Pitts*, opined that claims of PCRA counsel's ineffectiveness cannot be raised for the first time on appeal. This time, however, the Court's statement was directly related to the issue before it, *i.e.*, hybrid representation of counsel and the ability of a petitioner to raise claims of PCRA counsel effectiveness when still represented. *See also Commonwealth v. Hill*, 16 A.3d 484, 497 n.17 (Pa. 2011); *Commonwealth v. Potter*, 58 A.3d 752 (Pa. 2012) (*per curiam* order reversing Superior Court); *Commonwealth v. Robinson*, 139 A.3d 178, 184 n. 8 (Pa. 2016); *Commonwealth v. Henkel*, 90 A.3d 16 (Pa. Super. 2014) (*en banc*); *Commonwealth v. Ford*, 44 A.3d 1190 (Pa. Super. 2012).

Appointment of Counsel/Right to Counsel

An additional and significant flaw in not permitting claims of PCRA counsel ineffectiveness to be raised on appeal is that, at the time the PCRA statute was passed, **Commonwealth v. Grant**, 813 A.2d 726 (Pa. 2002), was not the law, and the legislature could not have anticipated that decision. Rather, **Commonwealth v. Hubbard**, 372 A.2d 687 (Pa. 1977), was the prevailing precedent. Accordingly, claims of ineffectiveness, including PCRA counsel, were required to be raised for the first time on appeal when the statute was promulgated. **Commonwealth v. Ford**, 44 A.3d 1190 (Pa. Super. 2012); **Commonwealth v. Jones**, 493 A.2d 662, 664 n.2 (Pa. 1985); **Commonwealth v. Klinger**, 470 A.2d 540 (Pa. Super. 1983); **Commonwealth v. Simmons**, 459 A.2d 14 (Pa. Super. 1983), *reversed on other grounds*, 475 A.2d 1310 (Pa. 1984); **Commonwealth v. Ramsey**, 446 A.2d 974 (Pa. Super. 1982).

It would seem that if the legislature did not intend for claims of PCRA counsel ineffectiveness to be raised on appeal, it would have contained a prohibition against leveling claims of PCRA counsel ineffectiveness. **Commonwealth v. Ford**, 44 A.3d 1190 (Pa. Super. 2012). Furthermore, the capital unitary system of review, which was passed at the same time the legislature made the 1995 amendments to the PCRA statute, permitted raising ineffective assistance claims of unitary review appeal counsel for the first time on appeal. *See* 42 Pa.C.S. 9571(c) ("Claims raised on collateral appeal shall be limited to claims that were preserved in the collateral proceeding in the trial court and to any other claim that could not have been raised previously, including claims of ineffective assistance of counsel on direct appeal.").

Earlier versions of the proposed statute actually read that "[o]nly claims raised in the unitary review petition shall be considered preserved for appellate review." Senate Bill No. 81, Special Session No. 1 of 1995, Printer's No. 109, March 21, 1995; *see also* Senate Bill No. 81, Special Session No. 1 of 1995, Printer's

No. 131, May 23, 1995. The CURA statute, unlike the PCRA, also included a provision entitled "Subsequent or untimely claims." 42 Pa.C.S. § 9573(b). These facts demonstrate that the legislature was able to distinguish between untimely claims instituting new PCRA trial level proceedings and claims of ineffectiveness that could only be raised for the first time on appeal. Thus, the legislative history does not support the Castille view.

Moreover, neither Chief Justice Castille or Justice Baer discussed that the PCRA statute does not bar raising PCRA counsel ineffectiveness claims, unlike the federal *habeas* statute and similar state *habeas* statutes. Additionally, Justice Baer did not analyze the constitutional implications of **Grant** relative to allegations of PCRA counsel ineffectiveness. Currently, the Pennsylvania Supreme Court has declined to address whether a petitioner has either a federal or state constitutional right to counsel during his or her first PCRA, instead relying on the rule-based right. *See* **Commonwealth v. Priovolos**, 715 A.2d 420 (Pa. 1998) (addressing claim of PCRA counsel ineffectiveness raised for first time on appeal); **Commonwealth v. Christy**, 656 A.2d 877 (Pa. 1995); **Commonwealth v. Peterson**, 683 A.2d 908 (Pa. Super. 1996).

Since **Grant** compels defendants to make all allegations of ineffectiveness during the PCRA process, it is possible that defendants have a constitutional right to counsel during a PCRA and therefore a corresponding constitutional right to effective assistance of counsel. *See* **Coleman v. Thompson**, 501 U.S. 722, 754-757 (1991); *see also id.* at 773-774 (Blackmun, J., dissenting with whom Justice Marshall and Justice Stevens joined); **Commonwealth v. Figueroa**, 29 A.3d 1177 (Pa. Super. 2011); **Martinez v. Ryan**, 132 S.Ct. 1309 (2012).

While the Supreme Court has held that there is no Sixth Amendment right or due process right to counsel during

Appointment of Counsel/Right to Counsel

collateral review, *Pennsylvania v. Finley*, 481 U.S. 551 (1987); *Murray v. Giarratano*, 492 U.S. 1 (1989); *Coleman v. Thompson*, 501 U.S. 722 (1991), the High Court did not foreclose the possibility that there is a constitutional right to counsel on a first time state collateral proceeding where that proceeding is the first opportunity the defendant will have to raise a particular issue, *i.e.*, ineffective assistance of trial counsel. **See Commonwealth v. Figueroa**, 29 A.3d 1177 (Pa. Super. 2011); *Martinez v. Ryan*, 132 S.Ct. 1309 (2012). In *Figueroa*, 29 A.3d 1177, the Superior Court briefly discussed one rationale for why a federal constitutional right to counsel might exist.[27]

Prior to **Grant**, defendants could set forth ineffectiveness claims on direct appeal where there exists an equal protection right to counsel and a concomitant due process right to effective assistance of counsel. **See Douglas v. California**, 372 U.S. 353 (1963); *Evitts v. Lucey*, 469 U.S. 387 (1985). After **Grant**, however, claims of ineffectiveness were deferred to collateral proceedings. Accordingly, by eliminating ineffectiveness claims from the ambit of direct review, **Grant** renders PCRA trial review as a first appeal as-of-right for trial counsel ineffectiveness issues.

Phrased another way, the PCRA is the first-tier review for Sixth Amendment ineffective assistance of counsel claims.[28] Additionally, by funneling claims of ineffectiveness into collateral review and eliminating the direct appeal avenue of

---

[27] The Third Circuit Court of Appeals has concluded that even where state law provides a right to counsel there is no federal due process constitutional right to effective counsel. **Caswell v. Ryan**, 953 F.2d 853, 862 (3d Cir. 1992); *see also Pursell v. Horn*, 187 F.Supp. 2d 260, 372-373 (W.D. Pa. 2002). The Third Circuit and its federal district courts have not addressed the constitutional issue in the context of the practice in Pennsylvania of all claims of ineffectiveness being deferred until collateral review.

relief for ineffectiveness claims, the Pennsylvania Supreme Court, in practice, removed the constitutional right to counsel for purposes of challenging prior counsel's effectiveness.

The United States Supreme Court discussed this precise rationale in *dicta* in the seven to two decision in ***Martinez v. Ryan***, 132 S.Ct. 1309 (2012). The ***Martinez*** decision arose out of Arizona, where much like Pennsylvania, ineffective assistance of counsel claims can only be raised in a state collateral proceedings and not during direct review. The defendant was convicted of sexually abusing his eleven year old step-daughter. The victim in an initial videotaped interview asserted that she was abused. In a subsequent interview, however, she denied the abuse occurred and she testified at trial that no abuse occurred. The victim's mother and grandmother also testified that the victim recanted. The defendant was unsuccessful during his direct review. During the defendants first state collateral review proceeding his counsel filed the equivalent of a ***Turner/Finley*** no-merit letter.

The state court permitted the defendant forty-five days to respond with a *pro se* petition, but he did not respond and the court dismissed the matter. The defendant contended that he was unaware of the proceeding and that counsel did not inform him that he needed to file a *pro se* petition. The Arizona intermediate court affirmed and the Arizona Supreme Court denied review.

The defendant, with the aid of counsel, filed a second collateral petition raising various claims of trial counsel ineffectiveness. The court denied the petition on the grounds that the issues were waived for not having been asserted in his original collateral

---

28 By eliminating an entire class of claims from direct review the ***Grant*** decision would also be rendered an unconstitutional violation of the Pennsylvania constitutional right to appeal unless another avenue of relief for such claims was provided. That avenue is the PCRA.

proceeding. This decision was again affirmed by the Arizona intermediate court. Arizona's Supreme Court did not grant review of the case.

The defendant subsequently filed a federal *habeas* petition arguing that he had a constitutional right to counsel during his initial state collateral matter, which he alleged overcame the rule of procedural default in his federal *habeas* case. Procedural default prevents a claim from being reviewed by a federal court where the state courts have denied the claim by relying on a independent and adequate state procedural rule. The federal district court and Ninth Circuit Court of Appeals declined to adopt the defendant's position. The Supreme Court granted *certiorari* and discussed **Coleman v. Thompson**, 501 U.S. 722 (1991), opining,

> **Coleman** had suggested, though without holding, that the Constitution may require States to provide counsel in initial-review collateral proceedings because "in [these] cases ... state collateral review is the first place a prisoner can present a challenge to his conviction." As **Coleman** noted, this makes the initial-review collateral proceeding a prisoner's "one and only appeal" as to an ineffective-assistance claim, and this may justify an exception to the constitutional rule that there is no right to counsel in collateral proceedings.

Martinez, 132 S.Ct. at 1315 (internal citations omitted).

Ultimately, the majority declined to decide whether such a exception existed. Instead, the High Court resolved the case on a more narrow issue, holding for the first time that ineffectiveness of collateral review counsel during an initial collateral proceeding, which serves as the first chance a defendant can raise ineffectiveness claims, may constitute cause for a

Appointment of Counsel/Right to Counsel

procedural default in a federal *habeas* matter.[29] The ***Martinez*** Court, nevertheless, reiterated the precise rationale explained in ***Commonwealth v. Figueroa***, 29 A.3d 1177 (Pa. Super. 2011), and also mentioned in ***Commonwealth v. Masker***, 34 A.3d 841, 846 n.4 (Pa. Super. 2011) (Bowes, J., concurring and dissenting), and ***Commonwealth v. Ford***, 44 A.3d 1190, 1199-1200 (Pa. Super. 2012). Both ***Figueroa*** and the ***Masker*** concurring and dissenting opinion were authored prior to the ***Martinez*** decision.

While the Pennsylvania Superior Court in ***Figueroa*** did not discuss whether a possible Pennsylvania constitutional right existed, in a concurring and dissenting opinion in ***Commonwealth v. Masker***, 34 A.3d 841 (Pa. Super. 2011) (*en banc*), four judges joined in noting that the Pennsylvania Constitution expressly entitles all defendants to an as-of-right direct appeal,[30] which at the time the Pennsylvania Constitution

---

29 In his ***Martinez*** dissent, Justice Scalia, joined by Justice Thomas, contended that the majority's decision was the equivalent of creating a constitutional right to initial collateral review counsel during the first proceeding, though not any appeal. The dissent continued that the majority's reasoning could be expanded to ***Brady*** claims, other newly-discovered evidence matters, and the ineffectiveness of direct appeal counsel since such issues cannot generally be raised until a state collateral proceeding.

Of course, if a federal constitutional right to counsel during the initial first-time collateral proceeding exists, *i.e.*, before a PCRA court in Pennsylvania, it would necessarily encompass the other examples Justice Scalia provided since the same proceeding would be used to raise those claims. At the same time, a newly-discovered fact claim presumably might not be discovered and brought during the initial PCRA case, thus, Justice Scalia's concern with whether counsel would be constitutionally required in this scenario is sound. Sadly, neither Justice Scalia or Justice Thomas engaged in any originalist analysis.

30 The Pennsylvania Constitution actually guarantees more than one

was amended to provide for that right included the ability to raise ineffectiveness claims on direct appeal. Thus, the same rationale for why a federal constitutional right to counsel would exist during collateral review also applies to the state constitutional right. However, it must be noted that Pennsylvania does technically still permit defendants to raise ineffectiveness claims during direct appeal if they waive PCRA review and the trial court develops an evidentiary record and discusses the issue(s) in an opinion. *See **Commonwealth v. Holmes**,* 79 A.3d 562 (Pa. 2013); ***Commonwealth v. Bomar***, 826 A.2d 831(Pa. 2003); *compare **Trevino v. Thaler***, 133 S.Ct. 1911 (2013).

An originalist would be hard-pressed to conclude that a Sixth Amendment right to counsel or an Article I, § 9 right to counsel exist during the PCRA. This is because the Sixth Amendment and Article I, § 9 right to counsel provisions, by their plain language, apply solely to prosecutions. *See **Evitts v. Lucey***, 469 U.S. 387, 408-410 (1985) (Rehnquist, J., dissenting). Historically, in Pennsylvania, unless there was a *request* for counsel, the court was only required to appoint a trial attorney in capital cases. *See **Commonwealth ex rel. McGlinn v. Smith***, 24 A.2d 1, 4-6 (Pa. 1942); ***but see Commonwealth ex rel. Schultz v. Smith***, 11 A.2d 656 (Pa. Super. 1940).

Of course, when the original Pennsylvania Constitution of 1776 and the subsequent constitution of 1790 were ratified, felonies such as murder, rape, robbery, burglary, and arson were all classified as capital crimes. ***Commonwealth v. Wade***, 33 A.3d 108 (Pa. Super. 2011) (citing ***Hackett v. Commonwealth***, 15 Pa. 95 (1850)). Thus, defendants were entitled to appointment of

---

as-of-right direct appeal as petitioners have a right to an appeal from PCRA matters. ***Commonwealth v. Morris***, 771 A.2d 721, 732 n.9 (Pa. 1996). In *Evitts v. Lucey*, 469 U.S. 387 (1985), the United States Supreme Court held that a right to effective assistance of counsel exists on an initial as-of-right appeal.

counsel for serious crimes, *i.e.*, felonies. Nonetheless, appointment of counsel was not required when seeking relief via *habeas corpus*. Indeed, the common law writ of *habeas corpus* was confined to challenging jurisdiction and not custody after a conviction, the latter being reserved for a writ of error/appeal. **Commonwealth ex rel. Lewis v. Ashe**, 7 A.2d 296 (Pa. 1939). Once *habeas corpus* became a frequent method of raising collateral claims, counsel was not required.

On the other hand, the due process of law clause of the federal constitution and the law of the land provision of the Pennsylvania Constitution have, even under a restricted view of those provisions, been read to require that proceedings follow written constitutional and statutory law. **See In re Winship**, 397 U.S. 358, 382 (1970) (Black, J., dissenting). Statutory law in Pennsylvania expressly guaranteed a right to counsel under the PCHA for indigent defendants, and the criminal rules of procedure currently assure that right under the PCRA. Hence, the "law of the land" requires counsel during a first-time PCRA proceeding. Of course, the legislature or Pennsylvania Supreme Court could choose to remove that requirement thereby removing it from the law of the land.

Only if removal of this right would infringe on a specific provision of the federal or Pennsylvania Constitution or the "settled usages and modes of proceeding existing in the common and statute law of England," **Murray v. Hoboken Land & Imp. Co.**, 59 U.S. 272, 277 (1855), would there be a constitutional violation. Therefore, an originalist argument for a constitutional due process right to counsel exists, but recognizes that the constitutional right could be removed if the state decided not to afford counsel to petitioners during the PCRA process.

In **Commonwealth v. Smith**, 121 A.3d 1049 (Pa. Super. 2015), the petitioner did allege that he had a federal due process right to effective PCRA counsel during his initial PCRA proceeding. In addition, he argued that the PCRA court's Rule 907 notice was inadequate because it did not inform him that he had to challenge PCRA counsel's ineffectiveness in response. He advanced these positions to overcome the fact that he had not presented his claims of PCRA counsel ineffectiveness before the PCRA court.

Although the *Smith* panel noted that procedural due process protections applied in the PCRA setting it did not fully confront the constitutional argument advanced above and concluded that the petitioner's claims of PCRA counsel ineffectiveness were waived. It highlighted that the PCRA court issued Rule 907 notice but did not dismiss the petition for approximately five months after that notice. The *Smith* Court reasoned that the petitioner could have consulted with an attorney or the court regarding presevering his PCRA counsel ineffectiveness issues. It held that the PCRA court was not required to specifically instruct the petitioner on the manner of raising claims of PCRA counsel ineffectiveness.

If petitioners have a constitutional right to effective assistance of counsel during a first time PCRA, the courts, it would seem, would be obligated to address issues of PCRA counsel's ineffectiveness even when raised for the first time on appeal so long as they are represented by new counsel or are proceeding *pro se*. (This is different from the situation where the defendant is represented during appeal and counsel files a brief and the defendant alleges appellate counsel has been ineffective. In this situation the bar against hybrid representation arises).

Having seen first hand, at both the trial and appellate levels the manner in which counsel handle PCRA petitions, I am sympathetic to Justice Baer's concern that not addressing a claim of PCRA counsel for the first time on appellate review effectively removes a defendant's right to effective

Appointment of Counsel/Right to Counsel

representation during the PCRA process. *See also Commonwealth v. Hill*, 16 A.3d 484 (Pa. 2011); *Id.* at 498 (Saylor, J., dissenting) ("in light of the ongoing developments in this area--including the apparent curtailment of an enforcement mechanism to assure the evenhanded enforcement of a capital post-conviction petitioner's rule-based right to assistance of counsel and the concomitant requirement of effective stewardship--I am unable to support the rigid application of *Lord's* bright line rule in the present [PCRA] setting."); *Commonwealth v. Paddy*, 15 A.3d 431, 479 (Pa. 2011) (Saylor, J., dissenting) ("a majority of the Court now appears to be suggesting that there effectively can be no state-level redress for such deficient stewardship.").

That same experience also lends support to Chief Justice Castille's concern that reviewing claims of PCRA counsel ineffectiveness does grant petitioners an as-of-right ability to litigate new, unlimited, claims on PCRA appeal. One solution to the problem is to amend the rules of criminal procedure to provide a requirement that PCRA courts provide a notice of dismissal in all cases, even after an evidentiary hearing, and mandate that any issues regarding PCRA counsel's effectiveness during the PCRA process be raised within a response requesting opportunity to file an amended petition or be waived. *See Commonwealth v. Henkel*, 90 A.3d 16 (Pa. Super. 2014) (*en banc*). Another alternative would be to entirely eliminate the notice of dismissal process and instead allow a post-PCRA motion following dismissal, and mandate the issue be raised therein. *Commonwealth v. Henkel*, 90 A.3d 16 (Pa. Super. 2014) (*en banc*).[31]

While these changes would not entirely resolve the matter as PCRA counsel could presumably be ineffective during the

---

[31] The courts could also decide to allow counsel to raise their own ineffectiveness.

Appointment of Counsel/Right to Counsel

appellate process, it would undoubtedly reduce claims of PCRA ineffectiveness being raised for the first time on appeal. (During the appellate process, counsel could fail to file a brief or file an inadequate brief, however, the appellate courts could simply require that attorney file an appropriate brief). Such a rule would also alleviate Chief Justice Castille's concern about substitute PCRA counsel entering a case after the appeal has been filed and alleging prior PCRA counsel was ineffective without affording the PCRA court a chance to address any issues regarding the effectiveness of PCRA counsel.[32]

It would, however, be problematic in the context that the petitioner on a first-time petition will be represented by counsel at the time and counsel is unlikely to file a response to the notice of dismissal (or a post-PCRA motion) alleging his own ineffectiveness. *See* Pa.R.Crim.P. 904(E) (appointment of counsel shall be effective throughout the post-conviction collateral proceedings, including any appeal). The PCRA court could, upon receipt of a *pro se* motion alleging ineffectiveness of PCRA counsel on a first-time PCRA, hold a colloquy to determine if the person wishes to proceed *pro se* and then address the issue. Otherwise, in some instances the issue of duel

---

[32] If counsel did enter the process after the appeal, the court could simply remand for the appropriate hearing on the issue or from its review of the record conclude that the issue did not warrant relief. *See* ***Commonwealth v. McBee***, 520 A.2d 10 (Pa. 1986); ***Commonwealth v. Grant***, 813 A.2d 726 (Pa. 2002) (Saylor, J., concurring). This situation would still give rise to Chief Justice Castille's jurisdictional concern with addressing such issues. Perhaps the best solution to the problem, in capital cases, would be to afford unitary review with specific competency and case load requirements for collateral/direct appeal counsel, close supervision by the court over collateral review representation, and mandatory evidentiary hearings. *See* ***Commonwealth v. Spotz***, 18 A.3d 244 (Pa. 2011) (Castille, C.J., concurring); *see also* 42 Pa.C.S. Section 9571-9579, suspended by Pennsylvania Supreme Court order of August 11, 1997.

representation that prevents courts from addressing *pro se* documents filed by defendants represented by counsel would have to be set aside for purposes of the filing of a *pro se* response to a notice of dismissal alleging ineffective assistance of PCRA counsel. This did not appear to be problematic for the Pennsylvania Supreme Court in **Commonwealth v. Pitts**, 981 A.2d 875 (Pa. 2009), although counsel therein was being permitted to withdraw.

There is, of course, no perfect solution to protecting a right to effective PCRA representation. Differing mandatory competency provisions for both non-capital and capital PCRA would prove beneficial, as would PCRA courts more closely monitoring the process and strictly following the procedural rules already promulgated.[33] For example, courts should regularly require defective petitions to be amended or mandate that counsel provide briefs/memorandum of law within a set time period and sanction counsel who fail to comply.[34]

The Supreme Court, for its own part, has recognized the implications of its holdings in **Commonwealth v. Holmes**, 79 A.3d 562 (Pa. 2013). It opined that the Court "has struggled with the question of how to enforce the 'enforceable' right to effective PCRA counsel within the strictures of the PCRA, as the statute was amended in 1995." *Holmes*, 79 A.3d at 584. The Court suggested that **Martinez v. Ryan**, 132 S.Ct. 1309 (2012), offered a solution at the federal level. It added that any state redress "should await either the action of the General Assembly —in response to **Martinez** and cases such as **Ligons**, and **Pitts**—

---

[33] Currently, capital PCRA counsel are required to meet certain criteria to serve as counsel. *See* Comment to Pa.R.Crim.P. 904 citing Pa.R.Crim.P. 801.

[34] Page limits should be closely monitored so as to force attorneys to winnow their arguments and not simply provide boilerplate allegations and overwhelm the courts with three hundred page briefs.

Appointment of Counsel/Right to Counsel

or a case where the issues is properly joined." *Holmes*, 79 A.3d at 584; *see also Commonwealth v. Henkel*, 90 A.3d 16 (Pa. Super. 2014) (*en banc*). Since PCRA counsel ineffectiveness was not at issue in *Holmes*, it declined to attempt a court remedy.

C. Hybrid Representation and Allegations of PCRA Counsel's Ineffectiveness after the Filing of a Brief on Appeal

The Superior Court, prior to the *Grant* decision, followed a general policy of forwarding defendant's *pro se* filings, alleging appellate counsel was ineffective for neglecting to raise a certain issue on appeal, to appellate counsel and requesting that counsel file a motion for remand detailing why they did not assert certain issues. *See Commonwealth v. Lawrence*, 596 A.2d 165 (Pa. Super. 1991). This policy was continued after the decision in *Grant* in *Commonwealth v. Battle*, 879 A.2d 266 (Pa. Super. 2005). In *Commonwealth v. Jette*, 947 A.2d 202 (Pa. Super. 2008), *abrogated in part by* 23 A.3d 1032 (Pa. 2011), and *Commonwealth v. Warren*, 979 A.2d 920 (Pa. Super. 2009) *abrogated by Jette*, 23 A.3d 1032, the majority cited to *Battle* in discussing the procedure to be followed during a PCRA appeal where a petitioner files a *pro se* document alleging that appellate PCRA counsel is ineffective. The procedure required counsel to file a petition for remand detailing the nature and extent of his review of the record, and provide a discussion with pertinent legal authority for why he did not raise certain issues on appeal. Essentially, counsel was to file a *Turner/Finley* no-merit letter relative to the issues that the appellant wanted to raise and that counsel had declined to set forth in his or her brief.

The Pennsylvania Supreme Court overturned the *Battle* procedure in *Commonwealth v. Jette*, 23 A.3d 1032 (Pa. 2011). In *Jette*, the defendant was convicted of various sex crimes involving abuse of an eight-year-old boy. During Jette's direct appeal he raised ineffective assistance of counsel claims that the Superior Court addressed. The Superior Court affirmed Jette's conviction in a published case. *See Commonwealth v. Jette*, 818 A.2d 533 (Pa. Super. 2003). Jette then filed a timely PCRA petition and counsel was appointed. Counsel initially filed a *Turner/Finley* no-merit letter. However, after Jette objected to the *Turner/Finley* no-merit letter, counsel filed an amended petition. The PCRA court conducted a hearing and denied Jette's petition. Counsel then filed an appeal and a brief with the Superior Court raising only one issue.

Jette thereafter submitted a *pro se* filing alleging PCRA counsel was ineffective for not raising additional issues on appeal. The Superior Court directed counsel to file a motion for remand addressing the *pro se* allegations. PCRA counsel complied and the Superior Court remanded for counsel to again file a motion for remand, but found that counsel could not argue that an issue was waived for not being included in a *pro se* petition since counsel's duty was to amend the petition.

Counsel filed a motion for remand and the Superior Court, in an unpublished memorandum, remanded for the appointment of new counsel. The Pennsylvania Supreme Court granted allowance of appeal and reversed. It held that there is no right to hybrid representation and, once counsel files an appellate brief, the Superior Court must address only the counseled brief and cannot require counsel to respond to *pro se* filings. *Commonwealth v. Jette*, 23 A.3d 1032 (Pa. 2011).[35]

---

35 The Supreme Court decision in *Jette* is sound with respect to barring hybrid representation. However, it declined to accept any responsibility for actually creating the problem. In *Commonwealth v. Ellis*, 626 A.2d 1137, 1139 (Pa. 1993), the decision relied on by the Superior Court in creating the *Battle* procedure, the Supreme Court specifically quoted from the Superior Court's *en banc Ellis* decision stating:

Appointment of Counsel/Right to Counsel

Another issue with ***Commonwealth v. Battle***, 879 A.2d 266 (Pa. Super. 2005), and the Superior Court's decision in ***Jette***, arose from the view among the majority of justices that ***Battle*** permitted defendants to file serial petitions raising new issues for the first time on appeal. According to the Supreme Court in ***Jette***, ***Battle*** permitted petitioners to circumvent the one-year time-bar and the serial petition miscarriage of justice standard.

> For these reasons, [the] Superior Court stated its holding as follows:
>
> We will accept for filing *pro se* appellate briefs, but we will not review a *pro se* brief if a counseled brief has been filed, either before, simultaneously with, or after the *pro se*, due to the judicial confusion and delay that ensues. Because we refuse to play a timing game or that of a mind reader, trying to determine what the *pro se really* wants, we see no difference as to when the *pro se* brief is filed in relation to the counseled brief. If a *pro se* brief is filed in a counseled appeal, we direct the prothonotary to send the *pro se* brief on to counsel who is best able to determine in her [sic] professional judgment which of the *pro se's* issues should be presented for our review. Counsel may argue such pertinent issues in her [sic] brief to the court, or if the appellate brief has been filed, she [sic] may file a supplemental brief addressing those same issues. If the *pro se* brief alleges ineffectiveness of appellate counsel or an affirmative desire to be heard *pro se,* we direct counsel to petition this court to remand the case to the trial court so that it may conduct a full hearing in order to determine appellant's knowing and intelligent waiver of his right to appellate counsel, and of his desire to proceed *pro se,* or in the case of ineffectiveness, an appointment of new appellate counsel.

Thus, the majority adopted Chief Justice Castille's position relative to raising claims of PCRA counsel ineffectiveness for the first time on appeal.

---

398 Pa. Super. at 550, 581 A.2d at 600-01. Accordingly, [the] Superior Court declined to review appellant's *pro se* brief. For the reasons that follow, we affirm.

The Supreme Court in *Ellis* did not find the Superior Court's procedure inappropriate; indeed, it concluded that the Superior Court "thoughtfully and fairly" addressed the issue. *Ellis*, 626 A.2d at 1141. Hence, it is not surprising that the Superior Court determined that the Supreme Court did not disapprove of the procedure that was subsequently overturned.

Chapter 18: Rule 905
Amendment and Withdrawal of Petition

(A) The judge may grant leave to amend or withdraw a petition for post-conviction collateral relief at any time. Amendment shall be freely allowed to achieve substantial justice.

(B) When a petition for post-conviction collateral relief is defective as originally filed, the judge shall order amendment of the petition, indicate the nature of the defects, and specify the time within which an amended petition shall be filed. If the order directing amendment is not complied with, the petition may be dismissed without a hearing.

(C) Upon the entry of an order directing an amendment, the clerk of courts shall serve a copy of the order on the defendant, the defendant's attorney, and the attorney for the Commonwealth.

(D) All amended petitions shall be in writing, shall comply substantially with Rule 902, and shall be filed and served within the time specified by the judge in ordering the amendment.

> *Comment*: "Defective," as used in paragraph (B), is intended to include petitions that are inadequate, insufficient, or irregular for any reason; for example, petitions that lack particularity; petitions that do not comply substantially with Rule 902; petitions that appear to be patently frivolous; petitions that do not allege facts that would support relief; petitions that raise issues the defendant did not preserve properly or were finally determined at prior proceedings.
>
> When an amended petition is filed pursuant to

paragraph (D), it is intended that the clerk of courts transmit a copy of the amended petition to the attorney for the Commonwealth. This transmittal does not require a response unless one is ordered by the judge as provided in these rules. *See* Rules 903 and 906.

Note: Previous Rule 1505 adopted January 24, 1968, effective August 1, 1968; rescinded December 11, 1981, effective June 27, 1982; rescission vacated June 4, 1982; rescinded February 1, 1989, effective July 1, 1989, and replaced by Rules 1506(b), 1508(a), and present Rule 1505(c). Present Rule 1505 adopted February 1, 1989, effective July 1, 1989; amended August 11, 1997, effective immediately; renumbered Rule 905 and amended March 1, 2000, effective April 1, 2001; *Comment* revised September 21, 2012, effective November 1, 2012.[36]

Annotated Comments

A. Leave to Amend

The PCRA court is permitted to allow amendment to a petition at any time. Pa.R.Crim.P. 905(A). In non-capital cases, the PCRA court will order appointed counsel to amend the *pro se* petition upon appointment. An amendment to a *pro se* petition is not separately subject to the one-year jurisdictional time bar, *i.e.*, the amended petition relates back to the filing of the *pro se* petition. **Commonwealth v. Flanagan**, 854 A.2d 489 (Pa. 2004); ***see also Commonwealth v. Swartzfager***, 59 A.3d 616 (Pa. Super. 2012). Typical practice also sees attorneys file supplemental amended petitions without requesting court

---

[36] A proposed new Rule 905 was considered in 2014, but not adopted. The new rule would have mandated the court allow one amended petition to be filed as of right. Thereafter, subsequent amendments were only to be granted upon cause shown. The proposed rule did not clarify if the court was to allow an amended petition as of right during serial PCRA proceedings, but appeared to do so. The proposed rules that were not adopted can be found in the 2015 edition of this work.

permission, although the rule requires the court to authorize amendments. Pa.R.Crim.P. 905(A). This practice was frowned upon in **Commonwealth v. Porter**, 35 A.3d 4 (Pa. 2012), where the Supreme Court opined that Rule 905 is not self-authorizing and that the PCRA court must either direct or grant leave to the petitioner to amend a petition. *See also* **Commonwealth v. Roney**, 79 A.3d 595, 615-616 (Pa. 2013); **Commonwealth v. Reid**, 99 A.3d 470 (Pa. 2014); **Commonwealth v. Baumhammers**, 92 A.3d 708 (Pa. 2014); **Commonwealth v. Mason**, 130 A.3d 601 (Pa. 2015).

In **Commonwealth v. Mason**, 130 A.3d 601, the capital petitioner filed an amended petition, several supplemental petitions, as well as a response to the Commonwealth's motion to dismiss over an approximate eleven year period. Neither PCRA judge who presided over the matter expressly granted the petitioner leave to amend the amended petition. The Commonwealth, nonetheless, did not raise any argument before the PCRA court that issues raised in the supplemental filings were not properly raised nor did the PCRA court dismiss any issues on that basis.

On appeal, the Commonwealth argued that those portions of Mason's claims that were raised in the supplemental filings were waived because the petitioner did not obtain leave of court to supplement his petition. The Supreme Court agreed, relying on **Commonwealth v. Baumhammers**, 92 A.3d 708 (Pa. 2014), **Commonwealth v. Reid**, 99 A.3d 470 (Pa. 2014), and **Commonwealth v. Porter**, 35 A.3d 4 (Pa. 2012), for the proposition that a claim must be raised in the petition itself or the court grant leave for amendment.

In **Commonwealth v. Brown**, 141 A.3d 491 (Pa. Super. 2016), the Superior Court cogently distinguished those cases from the situation where the petitioner supplemented the record with additional arguments and the PCRA court did not strike the filings and considered the arguments therein. In *Brown*, after the Commonwealth had filed a response to the petitioner's third amended petition, the petitioner filed a reply that supplemented his petition without express leave of court. Relying on *Commonwealth v. Boyd*, 835 A.2d 812 (Pa. Super. 2003), and *Commonwealth v. Dennis*, 950 A.2d 945, 959 n.11 (Pa. 2008), the *Brown* Court held that where a petitioner files supplemental materials and the court considers those positions, the argument is properly preserved.

It should be highlighted that in non-capital cases, counsel frequently develop their arguments and claims in briefs and supplmental filings and not the petition itself. Indeed, Rule 902, governing petitions, does not require argument or citation to authority. Where the petitioner's filings adequately raise the argument and relevant claim and the PCRA court addresses the issue, waiver should not be found. This is especially so where the Pennsylvania Supreme Court has essentially foreclosed review of PCRA counsel ineffectiveness claims.

The *Porter*, *Roney*, *Baumhammers*, *Reid*, and *Mason* decisions should not be read to require authorization to file an amended petition to raise claims of PCRA counsel ineffectiveness. *See Commonwealth v. Pitts*, 981 A.2d 875 (Pa. 2009); *cf. Commonwealth v. Rykard*, 55 A.3d 1177 (Pa. Super. 2012) (distinguishing between raising non-PCRA counsel ineffectiveness claims and other issues in a response to court's notice of dismissal).

In addition, a response to a notice of intent to dismiss is not considered an amended petition. *See Commonwealth v. Rykard*, 55 A.3d 1177 (Pa. Super. 2012); *Commonwealth v. Williams*, 732 A.2d 1167, 1191-1192 (Pa. 1999); *Commonwealth v. Paddy*, 15 A.3d 431, 471 (Pa. 2011); *Commonwealth v. Derrickson*, 923 A.2d 466 (Pa. Super. 2007); *compare Commonwealth v. Blackwell*, 936 A.2d 497 (Pa. Super. 2007)

Amendment and Withdrawal of Petition

(response to notice that seeks to withdraw the current petition and asks for reinstatement of appellate rights based on governmental interference treated as petition to withdraw and new petition). Hence, when filing a response to a notice of intent to dismiss, counsel should also request leave to amend the petition to correct any defects that precluded the court from reaching the merits, *i.e.*, inadequate development of the **Strickland/Pierce** test. However, a PCRA court's decision not to allow amendment after issuing a notice of dismissal is afforded significant deference. *See **Commonwealth v. Williams**,* 732 A.2d at 1192.

Counsel cannot amend a petition and add new claims following a remand from an appellate court where the remand is limited to a specific issue. ***Commonwealth v. Sepulveda***, 144 A.3d 1270 (Pa. 2016).

B. Amendments and Defective Petitions

A defective petition includes a petition that raises issues that were previously litigated or waived. *See* Comment to Rule 905. An untimely petition is not explicitly included in the definition of a defective petition found in the comment to Rule 905, but the list is non-exclusive. A petition that is on its face untimely, and does not argue a timeliness exception, may be considered defective.

Pursuant to Rule 905, a court shall order an amended petition if the original petition is defective. Pa.R.Crim.P. 905(B). As it currently stands, Rule 905 is complied with on first time PCRA petitions when the court appoints counsel and directs counsel to file an amended PCRA petition or ***Turner/Finley*** no-merit letter. Once counsel files an amended PCRA petition, the PCRA court is not mandated by Rule 905(C) to require counsel to file a subsequent petition if it finds the amended petition defective. ***Commonwealth v. Williams***, 782 A.2d 517, 527 n.7 (Pa.1999); **but see *Commonwealth v. Robinson***, 947 A.2d 710 (Pa. 2008) (*per curiam* order of Supreme Court holding that it is improper to dismiss an amended petition based on the failure to submit witness certifications without providing notice of that defect).

However, where a PCRA court dismisses a petition based on a pleading deficiency without affording counsel an opportunity to amend the petition, an appellate court may remand. *Cf. Commonwealth v. Fears*, 86 A.3d 795 (Pa. 2014) (no remand is necessary where it would be futile). Concomitantly, if the PCRA court does not find a pleading deficient and order an amendment, the Supreme Court has declined to find the issue waived on appeal due to pleading inadequacies at the PCRA level. *Commonwealth v. Simpson*, 66 A.2d 253, 261 (Pa. 2013).

The definition of "defective" discussed in the comments to Rule 905 is in conflict with typical practice pursuant to Rule 907, which permits a court to dismiss a petition in which the petitioner raises claims that are patently frivolous and do not raise any issues of material fact. Thus, on second or subsequent PCRA petitions where no counsel is appointed, the plain language of Rule 905 mandates that the PCRA court order amendment of a *pro se* PCRA if it finds the petition defective. Pa.R.Crim.P. 905(B). If a petitioner files a *pro se* petition it almost certainly will be defective and Rule 905 would require that the petitioner be given a chance to amend his petition. Where a petitioner's PCRA petition is filed utilizing the standard DC-198 pre-printed form, it automatically can be considered defective since it does not require the petitioner to cite or reference case law and boilerplate claims can result in dismissal.

A PCRA court, therefore, is advised that if the serial petition is filed via a pre-printed form, even where the petition appears untimely and only raises issues that have been waived or previously litigated, to order an amended petition setting forth a time period for the petitioner to file his amended petition. Pa.R.Crim.P. 905(B). Once this petition is filed, the court may

Amendment and Withdrawal of Petition

dispose of the petition accordingly. If the petition is not filed within the time-frame directed by the court, then the court may dismiss the PCRA petition. Pa.R.Crim.P. 905(B).

Rule 905's definition of "defective" should also be altered to reflect actual practice since there is ordinarily no reason to order an amended filing where the petition is not a first time petition and the petition is defective. Only where the serial defective petition appears to raise an issue of material fact should the court require a petitioner to amend his petition. Petitions that do not raise issues of fact do not require a hearing and can be decided as a matter of law. *See* Pa.R.Crim.P. 907. If an issue can be decided as a matter of law and no purpose would be served by permitting a petitioner to amend his petition, there should be no need to order an amended petition on a second or subsequent petition.

Rule 905 also permits a court to dismiss a petition without a hearing if it has directed an amended petition to be filed within a certain time frame and that order is not complied with by the petitioner. This portion of the rule only applies, in practice, after at least one amended petition has been filed. The reason for this is because the failure to file an amended petition is considered abandonment on the part of PCRA counsel and petitioners are entitled to at least one counseled PCRA petition. ***Commonwealth v. Williams***, 828 A.2d 981 (Pa. 2003); ***Commonwealth v. Duffey***, 713 A.2d 63 (Pa. 1998); ***Commonwealth v. Karanicolas***, 836 A.2d 940 (Pa. Super. 2003); ***Commonwealth v. Hampton***, 718 A.2d 1250 (Pa. Super. 1998). Thus, the rule is inconsistent with case law finding that a *pro se* petition cannot be dismissed where counsel never files an amended petition. The rule also does not provide any guidance for how long an attorney should have to file an amended petition; accordingly, it is up to the court to direct counsel to review the record and timely submit an amended petition.

Amendment and Withdrawal of Petition

Depending on the complexity of the case, anywhere from thirty to 120 days may be necessary to submit an amended petition. Should counsel fail to file a petition within the period set forth by the court, counsel has abandoned his client and should face sanctions, not limited to fines. Because an attorney may not wish to handle the case, removal may be inappropriate. In rare instances, referral to the Disciplinary Board may be necessary.

Chapter 19: Rule 906
Answer to Petition

(A) Except as provided in paragraph (E), an answer to a petition for post-conviction collateral relief is not required unless ordered by the judge. When the judge has not ordered an answer, the attorney for the Commonwealth may elect to answer, but the failure to file one shall not constitute an admission of the well-pleaded facts alleged in the petition.

(B) Upon the entry of an order directing an answer, the clerk of courts shall serve a copy of the order on the attorney for the Commonwealth, the defendant's attorney, or the defendant if unrepresented.

(C) If the judge orders an answer, the answer shall be in writing and shall be filed and served within the time fixed by the judge in ordering the answer. The time for filing the answer may be extended by the judge for cause shown.

(D) The judge may grant leave to amend or withdraw an answer at any time. Amendment shall be freely allowed to achieve substantial justice. Amended answers shall be in writing and shall be filed and served within the time specified by the judge in granting leave to amend.

(E) Answers in Death Penalty Cases

(1) First Counseled Petitions

(a) The Commonwealth shall file an answer to the first counseled petition for collateral review in a death penalty case.

(b) The answer shall be filed within 120 days of the filing and service of the petition. For good cause shown, the court may order extensions, of up to 90 days each, of the time for

Answer to Petition

filing the answer.

(2) Second and Subsequent Petitions

(a) An answer to a second or subsequent petition for post-conviction collateral relief is not required unless ordered by the judge. When the judge has not ordered an answer, the attorney for the Commonwealth may elect to file an answer.

(b) The answer shall be filed within 120 days of the filing and service of the petition. For good cause shown, the court may order extensions, of up to 90 days each, of the time for filing the answer.

(3) Amendments to Answer. The judge may grant the Commonwealth leave to amend the answer at any time, and amendment shall be freely allowed to achieve substantial justice. Amended answers shall be in writing, and shall be filed and served within the time specified by the judge in granting leave to amend.

> *Comment*: As used in the Chapter 9 rules, "answer" is intended to include an amended answer filed pursuant to paragraphs (D) and (E)(3) of this rule, except where the context indicates otherwise.
>
> Except as provided in paragraph (E), when determining whether to order that the attorney for the Commonwealth file an answer, the judge should consider whether an answer will promote the fair and prompt disposition of the issues raised by the defendant in the petition for post-conviction collateral relief.
>
> Paragraph (E)(1) was added in 1997 to require that the Commonwealth file an answer to the first counseled petition in a death penalty case. For second and subsequent petitions, paragraph (E)(2) would apply.

Answer to Petition

"First counseled petition," as used in paragraph (E)(1), includes petitions on which defendants have elected to proceed pro se pursuant to Rule 904(F)(1)(a). *See also* the Comment to Rule 903.

Note: Previous Rule 1506 adopted January 24, 1968, effective August 1, 1968; *Comment* revised April 26, 1979, effective July 1, 1979; rule rescinded December 11, 1981, effective June 27, 1982; rescission vacated June 4, 1982; *Comment* revised January 28, 1983, effective July 1, 1983; rule rescinded February 1, 1989, effective July 1, 1989, and replaced by Rule 1508. Present Rule 1506 adopted February 1, 1989, effective July 1, 1989; amended August 11, 1997, effective immediately; *Comment* revised January 21, 2000, effective July 1, 2000; renumbered Rule 906 and *Comment* revised March 1, 2000, effective April 1, 2001; amended March 3, 2004, effective July 1, 2004.

Annotated Comments

Only death penalty cases require that the Commonwealth file an answer to a first time PCRA petition. Pa.R.Crim.P. 906(E)(1)(a). In all other cases it is within the discretion of the PCRA court to order the Commonwealth to file an answer. Pa.R.Crim.P 906(A). Answers to second or subsequent capital petitions are not mandated. Pa.R.Crim.P. 906(E)(2)(a). The Commonwealth may voluntarily file an answer if it chooses. Pa.R.Crim.P. 906(A). The failure to file an answer, however, does not automatically result in the well-pled facts of a petition being admitted. Pa.R.Crim.P. 906(A). In death penalty matters, the Commonwealth has 120 days to file its answer after receiving a petition. Pa.R.Crim.P. 906(E)(1)(b).

However, the PCRA court can grant extensions of up to ninety days in order to allow the Commonwealth enough time to review the record and properly respond to a petitioner's PCRA petition. Pa.R.Crim.P. 906(E)(1)(b). When the PCRA court

Answer to Petition

believes that the petitioner has asserted a claim or claims of arguable merit it is recommended that the court direct the Commonwealth to file an answer. Answers in non-capital cases must be filed within the time frame directed by the PCRA court and the court may grant permission to amend an answer at any time. Pa.R.Crim.P. 906(D). Amendments to an answer must be submitted within the time frame designated by the PCRA court. Pa.R.Crim.P. 906(D); Pa.R.Crim.P. 906(E)(3).

Chapter 20: Rule 907

Disposition Without Hearing

Except as provided in Rule 909 for death penalty cases,

(1) The judge shall promptly review the petition, any answer by the attorney for the Commonwealth, and other matters of record relating to the defendant's claim(s). If the judge is satisfied from this review that there are no genuine issues concerning any material fact and that the defendant is not entitled to post-conviction collateral relief, and no purpose would be served by any further proceedings, the judge shall give notice to the parties of the intention to dismiss the petition and shall state in the notice the reasons for the dismissal. The defendant may respond to the proposed dismissal within 20 days of the date of the notice. The judge thereafter shall order the petition dismissed, grant leave to file an amended petition, or direct that the proceedings continue.

(2) A petition for post-conviction collateral relief may be granted without a hearing when the petition and answer show that there is no genuine issue concerning any material fact and that the defendant is entitled to relief as a matter of law.

(3) The judge may dispose of only part of a petition without a hearing by ordering dismissal of or granting relief on only some of the issues raised, while ordering a hearing on other issues.

(4) When the petition is dismissed without a hearing, the judge promptly shall issue an order to that effect and shall advise the defendant by certified mail, return receipt requested, of the right to appeal from the final order disposing of the petition and of the time limits within which

Disposition Without Hearing

the appeal must be filed. The order shall be filed and served as provided in Rule 114.

(5) When the petition is granted without a hearing, the judge promptly shall issue an order granting a specific form of relief, and issue any supplementary orders appropriate to the proper disposition of the case. The order shall be filed and served as provided in Rule 114.

> *Comment*: The judge is permitted, pursuant to paragraph (1), to summarily dismiss a petition for post-conviction collateral relief in certain limited cases. To determine whether a summary dismissal is appropriate, the judge should thoroughly review the petition, the answer, if any, and all other relevant information that is included in the record. If, after this review, the judge determines that the petition is patently frivolous and without support in the record, or that the facts alleged would not, even if proven, entitle the defendant to relief, or that there are no genuine issues of fact, the judge may dismiss the petition as provided herein. A summary dismissal would also be authorized under this rule if the judge determines that a previous petition involving the same issue or issues was filed and was finally determined adversely to the defendant. *See* 42 Pa.C.S. § 9545(b) for the timing requirements for filing second and subsequent petitions. Second or subsequent petitions will not be entertained unless a strong prima facie showing is offered to demonstrate that a miscarriage of justice may have occurred. *See Commonwealth v. Szuchon*, 534 Pa. 483, 486, 633 A.2d 1098, 1099 (1993) (citing *Commonwealth v. Lawson*, 519 Pa. 504, 549 A.2d 107 (1988)). This standard is met if the petitioner can demonstrate either:

Disposition Without Hearing

(1) that the proceedings resulting in the petitioner's conviction were so unfair that a miscarriage of justice occurred which no civilized society can tolerate; or (2) that the petitioner is innocent of the crimes charged. *See Commonwealth v. Szuchon*, 534 Pa. 483, 487, 633 A.2d 1098, 1100 (1993). When the disposition granting a petition reinstates a defendant's direct appeal rights nunc pro tunc, the judge must advise the defendant by certified mail, return receipt requested that a new notice of appeal must be filed within 30 days of the order. The clerk of courts must comply with the notice and docketing requirements of Rule 114 with regard to any orders entered pursuant to this rule. For the requirements for appointment of counsel on second and subsequent petitions, see Rule 904(B). Relief may be granted without a hearing under paragraph (2) only after an answer has been filed either voluntarily or pursuant to court order. A PCRA petition may not be dismissed due to delay in filing except after a hearing on a motion to dismiss. *See* 42 Pa.C.S. § 9543(b) and Rule 908. Nothing in this rule is intended to preclude a judicial district from utilizing the United States Postal Service's return receipt electronic option, or any similar service that electronically provides a return receipt, when using certified mail, return receipt requested.

Note: Previous Rule 1507 adopted January 24, 1968, effective August 1, 1968; rescinded December 11, 1981, effective June 27, 1982; rescission vacated June 4, 1982; amended January 28, 1983, effective July 1, 1983; rescinded February 1, 1989, effective July 1, 1989, and not replaced. Present Rule 1507 adopted February 1, 1989, effective July 1, 1989; amended August 11, 1997, effective immediately; renumbered Rule 907 and amended March 1, 2000, effective April 1, 2001; Comment

Disposition Without Hearing

revised September 18, 2008, effective February 1, 2009; amended July 27, 2012, effective September 1, 2012.

Annotated Comments

Following a review of the record, the PCRA court may dismiss a PCRA petition without holding a hearing if the court determines that there are no genuine issues of material fact and the petitioner is not entitled to relief. If there are no genuine issues of material fact then the petitioner is not entitled to an evidentiary hearing and no purpose would be served by a hearing. ***Commonwealth v. Albrecht***, 994 A.2d 1091 (Pa. 2010). When the court makes such a determination and decides to deny the petition, the judge shall give notice to the parties of the court's intent to dismiss. ***Commonwealth v. Feighery***, 661 A.2d 437 (Pa. Super. 1995); ***Commonwealth v. Morris***, 684 A.2d 1037 (Pa. 1996); ***Commonwealth v. Anderson***, 801 A.2d 1264 (Pa. Super. 2002) (case remanded where no Rule 907 notice was filed and no order in the record advised the defendant of his appellate rights); ***but see Commonwealth v. Pursell***, 749 A.2d 911 (Pa. 2000) (failure to issue notice of intent to dismiss is harmless where petition is untimely); ***Commonwealth v. Taylor***, 65 A.3d 462 (Pa. Super. 2013) (same); ***Commonwealth v. Lark***, 698 A.2d 43 (Pa. 1997) (where oral argument is held no notice of dismissal was required); ***Commonwealth v. Albrecht***, 720 A.2d 693 (Pa. 1998) (notice of intent to dismiss is not necessary where further proceedings are held on petition); *see also* ***Commonwealth v. Hutchinson***, 25 A.3d 277 (Pa. 2011); ***Commonwealth v. Barbosa***, 819 A.2d 81, 87 n.5 (Pa. Super. 2003).

In ***Commonwealth v. Bond***, 630 A.2d 1281 (Pa. Super. 1993), the Superior Court concluded that the PCRA court's failure to issue Rule 907 notice was harmless where counsel had filed a ***Turner/Finley*** no-merit letter and supplied that letter to Bond. ***Bond***, nonetheless, should not be read to eviscerate Rule 907 in

Turner/Finley cases. This is all the more important in light of the Pennsylvania Supreme Court's decision in ***Commonwealth v. Pitts***, 981 A.2d 875 (Pa. 2009), where the Court held that petitioners must raise any claims of PCRA counsel ineffectiveness in response to the PCRA court's notice of dismissal. Accordingly, ***Bond*** is now unsound where the petitioner wishes to contest PCRA counsel's representation.

When the court does not issue a notice of intent to dismiss but the petitioner fails to raise the issue on appeal, the matter will be waived and a remand will not be required. ***Commonwealth v. Carson***, 913 A.2d 220, 232 n.3 (Pa. 2006); ***Commonwealth v. Taylor***, 65 A.3d 462 (Pa. Super. 2013); ***Commonwealth v. Boyd***, 923 A.2d 513, 514 n.1 (Pa. Super. 2007); ***Commonwealth v. Guthrie***, 749 A.2d 502 (Pa. Super. 2000). A court that has been reassigned a PCRA matter cannot deny a petition without a hearing if the prior PCRA court handling the case ordered a PCRA hearing. ***Commonwealth v. King***, 999 A.2d 598 (Pa. Super. 2010). ***King*** was decided based on the coordinate jurisdiction rule.

The ***King*** panel reasoned that one judge already had determined that the petition raised an issue of material fact. Nonetheless, simply because the court enters a scheduling order before the appointment of counsel, as occurred in ***King***, does not mean the court concluded that an issue of material fact was raised. Indeed, the hearing could not have been an evidentiary hearing since counsel was not appointed. Where a PCRA court conducts a thorough review of the record and determines that no issues of material fact are present, it should be free to cancel a scheduled hearing. Nevertheless, in light of ***King***, if a PCRA court is assigned a PCRA case in which another judge has scheduled a hearing, the court must conduct that hearing.

Disposition Without Hearing

The comments to Rule 907 provide that, if the issues have been waived and or previously litigated, no evidentiary hearing is required and the court shall issue a notice of its intent to dismiss. Comment to Pa.R.Crim.P. 907. This comment, however, is in conflict with Rule 905 and its definition of a defective petition, which expresses that a court shall order a first time PCRA petition amended if it is defective. In the instance of a first time petition, no conflict exists because once the court appoints counsel, counsel must be directed to file either an amended petition or a *Turner/Finley* no-merit letter. *See Commonwealth v. Burkett*, 5 A.3d 1260 (Pa. Super. 2010).

However, in the case of a serial PCRA petition, there exists no requirement to appoint counsel. Pa.R.Crim.P. 904. Accordingly, if a petitioner files a petition that is defective, Rule 905 commands that the court direct the filing of an amended petition, whereas Rule 907 permits dismissal where the petition raises no issues of material fact. When defective petitions are filed in the context of a second or subsequent petition, it is common practice for courts to dismiss the petition without ordering an amended petition as mandated by Rule 905. Because a petitioner ordinarily is not prejudiced by a court's dismissal of a defective serial petition without ordering an amended petition and informing the petitioner of the defects in that petition, he will not be entitled to relief based upon a court's failure to direct the filing of an amended PCRA. (*See* annotated comments to Rule 905 for discussion of defective petitions).

Rule 907 and Rule 909 also provide that a notice of intent to dismiss shall state the reasons for the dismissal. The court cannot simply adopt the Commonwealth's position if the Commonwealth was ordered to file an answer, but must make its own determinations for the record. ***Commonwealth v. Williams***, 732 A.2d 1167 (Pa. 1999); *cf. **Commonwealth v. Williams***, 782 A.2d 517, 526 (Pa. 2001) (finding an adequate pre-dismissal notice is necessary); ***Commonwealth v. Rush***, 838

Disposition Without Hearing

A.2d 651 (Pa. 2003) (same). The defendant may respond to the proposed dismissal within twenty days of the filing of the notice. Pa.R.Crim.P. 907(1). Once twenty days have elapsed from the filing of the notice, the judge shall order the petition dismissed or grant leave to file an amended petition or direct the proceedings to continue. The PCRA court is not required to inform a petitioner in its notice that he must raise any claims of PCRA counsel ineffectiveness in response. ***Commonwealth v. Smith***, 121 A.3d 1049 (Pa. Super. 2015). Nonetheless, especially where counsel files a no-merit letter, such a practice by the PCRA court is recommended.

An issue not raised in a petition but raised in a response to a notice of intent to dismiss will not ordinarily entitle the petitioner to relief. ***Commonwealth v. Rykard***, 55 A.3d 1177 (Pa. Super. 2012); ***Commonwealth v. Williams***, 732 A.2d 1167, 1191 (Pa. 1999); ***Commonwealth v. Derrickson***, 923 A.2d 466 (Pa. Super. 2007); *but see* ***Commonwealth v. Pitts***, 981 A.2d 875 (Pa. 2009) (finding that when no evidentiary hearing is conducted, and counsel is granted permission to withdraw, a defendant must raise any issues of ineffectiveness of PCRA counsel to preserve the issue). Rather, the petitioner must request permission to file an amended petition and the court grant the request. ***Commonwealth v. Williams***, 732 A.2d 1167, 1191 (Pa. 1999); ***Commonwealth v. Porter***, 35 A.3d 4 (Pa. 2012); ***Commonwealth v. Derrickson***, 923 A.2d 466 (Pa. Super. 2007); *see also* ***Commonwealth v. Roney***, 79 A.3d 595, 615-616 (Pa. 2013) (issues raised in supplemental petition where PCRA court did not authorize amendment or accept supplemental petition were considered waived); *but see* ***Commonwealth v. Brown***, 141 A.3d 491 (Pa. Super. 2016); ***Commonwealth v. Boyd***, 835 A.2d 812 (Pa. Super. 2003); ***Commonwealth v. Dennis***, 950 A.2d 945, 959 n.11 (Pa. 2008)

The notice of intent to dismiss is similar to Pa.R.A.P. 1925(a), which requires a PCRA court to issue an opinion declaring its

Disposition Without Hearing

reasons for an order that is being appealed. The notice of intent to dismiss requirement can complicate the PCRA process and could be replaced by a rule that requires the final order indicate the reasons for dismissal and permit a PCRA petitioner to file a post-PCRA motion within twenty days challenging the denial.[37]

In the instance where counsel has not been permitted to withdraw, and the petitioner alleges in his response/post-PCRA motion that PCRA counsel was ineffective, the court should

---

[37] Proposed Amendment to Rule 907 abolishing Notice of Intent to Dismiss and establishing post-PCRA motion practice.

> Except as provided in Rule 909 for death penalty cases,
>
> the judge shall promptly review the petition, any answer by the attorney for the Commonwealth, and other matters of record relating to the petitioner's claim(s). If the judge is satisfied from this review that there are no genuine issues concerning any material fact and that the petitioner is not entitled to post-conviction collateral relief, and no purpose would be served by any further proceedings, the judge shall dismiss the petition and shall state the reasons for the dismissal in the manner of an opinion addressing each claim. The petitioner may respond to the final order within twenty days of the docketing of the final order. Where a *Turner/Finley* no-merit letter is filed and the petitioner believes that PCRA counsel rendered ineffective assistance he MUST raise the issue in a *pro se* response or the issue will be waived.
>
> The judge thereafter may grant leave to file an amended petition, schedule an evidentiary hearing, or direct that the proceedings continue.
>
> A petition for post-conviction collateral relief may be granted without a hearing when the petition and answer show that there is no genuine issue concerning any material fact and that the petitioner is entitled to relief as a matter of law.

Disposition Without Hearing

direct proceedings to continue and colloquy the defendant to determine if he wishes to proceed *pro se* to raise PCRA counsel's ineffectiveness. The filing of the post-PCRA motion would not, however, extend the thirty-day period for filing a notice of appeal unless the PCRA court grants the petitioner the right to file an amended petition, schedules a hearing, or directs the proceedings to continue. *See **Commonwealth v. Henkel**,* 90 A.3d 16 (*en banc*). Such a rule would largely eliminate

> The judge may dispose of only part of a petition without a hearing by ordering dismissal of or granting relief on only some of the issues raised, while ordering a hearing on other issues.
>
> When the petition is dismissed without a hearing, the judge promptly shall issue an order to that effect and shall advise the defendant by certified mail, return receipt requested, of the right to appeal from the final order disposing of the petition and of the time limits within which the appeal must be filed. The order shall be filed and served as provided in Rule 114.
>
> When the petition is granted without a hearing, the judge promptly shall issue an order granting a specific form of relief, and issue any supplementary orders appropriate to the proper disposition of the case. The order shall be filed and served as provided in Rule 114.
>
> *Comment*: This rule replaces the prior requirement that the PCRA court issue a notice of intent to dismiss when dismissing a petition without an evidentiary hearing. It also mandates that the PCRA court substantively analyze the issues raised by the petitioner rather than issue a boilerplate order. *See **Commonwealth v. Williams**,* 782 A.2d 517 (Pa. 2001); ***Commonwealth v. Rush**,* 838 A.2d 651 (Pa. 2003). The requirement that a petitioner raise allegations of the ineffectiveness of PCRA counsel when a ***Turner/Finley*** no-merit letter is filed is derived from ***Commonwealth v. Pitts**,* 981 A.2d 875 (Pa. 2009). This would provide petitioners an

Disposition Without Hearing

defendants frequent attempts to raise new non-PCRA counsel ineffectiveness issues in a reply, which is not permitted absent permission to file an amended petition. *Commonwealth v. Williams*, 732 A.2d 1167, 1191 (Pa. 1999); *Commonwealth v. Rykard*, 55 A.3d 1177 (Pa. Super. 2012); *cf. Commonwealth v. Reid*, 99 A.3d 470 (Pa. 2014). Further, courts sometimes neglect to issue a final order after issuing a notice of dismissal, leaving the petitioner in limbo. *See Commonwealth v. Swartzfager*, 59 A.3d 616 (Pa. Super. 2012). Additionally, a court could provide a comprehensive analysis of its reasons for its decision in its final order and incorporate that order in its Pa.R.A.P. 1925(a) opinion.

Nevertheless, a notice of intent to dismiss is an important part of the PCRA process and courts must be careful to issue one even if the defendant purports to be filing a writ of *habeas corpus* or other collateral motion. PCRA courts bearing a heavy caseload often issue a notice of intent to dismiss with the boilerplate language of Pa.R.Crim.P. 907 or the comment thereto, *i.e.*, that the petition is patently frivolous and no purpose would be served by holding an evidentiary hearing. These boilerplate notices do not provide reasons for the dismissal and skirt the reason the rule was crafted, *i.e.*, to allow a petitioner the opportunity to respond to the court's reasons for denying the petition.

Thus, the court has in practical effect failed to address the issues in the petition and has not actually stated the reasons for dismissal. This tactic should not be favored. *See*

---

opportunity to respond, including raising any issues of PCRA counsel's deficient stewardship while the PCRA court retains jurisdiction. Should the petitioner file a *pro se* response while represented by counsel where no *Turner/Finley* no-merit letter is filed it should simply be forwarded to counsel. *See e.g. Commonwealth v. Jette*, 23 A.3d 1032 (Pa. 2011).

Disposition Without Hearing

Commonwealth v. Rush, 838 A.2d 651, 658-660 (Pa. 2003); *Commonwealth v. Williams*, 782 A.2d 517 (Pa. 2001); *cf. Commonwealth v. Glover*, 738 A.2d 460 (Pa. Super. 1999) (PCRA court cannot adopt counsel's *Turner/Finley* no-merit letter in lieu of 1925(a) opinion); *see also Commonwealth v. Washington*, 927 A.2d 586 (Pa. 2007) (Saylor, J., dissenting); *Commonwealth v. Beasley*, 967 A.2d 376, 396 (Pa. 2009). Indeed, the Pennsylvania Supreme Court has held that a notice of intent to dismiss that does not put the petitioner on notice of the court's rationale for dismissing the petition is insufficient. *See Commonwealth v. Rush*, 838 A.2d 651, 658-660 (Pa. 2003); *Commonwealth v. Williams*, 782 A.2d 517 (Pa. 2001); *Commonwealth v. Williams*, 732 A.2d 1167 (Pa. 1999).

Although *Rush* and the *Williams* cases are capital cases pertaining to Rule 909, the rationale the courts provided for sufficiently detailing a PCRA court's reasons for dismissal within its notice of intent to dismiss, to permit counsel an opportunity to respond or amend the petition, applies equally to non-capital cases. *See Commonwealth v. Morris*, 684 A.2d 1037 (Pa. 1996). In 2014, there was a proposed addition to the comment to Rule 907 that included citations to *Commonwealth v. Rush*, 838 A.2d 651 (Pa. 2003), and *Commonwealth v. Williams*, 782 A.2d 517 (Pa. 2001), that set forth that the court issue a sufficient notice. The amendment, however, was not adopted.

In *Commonwealth v. Beasley*, 967 A.2d 376 (Pa. 2009), the Court stated that the general rule requires that the PCRA court adequately address a PCRA petition when it dismisses the petition and give a petitioner an opportunity to cure any defects in a petition. The *Beasley* Court remanded the case for the PCRA court to address all of the petitioner's issues because the PCRA court's reasons for dismissal expressed in its opinion were inadequate. *Beasley* provided that to affirm on another basis would have circumvented the notice of intent to dismiss

Disposition Without Hearing

rule. ***Beasley***, 967 A.2d at 396. While this seems to contradict the oft-stated *mantra* that a court may affirm the PCRA court on any basis supported by the record, *see* ***Commonwealth v. Fisher***, 870 A.2d 864, 870 n.11 (Pa. 2005), it ensures that a court provide adequate reasons for its decision. Of course, the relevant rule requiring a notice of intent to dismiss is only mandatory where an evidentiary hearing is not held, and ***Beasley*** was not a notice of intent to dismiss case.

In ***Beasley***, the court conducted a hearing; thus, a notice of intent to dismiss was not mandated. *See* ***Commonwealth v. Lark***, 698 A.2d 43 (Pa. 1997) (notice of intent to dismiss is not required where an evidentiary hearing is conducted); ***Commonwealth v. Hutchinson***, 25 A.3d 277 (Pa. 2011). Nevertheless, as discussed, in cases where the PCRA court decides to dismiss a petition without a hearing it must adequately address all of the issues raised in the PCRA petition. *See* ***Commonwealth v. Rush***, 838 A.2d 651, 658-660 (Pa. 2003); ***Commonwealth v. Williams***, 782 A.2d 517 (Pa. 2001); *but see* ***Commonwealth v. Smith***, 17 A.3d 873 (Pa. 2011) (inadequate PCRA opinion does not require remand where court can address claims based on record). Therefore, the PCRA court should, in its notice of dismissal, engage in a meaningful analysis of the claims. Such an exercise by the PCRA court will not ordinarily result in extra labor on the part of the court since the PCRA court will have to conduct an examination of the issues for purposes of filing a Pa.R.A.P. 1925(a) opinion.

Once the PCRA court engages in a comprehensive discussion of the issues in its notice of intent to dismiss it can either issue a Pa.R.A.P. 1925(a) order stating that the reasons for its final dismissal of the petition are contained in its notice of dismissal or simply copy and paste the notice of intent to dismiss into a section of its Pa.R.A.P. 1925(a) opinion. Regardless, the PCRA court's notice of intent to dismiss should be an opinion that actually addresses all of the issues raised by a PCRA petition

Disposition Without Hearing

and not a boilerplate statement quoting from the rule of criminal procedure. After the court issues its notice of intent to dismiss it still must issue a final order. The final order dismissing the PCRA petition must be sent to the parties via certified mail and provide notice of the right of appeal and the time in which the appeal may be taken. Pa.R.Crim.P. 907(4).

Where the record supports a petitioner's claim(s) and no additional fact-finding is necessary, a court may grant relief without conducting an evidentiary hearing after the Commonwealth files an answer. Pa.R.Crim.P. 907(2). This author has found no reported cases of the Commonwealth appealing from a decision that granted relief to a petitioner without an evidentiary hearing. The typical issue that will result in relief without an evidentiary hearing is the reinstatement of a defendant's direct appeal rights. In this event, the court is now required to inform the petitioner that he will have thirty days to appeal, unless post-sentence motion rights were also reinstated.

Chapter 21: Rule 908
Evidentiary Hearings

(A) Except as provided in Rule 907, the judge shall order a hearing:

(1) whenever the Commonwealth files a motion to dismiss due to the defendant's delay in filing the petition; or

(2) when the petition for post-conviction relief or the Commonwealth's answer, if any, raises material issues of fact. However, the judge may deny a hearing on a specific issue of fact when a full and fair evidentiary hearing upon that issue was held at trial or at any proceeding before or after trial. The judge shall schedule the hearing for a time that will afford the parties a reasonable opportunity for investigation and preparation, and shall enter such interim orders as may be necessary in the interests of justice.

(B) The judge, on petition or request, shall postpone or continue a hearing to provide either party a reasonable opportunity, if one did not exist previously, for investigation and preparation regarding any new issue of fact raised in an amended petition or amended answer.

(C) The judge shall permit the defendant to appear in person at the hearing and shall provide the defendant an opportunity to have counsel.

(D) Upon the conclusion of the hearing the judge shall determine all material issues raised by the defendant's petition and the Commonwealth's answer, or by the Commonwealth's motion to dismiss, if any.

(1) If the judge dismisses the petition, the judge promptly shall issue an order denying relief. The order shall be filed and served as provided in Rule 114.

Evidentiary Hearings

(2) If the judge grants the petition, the judge promptly shall issue an order granting a specific form of relief, and issue any supplementary orders appropriate to the proper disposition of the case. The order shall be filed and served as provided in Rule 114.

(E) If the judge disposes of the case in open court in the presence of the defendant at the conclusion of the hearing, the judge shall advise the defendant on the record of the right to appeal from the final order disposing of the petition and of the time within which the appeal must be taken. If the case is taken under advisement, or when the defendant is not present in open court, the judge, by certified mail, return receipt requested, shall advise the defendant of the right to appeal from the final order disposing of the petition and of the time limits within which the appeal must be filed.

Comment: The judge's power, under paragraph (A), to deny a hearing on a specific factual issue is intended to apply when an issue of fact already has been heard fully, but has never been determined. The judge need not rehear such an issue, but would be required to determine it under paragraph (D). The 1997 amendment to paragraph (A)(1) requires a hearing on every Commonwealth motion to dismiss due to delay in the filing of a PCRA petition. *See* 42 Pa.C.S. § 9543(b). When the disposition reinstates a defendant's direct appeal rights nunc pro tunc, the judge, pursuant to paragraph (E), also must advise the defendant that a new notice of appeal must be filed within 30 days of the order reinstating the direct appeal rights. The clerk of courts must comply with the notice and docketing requirements of Rule 114 with regard to any orders entered pursuant to this rule. *See also* Rule 909 for procedures in death penalty cases. Except as provided in Rule 902(E)(2) for first counseled petitions in death

Evidentiary Hearings

penalty cases, no discovery is permitted at any stage of the proceedings, except upon leave of the court with a showing of exceptional circumstances. *See* 42 Pa.C.S. § 9545(d)(2). Nothing in this rule is intended to preclude a judicial district from utilizing the United States Postal Service's return receipt electronic option, or any similar service that electronically provides a return receipt, when using certified mail, return receipt requested.

Note: Rule 1508 adopted February 1, 1989, effective July 1, 1989; amended August 11, 1997, effective immediately; renumbered Rule 908 and amended March 1, 2000, effective April 1, 2001; Comment revised September 18, 2008, effective February 1, 2009; amended July 27, 2012, effective September 1, 2012.

Annotated Comments

The Commonwealth is advised to file a motion to dismiss in exceptionally stale cases. This author has seen PCRA petitions that were filed pursuant to the predecessor to the current PCRA statute, which did not require the petition to be filed within one year of the final judgment, from cases originating in the 1970's and 1980's. Although filing such a motion will require the court to schedule a hearing, ***see Commonwealth v. Williams***, 980 A.2d 510 (Pa. Super. 2009), the Commonwealth in such instances can establish prejudice "either in its ability to respond to the petition or in its ability to re-try the petitioner." 42 Pa.C.S. § 9543(b); ***Commonwealth v. Renchenski***, 52 A.3d 251 (Pa. 2012); ***Commonwealth v. Markowitz***, 32 A.3d 706 (Pa. Super. 2011); ***Commonwealth v. Weatherill***, 24 A.3d 435 (Pa. Super. 2011).

As mentioned in discussing Rule 907, a petitioner is not automatically entitled to an evidentiary hearing; only where an issue of material fact is raised will a hearing be necessary.

Commonwealth v. Johnson, 139 A.3d 1257 (Pa. 2016); *Commonwealth v. Albrecht*, 994 A.2d 1091 (Pa. 2010); *Commonwealth v. Payne*, 794 A.2d 902 (Pa. Super. 2002). Where a proposed witness's testimony contradicts the testimony of a victim, an evidentiary hearing may be warranted. *Commonwealth v. Khalifah*, 852 A.2d 1238 (Pa. Super. 2004). A court may dismiss some issues prior to scheduling a hearing if it finds that those issues do not require fact-finding. *See* Pa.R.Crim.P. 907(3); *Commonwealth v. Collins*, 957 A.2d 237 (Pa. 2008). An order dismissing some but not all of the claims is not a final appealable order. Only after all of the petitioner's claims have been dismissed by the court may the petitioner appeal. Pa.Crim.P. 910; **but see *Commonwealth v. Porter*,** 35 A.3d 4 (Pa. 2012).

In addition, the court must decide all of the issues that a petitioner raises, not just the issues on which the evidentiary hearing is held, unless it reinstates a defendant's direct appeal rights. Pa.R.Crim.P. 908(D)(1) (judge shall determine all material issues raised by the defendant's petition); **compare *Commonwealth v. Hoyman*,** 561 A.2d 756 (Pa. Super. 1989) (PCRA court cannot consider merits of ineffectiveness claims where court determines the petitioner was deprived of his direct appeal); *Commonwealth v. Bronaugh*, 670 A.2d 147 (Pa. Super. 1995) (same). This, of course, raises an interesting problem when the *pro se* petition raises numerous claims and the amended petition does not assert each of those issues.

Where an amended petition incorporates all of the *pro se* issues, the PCRA court must address each of the issues alleged in the *pro se* petition, regardless of whether those issues are fully developed. *See generally Commonwealth v. Beasley*, 967 A.2d 376 (Pa. 2009); *Commonwealth v. Daniels*, 963 A.2d 409 (Pa. 2009); *Commonwealth v. Williams*, 950 A.2d 294, 305 (Pa. 2008) ("Deficient stewardship is manifest where, as here, successor lawyers raise the relevant claim but fail to develop it

Evidentiary Hearings

in a fashion which could possibly yield relief, thereby causing the claim to be rejected summarily."). Of course, the failure to fully develop an issue can be grounds for dismissal. ***Commonwealth v. Steele***, 961 A.2d 786 (Pa. 2008), though this precept should generally apply on appeal absent provding an opportunity for counsel to correct any pleading deficiency.

When the amended petition raises only some of the issues originally asserted in the *pro se* petition, only the issues in the amended petition need to be addressed, as the petitioner is not entitled to hybrid representation. ***Commonwealth v. Jette***, 23 A.3d 1032 (Pa. 2011); ***Commonwealth v. Pursell***, 724 A.2d 293 (Pa. 1999). The court must notify a petitioner of his appellate rights when dismissing a petition, which must be done by certified mail if the dismissal does not occur in open court. In ***Commonwealth v. Meehan***, 628 A.2d 1151 (Pa. Super. 1993), the Superior Court found that the failure to properly notify the petitioner of his appellate rights, under the predecessor to Rule 908, excused the petitioner's late notice of appeal. Essentially, the ***Meehan*** Court ruled that there was a breakdown in the judicial system and that it had jurisdiction to consider the appeal.

Chapter 22: Rule 909

Procedures for Petitions in Death Penalty Cases: Stays of Execution of Sentence; Hearing; Disposition

(A) Stays of Execution

(1) In a case in which the defendant has received a sentence of death, any request for a stay of execution of sentence should be made in the petition for post-conviction collateral relief.

(2) In all cases in which a stay of execution has been properly granted, the stay shall remain in effect through the conclusion of all PCRA proceedings, including review in the Supreme Court of Pennsylvania, or the expiration of time for seeking such review.

(B) Hearing; Disposition

(1) No more than 20 days after the Commonwealth files an answer pursuant to Rule 906(E)(1) or (E)(2), or if no answer is filed as permitted in Rule 906(E)(2), within 20 days after the expiration of the time for answering, the judge shall review the petition, the Commonwealth's answer, if any, and other matters of record relating to the defendant's claim(s), and shall determine whether an evidentiary hearing is required.

(2) If the judge is satisfied from this review that there are no genuine issues concerning any material fact, the defendant is not entitled to post-conviction collateral relief, and no legitimate purpose would be served by any further proceedings,

Procedures for Petitions in Death Penalty Cases: Stays of Execution of Sentence; Hearing; Disposition

> (a) the judge shall give notice to the parties of the intention to dismiss the petition and shall state in the notice the reasons for the dismissal.
>
> (b) The defendant may respond to the proposed dismissal within 20 days of the date of the notice.
>
> (c) No later than 90 days from the date of the notice, or from the date of the defendant's response, the judge shall issue an order:
>
> (i) dismissing the petition;
>
> (ii) granting the defendant leave to file an amended petition; or
>
> (iii) ordering that an evidentiary hearing be held on a date certain.
>
> The order shall be filed and served as provided in Rule 114.

(3) If the judge determines that an evidentiary hearing is required, the judge shall enter an order setting a date certain for the hearing, which shall not be scheduled for fewer than 10 days or more than 45 days from the date of the order. The judge may, for good cause shown, grant leave to continue the hearing. No more than 90 days after the conclusion of the evidentiary hearing, the judge shall dispose of the petition.

(4) When the 90-day time periods in paragraphs (B)(2)(c) and (B)(3) must be delayed, the judge, for good cause shown, may enter an order extending the period for not longer than 30 days.

Procedures for Petitions in Death Penalty Cases: Stays of Execution of Sentence; Hearing; Disposition

(5) If the judge does not act within the 90 days mandated by paragraphs (B)(2)(c) and (B)(3), or within the 30 day-extension permitted by paragraph (B)(4), the clerk of courts shall send a notice to the judge that the time period for disposing of the petition has expired. The clerk shall enter the date and time of the notice on the docket, and shall send a copy of the notice to the attorney for the Commonwealth, the defendant, and defense counsel, if any.

(6) If the judge does not dispose of the defendant's petition within 30 days of the clerk of courts' notice, the clerk immediately shall send a notice of the judge's non-compliance to the Supreme Court. The clerk shall enter the date and time of the notice on the docket, and shall send a copy of the notice to the attorney for the Commonwealth, the defendant, and defense counsel, if any.

(7) When the petition for post-conviction collateral relief is dismissed by order of the court,

> **(a) the clerk immediately shall furnish a copy of the order by mail or personal delivery to the Prothonotary of the Supreme Court, the attorney for the Commonwealth, the defendant, and defense counsel, if any.**
>
> **(b) The order shall advise the defendant of the right to appeal from the final order disposing of the petition, and of the time within which the appeal must be taken.**

> *Comment*: Paragraph (A)(1) was added in 1999 to provide the avenue by which a defendant in a death penalty case may request a stay of execution. Failure to include a request for a stay in the petition for post-conviction collateral relief may not be construed as a

waiver, and the defendant may file a separate request for the stay. In cases involving second or subsequent petitions when an application for a stay is filed separately from the PCRA petition, *Commonwealth v. Morris*, 565 Pa. 1, 33-34, 771 A.2d 721, 740-741 (2001) provides that the separate stay application "must set forth: a statement of jurisdiction; if necessary, a statement that a petition is currently pending before the court; and a statement showing the likelihood of prevailing on the merits."

Paragraph (A)(2) provides, if a stay of execution is properly granted, that the stay will remain in effect throughout the PCRA proceedings in the trial court and during the appeal to the Pennsylvania Supreme Court. Nothing in this rule is intended to preclude a party from seeking review of an order granting or denying a stay of execution. *See* Pa.R.A.P. 1702(d) (Stay of Execution) and Pa.R.A.P. 3316 (Review of Stay of Execution Orders in Capital Cases).

Paragraph (B)(3) permits the judge to continue the hearing when there is good cause, such as when the judge determines that briefing and argument are necessary on any of the issues, or when there is a problem with securing the defendant's appearance. It is intended that once a determination is made under paragraph (B)(3) of this rule that an evidentiary hearing is required, the provisions of Rule 908(C), (D), and (E) apply.

Paragraph (B)(4) was added in 2002 to permit the judge to enter an order for one 30-day extension of the 90-day time limit within which the judge must act pursuant to paragraphs (B)(2)(c) and (B)(3) of this rule.

Procedures for Petitions in Death Penalty Cases: Stays of Execution of Sentence; Hearing; Disposition

When the judge extends the time, the judge promptly must notify the clerk of courts of the extension order.

Paragraph (B)(5) addresses the situation in which the judge does not comply with the rule's time limits. The clerk of courts is required to give the judge notice that the 90-day time period, or the 30-day extension, has expired. Further non-compliance requires the clerk to bring the case to the attention of the Supreme Court, which is responsible for the administration of the unified judicial system. It is expected, if there are extenuating circumstances why the judge cannot act within the time limits of the rule, the judge will provide a written explanation to the Supreme Court.

Paragraph (B)(7) requires the clerk to immediately notify the Prothonotary of the Supreme Court, the attorney for the Commonwealth, the defendant, and defense counsel, if any, that the petition has been denied. This notice is intended to protect the defendant's right to appeal.

When the disposition reinstates a defendant's direct appeal rights nunc pro tunc, the judge must advise the defendant either in person or by certified mail, return receipt requested that a new notice of appeal must be filed within 30 days of the order. The clerk of courts must comply with the notice and docketing requirements of Rule 114 with regard to any orders entered pursuant to this rule.

Note: Previous Rule 1509 adopted February 1, 1989, effective July 1, 1989; renumbered Rule 1510 August 11, 1997, effective immediately. Present Rule 1509 adopted August 11, 1997, effective immediately; amended July 23, 1999, effective September 1, 1999; renumbered Rule 909 and amended March

Procedures for Petitions in Death Penalty Cases: Stays of Execution of Sentence; Hearing; Disposition

1, 2000, effective April 1, 2001; amended February 12, 2002, effective July 1, 2002; amended October 7, 2005, effective February 1, 2006; amended July 27, 2012, effective September 1, 2012.[38]

Annotated Comments

Rule 909 mandates that a capital petitioner request a stay of execution when filing his or her PCRA petition. In *Commonwealth v. Morris*, 771 A.2d 721 (Pa. 2001), the Pennsylvania Supreme Court determined that section 9545(c), relating to stays of execution, is the sole means of requesting a stay of execution. The High Court ruled that it was inappropriate to award a stay of execution where the PCRA court concluded that the PCRA petition did not warrant substantive relief. *Morris*, 771 A.2d 721.

Additionally, Rule 909 applies only to death penalty cases and is the sole PCRA rule of criminal procedure that sets forth specific time-frames that the Commonwealth and court are to follow. Although time periods are provided in the rule, death penalty cases routinely take years to decide because petitioners have no incentive to urge that the matter be heard and determined expediently. *See Commonwealth v. Spotz*, 18 A.3d 244 (Pa. 2011) (Castille, C.J., concurring); *Commonwealth v. Birdsong*, 24 A.3d 319 (Pa. 2011) (Castille, C.J., concurring); *Commonwealth v. Hill*, 16 A.3d 484, 494 (Pa. 2011).

Rule 909 must also be read in conjunction with Rule 906 with respect to the filing of an answer by the Commonwealth. Pa.R.Crim.P. 909(B)(1). The Commonwealth must file an

---

38 In 2014 a significant revision to Rule 909 was evaluated by the Pennsylvania Supreme Court, but not adopted. The proposed rule change would have mandated an evidentiary hearing in all first time capital PCRA proceedings and lengthened the period to decide a petition after the conclusion of the hearing from 90 to 180 days.

Procedures for Petitions in Death Penalty Cases: Stays of Execution of Sentence; Hearing; Disposition

answer in death penalty cases where it is the petitioner's first time petition. Pa.R.Crim.P. 906(E)(1)(a). According to Pa.R.Crim.P. 906, the Commonwealth has 120 days from the filing of the petition to file said answer. Once the Commonwealth files its answer, the court has twenty days to decide that an evidentiary hearing is necessary or issue a notice of intent to dismiss. Pa.R.Crim.P. 909(B)(1). If an evidentiary hearing is required, the court shall set the hearing not fewer than ten days from the scheduling order but not more than forty-five days from the date of the order. Pa.R.Crim.P. 909(B)(3). The PCRA court may continue the hearing upon good cause shown. Pa.R.Crim.P. 909(B)(3). Thereafter, the court has ninety days from the conclusion of the evidentiary hearing to decide the petition. Pa.R.Crim.P. 909(B)(3). One thirty-day extension may occur. Pa.R.Crim.P. 909(B)(4).

In the instance where a court issues a notice of intent to dismiss during a capital PCRA matter, the court has ninety days from either the issuance of its Pa.R.Crim.P. 909 pre-dismissal notice or the petitioner's response to file its final order. Pa.R.Crim.P. 909(B)(2)(c). Where no answer is required, *i.e*, during a serial PCRA proceeding, the court also has 140 days to determine if a hearing is necessary or issue a pre-dismissal notice. Pa.R.Crim.P. 909(B)(1); Pa.R.Crim.P. 906(E)(2)(b). For a discussion on the notice of intent to dismiss requirements see the annotated comments under Rule 907.

Delays in death penalty PCRA cases frequently occur where an evidentiary hearing is held but the hearing is not concluded on a single day and the matter is continued for additional hearings. In these instances, there are no time frames in which the court must schedule the second or subsequent date for the hearing and frequently there are lengthy delays in capital cases. Therefore, it would appear that additions to the procedural rules are necessary to help alleviate the problem. For example, if a judge continues

Procedures for Petitions in Death Penalty Cases: Stays of Execution of Sentence; Hearing; Disposition

a hearing for good cause or after a hearing is conducted and an additional hearing is necessary, that subsequent proceeding should be scheduled within 45 days of the previously scheduled matter.

Once ninety days have passed from the filing of the petition or conclusion of the hearing(s), or 120 days if an extension is granted, if no decision has been rendered, the clerk of courts must report the matter to the judge who has not determined the matter. Pa.R.Crim.P. 909(B)(5). If, within thirty days of that notice, the judge still has not acted, the clerk of courts is required to notify the Supreme Court that the trial judge has not complied with the rules. Pa.R.Crim.P. 909(B)(6). Although this rule only applies to death penalty cases, based on this author's practical experience with both the trial court and the Superior Court, the practice should be extended to non-capital cases.[39]

---

39 Proposed Rule (Where Notice of Intent to Dismiss is Maintained)

> In non-capital cases, upon receipt of an amended petition for post-conviction collateral relief, the court shall have ninety days to issue either a notice of intent to dismiss or schedule an evidentiary hearing or award relief. If the PCRA court awards relief in the nature of reinstatement of a defendant's direct appeal rights *nunc pro tunc* it shall issue an order indicating that the defendant has thirty days to perfect his appeal.
>
> If the judge does not act within the 90 days mandated, the clerk of courts shall send a notice to the judge that the time period for issuing a notice of intent to dismiss or schedule a hearing has expired. The clerk shall enter the date and time of the notice on the docket, and shall send a copy of the notice to the attorney for the Commonwealth, the defendant, and defense counsel, if any. If the judge fails to act within 30 days of the clerk of courts' notice, the clerk immediately shall send a notice of the judge's non-compliance to the

Procedures for Petitions in Death Penalty Cases: Stays of Execution of Sentence; Hearing; Disposition

Currently, attorneys and the courts often neglect to address PCRA petitions in a timely fashion. *See Commonwealth v. Burkett*, 5 A.3d 1260 (Pa. Super. 2010) (PCRA court took fifteen years to conduct an evidentiary hearing and sixteen years to decide matter).

PCRA courts also should be aware of dilatory tactics of capital PCRA counsel. *See Commonwealth v. Spotz*, 18 A.3d 244 (Pa. 2011) (Castille, C.J., concurring) (excoriating the Federal

> Supreme Court. The clerk shall enter the date and time of the notice on the docket, and shall send a copy of the notice to the attorney for the Commonwealth, the defendant, and defense counsel, if any.
>
> If the court determines that a hearing is necessary, the judge shall enter an order setting a date certain for the hearing, which shall not be scheduled for fewer than 10 days or more than 45 days from the filing date of the order scheduling the hearing. The judge may, for good cause shown, grant leave to continue the hearing. Where more than one hearing is necessary the court shall schedule any subsequent hearing no more than sixty days from the previous hearing. The judge shall dispose of the petition no more than 90 days after the conclusion of the evidentiary hearing. One thirty day extension may be granted.
>
> If the judge does not act within the 90 days mandated or within the 30 day-extension, the clerk of courts or an attorney in the matter shall send a notice to the judge that the time period for disposing of the petition has expired. The clerk shall enter the date and time of the notice on the docket, and shall send a copy of the notice to the attorney for the Commonwealth, the defendant, and defense counsel, if any. Where an attorney sends the notice he shall file it with the clerk of courts and provide a copy of the notice to the attorney for the Commonwealth and the defendant.

Procedures for Petitions in Death Penalty Cases: Stays of Execution of Sentence; Hearing; Disposition

Defenders for their tactics in PCRA matters); ***Commonwealth v. Birdsong***, 24 A.3d 319 (Pa. 2011) (Castille, C.J., concurring) (opining that the Federal Defenders advanced a frivolous argument to delay the case); ***Commonwealth v. Porter***, 35 A.3d 4 (Pa. 2012). As the Supreme Court noted in ***Commonwealth v. Hill***, 16 A.3d 484, 494 (Pa. 2011), delay itself can be a goal by capital PCRA counsel. The PCRA court is therefore charged with ensuring that the process proceeds in a timely manner. Accordingly, the court itself must be diligent in requiring both parties to act diligently.

In capital PCRA matters, a PCRA court will likely be faced with a PCRA petition that exceeds two hundred pages, as well as lengthy supplemental petitions. With the petitions, any possible supporting briefs, and other motions for discovery or recusal, as well as affidavits, the PCRA court could easily see documents exceeding four hundred pages. As a result, it is imperative that the PCRA court take charge of the proceedings. Most capital petitions contain numerous boilerplate claims that are entirely

> If the judge does not dispose of the petitioner's petition within 30 days of the notice, the clerk immediately shall send a notice of the judge's non-compliance to the Supreme Court. The clerk shall enter the date and time of the notice on the docket, and shall send a copy of the notice to the attorney for the Commonwealth, the petitioner, and defense counsel, if any.
>
> Failure of the judge to resolve the petition under this rule may result in sanctions.
>
> Should counsel fail to file an amended petition as directed, he shall be considered to have abandoned his client and rendered *per se* ineffective assistance of counsel and proper sanctions shall be imposed, including but not limited to being held in contempt and/or removal from the case without pay.

undeveloped, sometimes for strategic reasons. *See* ***Commonwealth v. Steele***, 961 A.2d 786 (Pa. 2008); ***Commonwealth v. Spotz***, 18 A.3d 244 (Pa. 2011).

Upon receipt of a capital PCRA petition, the court should order the petition be amended, direct that failure to develop a claim will result in it being dismissed, and require the amended petition not exceed a certain page limit. This would mandate PCRA counsel tailor the petition rather than submit two hundred page monstrosities. Prior to 2013, briefs on appeal were not to exceed seventy pages.

Therefore, PCRA petitions themselves could be limited to a similar page limit and any supplemental petitions should not exceed twenty-five or thirty pages depending on the complexity of the case. Similarly, the court should not allow PCRA counsel to file a lengthy brief in combination with the petition that is intended to raise additional claims. Where the petition contains argument, as most capital petitions do, a brief is unnecessary. However, a brief is needed where the petition does not develop the claims.

Chapter 23: Rule 910
Final Order

An order granting, denying, dismissing, or otherwise finally disposing of a petition for post-conviction collateral relief shall constitute a final order for purposes of appeal.

Comment: Disposition without a hearing under Rule 907(A) and (B), or under Rule 909(C)(3) (a), constitutes a final order under this rule. A partial disposition under Rule 907(C) is not a final order until the judge has fully disposed of all claims.

When the disposition reinstates a defendant's direct appeal rights *nunc pro tunc*, a new notice of appeal must be filed within 30 days of the order.

Note: Previously Rule 1509, adopted February 1, 1989, effective July 1, 1989; renumbered Rule 1510 and amended August 11, 1997, effective immediately; renumbered Rule 910 and *Comment* revised March 1, 2000, effective April 1, 2001; *Comment* revised July 27, 2012, effective September 1, 2012.

Annotated Comments

An order that denies relief on all issues or grants a new trial is a final appealable order. However, in ***Commonwealth v. Harper***, 890 A.2d 1078 (Pa. Super. 2006), the Superior Court held that a PCRA order granting a new trial, while final for purposes of appeal, is not final with respect to 42 Pa.C.S. § 5505. That statute precludes modification of a final order after thirty days.

A PCRA court's denial of relief of guilt phase claims in a death penalty case, which also awards relief on a sentencing issue is a final order appealable to the Pennsylvania Supreme Court. ***Commonwealth v. Bryant***, 780 A.2d 646 (Pa. 2001). In ***Commonwealth v. Gaines***, 127 A.3d 15 (Pa. Super. 2015) (*en*

Final Order

banc), the Superior Court was divided over whether an appeal was timely where the PCRA court had granted sentencing relief but denied relief in all other respects in a non-capital case. The petitioner did not appeal within thirty days of the PCRA order. Instead, the petitioner appealed within thirty days from being resentenced. In that appeal, he attempted to contest the PCRA court's denial of PCRA relief. The lead opinion, with three judges agreeing in the rationale, relied on Rule 910 and ***Commonwealth v. Bryant***, 780 A.2d 646 (Pa. 2001), and quashed the appeal as untimely. Two judges concurred on separate grounds. Three judges dissented, and would have found that the appeal from the denial of PCRA relief was a timely appeal from the new judgment of sentence. The dissent, ignoring the plain language of Rule 910, and the fact that the rule applies equally to non-capital petitioners, opined that ***Bryant*** only applied in the capital setting.

The ***Gaines*** lead opinion is more faithful to Rule 910 and the applicable appellate rules of procedure. An order that denies relief in part and grants sentencing relief is a final order so long as it disposes of all claims. Accordingly, where a PCRA court files an order that grants relief in part and denies relief in part, a petitioner must file an appeal within thirty days of the PCRA court's order.

Orders that dispose of some but not all of the claims are not final orders. *See* Pa.R.Crim.P. 907(3) (permitting a PCRA court to dismiss certain claims without an evidentiary hearing and conduct a hearing on other claims); Comment to Pa.R.Crim.P. 910; ***but see Commonwealth v. Porter***, 35 A.3d 4 (Pa. 2012). The Court in ***Porter*** was faced with determining whether the order appealed from was interlocutory or final. In ***Porter***, the petitioner originally filed a serial petition alleging that he was mentally challenged, *i.e.*, an ***Atkins*** claim. He subsequently filed a supplemental petition, without

Final Order

authorization from the PCRA court, which raised a *Brady* claim. At the same time, he achieved *habeas* relief in the lower federal courts on a *Mills v. Maryland*, 486 U.S. 367 (1988) jury instruction violation issue. The Commonwealth appealed that federal decision. Porter's attorney argued before the federal court that the federal court should await deciding the case until the PCRA court decided the *Brady* matter. However, he also contended before the PCRA court that it should not resolve the *Atkins* claim until the federal court decided the *Mills* issue. The PCRA court addressed the *Brady* claim, but expressly declined to review the *Atkins* issue. Porter appealed, but on appeal argued that the appeal was interlocutory. The Supreme Court held that the supplemental petition was a separate petition, not a mere amendment to the original *Atkins* petition, and that the PCRA court's resolution of the *Brady* claim was a final order.

Justice Baer penned a dissent in *Porter*, opining that the majority holding could result in multiple final orders and separate appeals for each distinct claim. Indeed, if a petitioner is required to file a new separate serial petition each time he discovers new information, relative to a different claim, rather than merely amend the prior petition, the result would be a procedural quagmire. *See Porter*, 35 A.3d at 28 (Baer, J., dissenting). Petitioners would have to appeal each order denying a single claim separately, resulting in inevitable delay. PCRA courts should, in general, permit petitioners to amend the original petition with any new information and consider supplemental filings, and issue a single final order disposing of each claim. In the event the Commonwealth fails to object to the petitioner's submission of an amended petition and the court addresses the issue, then any claim by the Commonwealth that the PCRA court failed to authorize the amendment should be waived.

In capital cases, the final order is directly appealable to the Pennsylvania Supreme Court, *see Commonwealth v. Morales*,

701 A.2d 516 (Pa. 1997), in all other instances the appeal must be filed with the Superior Court. *See **Commonwealth v. Rompilla***, 983 A.2d 1207 (Pa. 2009) (finding that, after death sentence was overturned and person was sentenced to life imprisonment, the Superior Court had jurisdiction over appeal). An order granting a defendant's request for DNA testing filed pursuant to 42 Pa.C.S. § 9543.1 was held by the Pennsylvania Supreme Court to be a final appealable order. ***Commonwealth v. Scarborough***, 64 A.3d 602 (Pa. 2013).

The Pennsylvania Supreme Court also has concluded that it has jurisdiction to determine a Commonwealth appeal from a decision to stay an execution after the PCRA court dismissed the petition, although the order staying the execution was not a final order. ***Commonwealth v. Morris***, 771 A.2d 721 (Pa. 2001). In addition, a notice of intent to dismiss is not a final order and any appeal filed from such an order is premature. *See **Commonwealth v. Swartzfager***, 59 A.3d 616 (Pa. Super. 2012). However, if the PCRA court subsequently enters a final order the appeal from the notice of intent to dismiss will be considered proper under Pa.R.A.P. 905.

Author's note: The Comment to Rule 910 includes a reference to Rule 909(C)(3)(a). There no longer is a Rule 909(C)(3)(a), and the analogous provisions are Rule 909(B)(2)(c) and Rule 909(B)(7).

Chapter 24:
Standard and Scope of Review

On appeal, the appellate courts have set forth that their standard of review is limited to deciding whether the PCRA court's findings are supported by the record and free of legal error. *Commonwealth v. Johnson*, 966 A.2d 523 (Pa. 2009). When evaluating a PCRA court's decision, the courts have also delineated their scope of review as being limited to the findings of the PCRA court and the evidence of record, viewed in the light most favorable to the prevailing party at the PCRA level. *Commonwealth v. Colavita*, 993 A.2d 874 (Pa. 2010). The courts have, however, conflated the scope and standard of review, which are two distinct terms.

Scope of review is "what" the court examines, whereas, standard of review is "how" that analysis is conducted. *See* **Summers v. Certainteed Corp.**, 997 A.2d 1152, 1160 n. 11 (Pa. 2010). The latter part of the scope of review delineated by the Supreme Court and followed by the Superior Court, *i.e.*, reviewing the record in a light most favorable to the prevailing party at the PCRA court level, is actually more properly part of the court's standard of review.

Where an appellate court's review focuses on the PCRA court's application of the proper legal principles and a petitioner's appeal raises solely questions of law, the appropriate standard of review is *de novo* and the scope of review plenary. *Commonwealth v. Colavita*, 993 A.2d 874 (Pa. 2010); *Commonwealth v. Fahy*, 959 A.2d 312 (Pa. 2008) (scope of timeliness provisions presents question of law and standard of review is therefore *de novo*); *Commonwealth v. Mallory*, 941 A.2d 686 (Pa. 2008); *Commonwealth v Smith*, 818 A.2d 494 (Pa. 2003). Additionally, when the issue presents a mixed question of law and fact, as stated in *Commonwealth v. Reaves*,

Standard and Scope of Review

923 A.2d 1119, 1124 (Pa. 2007), "[t]he level of deference to the hearing judge may vary depending upon whether the decision involved matters of credibility or matters of applying the governing law to the facts as so determined." *See also Commonwealth v. Martin*, 5 A.3d 177, 198-199 (Pa. 2010); *Commonwealth v. Cox*, 983 A.2d 666 (Pa. 2009).

Where the court summarily dismisses a petition without an evidentiary hearing, the petitioner must demonstrate that he raised a genuine issue of fact that if resolved in his favor would warrant relief. The appellate court will review a PCRA court's determination that an evidentiary hearing is not required under an abuse of discretion standard. *Commonwealth v. Baumhammers*, 92 A.3d 708, 726-727 (Pa. 2014).

Appellate courts defer to the factual findings of the PCRA court where the record supports those findings, even if the record may support contrary findings. *Commonwealth v. Rathfon*, 899 A.2d 365 (Pa. Super. 2006); *Commonwealth v. Carr*, 768 A.2d 1164 (Pa. Super. 2001). A PCRA court's credibility determinations are also binding upon our courts of appeals. *Commonwealth v. Clark*, 961 A.2d 80 (Pa. 2008). Of course, an appellate court may affirm a PCRA court's determination on any basis supported by the record. *Commonwealth v. Fisher*, 870 A.2d 864, 870 n.11 (Pa. 2005); *Commonwealth v. Burkett*, 5 A.3d 1260 (Pa. Super. 2010).

Chapter 25:
A Brief Word on Juvenile Matters

Juveniles are entitled to effective assistance of counsel during an adjudicatory and dispositional hearing. *Matter of Smith*, 573 A.2d 1077 (Pa. Super. 1990) (*en banc*) (majority of judges agreed that juveniles have right to effective counsel). However, a juvenile who is not charged as an adult is not entitled to PCRA relief or review. *In re A.J.*, 829 A.2d 312 (Pa. Super. 2003); *In re B.S.*, 831 A.2d 151 (Pa. Super. 2003). Accordingly, juveniles must raise any issues of counsel's ineffectiveness on direct appeal. This may require counsel to allege his own ineffectiveness. *In re B.S.*, 831 A.2d 151 (Pa. Super. 2003). Neither *Commonwealth v. Grant*, 813 A.2d 726 (Pa. 2002), nor *Commonwealth v. Hubbard*, 372 A.2d 687 (Pa. 1977), apply to when the claims must be asserted. *In re B.S.*, 831 A.2d 151 (Pa. Super. 2003) (discussing inapplicability of *Grant*); *Matter of Smith*, 573 A.2d 1077 (Pa. Super. 1990); *In re K.A.T.*, 69 A.3d 691 (Pa. Super. 2013) (Bowes, J., concurring).

Moreover, *Hubbard* never applied to juvenile cases because post-dispositional motions were not mandated. *In re K.A.T.*, 69 A.3d 691 (Pa. Super. 2013) (Bowes, J., concurring). Indeed, at the time *Hubbard* was decided, issues in adult cases were required to be preserved in post-trial motions. Since counsel is not required under the juvenile rules to file post-dispositional motions, the issues possibly could properly be raised for the first time in a Pa.R.A.P. 1925(b) statement. *See Matter of Smith*, 573 A.2d 1077 (Pa. Super. 1990); *In re K.A.T.*, 69 A.3d 691 (Pa. Super. 2013). Nevertheless, best practice is to file a post-dispositional motion containing any of-record ineffectiveness claims.

The failure to include a claim in a post-dispositional motion when counsel files such a motion could be considered grounds for waiver where the claim appears of record. If counsel files a post-dispositional motion raising some ineffectiveness claims but does not raise an issue that has merit, he should raise the issue in his Pa.R.A.P. 1925(b) statement and alternatively assert his own derelict in neglecting to raise the claim earlier. *In re B.S.*, 831 A.2d 151 (Pa. Super. 2003). On appeal, in this situation, counsel should again assert his own ineffectiveness to avoid any chance of the appellate court finding waiver.

The applicable test for ineffectiveness in juvenile matters is the same as in adult cases. *See In re A.J.*, 829 A.2d 312 (Pa. Super. 2003). When counsel alleges ineffectiveness on appeal in a juvenile matter, if there has not been an evidentiary hearing addressing the issues, the appellate court may remand for a hearing and opinion to address the claims. Juvenile courts faced with allegations of ineffective assistance of counsel in a post-dispositional motion should conduct a hearing on the issue whenever it appears to have arguable merit so as to properly develop the record. Failing to hold a hearing or address the matter may result in a remand for the juvenile court to make the proper record and address the question or questions of ineffective assistance of counsel. However, where the issue is raised for the first time in a Pa.R.A.P. 1925(b) statement, the court is without jurisdiction to conduct hearings and should address the issue as thoroughly as possible in its Pa.R.A.P. 1925(a) opinion. Whenever the ineffectiveness claim involves extra-record issues, *i.e.*, advice provided by counsel to his client, an evidentiary hearing is normally required.

Extra-record claims likely should not be considered waived as the result of the failure to file a post-dispositional motion. *See e.g. Commonwealth v. Dancer*, 331 A.2d 435 (Pa. 1975). The decision in *Dancer* was pre-*Hubbard* and did not apply to juvenile matters. However, it made clear that ineffectiveness claims that do not appear of record are not waived for failing to raise them in a post-trial motion.

A Brief Word on Juvenile Matters

It is also conceviable that claims of ineffective assistance of counsel during juvenile proceedings could be raised via *coram nobis* or *habeas corpus* since the juvenile would not be contesting a conviction or sentence.

Chapter 26: Summary and Checklists

Once a court receives a *pro se* PCRA petition or a motion that should be construed as a PCRA petition, the court must appoint counsel if it is a first-time petition. Pa.R.Crim.P. 904. Counsel, however, is not required to be appointed where the petitioner files a DNA motion under section 9543.1. ***Commonwealth v. Brooks***, 875 A.2d 1141 (Pa. Super. 2005). In first-time capital cases, PCRA counsel is appointed following completion of direct review and before the filing of any petition. *See* Pa.R.Crim.P. 904(H)(1). If the petition is a second or subsequent petition, the court need not appoint counsel unless it believes that an evidentiary hearing is necessary. After a court receives an amended PCRA petition, if it finds that the amended petition is defective, it may, but is not required to direct counsel to file a subsequent petition. Pa.R.Crim.P. 905.

The PCRA court may also direct the Commonwealth to file an answer if the case is not a first time petition in a capital case. Pa.R.Crim.P. 906(A). In a capital case, the Commonwealth must file an answer for a first-time petition. Pa.R.Crim.P. 906(E)(1)(a). In the case of a PCRA petition that appears to have merit, it is suggested that the PCRA court order the Commonwealth file an answer. Additionally, the PCRA court must review the record and make its own conclusions and findings of fact and cannot merely adopt the Commonwealth's position when deciding the case. ***Commonwealth v. Williams***, 732 A.2d 1167 (Pa. 1999); ***Commonwealth v. Fulton***, 876 A.2d 342 (Pa. 2002). The court must also determine whether the petition is timely. Untimely petitions render the PCRA court without jurisdiction to afford relief. ***Commonwealth v. Yarris***, 731 A.2d 581 (Pa. 1999).

Where no evidentiary hearing is held and the petition is dismissed, the PCRA court must issue a notice of dismissal addressing all of the issues raised in the petition. Pa.R.Crim.P. 907; Pa.R.Crim.P. 909; ***Commonwealth v. Brown***, 830 A.2d 536 (Pa. 2003); ***Commonwealth v. Morris***, 684 A.2d 1037 (Pa. 1996); ***Commonwealth v. Diaz***, 913 A.2d 871 (Pa. Super. 2006); ***Commonwealth v. Feighery***, 661 A.2d 437 (Pa. Super. 1995). Failure to give the required notice of intent to dismiss has been held to deprive a petitioner of his right to have the PCRA court review the claims. ***Commonwealth v. Anderson***, 801 A.2d 1264 (Pa. Super. 2002).

Importantly, an amended petition is merely an extension of an existing petition and not a new and distinct petition. ***Commonwealth v. Tedford***, 781 A.2d 1167, 1171 (Pa. 2001); ***Commonwealth v. Padden***, 783 A.2d 299 (Pa. Super. 2001); **but see *Commonwealth v. Porter***, 35 A.3d 4 (Pa. 2012). The court need not consider *pro se* filings where the defendant is **adequately** represented by counsel and a defendant has a history of filing lengthy *pro se* documents. ***See Commonwealth v. Pursell***, 724 A.2d 293, 302 (Pa. 1999) (stating, "we will not require courts considering PCRA petitions to struggle through the *pro se* filings of defendants when qualified counsel represent those defendants.") (emphasis added).

Where a petition is filed and the court has not entered a final order, and the petitioner or counsel files an amended petition, the amended petition is not subject to the time requirements of the PCRA if the original petition was timely filed. ***Commonwealth v. Flanagan***, 854 A.2d 489 (Pa. 2004); ***Commonwealth v. Swartzfager***, 59 A.3d 616 (Pa. Super. 2012). A PCRA petition should NOT be dismissed if counsel has not filed an amended petition, even more so where no evidentiary hearing was held. The failure of counsel to file an amended petition or a ***Turner/Finley*** no-merit letter is the equivalent of allowing the petitioner to proceed without counsel. ***Commonwealth v. Williams***, 828 A.2d 981 (Pa. 2003); ***Commonwealth v. Duffey***, 713 A.2d 63 (Pa. 1998);

Commonwealth v. Hampton, 718 A.2d 1250 (Pa. Super. 1998).

A court should remove counsel if he or she fails to act within a certain time frame and may also report an attorney to the disciplinary board. An appointed attorney who neglects to file an amended petition or ***Turner/Finley*** letter should not be authorized to receive any payment. If a *pro se* petition is incorporated by reference in an amended petition, the PCRA court must address the issues raised in the *pro se* document or require counsel to file another amended petition which addresses the issues raised in the *pro se* petition. ***Commonwealth v. Wallace***, 724 A.2d 916, 923 n.9 (Pa. 1999).

Issuing a notice of intent to dismiss that merely quotes from Rule 907 but does not give the legal reasoning behind the dismissal is discouraged because it does not indicate a thorough review of the record, nor does it serve the purpose of the rule to give the petitioner notice of the reasoning for the dismissal. Rather, such an order is conclusory in nature. *See* Annotated Comment on Rule 907; *see also **Commonwealth v. Beasley***, 967 A.2d 376 (Pa. 2009); ***Commonwealth v. Rush***, 838 A.2d 651 (Pa. 2003); ***Commonwealth v. Williams***, 782 A.2d 517 (Pa. 2001). Failure to issue a notice of dismissal can result in a remand from the appellate courts. ***Commonwealth v. Guthrie***, 749 A.2d 502 (Pa. Super. 2000); ***Commonwealth v. Morris***, 684 A.2d 1037 (Pa. 1996). However, in cases where the petition was untimely, it has been held to be harmless error for the PCRA court to fail to issue a notice of its intent to dismiss. ***Commonwealth v. Pursell***, 749 A.2d 911 (Pa. 2000).

Furthermore, a petitioner's failure to raise the court's error in neglecting to supply a notice of intent to dismiss results in waiver of the issue. ***Commonwealth v. Carson***, 913 A.2d 220, 232 n.3 (Pa. 2006); ***Commonwealth v. Boyd***, 923 A.2d 513, 514 n.1 (Pa. Super. 2007); ***Commonwealth v. Guthrie***, 749 A.2d 502 (Pa. Super. 2000). Upon remand, the PCRA court must wait until the record is returned before issuing its notice of dismissal. The Superior Court will not return the record by rule for thirty days after issuing its order. The PCRA court does not have jurisdiction until the record is returned. *See generally* **Commonwealth v. Salley**, 957 A.2d 320 (Pa. Super. 2008). Therefore, if the PCRA court issues its notice of dismissal prior to the record being remanded, the notice of intent to dismiss will be void as the court may not have had jurisdiction.

After filing a notice of intent to dismiss, the court must wait twenty days before filing a final order. This twenty day period gives a petitioner the opportunity to respond to the dismissal. The relevant rule of criminal procedure provides that a petitioner may respond, but is not required to respond. However, if a petitioner is dissatisfied with PCRA counsel, case law has held that after receiving the notice of dismissal he must file a response and raise any issue of ineffectiveness of his PCRA counsel or risk waiver. **Commonwealth v. Pitts**, 981 A.2d 875 (Pa. 2009); **Commonwealth v. Henkel**, 90 A.3d 16 (Pa. Super. 2014) (*en banc*); **but see Commonwealth v. Williams**, 732 A.2d 1167 (Pa. 1999) (holding that raising a subsequent claim in response to a notice of dismissal is too late unless the PCRA court grants the defendant a chance to file an amended petition).

In *Williams*, the Supreme Court held that the PCRA court did not abuse its discretion in not granting the defendant a chance to amend his petition after he raised a *Batson* claim in his response to the court's notice of dismissal. *See also* **Commonwealth v. Derrickson**, 923 A.2d 466 (Pa. Super. 2009). The Superior Court in **Commonwealth v. Rykard**, 55 A.3d 1177 (Pa. Super. 2012), differentiated between ineffective assistance of PCRA counsel claims and other claims asserted in a Rule 907/909 response, holding that the PCRA counsel ineffectiveness issues are preserved but that the PCRA court is not required to address other types of claims unless it permits the filing of another amended petition.

Of course, after the issuance of a notice of intent to dismiss, the trial court cannot forget to issue a final order. Without a final order, the PCRA petition has never formally been dismissed. ***See Commonwealth v. Swartzfager***, 59 A.3d 616 (Pa. Super. 2012). A final order must inform the defendant of his right to appeal and the time he has to file the appeal. Pa.R.Crim.P. 908(E); Pa.R.Crim.P. 909(B)(7)(b). However, if the court determines that there are issues of genuine material fact, it must schedule a hearing relative to those issues. Pa.R.Crim.P. 907; Pa.R.Crim.P. 909. A court may dismiss some issues and schedule a hearing in relation to others. Pa.R.Crim.P. 907(3); Comment to Pa.R.Crim.P. 910; ***Commonwealth v. Collins***, 957 A.2d 237 (Pa. 2008).

In making a decision following an evidentiary hearing, the court must include in its findings its credibility determinations relative to the witnesses who testified, ***see Commonwealth v. Johnson***, 966 A.2d 523 (Pa. 2009), and address all issues raised in the amended PCRA petition, even those issues that were not addressed at the hearing. Pa.R.Crim.P. 908(D)(1); ***Commonwealth v. Beasley***, 967 A.2d 376 (Pa. 2009). Assessing credibility for purposes of deciding an ineffectiveness claim does not require the court to conclude that a jury would find the witness credible. ***Commonwealth v. Stewart***, 84 A.3d 701 (Pa. Super. 2013) (*en banc*); ***see also Commonwealth v. Johnson***, 966 A.2d at 541.

On claims of ineffectiveness, if the court finds that a petitioner was not prejudiced by counsel's actions, the court need not address the other elements of the ineffectiveness test. ***Commonwealth v. Travaglia***, 661 A.2d 352 (Pa. 1995). Additionally, when an issue does not have arguable merit or fails any of the requirements of the ***Strickland/Pierce*** test, a petitioner is not entitled to relief. ***Commonwealth v. Steele***, 961 A.2d 786 (Pa. 2008).

Summary and Checklists

A PCRA court should also be cognizant of Rule 905(B), and liberally order amendment to petitions which, although deficient in some manner, appear to raise an issue of arguable merit. *See generally **Commonwealth v. Jette**,* 947 A.2d 202 (Pa. Super. 2008), *abrogated on other grounds,* 23 A.3d 1032 (Pa. 2011) (stating that a court should permit petitioners to amend a petition to avoid dismissal due to a correctable defect in the pleading). Additionally, if a petition is facially untimely and no timeliness exception has been specifically alleged, but the petition raises facts which could support a timeliness exception, amendment should be ordered by the court to address the possible timeliness issue. ***But see Commonwealth v. Beasley***, 741 A.2d 1258 (Pa. 1999) (timeliness exception must be specifically pleaded). Further, the PCRA court is permitted to award relief without granting a hearing if it finds that the petition and any answer filed in response do not raise material issues of fact and the petitioner is entitled to relief. Pa.R.Crim.P. 907(2). Therefore, if the court finds, based on the record, that a petitioner's claim(s) warrant relief, it may grant relief without an evidentiary hearing.

The PCRA court should also be aware that delay in addressing a PCRA petition is a cognizable claim under the PCRA and may entitle a petitioner to relief if the delay caused prejudice to the petitioner. ***Commonwealth v. Burkett***, 5 A.3d 1260 (Pa. Super. 2010). In ***Burkett***, the Superior Court ultimately concluded that a fifteen-year delay in holding a hearing and a sixteen-year period taken to finally decide a PCRA petition did not result in prejudice because the petitioner's underlying claims were not affected by the delay but cautioned against lengthy delays in addressing non-capital PCRA petitions. ***See also Commonwealth v. Volk***, 138 A.3d 659 (Pa. Super. 2016); ***Commonwealth v. Anderson***, 995 A.2d 1184 (Pa. Super. 2010) (Rule 600 does not apply to PCRA proceedings but an evidentiary hearing must be held within a reasonable time).

Summary and Checklists

PCRA Court Checklist

1. Determine if the motion/filing is a PCRA petition-- does it seek relief from a conviction, challenge the sentence being served, or request a *nunc pro tunc* direct appeal? The vast majority of post-conviction filings will fall into the PCRA category; however, there are an extremely small number of motions that do not come within the parameters of the PCRA.

2. If the petition is a first time PCRA petition, counsel must be appointed. (In capital cases, counsel will file the initial petition). Make sure that the order appointing counsel includes the attorney's name, work address, and contact number. The order should specify a specific time frame in which counsel has to file an amended petition or ***Turner/Finley*** no-merit letter. In addition, it may be beneficial to direct that transcripts be provided to counsel if they are not part of the record and provide a copy of the petition with the appointment order. Where the petition is a second or subsequent petition, do not appoint counsel unless an evidentiary hearing is necessary.

3. Upon receipt of an petition, if necessary, the court may issue an order directing the Commonwealth to file an answer within a set period. In capital cases, an answer from the Commonwealth is mandatory. On second or subsequent petitions, where the petition is timely but defective, direct the petitioner or counsel, if the petitioner is represented, to submit a proper petition. Should the court receive a ***Turner/Finley*** no-merit letter, the PCRA court must review the *pro se* petition to ensure that counsel has discussed each issue raised in the *pro se* petition or raised elsewhere in the record during the PCRA process. Do not schedule an

Summary and Checklists

evidentiary hearing when a no-merit letter is filed. If the no-merit letter is deficient, direct counsel to file a proper no-merit letter or an advocate's petition. Where an amended petition is defective for failing to include witness certifications the court must direct counsel to provide witness certifications.

4. Review the record, including petitions and any answers. If an amended petition and any briefs have been filed which are excessive in length (over seventy pages), order counsel to file an amended petition/brief within a set time frame and specify a page limit.

5. Determine if the petition is timely. If untimely, the court is without jurisdiction to afford relief.

6. Where there are no issues of material fact and no need for an evidentiary hearing, the court must issue a notice of intent to dismiss and should send it via certified mail. This notice should provide legal discussion of why the petition is being dismissed so as to enable counsel a meaningful opportunity to respond. Where a notice of intent to dismiss is filed and sent to the petitioner, the court must wait twenty days before issuing its final order. The court is advised that, when a proper *Turner/Finley* no-merit letter is filed, best practice is to allow counsel to withdraw when issuing the notice of intent to dismiss. This prevents hybrid representation issues.

7. If a petition raises an issue of material fact, schedule an evidentiary hearing. Alternatively, the court may dismiss certain issues without a hearing and schedule a hearing for the remaining issues. For example, a defendant may raise issues of law that do not require fact-finding that may be disposed of without a hearing, but also set forth claims that do require fact-finding.

8. Conduct hearing. If more than one hearing is necessary, specify exact date of future hearing at the conclusion of the evidentiary hearing.

9. Where dismissal is appropriate, issue a final order and advise defendant of his appellate rights. If the court dismisses the petition outside the presence of the defendant, it must notify the petitioner by certified mail. Where a proper **Turner/Finley** no-merit letter is filed, the court must specify that it is permitting counsel to withdraw if it has not done so previously.

11. Where an appeal is filed, direct the appellant to file and serve a Pa.R.A.P. 1925(b) statement. If counsel has been permitted to withdraw, order the *pro se* petitioner to file and serve the statement.

12. Author Pa.R.A.P. 1925(a) opinion—may incorporate reasoning from notice of intent to dismiss if relevant. Do not accept a *pro se* 1925(b) statement when the petitioner is represented by counsel.

Prosecutor's Checklist

1. Review petition to determine if it is timely. Where untimely, file a motion to dismiss, regardless of whether the court has directed you to file a response. However, ensure that the court appoints counsel on first time PCRA petitions before it disposes of the petition even if the petition is untimely.

2. If the petition is timely because of a timeliness exception or a timely petition was originally filed but a long delay has occurred in the filing of an amended petition, and significant time has passed since the trial/plea and the Commonwealth would be prejudiced if it is required to re-try or try the petitioner, request an

Summary and Checklists

evidentiary hearing to establish prejudicial delay.

3. Review record and file an answer if directed by the court. Where it is a capital PCRA, you must file an answer. In capital PCRA matters, pay close attention to applicable time frames.

4. Request removal of counsel or a court order directing counsel to take action if significant delay occurs.

PCRA Counsel Checklist (Non-capital case)

1. When appointed, write client to inform him of your representation. Request any additional documents or information from client that he believes is pertinent. If retained, enter your appearance and make sure you file a timely petition or a petition asserting a timeliness exception.

2. Review record and request any necessary transcripts, including transcripts of opening and closing statements, which sometimes are not transcribed. Conduct necessary extra-record investigations (prison visitation records, other potential witnesses, correspondence between your client and his previous counsel, the record in cases of any co-defendants, interview/correspond with prior counsel, etc…).

3. Draft amended petition or *Turner/Finley* no-merit letter. Provide copies of amended petition to client for review. Client may request additional issues be raised in an amended petition. Indicate in a letter, with legal analysis, why such additional issues are without legal merit if the issues lack merit. Create witness certifications when necessary and obtain affidavits.

4. File amended petition or *Turner/Finley* no-merit

Summary and Checklists

letter. If a no-merit letter is filed, also file of record a request to withdraw. Provide defendant with copy of the ***Turner/Finley*** no-merit letter before filing. The amended petition should include a request for an evidentiary hearing. Further, counsel must attach any witness certifications to the petition. Where counsel does not develop argument under the ineffective assistance of counsel test in the petition, counsel should file a brief properly developing the claims.

5. If you do not withdraw, you are still in the case. Consult with client about possible appeal if petition is dismissed and file any appeal that is requested. If you filed a ***Turner/Finley*** no-merit letter and the court did not allow you to withdraw, request the PCRA court permit you to withdraw or file a notice of appeal and submit a ***Turner/Finley*** no-merit letter on appeal.

Denied petition for Early parole
might let him out later

Chapter 27:
Closing Remarks

In his dissenting opinion in ***Commonwealth v. Smith***, 17 A.3d 873, 915-916 (Pa. 2011), Justice Saylor wrote that the case:

> reflects multiple irregularities, which are far too prevalent in the capital post-conviction arena. The matter has languished in the PCRA court for the better part of two decades. Several attorneys who have represented Appellant on post-conviction did very little or nothing to advance the case. ***See*** Majority Opinion, *Op.* at 880–81. After the Defender Association of Philadelphia entered their appearance, the PCRA court attempted to dismiss the amended petition in a perfunctory fashion, yielding a remand. ***See id.*** at 881. Such dismissal was obviously unjustified, as, in the ensuing proceedings—albeit five years later—the Commonwealth stipulated to penalty relief based on deficient performance by Appellant's trial counsel. ***See id.*** at 882. Presently, we are confronted with an incomplete PCRA court opinion after a second summary dismissal of guilt-phase claims. ***See id.*** at 883–84.

Similar problems are found in non-capital cases. Indeed, delay in post-conviction practice in Pennsylvania is nothing new. In his 1970 article, State Post-Conviction Remedies and Federal Habeas Corpus, 12 Wm. & Mary L. Rev. 147, William F. Swindler quoted from a Pennsylvania attorney in 1969 discussing the PCHA, stating,

> the major problem in these cases concerns delay. It is not uncommon for final disposition to be delayed for years, even in cases which have potential merit....Because of the volume, it is not uncommon for

several months to pass before a matter is set for initial hearing. The hearing, preparation and filing of briefs, appeals, and postponements for reasons such as unavailability of witnesses can result in unbelievable delays.

Id. at 216 (quoting letter from Samuel J. Reich, November 10, 1969).

Justice Saylor has called for more "strict adherence to the requirements of pre-dismissal notice containing reasonably specific notice of pleading deficiencies or other reasons for summary dismissal and uniformly dispense hearings where credibility matters are materially in issue." *Smith*, 17 A.3d at 916. He is correct. The time has come for PCRA courts to carefully delineate the reasons for PCRA dismissal in a reasoned fashion and not boilerplate orders, or for the notice of intent to dismiss be replaced by a more traditional post-PCRA motion practice.

This book is intended to ensure that judges, clerks and attorneys are educated on the proper method of handling post-conviction proceedings. Attorneys must pay closer attention to the procedural rules, and courts must monitor and direct counsel and the Commonwealth to take specific and timely action. Orders directing the production of necessary transcripts, a time frame for submitting an amended petition and any supporting briefs, should become the rule and not the exception. Oversight by the courts will alleviate delay and the need for remands as well as help to protect the right to effective representation during the collateral proceeding.

Justice Saylor also cogently set forth that the courts must improve enforcement of the criminal procedural rules timing mechanisms in capital cases. I believe that these time tracking mechanisms must be extended to non-capital cases. Currently, non-capital cases languish because attorneys, prosecutors and the courts fail to act in a reasonably timely manner. It is uncon-

Closing Remarks

scionable for a PCRA matter to take three, four, five, or more years to conclude. It is a disservice to victims, prosecutors, and petitioners for cases to sit idly. PCRA practitioners must take seriously their responsibility to the courts and their clients and the courts must also efficiently handle PCRA cases and monitor the inaction of both the government and counsel.

Diligent efforts by PCRA attorneys can alleviate the frequent problems that have arisen in enforcing the right to effective PCRA representation. Knowledge of the basic rules and statutory provisions are essential to providing effective representation. The fact that petitioners are rarely "factually innocent" should not discourage counsel, nor should it cause judges or prosecutors to view PCRA petitions as less important than other matters. A courts correct handling of a first-time petition that does not entitle a petitioner to relief makes subsequent frivolous or untimely petitions easy to resolve.

In the capital arena, the Pennsylvania Supreme Court should consider adoption of the unitary system of review that was originally passed by the legislature and suspended by the Supreme Court. Adoption of more stringent competency requirements for all PCRA cases and mandatory oversight by the courts, as well as mandatory evidentiary hearings in first time PCRA capital cases, would greatly reduce the possibility of ineffective assistance by collateral review counsel.

Samples

Sample Order Appointing Counsel

IN THE COURT OF COMMON PLEAS OF _____
COUNTY, PENNSYLVANIA

COMMONWEALTH OF PENNSYLVANIA

vs.

ED E,

Petitioner

ORDER OF COURT

AND NOW, this _____ day of _____, 20__, upon review of the Petitioner's petition for Post Conviction Collateral Relief, it is hereby **ORDERED**, **ADJUDGED**, and **DECREED** that _____, Esquire (Phone Number/Address) is appointed to counsel Petitioner throughout his PCRA proceedings, and that an amended PCRA petition, or a "no-merit" letter in accordance with *Commonwealth v. Turner*, 544 A.2d 927 (Pa. 1988), and *Commonwealth v. Finley*, 550 A.2d 213 (Pa. Super. 1988) (*en banc*), shall be filed within sixty (60) days of this Order.

BY THE COURT:

_____, J

cc:

ADA Johnny Smith

Ed E

Sample PCRA Questionairre for Client

(Supplement with additional questions specific to the case at issue)

Other than the attorneys listed in your *pro se* petition, were you represented in this case by any other attorneys? If so, please list their names and at what stage they represented you, *i.e.*, sentencing, direct appeal, etc...

Were you convicted of any other crimes at the time of your trial/plea at another case number? If so, indicate what those convictions were for and the case number if known.

How many times did your attorney meet with you prior to your trial/plea? Include any meetings at your preliminary hearing or arraignment.

How long were the face-to-face meetings?

Did you discuss substantively a trial strategy? For example, did you discuss what witnesses that you intended to call--character witnesses, alibi witnesses, expert witnesses?

If relevant, did counsel discuss any potential suppression issues?

Did you and your attorney discuss whether you would testify, how your criminal history, if any, might impact that decision?

Do you or your family have any letters or correspondence between you and your attorney? Provide any copies that you may have.

Did you have telephone conversations with your attorney? Approximately how many discussions over the telephone did you have? What did you discuss?

Did counsel discuss with you any plea offers, sentencing maximums, sentencing guideline ranges?

Sample PCRA Questionairre for Client

Were the elements of the crimes charged explained to you?

If you are a minority (or female) were there any members of your race/gender on the jury? How many?

If you recall, did the Commonwealth strike prospective jurors of the same race/gender?

Did you provide a list of witnesses to call to your lawyer that were not utilized? If yes, are those witnesses listed in your *pro se* petition? If not, please provide a list of those witnesses and their address if known.

If you proceeded to trial and did not testify, what reasons did counsel give for advising you not to testify?

Have you learned of any evidence that was not available at the time of trial that would have aided your defense?

[Where a direct appeal was filed]

Do you have a copy of any appellate briefs filed on your behalf? (Trial briefs should be contained within the trial court record). If so, please provide a copy.

Did you ask counsel to file a petition for allowance of appeal with the Pennsylvania Supreme Court after the Superior Court decided your direct appeal?

[If no direct appeal was filed]

Did you request your attorney file an appeal?

Did your attorney discuss with you your appellate rights? If so what advice did he present to you?

<u>Sample Petition</u>

COMMONWEALTH of PENNSYLVANIA

v. CASE NUMBER

PETITIONER

<u>(NON-CAPITAL) PETITION FOR POST-CONVICTION RELIEF</u>

AND NOW comes the Petitioner, (NAME), by and through his Counsel, (Name), and files this Petition for Post-Conviction Relief pursuant to 42 Pa.C.S. §§ 9541-9546:

1. Petitioner, JOHN DOE, is currently housed in (Name and Address of Prison).

2. Mr. Doe was (convicted by a jury, judge without jury or pleaded guilty or *nolo contendere* of) the following crimes:

3. On (DATE) Mr. Doe was sentenced to a term of incarceration of _____ by the Honorable _____. (Specify on which counts the petitioner was sentenced by the court).

4. Mr. Doe filed a direct appeal at APPEAL CASE NUMBER, raising the following issues:_____.

The direct appeal was denied by order of court on DATE. **Commonwealth v. Doe**, __ A.3d __ (Pa. Super. ____) (unpublished memorandum). The Pennsylvania Supreme Court denied Petitioner's petition for allowance of appeal by order of court on DATE. **Commonwealth v. Doe**, __ A.3d __ (Pa. ____). Mr. Doe did not seek review by the U.S. Supreme Court. The date of final judgment therefore was ninety (90) days from the Pennsylvania Supreme Court's denial of allowance of appeal. A petition must be filed within one year of the date of final judgment. The petition was filed on _____; therefore, it is timely.

(If the petitioner did not file a direct appeal, the date of final judgment would be thirty days from the date of his sentencing. Also, if the petition is not timely, a petitioner must allege one of three exceptions to the timeliness requirement or the court will not have jurisdiction to reach the merits of the petition).

5. Mr. Doe was previously represented by: (NAMES of any attorney who represented the defendant at any time after his arrest, and the stage of the case represented--trial, direct appeal, etc...).

6. Mr. Doe requests the following relief: (New trial, withdrawal of guilty plea).

7. The grounds for the relief requested have not been raised before and are therefore not previously litigated nor could they have been raised prior, thus they are not waived.

8. Attorney _____ filing the petition is authorized to do so on Petitioner's behalf.

9. Mr. Doe raises the following grounds for relief:

(ineffective assistance of counsel, violation of constitutional rights, sentence that exceeds the lawful maximum, etc...)

Issue 1: Discuss facts supporting request for relief and places in the record where they appear, and if they do not appear in the record identify any affidavits, documents, or other evidence showing such facts. Make sure to either fully develop any ineffectiveness claims based on the *Pierce* test or file a brief fully developing the issues. *See Commonwealth v. Davis*, 526 A.2d 440 (Pa. Super. 1987). (The rule states citation to authorities is not required in the petition; however, argument and supporting citations must be provided to the court or the issue may be waived).

Sample Petition

DO NOT USE BOILERPLATE CLAIMS in an accompanying brief.

SUBSEQUENT ISSUES

10. Mr. Doe requests an evidentiary hearing on the following issues: LIST ISSUES

11. Counsel intends to call the following witnesses: (List of witness names, addresses, date of birth, and substance of proposed witnesses' testimony). (Attach any documents, including witness certifications or affidavits, material to the witnesses proposed testimony. An attorney or the petitioner can create the witness certification setting forth what the proposed witnesses' testimony would be).

12. Petitioner asks that upon leave of court he be permitted discovery of the following:

(In a non-capital case, a petitioner must make a showing of exceptional circumstances to warrant discovery. In a capital case, discovery will be granted upon leave of court if the petitioner can show good cause).

13. Attach Verification statement.

14. Attach Witness Certifications and/or affidavits.

Envelope

Sample Witness Certification

Sample Witness Certification

IN THE COURT OF COMMON PLEAS OF _____ COUNTY, PENNSYLVANIA

COMMONWEALTH   :   Case No.

v.   :

Joe Petitioner   :

WITNESS CERTIFICATIONS

AND NOW comes the Petitioner, JOE PETITIONER, by and through his Counsel, _____, Esquire and files these Witness Certifications. Counsel reserves the right to amend these certifications if additional witnesses or evidence is necessary based on the testimony of certain witnesses or other evidence arises during the PCRA process, including but not limited to Mr. Petitioner's evidentiary hearing(s).

Certification of Petitioner

Mr. Petitioner was born on DATE, 1981. He currently resides at SCI Greene, 175 Progress Drive, Waynesburg, PA 15370. Counsel certifies that Mr. Petitioner will testify consistently with the facts contained in his petition and brief. Specifically, Mr. Petitioner would testify that he did request that trial counsel file a direct appeal on his behalf. Mr. Petitioner would set forth that despite his requests, as well as requests from family members, trial counsel failed to file an appeal nor did she consult with him regarding his appellate rights.

Sample Witness Certification

In addition, Mr. Petitioner would submit that he did not testify in his own defense based on the advice of counsel, and that counsel informed him that he could be questioned regarding his prior non-*crimen falsi* criminal history. He would further add that the Court also indicated as such in the Court's colloquy. Mr. Petitioner would testify that if not for counsel's legally erroneous advice, he would have taken the stand in his defense and denied possessing the weapon.

Certification of Trial Attorney

Trial attorney's professional address is _____. Counsel certifies to the best of counsel's knowledge and belief, it is believed that trial counsel will testify that she represented Mr. Petitioner in this matter and that she did advise Mr. Petitioner not to testify. To the best of counsel's knowledge and belief, trial counsel would confirm the existing record and that her advice was based on the belief that Mr. Petitioner could be impeached and cross-examined based on his criminal history.

To the best of counsel's knowledge, trial counsel would also testify regarding the circumstances leading to the juvenile witness not testifying based on her counsel and the court's belief that the witness's mother also had to waive the juvenile's right against self-incrimination. To the best of counsel's knowledge and belief, trial counsel would testify concerning any communications she had with Mr. Petitioner and/or his family regarding filing an appeal and whether she researched case law relative to the sufficiency of the evidence.

Certification of Ms. Petitioner

Ms. Petitioner is Mr. Petitioner's sister. She resides at _____ and was born on _____. She would testify as to her efforts to communicate with trial counsel and that she asked about an appeal on Mr. Petitioner's behalf. She would submit that she called trial counsel repeatedly regarding an

Sample Witness Certification

appeal and that those calls went unreturned. Ms. Petitioner would also testify that she e-mailed trial counsel regarding post-sentence motions and an appeal. She would submit that trial counsel responded one time regarding an inquiry, but that it was not related to Mr. Petitioner's appeal or appellate rights.

      Respectfully submitted:

      Name
      Pa. I.D.
      Address
      Phone
      E-mail

Sample No Merit Letter (Where trial was held)

<u>Sample No Merit Letter (Where trial was held)</u>

COMMONWEALTH of PENNSYLVANIA

v.   CASE NUMBER

PETITIONER

<u>Turner/Finley No-Merit Letter</u>

AND NOW comes Joe Esquire, Esq. and files this ***Turner/Finley*** no-merit letter pursuant to ***Commonwealth v. Turner***, 544 A.2d 927 (Pa. 1988) and ***Commonwealth v. Finley***, 550 A.2d 213 (Pa. Super. 1988) (*en banc*).

After careful review of the entire Podunk County, Pennsylvania record at case number _____, including the transcripts of both the trial and sentencing and Petitioner's *pro se* PCRA petition, and correspondence and materials supplied by Petitioner and prior counsel, counsel finds that the issues Petitioner wishes to raise do not entitle him to PCRA relief and counsel has determined that no other meritorious issues exist. Counsel, therefore, requests that he be permitted to withdraw from representation.

Petitioner was found guilty following a jury trial of attempted murder, aggravated assault, reckless endangerment of another person ("REAP"), carrying an unlicensed firearm, and simple assault and sentenced to a term of incarceration of twenty to forty years by the Honorable Judd Ge.

In the early morning hours of December 26, 2008, Petitioner was involved in an altercation with three men: John Smith, Billy Baggins, and Dwight Baddin. Two of the men, Baggins and Baddin, were known by Petitioner to be local drug dealers and he suspected that they were armed. The confrontation began after John Smith, the person unknown to Petitioner, began to flirt with Petitioner's girlfriend inside of a local establishment called Po' & Drunk. The two men were asked to leave after the

Sample No Merit Letter (Where trial was held)

confrontation turned physical with some brief shoving. Petitioner, his girlfriend, and another couple exited the bar. John Smith also exited with Billy Baggins and Dwight Baddin. According to Petitioner, Smith, Baggins and Baddin began to taunt him and his girlfriend as the three men walked toward him. Petitioner, believing Baggins and Baddin were armed, pulled out an unlicensed .40 caliber Glock handgun and told the men to stop moving. At this point, Petitioner alleges that Baddin and Baggins hands moved toward the back waist area of their body. Believing the men were going for guns, Petitioner fired four shots, wounding Smith three times and Baddin once. Baggins escaped unharmed.

At trial, Smith, Baggins and Baddin testified that as soon as they exited the bar, Petitioner pulled a handgun on Smith and threatened them before firing three shots at Smith. Baggins and Baddin ran for cover and Petitioner fired another round, hitting Baddin, before Petitioner sped away in his vehicle. Trial counsel impeached these three men with prior *crimen falsi* convictions. Four other individuals in the parking lot testified to seeing Petitioner exit the bar and immediately pull a gun. They each stated that some words were exchanged between Smith and Petitioner before Petitioner opened fire. The couple that exited with Petitioner also testified against Petitioner, stating that he fired the shots without warning. A videotape was also shown of the incident. The tape corroborated the testimony of the victims and the other Commonwealth witnesses.

Trial counsel's theory at trial was imperfect self defense. During Petitioner's case-in-chief, Petitioner and his girlfriend both took the stand and gave identical accounts of the altercation, averring that Smith threatened them inside the bar and Baggins and Baddin appeared to go for what they believed were their firearms once outside. Additionally, trial counsel for Petitioner called three character witnesses that Petitioner requested to be called on his behalf. These witnesses each testified that

Sample No Merit Letter (Where trial was held)

Petitioner had a reputation in the community for being a peaceful and law-abiding citizen.

During the cross-examination of the first character witness, the prosecution improperly inquired with the witness if he knew Petitioner had been arrested three times. Trial counsel objected, the trial judge sustained the objection, and called both counsel to side-bar and admonished the prosecutor that such questioning was inappropriate. Trial counsel requested a mistrial, but the court declined that motion and indicated that he would give a curative instruction if counsel wished. Counsel declined, stating that the instruction would only highlight the issue.

The jury returned a guilty verdict on the charge of attempted murder-serious bodily injury and aggravated assault pertinent to John Smith. They also found Petitioner guilty of aggravated assault, simple assault, and REAP of Dwight Baddin. Petitioner was also convicted of carrying a firearm without a license. Thereafter, Petitioner was sentenced to a term of imprisonment of twenty to forty years for attempted murder. The trial court imposed no further sentence. Petitioner filed a timely post-sentence motion, raising weight and sufficiency claims, a discretionary sentencing claim that the sentence was excessive, as well as a challenge to the trial court's decision not to grant a mistrial. The trial judge denied the post-sentence motion without a hearing. Petitioner filed a timely direct appeal raising weight and sufficiency of the evidence issues as well as the mistrial claim. The Superior Court affirmed the decision of the trial court and the Pennsylvania Supreme Court denied his petition for allowance of appeal. This PCRA petition followed.

Before reaching the merits of any claim under the PCRA, the petition must be timely. A petition which is untimely renders the court without jurisdiction to consider the merits of the claims, unless the petitioner can plead and prove that the claim falls within one of the PCRA timeliness exceptions. Instantly, petitioner was sentenced by the trial court on January 10, 2010. A post-sentence motion was filed on January 19, 2010, and denied without hearing on January 30, 2010. Petitioner filed a timely direct appeal on February 8, 2010. The judgment of sentence was affirmed on May 10, 2011, and Petitioner filed a timely petition for allowance of appeal. Petitioner's allowance of appeal was denied on June 21, 2011. Petitioner had ninety days to seek review in the United States Supreme Court, but did not do so. Thus, the date of final judgment was on or about September 19, 2011. The instant petition was filed August 14, 2012. Therefore, the petition is timely. Petitioner in his *pro se* petition raised the following issues:

> 1. Ineffective assistance of trial counsel for not objecting to the prosecutor's questioning of his first character witness.
>
> 2. Ineffectiveness of trial counsel for failing to object to the prosecutor's improper remark during closing statements that Petitioner was a "thug."

Pro se petition, DATE, at page number.

Petitioner's first issue is whether trial counsel was ineffective for neglecting to object to the district attorney's improper questioning of a character witness regarding Petitioner's prior arrests. Counsel is presumed effective and will only be deemed ineffective if the petitioner demonstrates that counsel's performance was deficient and he was prejudiced by the deficient performance. ***Commonwealth v. Steele***, 961 A.2d 786, 797 (Pa. 2008). Prejudice is established if there is a reasonable probability that but for counsel's errors the result of the proceeding would have been different. ***Id.***

To properly plead ineffective assistance of counsel, a petitioner must plead and prove that the underlying issue has arguable merit; counsel's actions lacked an objective reasonable basis;

and actual prejudice resulted from counsel's act or failure to act. ***Commonwealth v. Tedford***, 960 A.2d 1 (Pa. 2008) (citing ***Commonwealth v. Pierce***, 527 A.2d 973, 975 (Pa. 1987) adopting the U.S. Supreme Court's holding in ***Strickland v. Washington***, 466 U.S. 668 (1984)). If a petitioner fails to plead or meet any elements of the above cited test his claim must fail. ***Steele, supra.*** The Pennsylvania Supreme Court has consistently deemed cross-examination of a character witness regarding the witness's knowledge of a defendant's prior arrests improper. *See* ***Commonwealth v. Morgan***, 739 A.2d 1033 (Pa. 1999); ***Commonwealth v. Scott***, 436 A.2d 607 (Pa. 1981); *see also* ***Commonwealth v. Yeager***, 461 A.2d 281 (Pa. Super. 1983). Moreover, Pa.R.E. 405(a) bars cross-examination of a witness with respect to allegations of criminal misconduct that did not result in a conviction.

However, counsel did object to the questioning, the court immediately halted the questioning, did not allow the witness to answer the inquiry, and told the jury to disregard the question. Counsel at side-bar requested a mistrial, which the court declined and instead offered to give a further curative instruction. Counsel declined, stating on the record that the instruction would merely highlight the improper question that had not yet been answered. Thus, counsel did object and the trial judge properly interrupted the prosecutor and told the jury to disregard the question immediately after the improper question. Additionally, besides the two victims, multiple other witnesses testified that Petitioner began the altercation and pulled a firearm and fired the weapon numerous times. Furthermore, a video camera captured the incident on tape and demonstrated that Petitioner was the clear aggressor. Because counsel did object, stated on the record a reasonable basis for declining a curative instruction, and overwhelming evidence was introduced, this issue does not entitle Petitioner to relief.

Petitioner's second issue is that trial counsel was ineffective in

Sample No Merit Letter (Where trial was held)

failing to object to the prosecutor's statement during his closing argument that Petitioner was a "thug." Where the allegation is that the prosecutor committed misconduct during trial, and no objection was made, the claim must be argued as an ineffective assistance of counsel claim. The Pennsylvania Supreme Court in *Commonwealth v. Tedford*, 960 A.2d 1 (Pa. 2008), clearly outlined what a petitioner must prove to successfully raise an ineffectiveness claim for failure to object to a prosecutor's comments. The Court in *Tedford* stated, "ineffectiveness claims stemming from a failure to object to a prosecutor's conduct may succeed when the petitioner demonstrates that the prosecutor's actions violated a constitutionally or statutorily protected right, such as the Fifth Amendment privilege against compulsory self-incrimination or the Sixth Amendment right to a fair trial, or a constitutional interest such as due process." *Id.* at 29.

Additionally, the prosecutorial misconduct must be of sufficient significance to result in the denial of the defendant's right to a fair trial. A prosecutor's comments will only be reversible error when the comments effect is to unavoidably prejudice the jury, "forming in their minds a fixed bias and hostility toward the defendant such that they could not weigh the evidence objectively and render a fair verdict." *Id* at 33. If a prosecutor's comments "are based on the evidence or proper inferences therefrom, or represent mere oratorical flair," they are not objectionable. *Id.* Instantly, the Commonwealth's reference to the word thug occurred in the context of describing the victims and not Petitioner; hence, the issue has no arguable merit. N.T., DATE, page number.

Wherefore, counsel, pursuant to *Turner/Finley*, respectfully requests to be permitted to withdraw from representation of Petitioner.

CC:

Sample Petition to Withdraw

IN THE COURT OF COMMON PLEAS OF _____ COUNTY, PENNSYLVANIA, CRIMINAL DIVISION

COMMONWEALTH OF PENNSYLVANIA,

vs.   No:

John Q. Smith

    Petitioner

PETITION TO WITHDRAW

AND NOW, this _____ day of _____, comes NAME OF ATTORNEY, Esq., and respectfully requests that this Honorable Court permit counsel to withdraw from representation based on compliance with *Turner/Finley*. A copy of counsel's *Turner/Finley* no-merit letter is attached. Counsel has notified Petitioner of his right to retain private counsel or to continue *pro se*. A copy of the letter notifying Petitioner of his rights is attached.

Respectfully submitted,

_____

Name

Supreme Court ID No.

Name of Firm/Public Defender Office

Address

Phone Number

cc:

Name of DA on case

Sample Order Allowing Withdrawal

IN THE COURT OF COMMON PLEAS OF _____ COUNTY, PENNSYLVANIA

COMMONWEALTH OF PENNSYLVANIA,

vs.　　　　　　　　　　No:

John Q. Smith

 Petitioner

ORDER

AND NOW, this ____ day of _____, it is hereby ORDERED that _____, Esq. is permitted to withdraw from representation in this case having filed a no-merit letter in compliance with the dictates of **Commonwealth v. Finley**, 550 A.2d 213 (Pa. Super. 1988) (*en banc*) and **Commonwealth v. Turner**, 544 A.2d 927 (Pa. 1988).

BY THE COURT

_____ J.

Letter to Client about Withdrawal before PCRA Court

LETTERHEAD

Date
John Q. Smith
Prisoner Number
Address
Re: Commonwealth v. John Q. Smith, CASE NUMBER

Dear John Q. Smith:

After carefully reviewing your case, including the transcripts, your *pro se* petition, the remainder of the certified record, correspondence between you and trial counsel, as well as interviewing witnesses, and examining other documentation that you have supplied to me, I have determined that your petition is meritless and that there are no other issues of merit appearing in the record. Accordingly, I will be filing a **Turner/Finley** no-merit letter with the court. I have attached a copy of that no-merit letter. Furthermore, I am notifying you that you have the right to hire private counsel to proceed on your behalf, including filing any appeal. In addition, you may elect to proceed on your own without the assistance of an attorney before the PCRA court or on appeal.

Respectfully,

NAME

Attorney ID No.

Letter to Client about Withdrawal before PCRA Court

Letter to Client about Withdrawal before Superior Court

LETTERHEAD

Date
John Q. Smith, Prisoner Number
Jail Address
Re: Commonwealth v. John Q. Smith, CASE NUMBER

Dear John Q. Smith:

After careful review of your case, I have determined that any appeal would be without merit. Enclosed find a copy of my **Turner/Finley** no-merit brief and petition to withdraw that I will file with the Superior Court on DATE. Pursuant to Superior Court precedent, I am also notifying you that you have the right to hire private counsel or continue *pro se*, that is, on your own, before the Superior Court. Further, should the Superior Court permit me to withdraw, you may hire a private attorney or proceed *pro se* by filing a petition for allowance of appeal with the Pennsylvania Supreme Court within thirty days of the Superior Court decision.

If you would like to file, or have private counsel file, a merits brief on your behalf with the Superior Court, you should include your docket number, [include docket number], on the filing, and send the document to the following address:

Address

The Superior Court does not have a deadline for a *pro se* brief but if you intend to file a merits brief on your own behalf you should submit it within forty-five days. Upon receipt of the Superior Court decision, I will send you a copy of the determination.

Sincerely,

Sample Petition to Withdraw before Superior Court

COMMONWEALTH OF PENNSYLVANIA,

vs. No: ____ WDA ____

John Q. Smith

Petitioner

PETITION TO WITHDRAW

AND NOW comes NAME OF ATTORNEY, Esq., and respectfully requests that this Honorable Court permit counsel to withdraw from representation based on compliance with **Commonwealth v. Turner**, 544 A.2d 927 (Pa. 1988) and **Commonwealth v. Finley**, 550 A.2d 213 (Pa. Super. 1988) (*en banc*). After careful review of the entire Podunk County, Pennsylvania record at case number _____, including the transcripts of both the trial and sentencing and Appellant's *pro se* PCRA petition, and correspondence and materials supplied by Appellant and prior counsel, counsel finds that the issues Appellant wishes to raise do not entitle him to PCRA relief and counsel has determined that no other meritorious issues exist. Counsel, therefore, requests that he be permitted to withdraw from representation. A copy of counsel's **Turner/Finley** no-merit brief is attached. Counsel has notified Appellant of his right to retain private counsel or to continue *pro se*. A copy of the letter notifying Appellant of his rights is attached.

Respectfully submitted,

_____

Name
Supreme Court ID No.
Name of Firm/Public Defender Office
Address/Phone Number
cc: Name of DA on case

Sample Letter to Client

<u>Sample Letter to Client</u>
NAME OF ATTORNEY
OFFICE ADDRESS
OFFICE PHONE NUMBER
OFFICE EMAIL ADDRESS

Name of Client and Prison Identification Number
Prison Facility Address

Dear Sir [name of client],

My name is _____ and I have been appointed to represent you in your PCRA proceeding. I have examined your *pro se* petition and [will be reviewing/ or have reviewed the certified record in this case, including the available transcripts]. Enclosed is a questionnaire for you to complete along with two stamped envelopes for your convenience that are to be used to return the completed questionnaire as well as any other documents that you may have that are relevant to your case. Please do not send any prison briefs authored by a fellow inmate. I intend to fully research your case and complete a thorough amended petition and supporting brief on your behalf [after meeting with you]. Any filings will be sent to you to review.

Achieving PCRA relief in the nature of a new trial is often difficult and always rare, but I will zealously and ethically represent you at both the PCRA level and throughout any state appellate proceedings. This includes developing and arguing meritorious issues that may not have been included in your *pro se* petition as well as any arguably meritorious claims set forth

Sample Letter to Client

in your petition. Issues that lack merit will not be advanced. In the event that I do not pursue an issue that you have raised in your *pro se* petition, I will explain the justification for focusing on other issues. You will be fully apprised of all developments in your case as it proceeds. Please remember that while you are one of the foremost experts on the facts related to your case, it is my duty as your attorney to determine which legal issues to raise. I have already contacted your prior attorney(s) and requested his/her file in this matter. Attached is a copy of a letter sent to previous counsel regarding your case.

If you have any questions please send them with your completed questionnaire. Thank you.

Respectfully,

_____, Esq.

Sample Notice of Intent to Dismiss

IN THE COURT OF COMMON PLEAS OF _____ COUNTY, PENNSYLVANIA, CRIMINAL DIVISION

COMMONWEALTH OF PENNSYLVANIA,

vs.   No:

Jim Bow

Petitioner

Pa.R.Crim.P. 907 Notice of Intent to Dismiss

AND NOW, this ____ day of _____, 20__, after due consideration of Petitioner's petition for post-conviction relief ("PCRA") and the no-merit letter filed by court appointed counsel, _____, Esquire, pursuant to **Commonwealth v. Finley**, 550 A.2d 213 (Pa. Super. 1988) (*en banc*) and **Commonwealth v. Turner**, 544 A.2d 927(Pa. 1988) ("*Turner/Finley*"), this Court agrees with the characterization of the issues contained in the *Turner/Finley* no-merit letter and holds that Petitioner is not entitled to relief. Pursuant to Pa.R.Crim.P. 907(1), this Court hereby gives notice to Petitioner that his petition for post-conviction relief will be DISMISSED without an evidentiary hearing.

The *Turner/Finley* decisions mandate that competent counsel independently review the record before a PCRA court may grant an attorney's request to withdraw. **Commonwealth v. Pitts**, 981 A.2d 875, 876 n.1 (Pa. 2009). This independent review requires counsel to file a no-merit letter detailing the nature and extent of his review, listing each issue the petitioner wishes the court to examine, and explain why those issues are meritless. *Id.* This Court then must conduct its own independent examination of the record and agree with counsel that the petition is without merit. *Id.* Additionally, the Superior Court has imposed additional procedural requirements on counsel. Counsel must serve upon his client his no-merit letter and petition to withdraw along with a statement informing his client that if the court grants the withdrawal request, the petitioner may proceed with a privately retained attorney or *pro se*. **See Commonwealth v. Widgins**, 29 A.3d 816 (Pa. Super. 2011). Counsel has complied with the procedural requirements of **Turner/Finley** and **Widgins**. We therefore undertake our independent review.

Petitioner timely filed a *pro se* PCRA petition on September 25, 2011. The following day, this Court appointed counsel and directed that he file an amended petition or **Turner/Finley** no-merit letter within forty-five days. As noted, counsel submitted a **Turner/Finley** no-merit letter addressing the issue Petitioner raised in his *pro se* motion. Specifically, Petitioner contended that he was unlawfully induced into entering a guilty plea. Before addressing this issue, counsel noted that this Court sentenced Petitioner to six (6) months probation on September 26, 2010. Accordingly, Petitioner is no longer serving his sentence in the case *sub judice*. Counsel, therefore, reasoned that Petitioner is ineligible for relief.

To be eligible for relief under the PCRA, a petitioner must be serving a sentence of imprisonment, probation, or parole for the crime. **See** 42 Pa.C.S. § 9543(a)(1)(i). The petitioner must be eligible at both the time he files the petition and the time that relief is due. In the present case, Petitioner's sentence expired on or about March 29, 2011. Because Petitioner's sentence has expired, he is not eligible for relief. **See Commonwealth v. Ahlborn**, 699 A.2d 718 (Pa. 1997). This Court further advises Petitioner that if he desires to respond to the proposed dismissal of said petition, he must respond within twenty days of the filing date of this notice. Counsel, having complied with the dictates of **Turner/Finley**, is permitted to withdraw. The clerk of courts is directed to serve this order by certified mail, return receipt requested.

Sample Notice of Intent to Dismiss

BY THE COURT:

_____ J.

Sample Notice of Intent to Dismiss

IN THE COURT OF COMMON PLEAS OF _____
COUNTY, PENNSYLVANIA, CRIMINAL DIVISION

COMMONWEALTH OF PENNSYLVANIA,

vs.   No.

JOHN DOE

NOTICE OF DISMISSAL

AND NOW, this ____ day of _____, 20__, after careful review, and finding that Petitioner's writ of *habeas corpus* should be treated as an application for post-conviction relief ("PCRA"), the Court finds that the petition lacks any new genuine issues of material fact, and the issues raised have been previously litigated. For the reasons set forth below and pursuant to Pa.R. Crim.P. 907(1), this Court hereby gives notice to Petitioner that his PCRA petition will be DISMISSED without an evidentiary hearing.

Petitioner pled guilty to aggravated assault and robbery arising out of two separate incidents and was sentenced on February --, 2007, to eight to sixteen years imprisonment. No direct appeal was filed. Petitioner filed a PCRA petition on May 18, 2007. Subsequently, _____, Esq. was appointed PCRA counsel and filed an amended petition on June --, 2007. The Court conducted an evidentiary hearing on July --, 2007, and denied the petition on August --, 2007. Petitioner timely appealed. However, the Superior Court filed a notice of discontinuance of the action on November --, 2007, after Petitioner withdrew his appeal. Petitioner then filed a writ of *habeas corpus* on January --, 2008, reiterating the identical claims he made in his original

PCRA. Specifically, he alleged that his constitutional right to a direct appeal was infringed and that he was entitled to a direct appeal *nunc pro tunc*, his guilty plea to robbery was unlawfully induced, and that his counsel's refusal to file an appeal was governmental interference with that right.

Regardless of the title of a pleading asking for post conviction relief, the pleading is to be treated as if it were a PCRA petition. ***Commonwealth v. Jackson***, 30 A.3d 516 (Pa. Super. 2011); ***Commonwealth v. Fowler***, 930 A.2d 586 (Pa. Super. 2007); ***Commonwealth v. Kutnyak***, 781 A.2d 1259 (Pa. Super. 2001); ***Commonwealth v. Guthrie***, 749 A.2d 502 (Pa. Super. 2000); ***Commonwealth v. Evans***, 866 A.2d 442 (Pa. Super. 2005); *compare* ***Commonwealth v. Deaner***, 779 A.2d 578 (Pa. Super. 2001). Under Pennsylvania law, the PCRA subsumes the writ of *habeas corpus* unless the claim does not fall under the PCRA. 42 Pa. C.S. § 9542. Since Petitioner claims: (1) violations of the Constitution of the United States and the Pennsylvania Constitution; (2) that his plea of guilty to robbery was unlawfully induced; (3) and improper obstruction by government officials of the petitioner's right of appeal, the issues raised are cognizable under the PCRA. *See* 42 Pa. C.S. § 9543.

Petitioner is not entitled to a PCRA hearing as a matter of right; the Court may decline to hold hearing where there is no genuine issue concerning any material fact and the petitioner is not entitled to post-conviction collateral relief, and no purpose would be served by any further proceedings. ***Commonwealth v. Hardcastle***, 701 A.2d 541 (Pa. 1997). In order to be eligible for relief under the PCRA, a petitioner must plead and prove by a preponderance of the evidence, that the issues raised have not been previously litigated. ***Commonwealth v. Senk***, 582 A.2d 1119 (Pa. Super. 1990). Under 42 Pa. C.S. § 9544(a)(3), an issue is previously litigated if it was raised and decided in a proceeding collaterally attacking the conviction or sentence.

Sample Notice of Intent to Dismiss

Petitioner has not pled or proved that the issues raised were not previously litigated in his original PCRA, further a review of the record indicates that each of his issues were previously raised. In addition, Petitioner has not raised any new issues of material fact. As Petitioner has raised no new genuine issues of material fact, and the claims raised were previously litigated in his original PCRA, the Court finds his petition warrants dismissal without an evidentiary hearing. This Court further advises Petitioner that if he desires to respond to the proposed dismissal of said petition, he must respond within twenty (20) days of the date of this notice. The clerk of courts is directed to serve this order by certified mail, return receipt requested.

BY THE COURT:

_____ J.

Sample Notice of Intent to Dismiss

IN THE COURT OF COMMON PLEAS OF _____ COUNTY, PENNSYLVANIA, CRIMINAL DIVISION

COMMONWEALTH OF PENNSYLVANIA,

vs.   CASE #

PETITIONER

October___, 20__

NOTICE OF INTENT TO DIMISS PURSUANT TO PENNSYLVANIA RULE OF CRIMINAL PROCEDURE 907(1)

This is an amended PCRA petition filed on _____. After careful review, this Court will dismiss the petition.

On December __, 19__, police officers from _____, Pennsylvania responded to a shooting at a local convenience store. Statements were given to the police by four passengers

Sample Notice of Intent to Dismiss

riding with Petitioner at the time of the incident. According to their statements, they had driven to the store with Petitioner before he entered the convenience store with a shotgun. Petitioner himself stated he removed a shotgun from his trunk and took it into the store. Additional statements from an eyewitness described a person fitting the general description of Petitioner enter the store with a shotgun, approach the counter, point the shotgun at the store's clerk and demand money. After taking money from the cash register, Petitioner attempted to fire his shotgun, but the weapon misfired. He then adjusted the weapon and fired again, this time hitting the clerk with the shotgun blast, causing the clerk's death.

An eyewitness outside of the convenience store described the getaway car, followed the car, and recorded a partial license plate number. Police, upon receipt of this information, were led to Petitioner. Store surveillance cameras also captured the crime on tape and clothes matching those seen on the assailant in the video tape were found in Petitioner's possession. Police also recorded Petitioner in a conversation with another individual in which he discussed the robbery and shooting. In addition, police interviewed Petitioner. After waiving his right to remain silent, and his right to counsel, Petitioner admitted to the commission of the robbery and the shooting. Thereafter, Petitioner was arrested and charged with first degree murder and the district attorney's office indicated that it would be seeking the death penalty.

Trial counsel for Petitioner sought to suppress both the confession and the wiretap conversation. The trial court denied that motion. After the court ruled the confession and wiretap conversation admissible, Petitioner proceeded to a non-jury trial. In preparation, trial counsel sought a psychiatric evaluation of Petitioner from Dr. _____ for purposes of putting forth a diminished capacity defense. Counsel also conducted extensive discovery.

Sample Notice of Intent to Dismiss

Faced with the possibility of a death sentence, Petitioner entered into a negotiated plea agreement with the Commonwealth and pled guilty to second degree murder and robbery. Petitioner, with the advice of counsel, completed a seven page, forty-three question written guilty plea colloquy. Within the written guilty plea colloquy, Petitioner stated that he was voluntarily, knowingly, and intelligently entering the plea. He also indicated he was not suffering from any mental disorders nor was he under any medication. Subsequently, the court conducted an oral colloquy. Petitioner testified, under oath, that his guilty plea was voluntary, knowing, and intelligent. Immediately thereafter, the court sentenced Petitioner to life imprisonment for second-degree murder.

Petitioner, represented by new counsel, filed a timely notice of appeal with the Superior Court alleging ineffective assistance of counsel, the unconstitutionality of the Pennsylvania felony murder statute, and that his history of psychiatric treatment made him incapable of entering a knowing, voluntary, and intelligent plea. Specifically, Petitioner alleged: (1) that trial counsel was ineffective in failing to move to withdraw his guilty plea, for not raising an issue of competency to stand trial; (2) and that his history of psychiatric treatment rendered him incapable of entering a proper guilty plea.

The Superior Court found no merit to his arguments and concluded that the evidence against Petitioner was overwhelming. ***See Commonwealth v.*** _____, __ A.2d __ (Pa. Super. 1998) (unpublished memorandum). On the issue of Petitioner's mental condition at the time of his plea, the Superior Court found that he answered the written questions in the seven page colloquy and responded orally at his plea hearing to understanding the charges and the evidence against him. Further, the Superior Court held that his plea was voluntarily, knowingly, and intelligently entered. In addition, the Superior Court concluded that there were no grounds to support a finding that a competency hearing was necessary, stating that Petitioner confused his right to present a diminished capacity defense if he went to trial with the necessity of a competency hearing. *Id.* at __. The Superior Court also pointed out that Petitioner gave extensive oral statements regarding his guilt. Finally, the panel held that trial counsel was not ineffective for failing to file a post-sentence motion to withdraw the guilty plea or failing to raise the competency question.

Thereafter, Petitioner filed a timely petition for allowance of appeal to the Pennsylvania Supreme Court. The Supreme Court denied his petition and he filed a timely *pro se* motion for post-conviction relief. The court appointed a series of attorneys to represent Petitioner. Petitioner's third attorney submitted an amended petition and requested an evidentiary hearing. No hearing was conducted and the original PCRA court issued a notice of dismissal, almost five years after the filing of the initial petition. In response, Petitioner hired his own attorney, who prior to the issuance of the final order, sought leave and was permitted to file an amended PCRA petition. That petition alleged ineffective assistance of counsel on the basis that counsel had incorrectly advised Petitioner that he would be eligible for parole if he accepted the guilty plea.

> [1] Any alleged statements by counsel about a likely sentence could not have induced the plea where the written guilty plea colloquy and oral colloquy would have dispelled any misconceptions about the defendant's possible sentence. ***See Commonwealth v. Fowler***, 843 A.2d 758, 765 (Pa. Super. 2006).

The prior court took no action on this petition and this Court was assigned the matter in February 2009. The current amended PCRA petition was filed that same month by yet another attorney, after this Court granted counsel's request to file an amended petition. The petition alleged that Petitioner's plea of

Sample Notice of Intent to Dismiss

guilty was unlawfully induced by both ineffective assistance of counsel and prosecutorial misconduct, specifically an alleged false pre-trial statement given by a juvenile witness that was allegedly induced by a former district attorney. In addition, attached to Petitioner's amended petition was a document titled "Writ of *Habeas Corpus Ad Subjiciendum*," which alleges that the entire 1968 Pennsylvania Constitution is unconstitutional, and therefore this Court was without jurisdiction. This opinion addresses the issues raised in Petitioner's most recent amended petition, including his supplemental *habeas corpus* petition.

Before considering the merits of any PCRA petition, this Court must first address whether the petition was timely filed. If the petition is not timely filed then the Court has no jurisdiction to reach the merits of the case. ***Commonwealth v. Fisher***, 870 A.2d 864 (Pa. 2005). Under the PCRA, a petition is timely filed if submitted within one year of the final judgment of sentence or if it falls within one of three timeliness exceptions, and was filed within sixty (60) days of the date the claim could have been presented. 42 Pa. C.S. § 9545.

Petitioner's date of final judgment of sentence was February __, 1999.[2] Therefore, pursuant to the PCRA statute, Petitioner had until February __, 2000, to file a timely petition and his first petition met the timeliness requirement. Also, while the current petition was filed beyond the one year period, the current petition may be considered an amended petition of the original PCRA, since no final order was entered by this Court and this Court allowed the amendments. Because the original PCRA petition was never acted upon and was timely filed and this Court allowed counsel to amend the most recent petition, the petition is timely.

[2] This is 90 days after the November __, 1998 denial of allowance of appeal by the Pennsylvania Supreme Court, the period in which Petitioner could have sought

review by the United States Supreme Court.

Petitioner in the most recent amended petition asserted that he was entitled to the withdrawal of his guilty plea because: (1) his constitutional rights were violated, (2) his plea of guilty was unlawfully induced, and (3) the unavailability at the time of trial of exculpatory evidence that would have changed the outcome of the trial. In addition, Petitioner made a boilerplate allegation of ineffective assistance of counsel. Since boilerplate allegations of ineffective assistance of counsel are insufficient, trial counsel will not be deemed ineffective on that basis. ***Commonwealth v. Lambert***, 797 A.2d 232 (Pa. 2001).[3] Since Petitioner raised ineffectiveness claims on direct appeal he also was required to layer his claims. ***Commonwealth v. Chmiel***, 30 A.3d 1111, 1128 (Pa. 2011). We have looked through his failure to do so, and conclude that the underlying ineffectiveness claim fails for reasons outlined in our discussion of his remaining arguments.

[3] To properly plead and establish a claim of ineffective assistance of counsel, a petitioner must show: (1) the underlying claim has arguable merit; (2) that counsel's performance was not reasonably designed to effectuate the petitioner's interests; and (3) that counsel's unreasonable performance prejudiced the petitioner. ***Commonwealth v. Hall***, 872 A.2d 1177 (Pa. 2005). If a petitioner fails to plead or meet any elements of the above cited test his claim must fail. ***Commonwealth v. Sneed***, 899 A.2d 1067 (Pa. 2006). A petitioner also must plead that the claims were not waived or previously litigated during either direct review or collateral review. ***Commonwealth v. Rios***, 920 A.2d 790 (Pa. 2007).

Petitioner claims that his guilty plea was unlawfully induced by prosecutorial misconduct and pursuant to 42 Pa. C.S. § 9543(a)(2)(iii), he is entitled to the withdrawal of his guilty plea.[4] To withdraw a plea on the grounds that the plea was unlawfully induced, the defendant must prove that the plea was the result of manifest injustice. ***Commonwealth v. Holbrook***, 629 A.2d 154 (Pa. Super. 1993). To demonstrate a manifest injustice, Petitioner must show that the plea was involuntary or was entered without knowledge of the charges. ***Commonwealth v. Fluharty***, 632 A.2d 312 (Pa. Super. 1993). Petitioner also alleges prosecutorial misconduct on the part of a former district attorney. According to Petitioner, a juvenile witness recanted and stated he was offered a choice of jail or cooperation with the district attorney's office. Police then instructed him to write out and sign a statement implicating Petitioner in the crimes of robbery and homicide.

> [4] Under the provision cited, and unlike an ineffectiveness claim, Petitioner must plead that he is innocent of the charges. ***Commonwealth v. Lynch***, 820 A.2d 728 (Pa. Super. 2003); 42 Pa.C.S. 9543(a)(2)(iii). Petitioner did not state anywhere in his petition that he was innocent of the charges, however, this Court treated the petition as though he properly pled the issue.

Petitioner attached a notarized affidavit in which the juvenile witness recanted his earlier statements. Nowhere in the affidavit was there mentioned any allegations of misconduct by the district attorney. The affidavit does not identify the detectives involved, nor does it indicate the district attorney was present at the time of the statement. Neither Petitioner nor the affidavit offer anything more than generalized allegations of prosecutorial misconduct. Assuming *arguendo* that these statements were improperly induced, Petitioner admitted to committing the crimes and there was substantial other evidence indicating he committed the crimes. The record contains statements of a full account of the shooting by friends of Petitioner and a six page document the police reduced to writing

Sample Notice of Intent to Dismiss

based on Petitioner's oral confession detailing his involvement in the robbery and shooting. This Court finds it highly improbable that a statement made by a single witness induced Petitioner to plead guilty.

Importantly, the fact that the recantation witness claimed that he had no knowledge of the crime, and recanted having previously implicated Petitioner in a statement to police, does not establish Petitioner's innocence, nor does it exculpate the defendant. *See* ***Commonwealth v. Bond***, 819 A.2d 33, 49-50 (Pa. 2002). Indeed, the only thing the witness's affidavit conclusively established was that he "is guilty of fabrication -- either in his initial statement to police or in his post-conviction recantation." *Id.* at 50. Thus, Petitioner's claim that the newly-discovered evidence was exculpatory is, as a matter of law, inaccurate, and does not entitle him to relief.

Moreover, conviction after a guilty plea is not based on the evidence in the hands of the Commonwealth, but is based on a defendant's open court admission. ***Commonwealth v. Vealey***, 581 A.2d 217 (Pa. Super. 1990). Therefore, Petitioner's conviction is based on his open court admission of guilt. Hence, Petitioner must show that his open court admission was induced under circumstances that make it likely that the inducement caused him to plead guilty where he was innocent. The juvenile witness's original police statement alone could not have been the reason for Petitioner's guilty plea, since Petitioner himself confessed to the crime and there were numerous other witnesses who gave statements implicating Petitioner.

Since the reason for Petitioner's guilty plea was not the single statement made by the juvenile witness, it would be improper to allow his guilty plea to be withdrawn based solely upon this recantation. *See* 42 Pa.C.S. § 9543 (a)(2)(iii) (stating that in order to be eligible for relief a person must plead that "*the circumstances make it likely* that the inducement caused the petitioner to plead guilty when he is innocent") (emphasis added). The recantation evidence here is insufficient to overcome the overwhelming evidence of Petitioner's guilt and his own open court admission.

Petitioner also asserts that, because the Pennsylvania Constitution of 1776 prohibited the legislature from altering that constitution, the current Pennsylvania Constitution is unconstitutionally void. Accordingly, he contends that this Court was without jurisdiction in his original criminal case. Section 9 of the 1776 Pennsylvania Constitution did provide that the General Assembly "shall have no power to add to, alter, abolish, or infringe any part of this constitution." Pa.Const. Chapt. II, § 9 (1776). Indeed, a similar claim to that leveled by Petitioner was politically debated and rejected in 1789, and several commentators have asserted that the 1790 constitutional convention was extra-legal. John Alexander Jameson, A TREATISE ON THE PRINCIPLES OF CONSTITUTIONAL LAW AND LEGISLATION: THE CONSTITUTIONAL CONVENTION, (Myers & Co. 2d ed. 1869); Matthew J. Herrington, *Popular Sovereignty in Pennsylvania 1776-1791*, 67 Temple L. Rev. 575 (1994); Christian G. Fritz, *Recovering the Lost Worlds of America's Written Constitutions*, 68 Alb. L. Rev. 261 (2005). However, as Professor Thomas Raeburn White, one of Pennsylvania's most eminent constitutional scholars, pointed out, "subsequent judicial opinion upholds the views of the majority of the General Assembly of 1789." Thomas Raeburn White, COMMENTARIES ON THE CONSTITUTION OF PENNSYLVANIA, 35 (1907).

Similar to Petitioner's argument, a minority of the General Assembly objected to the calling of a constitutional convention for the amending of the 1776 constitution, contending that the 1776 constitution could only be altered by an entity labeled the Council of Censors, and that the members of the house were not competent to call a convention. *See* White, ***supra*** at 34; Proceedings Relative to Calling the Conventions of 1776 and 1790: Chapter 1, Proceedings Relative to Calling the Convention of 1789-90, at 131 (1825). In this regard, Section 47 of the 1776 Constitution granted authority to an elected body known as the Council of Censors to "enquire whether the constitution has been preserved inviolate in every part[.]" Pa.Const. Chapt. II, § 47 (1776). The Council of Censors was to be elected every seven years, and had the power to call a constitutional convention. ***Id.*** Section 47 specifically provided in relevant part,

> if there appear to them an absolute necessity of amending any article of the constitution which may be defective, explaining such as may be thought not clearly expressed, and of adding such as are necessary for the preservation of the rights and happiness of the people; But the articles to be amended, and the amendments proposed, and such articles as are to be proposed to be added or abolished, shall be promulgated at least six months before the day appointed for the election of such convention, for the previous consideration of the people, that they may have an opportunity of instructing their delegates on the subject.

According to the minority, constitutional amendment could only be achieved via the method outlined in Section 47. A majority of Pennsylvania representatives rejected that limitation and, on March 24, 1789, adopted a resolution for the calling of a constitutional convention. *See* Proceedings Relative to Calling the Conventions of 1776 and 1790: Chapter 1, Proceedings Relative to Calling the Convention of 1789-90, at 129-130 (1825). Citing both the Declaration of Independence and

Pennsylvania's bill of rights, the majority proposed that the people, if it be their will, elect members to a constitutional convention. Article V of the Pennsylvania Declaration of Rights specifically delineated,

> That government is, or ought to be, instituted for the common benefit, protection and security of the people, nation or community; and not for the particular emolument or advantage of any single man, family, or set of men, who are a part only of that community: And that the community hath an indubitable, unalienable and indefeasible right to reform, alter, or abolish government in such manner as shall be by that community judged most conducive to the public weal.

Pa.Const. Chapt. I, § V (1776).

This clause, known today as the People's Sovereignty clause, has been determined by the Pennsyvlania Supreme Court to authorize subsequent legislatively called constitutional conventions. **Wells v. Bain**, 75 Pa. 39 (1874); **Appeal of Woods**, 75 Pa. 59 (1874); **Stander v. Kelley**, 250 A.2d 474 (Pa. 1969). With respect to the 1790 convention, despite the minority objections, within four months of the resolution, the General Assembly reported that a majority of Pennsylvania citizens approved the calling of a constitutional convention. John L. Gedid, Pennsylvania's Constitutional Conventions—Discarding the Myths, Pa. Bar. Assoc. Quarterly, October 2011, at 157. Accordingly, a general election for delegates to the convention ensued. *Id.* That convention proposed the 1790 Constitution and then adjourned for six months to allow the people to review the changes. *Id.* at 155.

The members of the convention then ratified the 1790 Constitution and pronounced it the new constitution of this

Commonwealth. As one commentator has astutely noted, "the call for election of delegates by the legislature and the election that followed constituted action by citizens and their legal representatives to change the then existing [1776] constitution." *Id*. at 157.

In addition to the People's Sovereignty Clause, the preamble to the 1776 Constitution echoed the sentiments of the Declaration of Independence, stating, "the people have a right by common consent to change" their form of government. Pa.Const. Preamble (1776). It further provided that the Constitution was "to remain in force therein forever, unaltered, except in such articles as shall hereafter on experience be found to require improvement and which shall be the same authority of the people, fairly delegated as this frame of government directs, be amended or improved for the more effectual obtaining and securing the great end and design of all government[.]" *Id*.

These provisions are consistent with the general principle that all power to create, destroy, or alter government is inherent in the people. Thus, "[i]f the minority [in 1789] were correct in their view of the functions of the Legislature, the convention of 1790 was contrary to law, and the constitution, which it enacted, by the subsequent assent of the majority of the people, became the product of a real though bloodless revolution." White, *supra* at 35 n. 7. Indeed, as Professor White cogently stated over a century ago,

> The constitution being the written will of the people, of course the method provided therein may be safely followed. It is not exclusive, however, as the people cannot be deemed to have deprived themselves of any of their fundamental right to change the government in any manner they may determine unless they have expressly

so stated. They may, therefore, bring about a change of government by calling a convention in any way in which it is possible for them as a whole to express their will.

Id. at 37.

This view is not merely consistent with early constitutional theory and the principle of the people's sovereignty, but as noted earlier, is binding law announced by the Pennsylvania Supreme Court. In ***Wells, supra***, the Court was faced with determining whether it should issue an injunction to prevent commissioners in Philadelphia from voting on ratification of the constitution in a manner that was not authorized by the enabling act of the constitutional convention. The Court, in issuing an injunction, began its decision, opining:

> Since the Declaration of Independence in 1776, it has been an axiom of the American people, that all just government is founded in the consent of the people. This is recognised in the second section of the declaration of rights of the Constitution of Pennsylvania, which affirms that the people "have at all times an inalienable and indefeasible right to alter, reform or abolish their government in such manner as they may think proper."

Id. at 46.

The High Court continued, stating that the constitution could be amended by the method included within the constitution, a legislatively called constitutional convention, or revolution. The ***Wells*** Court noted that, "[t]he first two are peaceful means through which the consent of the people to alteration is obtained, and by which the existing government consents to be displaced without revolution. The government gives its consent, either by pursuing the mode provided in the constitution, or by passing a law to call a convention." *Id*. at 47. Discussing the constitutional convention that resulted in the 1874 Pennsylania Constitution, the **Wells** Court set forth, "The people having adopted a proceeding by law as the means of executing their will, having acted under it and chosen their delegates by virtue of its authority, submitted themselves to it, as their own selected and approved means of carrying out peacefully their purpose of amendment." *Id*. at 48.

In addition, in ***Appeal of Woods***, *supra*, the High Court reasoned:

> The calling of a convention, and regulating its action by law, is not forbidden in the constitution. It is a conceded *manner*, through which the people may exercise the right reserved in the bill of rights. It falls, therefore, within the protection of the bill of rights as a very manner in which the people may proceed to amend their constitution[.]

Id. at 72.

Additionally, after the 1968 Constitution was adopted, the method in which it was adopted was challenged. In ***Stander***, *supra*, the Pennsylvania Supreme Court rejected the argument that the Pennsylvania Constitution could only be amended via the method delineated in that document. Although three judges concurred in the result and wrote further on an issue not pertinent hereto, and one judge dissented, neither the dissent nor the concurring justices disputed that a constitutional convention was a legitimate method for altering the constitution. The lead opinion provided,

> this Court has several times previously held that

Sample Notice of Intent to Dismiss

amendments to our prior and existing Constitution may be initiated by the calling of a Constitutional Convention, provided a majority of the electors vote in favor of such a call. Unmindful of the fact that the Constitution of 1874, which has been the framework of our State Government for over 90 years, was adopted by the convention method at a time when the amendatory provisions of the then existing Constitution did not prescribe a convention as a method for Constitutional change, appellants contend that nowhere in any Article or provision of the Constitution is there any authority for the calling of a Constitutional Convention for the purpose of permitting the people to amend the Constitution. Appellants also forget that the provisions for the adoption of the Constitution of the United States directly contravened Article XIII of the Articles of Confederation which were drawn up and submitted to the people through a Constitutional Convention, and that 12 of the original 13 State Constitutions contained no amendment provisions, yet all of them were amended from time to time by the Convention method.

Stander, *supra* at 478-479 (footnote omitted). The Court specifically held that "so long as a Constitutional Convention is not expressly prohibited by the then existing Constitution it represents a proper manner and method in which the citizens of Pennsylvania may initiate an amendment of their Constitution." *Id.* at 479. Under this rationale, past constitutions and the current 1968 Constitution were properly adopted.

Sample Notice of Intent to Dismiss

Because the people in this Commonwealth retain the right to amend and change their constitution, and nothing in the federal constitution prohibits a state from amending its constitution, and case law has upheld the validity of legislatively called constitutional conventions and the 1968 Constitution, the Pennsylvania Constitution is constitutional. This Court, therefore, gives notice that Petitioner's PCRA petition will be dismissed without an evidentiary hearing.

BY THE COURT:

_____, J.

ORDER

AND NOW, this ____ day of_____, 20__, after due consideration of Petitioner's Amended Petition for Post-Conviction Relief and careful review of the certified record herein, this Court holds that the issues raised by Petitioner do not entitle him to relief or an evidentiary hearing. Pursuant to Pa.R.Crim.P. 907, this Court hereby gives notice to Petitioner that his petition will be DISMISSED without an evidentiary hearing. Petitioner may respond within twenty days of the filing of this order. The clerk of courts is directed to serve this order by certified mail, return receipt requested.

BY THE COURT

_____J.

Sample Final Order

<u>Sample Final Order</u>

IN THE COURT OF COMMON PLEAS OF _____ COUNTY, PENNSYLVANIA

COMMONWEALTH OF PENNSYLVANIA

vs.   No:

ROSS COE

<u>ORDER</u>

AND NOW, this ____ day of March, 20__, for the reasons set forth in this Court's Notice of Intent to Dismiss dated March __, 20__, it is hereby ORDERED, ADJUDGED AND DECREED that Petitioner's PCRA is DENIED. Pursuant to Pa.R.Crim.P. 907, the Court further advises Petitioner that if he wishes to appeal this final order he has thirty days from the date of the filing of this order to file his appeal. The Court directs the clerk of courts to send this order by certified mail, return receipt requested.

BY THE COURT:

_____J.

Sample Notice of Appeal

Sample Notice of Appeal

_____ County Court of Common Pleas

Commonwealth   )
      v.   )   Case No(s):
)
_____   )
Petitioner   )

NOTICE OF APPEAL

Notice is hereby given that _____, the above named petitioner, appeals to the Pennsylvania Superior Court from the order entered on _____. Pursuant to Pa.R.A.P. 904(c), I, _____, Esq., certify that the order for transcript is attached. The order appealed from has been entered on the docket as evidenced by the attached copy of the docket entry.

_____
Signature

_____
Print

_____
Attorney ID Number

_____
Firm Name

_____
Address

_____
Email Address

_____
Telephone Number

Sample 1925(a) Opinion

Sample 1925(a) Opinion
IN THE COURT OF COMMON PLEAS OF
_____ COUNTY, PENNSYLVANIA, CRIMINAL DIVISION

COMMONWEALTH OF PENNSYLVANIA,

vs.   No. CASE #

PETITIONER'S NAME

June___, 20__

OPINION PURSUANT TO PENNSYLVANIA RULE OF APPELLATE PROCEDURE 1925 (a)

This is an appeal from the denial of Appellant's first post-conviction petition ("PCRA"). After careful review, this Court dismissed the petition. This Court should be affirmed.

The facts of the case arise from the sexual assaults of three minor female victims, ages eight, seven, and five at the time of the assaults. The underlying factual details are outlined in this Court's earlier Pa.R.A.P. 1925(a) opinion. T.C.O., 1/--/04. Appellant, on October --, 2003, following jury trial, was convicted of rape, attempted rape, statutory sexual assault, involuntary deviate sexual intercourse, sexual assault, aggravated indecent assault, indecent assault, intimidation of witnesses or victims, and corruption of minors. Appellant, thereafter, was sentenced on December __, 2003, to a term of incarceration of twenty seven years to fifty four years. Appellant filed a timely direct appeal raising four issues. Those issues were: (1) whether the trial court abused its discretion by permitting a Children and Youth Services ("CYS") caseworker to sit on the jury; (2) whether the prosecutor engaged in misconduct by failing to timely produce and provide discovery materials; (3) whether the trial court abused its discretion in prohibiting Appellant from introducing evidence of prior instances of sexual assault against the victims; and (4) sufficiency and weight of the evidence claims. After review, the Superior Court affirmed the trial court's judgment of sentence.

Subsequently, Appellant filed a timely post-conviction petition ("PCRA"), raising twenty issues. A series of different attorneys were appointed to represent Appellant, but no amended petition was ever filed. On December __, 2005, the court dismissed Appellant's PCRA, and he filed an appeal on or about January __, 2006. For reasons unknown to this Court, the record was not received by the Superior Court until June 2006. Counsel requested and was granted withdrawal by the Superior Court, and the record was remanded for the appointment of new counsel. Current counsel was then appointed on October __, 2006.

On May -, 2007, the Superior Court, having received no brief from appointed counsel, remanded for a determination as to whether counsel had abandoned Appellant. Counsel indicated he had not abandoned Appellant and filed a brief on behalf of Appellant on August __, 2007. Although prior counsel filed multiple briefs in support of Appellant's claims, counsel did not file a document entitled as an amended petition and the Superior Court remanded the case on or about March __, 2008. It further ordered appointed counsel to file an amended petition within 60 days of receipt of the record.

This Court was then assigned to the case because the trial judge who had previously handled both the trial and the PCRA hearings had retired. On August __, 2009, appointed counsel having failed to file an amended petition, the Court issued an order directing counsel to file an amended petition, and further directing that failure to file a petition would result in removal from the case as it was *per se* ineffectiveness. Counsel filed his amended petition on August --, 2009. Thereafter, this Court issued a notice of dismissal on September __, 2009, setting forth

Sample 1925(a) Opinion

the reasons for the denial of PCRA relief. Subsequently, a final order was issued on October __, 2009. Appellant filed the instant appeal on November __, 2009. This Court issued an order directing counsel to file a Pa.R.A.P. 1925(b) concise statement of the errors complained of on appeal and counsel complied. Appellant raises the following issues.

    1. Trial counsel was ineffective in failing to challenge a juror who was alleged to be an employee of CYS.

    2. Trial counsel was ineffective for failing to make an objection to the trial court's refusal to introduce testimony from others charged with independently sexually assaulting two of the child victims.

Appellant's Pa.R.A.P. 1925(b) concise statement.

This court may dismiss a PCRA petition without an evidentiary hearing where there is no genuine issue of material fact, the petitioner is not entitled to post-conviction collateral relief, and no purpose would be served by any further proceedings. ***Commonwealth v. Hardcastle***, 701 A.2d 541 (Pa. 1997); Pa.R.Crim.P. 907(1). To properly plead and establish a claim of ineffective assistance of counsel a defendant must show: (1) the underlying claim has arguable merit; (2) that counsel's performance was not reasonably designed to effectuate the Appellant's interests; and (3) that counsel's unreasonable performance prejudiced Appellant. ***Commonwealth v. Hall***, 872 A.2d 1177 (Pa. 2005). If a defendant fails to plead or meet any elements of the above cited test his claim must fail. ***Commonwealth v. Sneed***, 899 A.2d 1067 (Pa. 2006). Boilerplate allegations of ineffective assistance of counsel are insufficient. ***Commonwealth v. Lambert***, 797 A.2d 232 (Pa. 2001). A defendant also must plead that the claims were not waived or previously litigated on either direct review or collateral review. ***Commonwealth v. Rios***, 920 A.2d 790 (Pa. 2007).

Appellant's initial issue is that trial counsel was ineffective in failing to challenge a juror who was alleged to be an employee of CYS. This issue must fail because the underlying merits of the claim were previously litigated and determined to be without merit. Though an ineffectiveness claims is distinct from the underlying issue, *see Commonwealth v. Collins*, 888 A.2d 564 (Pa. 2005), counsel cannot be held ineffective for failing to raise an issue that was held to be without merit. The Superior Court found that the juror in question did not indicate she knew anything about the facts of the case, the attorneys, or the parties. *See Commonwealth v. _____*, 000 A.2d 000 (Pa. Super. YEAR) (unpublished memorandum, at 5).

The Court also noted that the juror indicated she could determine Appellant's guilt or innocence without bias or prejudice. *Id.* In concluding its discussion on the issue, the Superior Court found that the record did not "demonstrate a close relationship between the juror and the case such that a likelihood of prejudice would be presumed." *Id.* (citing *Commonwealth v. Wilson*, 672 A.2d 293, 299 (Pa. 1996)). Because the underlying issue has been previously litigated, Appellant cannot establish arguable merit on his ineffectiveness claim and he is not entitled to relief on that basis.

The second claim Appellant levels is that trial counsel was ineffective in failing to pursue an objection to the trial court's refusal to introduce testimony from other individuals independently charged with assaulting two of the victims. Appellant alleges that this testimony could have established how the victims acquired sexual knowledge and that he was the victim of mistaken identity. Initially, we note that trial counsel did object to the refusal of the trial court to allow testimony about allegations made by the victims against other individuals charged with similar crimes.

Sample 1925(a) Opinion

The trial court refused to allow trial counsel to pursue that line of questioning and the Superior Court held that the trial court did not abuse its discretion in refusing to permit Appellant to cross-examine one of the victims and a child victim specialist regarding prior sexual abuse by two other individuals charged with assaulting two of the young victims. Specifically, the Superior Court found that trial counsel had not argued or shown that the evidence was relevant and also determined the prior sexual allegation evidence was irrelevant.

Insofar as PCRA counsel implies that trial counsel was ineffective in failing to set forth why the evidence was relevant, the proffered testimony would be irrelevant unless there was evidence that the accusations made were false. ***Commonwealth v. Boyles***, 595 A.2d 1180 (Pa. Super. 1991); *see also **Commonwealth v. Holder***, 815 A.2d 1115 (Pa. Super. 2003) (while rape shield law did not prevent introduction of evidence that the victim was previously assaulted the matter was collateral and irrelevant as previous allegation did not bear on whether defendant raped the victim); ***Commonwealth v. L.N.***, 787 A.2d 1064 (Pa. Super. 2001) (evidence that victim previously asserted that he was sexually assaulted by someone other than the defendant was irrelevant).

In ***Boyles***, the Court found that evidence that a victim made accusations of sexual assault against other men was irrelevant because there was no evidence that those accusations were false. Subsequent to Appellant's trial, the additional men alleged to have assaulted the victims in the present case pled guilty to various sexual crimes against the victims. Since there was no indication that the allegations made against the other men were untrue in the present case, the evidence was irrelevant and Appellant was not prejudiced. *See also **Commonwealth v. Allburn***, 721 A.2d 163 (Pa. Super. 1998) (determining that evidence of other sexual contact is not admissible to provide an alternative source of sexual knowledge of a young victim).[1]

Sample 1925(a) Opinion

For the foregoing reasons, Appellant cannot establish actual prejudice and Appellant's PCRA petition was properly dismissed.

BY THE COURT:

_____, J.

1 The court is cognizant that evidence of prior sexual assaults or allegations against others maybe admissible under limited circumstances to show motive or bias. *See Commonwealth v. Johnson*, 638 A.2d 940 (Pa. 1994); *Commonwealth v. Spiewak*, 617 A.2d 696 (Pa. 1992). In the instant case, the evidence was being sought by trial counsel and now by PCRA counsel for purposes of showing mistaken identity or sexual knowledge from an alternative source.

Sample Appellate Briefs

(Author's note: These briefs are not intended to be a complete discussion of the pertinent issues; rather, they are condensed versions of both an appellant's and appellee's brief. In addition, the sections of these sample briefs are condensed onto the same page, which is inappropriate for an actual brief.)

IN THE SUPERIOR COURT

FOR THE WESTERN DISTRICT OF PENNSYLVANIA

No. --- WDA YEAR

COMMONWEALTH OF PENNSYLVANIA

v.

Ah Pell Ant

APPELLANT'S BRIEF

This is an appeal from the order entered May 15, 2014, dismissing Appellant's PCRA petition without a hearing by the Honorable NAME of the _____ County Court of Common Pleas at CP-00-CR-NUMBER

Table of Contents

Table of Citations

Statement of Jurisdiction

Statement of Scope and Standard of Review

Order in Question

Statement of Questions Involved

Statement of Case

Summary of Argument

Argument

Conclusion

Proof of Service

Appendix A- Pa.R.A.P. 1925(a) opinion

Appendix B- Pa.R.A.P. 1925(b) concise statement

Appendix C- Final Order

Table of Citations

Names of Cases

Statutory Provisions

Rules of Criminal Procedure

Federal and State Constitutional Amendments

Statement of Jurisdiction

The Superior Court has jurisdiction over appeals from final orders in PCRA matters pursuant to 42 Pa.C.S. § 742.

Statement of Scope and Standard of Review

The Superior Court reviews an order dismissing a PCRA petition in the light most favorable to the prevailing party at the PCRA level. ***Commonwealth v. Burkett***, 5 A.3d 1260 (Pa. Super. 2010). Its review is limited to the findings of the PCRA court and the evidence of record. *Id*. However, where the petitioner raises questions of law, the standard of review is *de novo* and scope of review plenary. *Id*.

Order in Question

This is an appeal from the May 15, 2014 order dismissing Mr. Ant's PCRA petition without a hearing. A copy of the order is attached at Appendix C.

Statement of Questions Involved

1. Did the PCRA court err in concluding that Mr. Ant's second petition was not a timely first petition because initial PCRA counsel failed to file an amended petition?

The PCRA court answered in the negative.

2. Whether the PCRA court erred in finding Mr. Ant's petition did not meet the newly-discovered fact timeliness exception or that the PCRA time-bar was unconstitutional as applied where he alleged that original PCRA counsel abandoned him.

The PCRA court answered in the negative.

3. Was PCRA counsel ineffective by failing to argue trial counsel's ineffectiveness in neglecting to assert that Mr. Ant's Fifth Amendment right to counsel and his corresponding state constitutional right to counsel were violated when police questioned him after he asked for an attorney?

The PCRA court answered in the negative.

Statement of the Case

On August 19, 2008, four-year-old George Jungle was shot inside a diner in Pennsylvania. Jungle suffered a single gunshot wound to the chest and was pronounced dead the following day. The shooting occurred after an altercation erupted inside the diner between two groups of juveniles over the purported robbery of Mr. Ant's friend, Jack Ripper. Following the shooting, several eyewitnesses identified Mr. Ripper as the shooter. Mr. Ripper claimed that another juvenile member of the group, Anibal Hector, shot Jungle. The girlfriend of Mr. Ripper identified the gunman as Mr. Ant and said he admitted to firing a gun.

At 2:00 a.m., on August 21, 2008, police brought then seventeen-year-old Mr. Ant to the police station for questioning.

Sample Appellate Briefs

Upon Mr. Ant's arrival, police gave him *Miranda* warnings. Mr. Ant initially asked for a lawyer or to speak with his mother. The officer questioning Mr. Ant left the room and a different officer entered. He informed Mr. Ant that his mother was not going to come to the station, but that his three friends indicated that he fired all of the shots. Mr. Ant's accomplices actually had not provided police with any information. Without having an opportunity to consult with his mother or an attorney, Mr. Ant admitted to being part of the group that engaged in the gun battle, but stated that he did not have a gun.

Police questioning continued for approximately six hours. Although Mr. Ant denied having a gun for five and one-half hours, he eventually stated that he fired one shot in the air. The entire interview process took over seven hours. According to one officer, Mr. Ant was nervous and denied firing a weapon for an extended period. Mr. Ant had no prior experience with police interrogation or any criminal or juvenile record. His IQ was sixty-four.

In his statement, Mr. Ant stated that he and his friends went to the diner looking for the individuals who robbed Mr. Ripper. After they entered, he explained that a fight erupted and the other group drew weapons and began to fire at his friends. He admitted firing one shot before running out. Mr. Ant could not identify the type of weapon he used. Police did not recover a firearm. The Commonwealth charged Mr. Ant with murder, criminal conspiracy to commit both murder and aggravated assault, possession of an instrument of crime ("PIC"), and two violations of the Uniform Firearms Act.

After the trial court denied Mr. Ant's motion for decertification to juvenile court, Mr. Ant filed a suppression motion solely on the basis that he did not talk to his mother or another interested adult before confessing. The trial court denied that motion. Mr. Ant then requested permission to use expert testimony on false

Sample Appellate Briefs

confessions. The trial court prohibited the expert from testifying. The matter proceeded to trial. Since the trial court allowed Mr. Ant's confession, Mr. Ant took the stand and contended that he falsely confessed. The jury rejected Mr. Ant's testimony and convicted him of third degree murder, conspiracy to commit murder and aggravated assault, PIC, and both firearms violations.

Mr. Ant filed a timely post-sentence motion, which the court denied. His timely appeal ensued. Therein, he challenged the trial court's denial of his request to call an expert on false confessions, the dismissal of his suppression motion, and the sufficiency of the evidence. The Superior Court affirmed in an unpublished decision. *Commonwealth v. Ah Pell Ant*, ### A.2d #### (Pa. Super. 2009) (unpublished memorandum). The Pennsylvania Supreme Court denied allowance of appeal on March 3, 2009. *Commonwealth v. Ah Pell Ant*, ### A.2d #### (Pa. 2009). Mr. Ant did not seek review by the United States Supreme Court.

Thereafter, Mr. Ant filed a timely *pro se* PCRA petition contending that trial counsel was ineffective in litigating his suppression motion by declining to argue that his right to counsel was violated. The PCRA court appointed counsel. PCRA counsel failed to file an amended petition, but did represent Mr. Ant at a hearing. Counsel did not present any witnesses and indicated that the suppression issue, though distinct from the issue raised on direct appeal, was previously litigated. However, he argued that trial counsel was ineffective for failing to challenge the court's accomplice liability instruction for murder.

The PCRA court dismissed Mr. Ant's petition. Mr. Ant's counsel filed a timely notice of appeal. The PCRA court directed counsel to file a Pa.R.A.P. 1925(b) concise statement of errors complained of on appeal. PCRA counsel did not file a Pa.R.A.P.

Guilty Until Proven Innocent

1925(b) concise statement; however, Mr. Ant filed a *pro se* concise statement. In that statement, Mr. Ant alleged that PCRA counsel was ineffective in declining to file an amended petition and that counsel and the court were incorrect in finding that his suppression issue was previously litigated.

Although still ostensibly represented by counsel, the PCRA court filed a 1925(a) opinion addressing Mr. Ant's claims. **But see *Commonwealth v. Ali*,** 10 A.3d 282 (Pa. 2010). The Superior Court did not direct counsel to file a brief or remand for the appointment of new counsel, despite Mr. Ant requesting a remand for appointment of new counsel. **See *Commonwealth v. Quail*,** 729 A.2d 571 (Pa. Super. 1999). Instead, the panel affirmed the PCRA court, concluding that Mr. Ant could not prove actual prejudice. ***Commonwealth v. Ah Pell Ant*,** ### A.2d ### (Pa. Super. 2011) (unpublished memorandum) (filed May --, 20__).

Mr. Ant did not file a petition for allowance of appeal; instead, within sixty days of receipt of that decision, he submitted a second *pro se* PCRA petition. Mr. Ant's family then retained current counsel, who entered his appearance and filed an amended petition. Therein, Mr. Ant alleged that his petition should be treated as his first since no amended petition was ever filed on his behalf. In the alternative, he averred that he timely filed his second petition based on the abandonment of PCRA counsel and that applying the time-bar against him would render the PCRA statute's jurisdictional time-provision unconstitutional as applied, due to it depriving him of his constitutional right to effective trial and PCRA counsel.

In addition, he again asserted the ineffectiveness of suppression counsel. The PCRA court issued a boilerplate notice of intent to dismiss, concluding that the petition was untimely. Counsel filed a response to the notice of intent to dismiss within twenty days. The court filed a final order on May 15, 2014. This appeal ensued. The PCRA court directed counsel to file and serve a Pa.R.A.P. 1925(b) concise statement of errors complained of on appeal. Mr. Ant complied, raising the same issues presented in this appeal. The matter is now ripe for this Court's review.

Summary of Argument

Since Mr. Ant's first petition was dismissed without the filing of an amended petition or a *Turner/Finley* no-merit letter, his second petition should be treated as a timely first petition. ***Commonwealth v. Tedford***, 781 A.2d 1167 (Pa. 2001). Even if Mr. Ant's second petition is not treated as a timely first petition, he timely filed his second petition based on the newly-discovered fact exception, *i.e.*, PCRA counsel's abandonment. *See* ***Commonwealth v. Bennett***, 930 A.2d 1264 (Pa. 2007). Moreover, because original PCRA counsel abandoned Mr. Ant by both failing to file an amended petition and declining to represent Mr. Ant on appeal, he was deprived of both his rule-based and Pennsylvania and federal due process right to effective PCRA counsel. As the only means for enforcing these rights is within a serial petition, since the issue cannot be raised for the first time on appeal, applying the time-bar is unconstitutional as applied.

In addition, PCRA counsel was ineffective in neglecting to submit an amended petition or provide argument on Mr. Ant's trial counsel ineffectiveness suppression issue, which, because it was both an ineffectiveness claim and pertained to a distinct legal argument, was not previously litigated. *See* ***Commonwealth v. Collins***, 888 A.2d 564 (Pa. 2005). Lastly, trial counsel provided ineffective representation in not seeking to suppress Mr. Ant's confession after he asked to speak with an attorney and police continued interrogating him, despite filing a suppression motion on other grounds. ***Commonwealth v. Boyer***, 962 A.2d 1213 (Pa. Super. 2008); ***Commonwealth v. Champney***, 65 A.3d 386 (Pa. 2013) (Opinion in Support of

Affirmance); ***Commonwealth v. Kilgore***, 719 A.2d 754 (Pa. Super. 1998) (counsel found ineffective for filing a suppression motion but failing to argue meritorious violation of the Pennsylvania Constitution).

<u>Argument</u>

<u>1. The PCRA court erred by not concluding that Mr. Ant's second petition should be treated as a timely first petition.</u>

The Pennsylvania Supreme Court has held that when a PCRA court dismisses a petition before an amended petition is filed by counsel, a PCRA court must treat a subsequent petition as an amendment of the first timely petition. ***Commonwealth v. Tedford***, 781 A.2d 1167 (Pa. 2001); ***Commonwealth v. Duffey***, 713 A.2d 63 (Pa. 1998); *compare also* ***Commonwealth v. Williams***, 828 A.2d 981, 990 (Pa. 2003) (*"**Tedford** and **Duffey** stand for the proposition that if a court dismisses a pro se petition prior to the appointment of counsel, a subsequent counseled petition may not be treated as an untimely second petition."*). Although the PCRA court did appoint counsel herein, appointment is meaningless absent actual representation. Here, the record does not demonstrate that initial PCRA counsel represented Mr. Ant in any meaningful manner during the PCRA proceedings. *See **Commonwealth v. Davis***, 526 A.2d 440 (Pa. Super. 1987) (failure to file amended petition or supporting brief constructively denied petitioner right to PCHA counsel even though counsel did appear before court to make argument); *see also **Commonwealth v. Wiley***, 966 A.2d 1153 (Pa. Super. 2009) (despite petition being facially untimely, the Superior Court remanded after counsel failed to participate meaningfully).

Much like in ***Davis***, counsel did not file an amended petition or brief. Thus, Mr. Ant was constructively denied representation during his first petition before the court improperly dismissed his *pro se* petition, and his second counseled petition must be treated as a timely first petition.

2. In the alternative, the PCRA court erred in finding Mr. Ant's petition did not meet the newly-discovered fact timeliness exception or that the PCRA time-bar was unconstitutional as applied where he alleged that original PCRA counsel abandoned him.

Herein, the only means of enforcing Mr. Ant's Sixth Amendment constitutional right to counsel and his federal and state constitutional due process rights to effective PCRA counsel, as well as his rule based right to effective collateral counsel, is via a serial petition. That petition, while not filed within one-year of the finality of Mr. Ant's judgment of sentence, does meet a timeliness exception. Specifically, Mr. Ant alleged that PCRA counsel's abandonment at both the PCRA level and on appeal is a newly-discovered fact for purposes of 42 Pa.C.S. § 9545(b)(1)(ii). ***Commonwealth v. Bennett***, 930 A.2d 1264 (Pa. 2007).

Original PCRA counsel's failure to represent Mr. Ant before the PCRA court by neglecting to file an amended petition and his abandonment of Mr. Ant on appeal demonstrate *per se* ineffectiveness. ***Commonwealth v. Hampton***, 718 A.2d 1250 (Pa. Super. 1998); ***Bennett, supra***. Since Mr. Ant filed the instant petition within sixty days of the resolution of his prior PCRA appeal, ***Commonwealth v. Lark***, 746 A.2d 585 (Pa. 2000), and he properly averred and proved abandonment of counsel as a timeliness exception, he timely filed his petition and the PCRA court erred in concluding that it did not have jurisdiction.

Moreover, applying the time-bar to Mr. Ant renders it unconstitutional as applied. *See **Commonwealth v. Brown***, 943 A.2d 264, 268 n.4 (Pa. 2008) ("The Court, however, has recognized the potential availability of an as-applied constitutional challenge to the application of the PCRA's time restriction"). This is because the Pennsylvania Supreme Court no longer permits defendants to raise ineffectiveness claims for the first-time on appeal, which not only deprives Mr. Ant of his constitutional right to effective PCRA counsel, but also his Sixth Amendment right to effective trial counsel.

Admittedly, the Pennsylvania Supreme Court has declined to address whether a petitioner has either a federal or state constitutional right to counsel during his or her first PCRA. *See* ***Commonwealth v. Priovolos***, 715 A.2d 420 (Pa. 1998). Further, the Supreme Court has held that there is no Sixth Amendment right or due process right to counsel during collateral review. ***Pennsylvania v. Finley***, 481 U.S. 551 (1987); ***Coleman v. Thompson***, 501 U.S. 722 (1991). However, the High Court did not foreclose the possibility that there is a constitutional right to counsel on a first time state collateral proceeding where that proceeding is the first opportunity the defendant will have to raise a particular issue, *i.e.*, ineffective assistance of trial counsel. *See* ***Commonwealth v. Figueroa***, 29 A.3d 1177 (Pa. Super. 2011); ***Martinez v. Ryan***, 132 S.Ct. 1309 (2012).

In ***Figueroa***, the Superior Court delineated, in a footnote, one rationale for why a federal constitutional right to counsel might exist. Since ***Commonwealth v. Grant***, 813 A.2d 726 (Pa. 2002), compels defendants to make all allegations of ineffectiveness during the PCRA process, defendants have a constitutional right to counsel during a PCRA and therefore a corresponding constitutional right to effective assistance of counsel. *See* ***Coleman supra*** at 754-757 (1991); *see also id*. at 773-774 (Blackmun, J., dissenting with whom Justice Marshall and Justice Stevens joined); ***Figueroa, supra***; ***Martinez, supra***. Prior to ***Grant***, defendants could set forth ineffectiveness claims on direct appeal where there exists an equal protection right to counsel and a concomitant due process right to effective assistance of counsel. *See* ***Douglas v. California***, 372 U.S. 353

(1963); ***Evitts v. Lucey***, 469 U.S. 387 (1985). After **Grant**, however, claims of ineffectiveness were deferred to collateral proceedings. Accordingly, by eliminating ineffectiveness claims from the ambit of direct review, **Grant** renders PCRA trial review as a first appeal as-of-right for trial counsel ineffectiveness issues.

The United States Supreme Court discussed the same rationale in *dicta* in **Martinez**. The **Martinez** decision arose out of Arizona, where like Pennsylvania, ineffective assistance of counsel claims can only be raised in a state collateral proceeding and not during a direct appeal. Ultimately, the majority declined to decide whether constitutional right existed. Instead, the High Court resolved the case on a more narrow issue, holding for the first time that ineffectiveness of collateral review counsel during an initial proceeding, which serves as the first chance a defendant can raise ineffectiveness claims, may constitute cause for procedural default in a federal *habeas* matter. ***See also Trevino v. Thaler***, 133 S.Ct. 1911 (2013).

The **Martinez** Court, nevertheless, reiterated the identical grounds explained in **Figueroa** and also discussed in **Commonwealth v. Masker**, 34 A.3d 841, 846 n.4 (Pa. Super. 2011) (Bowes, J., concurring and dissenting) and **Commonwealth v. Ford**, 44 A.3d 1190, 1199-1200 (Pa. Super. 2012). Both **Figueroa** and the **Masker** concurring and dissenting opinion were authored prior to the **Martinez** decision. In **Ford**, the Superior Court highlighted:

> no Pennsylvania Supreme Court decision has opined on the implications of **Grant**, with regard to whether that decision effectively fashioned either a federal or Pennsylvania constitutional right to counsel for purposes of a first-time PCRA. For its part, the United States Supreme Court left open the possibility that where a state mandates that ineffectiveness claims can

only be raised in a collateral proceeding, there could be a constitutional right to counsel in the initial proceeding. *Coleman v. Thompson*, 501 U.S. 722, 755-757 (1991); *id.* at 773-774 (Blackmun, J., dissenting) ("if a State desires to remove from the process of direct appellate review a claim or category of claims, the Fourteenth Amendment binds the State to ensure that the defendant has effective assistance of counsel for the entirety of the procedure where the removed claims may be raised."); *see also Commonwealth v. Priovolos*, 715 A.2d 420, 422, n. 2 (Pa. 1998). Thus, it is not altogether clear that the decision in *Grant* does not create a federal or state constitutional right to counsel on a first-time PCRA.

Additionally, no Pennsylvania court has expounded on whether either the federal due process clause or its Pennsylvania equivalent, *see* Art. I, § 9 ("nor can he be deprived of his life, liberty or property, unless by the judgment of his peers or the law of the land"), protects a constitutional right to effective assistance of counsel during collateral review where state law mandates counsel for first-time PCRA matters. The federal courts have, in mostly cursory fashion, held that the federal due process clause does not guarantee a constitutional right to effective counsel even where state law requires the appointment of counsel. *Caswell v. Ryan*, 953 F.2d 853 (3d Cir. 1992) ("Ineffectiveness of [PCRA] counsel does not provide sufficient cause to excuse procedural default when counsel is not constitutionally mandated); *Pursell v. Horn*, 187 F.Supp.2d 260, 373 (W.D. 2002) ("the due process clause does not require counsel for state post-conviction proceedings, whether state law requires such counsel or not."); *In re Goff*, 250 F.3d 273 (5th Cir. 2001). Thus, federal courts have concluded that fundamental fairness does not include effective assistance of post-conviction counsel during an initial collateral attack. Whether Pennsylvania courts will follow suit has yet to be decided. This is likely because it was previously presumed that the rule-based right to effective assistance of counsel is enforceable in some manner. *Priovolos, supra* at 422.

Ford, supra at 1199-1200 (footnotes omitted).

The federal court decisions referenced in *Ford* were all pre-*Grant* cases. Indeed, Pennsylvania Supreme Court decisions finding no federal constitutional right to counsel in the PCRA all were handed down based on a pre-*Grant* framework. *Commonwealth v. Jones*, 815 A.2d 598, 611 (Pa. 2002) (OAJC) (decided same date as *Grant, supra*); *Priovolos, supra*, at 421-422; *Commonwealth v. Lambert*, 797 A.2d 232, 244 (Pa. 2001) (OAJC); *Commonwealth v. Albrecht*, 720 A.2d 693, 699 (Pa. 1998); *Commonwealth v. Travaglia*, 661 A.2d 352, 367 (Pa. 1995); *Commonwealth v. Christy*, 656 A.2d 877, 881 (Pa. 1995); *see also Commonwealth v. Peterson*, 683 A.2d 908 (Pa. Super. 1996).

Equally important, the due process clause of the federal constitution and the law of the land provision of the Pennsylvania Constitution have, even under a restricted view of those provisions, been read to require that proceedings follow written constitutional and statutory law. *See In re Winship*, 397 U.S. 358, 382 (1970) (Black, J., dissenting). Statutory law in Pennsylvania expressly guaranteed a right to counsel under the PCHA for indigent defendants and the criminal rules of procedure currently assure that right under the PCRA. Hence, the "law of the land" requires counsel during a first-time PCRA.

Therefore, under an originalist interpretation of both the federal and Pennsylvania Constitution, Mr. Ant had a constitutional right to counsel in his first PCRA proceeding before the PCRA court and a corresponding right to effective counsel. Pointedly, while a state has no constitutional obligation to provide a means for collaterally attacking a conviction, when it does, its "procedures must comport with the fundamental fairness mandated by the Due Process Clause." ***Commonwealth v. Haag***, 809 A.2d 271, 283 (Pa. 2002). Aside from a constitutional right to PCRA counsel before the PCRA court, Mr. Ant clearly had a rule-based right to effective counsel at that level and on appeal. ***See Priovolos***, ***supra***.

Finding Mr. Ant's petition untimely not only deprives him of a rule-based and constitutional right to effective PCRA counsel, since he could not enforce that right during his prior appeal, it also results in a violation of his Sixth Amendment right to effective trial counsel as is outlined in the next issue. Accordingly, interpretation of the time-bar to prohibit Mr. Ant's current petition would render the PCRA time-bar unconstitutional as applied.

<u>3. PCRA counsel was ineffective by failing to argue trial counsel's ineffectiveness in neglecting to assert that Mr. Ant's Fifth Amendment right to counsel and his corresponding state constitutional right to counsel were violated when police questioned him after he asked for an attorney.</u>

This issue is not previously litigated because Mr. Ant's suppression issue raised on direct appeal was not an ineffectiveness claim and, more importantly, pertained only to law enforcement's failure to permit him to speak with an interested adult. Furthermore, although Mr. Ant raised the underlying trial counsel ineffectiveness issue in his original *pro se* PCRA petition, counsel never filed an amended petition arguing this issue and incorrectly contended that the claim was previously litigated.

As neither the layered claim, the trial counsel ineffectiveness claim, or the underlying suppression issue has ever been resolved on its merits, it is not previously litigated. Additionally, the claim is not waived since no notice of dismissal was required after Mr. Ant's initial PCRA proceeding and Mr. Ant raised it at the first opportunity in his *pro se* PCRA 1925(b) statement, and maintained his position in both his prior appeal and in this PCRA matter. To the extent the *pro se* concise statement is a nullity, binding precedent precluded Mr. Ant from asserting the layered claim for the first time on appeal and therefore this was his first opportunity to assert the issue. ***Commonwealth v. Jette***, 23 A.3d 1032 (Pa. 2011); ***Commonwealth v. Colavita***, 993 A.2d 874 (Pa. 2010); ***Commonwealth v. Pitts***, 981 A.2d 875 (Pa. 2009).

In the context of alleging PCRA counsel ineffectiveness, the claim must be layered. ***See Commonwealth v. McGill***, 832 A.2d 1014 (Pa. 2003) (discussing layering claims). Proving trial counsel's ineffectiveness establishes arguable merit to PCRA counsel's lack of effective representation. ***Commonwealth v. Reyes***, 870 A.2d 888 (Pa. 2005). The Pennsylvania Supreme Court has set forth a three-prong test to evaluate ineffective assistance of counsel claims under the PCRA. ***Commonwealth v. Pierce***, 527 A.2d 973 (Pa. 1987).

Pierce requires the underlying substantive claim have arguable merit; that the counsel whose effectiveness is being challenged had no reasonable basis for his action or lack of action; and that the Petitioner suffered prejudice as a result of counsel's deficient performance. *Id.* at 975-76. A showing of prejudice requires only that there existed a reasonable probability that but for counsel's error, the outcome of the proceeding would have been different. ***Commonwealth v. Rathfon***, 899 A.2d 365 (Pa. Super. 2006). The reasonable probability test is not stringent and requires a probability sufficient to undermine confidence in the outcome. *Id.*

Mr. Ant's underlying trial counsel claim has arguable merit because, under both federal and Pennsylvania law, once a person invokes his Fifth Amendment right to counsel, questioning cannot continue or be reinitiated without the person being provided with an attorney, regardless of the signing of a waiver. *See Commonwealth v. Wyatt*, 669 A.2d 954 (Pa. Super. 1996) (stating, "once a suspect asserts the right to counsel, not only must the current interrogation cease, but he may not be approached until counsel has been made available to him"); *see also Commonwealth v. Santiago*, 599 A.2d 200 (Pa. 1991); *Champney, supra*. Since Mr. Ant had invoked his right to counsel and questioning continued, the questioning was in violation of his constitutional rights and Mr. Ant's confession should have been suppressed.

After an individual invokes his right to counsel under the Fifth Amendment all interrogation must cease. Additionally, the reading of a third party statement implicating the defendant in the crime constitutes an interrogation. *Commonwealth v. Mercier*, 302 A.2d 337 (Pa. 1973). In this case, the officer told Mr. Ant that another person was implicating him in the crime, which qualifies as police initiated questioning, *i.e.*, questions that the police should know are reasonably likely to elicit an incriminating response. *Commonwealth v. Ramos*, 532 A.2d 465 (Pa. Super. 1988). Also, it has been held that a waiver of the right to counsel is invalid even if it is seemingly knowing, intelligent and voluntary, where the defendant invokes his right to counsel and later confesses following a police initiated interview. *See Ramos, supra*; *see also Commonwealth v. Templin*, 795 A.2d 959 (Pa. 2002).

The facts of this case are remarkably similar to the facts of *Mercier, supra*. The defendant in *Mercier* went to police headquarters and was apprised of his rights and requested counsel. The police left the defendant alone and then returned and read a statement of a co-accused implicating the defendant in a robbery and murder. The defendant in *Mercier* then confessed. On appeal, the Supreme Court of Pennsylvania held that the confession should have been suppressed. In the instant case, the police did not read the statement, but remarked that the co-defendants had made statements implicating Mr. Ant. Further, counsel would have had no reasonable basis for not filing a suppression motion on the right to counsel issue when counsel sought suppression on other grounds and there is clear case law on the issue. *See e.g. Kilgore, supra.*

In a more recent case, *Boyer, supra*, the Superior Court held counsel ineffective for not seeking to suppress a confession under analogous circumstances. There, the defendant indicated to one officer that he did not wish to talk. A second officer asked if he could have a shot at the defendant and reinitiated questioning. The panel concluded that trial counsel was ineffective in not seeking to suppress the subsequent confession. Finally, trial counsel's action resulted in actual prejudice because Mr. Ant's confession was the Commonwealth's most compelling evidence as no eyewitness identified Mr. Ant and none of his co-defendants indicated that he fired any shots. Since the strongest evidence against Mr. Ant was his confession, and it should have been suppressed, there is a reasonable probability that the likelihood of the trial would have been different.

Having established trial counsel's ineffectiveness, the issue has arguable merit as to PCRA counsel. *Reyes, supra.* PCRA counsel could not have had any reasonable basis for not litigating this issue where clear precedent indicates that ineffectiveness claims are distinct from non-ineffectiveness claims and the issue was not previously litigated. *Collins, supra.* Further, the previously litigated suppression issue is actually, as discussed *supra*, distinct from the current issue. Thus, counsel's legal conclusion that Mr. Ant previously litigated this issue was legally erroneous and therefore unreasonable. *See*

Commonwealth v. Reed, 42 A.3d 314, 323 (Pa. Super. 2012) (legally erroneous grounds for not objecting is unreasonable). Finally, because prejudice is established relative to trial counsel, it necessarily follows that prejudice exists as it pertains to PCRA counsel. Phrased differently, the result of the PCRA proceeding would have likely been different since trial counsel's failure to suppress the confession resulted in the most damning evidence against Mr. Ant. ***See Boyer, supra***.

Conclusion

For the aforementioned reasons, Mr. Ant respectfully requests that this Court reverse the PCRA court's order below and award Mr. Ant a new trial.

Proof of Service

A copy of this brief has been served upon the following by certified mail/personal delivery, this DATE:

Name of DA/ADA

Address of District Attorney's Office

Appendix

Attach relevant documents.

Sample Appellate Briefs

<u>Sample Appellee Brief</u>

IN THE SUPERIOR COURT

FOR THE WESTERN DISTRICT OF PENNSYLVANIA

No. --- WDA 2014

COMMONWEALTH OF PENNSYLVANIA

v.

Ah Pell Ant

APPELLEE'S BRIEF

This is an appeal from the order entered May 15, 2014, dismissing Appellant's PCRA petition without a hearing by the Honorable NAME of the _____ County Court of Common Pleas at CP-00-CR-NUMBER

Table of Contents

Table of Citations

Statement of Jurisdiction

Statement of Scope and Standard of Review

Order in Question

Statement of Questions Involved

Statement of Case

Summary of Argument

Argument

Conclusion

Proof of Service

Appendix

Sample Appellate Briefs

Table of Citations

Names of Cases

Statutory Provisions

Rules of Criminal Procedure

Federal and State Constitutional Amendments

Counter Statement of Questions Involved

1. The PCRA court correctly determined that Appellant's petition was a second petition subject to the jurisdictional time-bar and miscarriage of justice standard.

2. No constitutional right to collateral review counsel exists and, assuming Appellant's petition was timely filed, he suffered no prejudice.

Counter Statement of the Case

Appellant and three other juveniles opened fire on rival gang members in a diner, killing a four-year old boy in the process. After an initial investigation, police located Appellant at the home of a friend and brought him in for questioning. Police provided Appellant his *Miranda* warnings and telephoned his mother. She indicated that police could question her son without her presence and that she was not going to come to the police station. Appellant initially said he might need a lawyer and would like to talk with his mother. After being told that his mother was not going to come to the station, he began to talk to the officers. Eventually, Appellant admitted to firing a single shot in the air.

Following the unsuccessful litigation of a decertification motion, a motion *in limine*, and a suppression motion, the case proceeded to trial. The Commonwealth introduced Appellant's statement, a statement by a girlfriend of one of the other juveniles, wherein Appellant admitted to her to firing a gun, and the testimony of numerous investigating officers, a ballistics expert, and the medical examiner. Appellant also testified, denying that he ever fired a shot, and stating that he falsely admitted to shooting the weapon.

The trial court instructed the jury on accomplice liability relative to murder and the jury convicted Appellant of third degree murder. On appeal, the Superior Court ruled that Appellant's suppression issue, that his confession was improperly obtained where he did not have the opportunity to speak to an adult, did not warrant relief. Appellant timely filed a *pro se* PCRA petition and the court appointed counsel. Although counsel did not formally file an amended petition, he provided legal argument at a hearing. The court rejected this position and Mr. Ant filed a *pro se* appeal.

A panel of the Superior Court declined to remand for the appointment of counsel, reached the merits of Mr. Ant's issue, and affirmed. Appellant then submitted a serial PCRA petition within sixty days of that decision and retained counsel. After the submission of an amended petition, the PCRA court issued a Pa.R.Crim.P. 907 notice. Appellant replied, and the court dismissed the petition holding it both untimely and that he failed to establish a miscarriage of justice since the confession actually aided the truth-determining process. This appeal followed.

Summary of Argument

Since the PCRA court appointed counsel and counsel appeared and presented argument on behalf of Appellant, this case is distinguishable from the cases relied upon by Mr. Ant for the proposition that his second petition should be treated as his first. Thus, Appellant's petition was a second petition subject to both the timeliness provision of the PCRA and the miscarriage of justice standard applicable to serial petitions. As Appellant cannot establish a miscarriage of justice, he is not entitled to relief.

There is no constitutional right to counsel during PCRA review, but admittedly there is a rule based right to effective PCRA counsel. However, even assuming *arguendo* that ***Commonwealth v. Bennett***, 930 A.2d 1264 (Pa. 2007), was correctly decided, and Appellant's petition was timely, Appellant still cannot establish actual prejudice relative to his suppression issue. Therefore, PCRA counsel's representation during the PCRA proceeding cannot be construed as ineffective assistance.

Argument

1. The PCRA court correctly determined that Appellant's petition was a second petition subject to the time-bar and miscarriage of justice standard.

Appellant's first position rests on case law that is factually distinguishable from the case *sub-judice*. In ***Commonwealth v. Tedford***, 781 A.2d 1167 (Pa. 2001), the petitioner filed a *pro se* petition. While the PCRA court appointed counsel, it dismissed the petitioner's *pro se* petition and ordered counsel to file a new petition within thirty days. Counsel requested and received several extensions before filing a petition. The PCRA court *sua sponte* denied the counseled petition as untimely, stating that the petition was not filed within one-year of the appellant's judgment of sentence becoming final. The Supreme Court reversed, holding that the petitioner timely filed his original *pro se* petition and that the later counseled petition should have been treated as an amended petition.

In ***Commonwealth v. Duffey***, 713 A.2d 63 (Pa. 1998), the Pennsylvania Capital Case Resource Center provided an original and courtesy copy of the petitioner's *pro se* motion for stay of execution and request for appointment of counsel. The organization neither entered its appearance nor did the court appoint it to represent Duffey. The PCRA court dismissed the petition without appointing counsel. Two days after the dismissal, the petitioner filed a *pro se* motion for reconsideration and attached a completed pre-printed PCRA petition form.

The PCRA court denied the motion for reconsideration. Duffey later filed a subsequent petition that he labeled as an amended petition. The Supreme Court determined that because the court never appointed counsel, the latter amended petition should not have been dismissed. Duffey, however, was decided before the implementation of the one-year jurisdictional time-bar.

Similarly, in **Commonwealth v. Williams**, 828 A.2d 981 (Pa. 2003), the petitioner filed a *pro se* petition on December 26, 1995, but the court did not appoint counsel. The petitioner then filed a *pro se* motion to discontinue, which the court never acted on. The petitioner, one year later, filed a second *pro se* petition, but on February 4, 1997, filed a petition to discontinue that petition if it would affect his federal *habeas* proceeding. Eventually, on March 27, 1997, counsel representing the petitioner on federal *habeas* review filed a counseled motion for a stay and leave to amend, although he was not appointed and did not enter an appearance.

The PCRA court conducted numerous evidentiary hearings and the petitioner submitted, but did not file, an amended petition on September 30, 1997. The court, from the bench, ordered that petition docketed. It later concluded that Appellant had withdrawn his PCRA on January 31, 1996, and that the subsequent filings were untimely. The Supreme Court reversed, concluding that because the court never appointed an attorney and did not act on the motions to discontinue, the later petitions were timely amendments to his first *pro se* petition.

Contrary to **Tedford** and **Williams**, Appellant's first petition was not dismissed as untimely; rather, after appointed counsel presented argument at a hearing it was denied on the merits.

Concomitantly, ***Duffey*** involved a case where counsel was never appointed. Appellant's citation to ***Commonwealth v. Davis***, 526 A.2d 440 (Pa. Super. 1987), is equally unavailing. Therein, the court specifically commented on counsel's failure at an evidentiary hearing to have a rudimentary understanding of the case.

Instantly, the court addressed the merits of Appellant's petition after it appointed counsel and counsel represented Appellant at a hearing. At the hearing, counsel provided thorough argument on whether the accomplice liability instruction was improper and demonstrated extensive knowledge of the facts of the case. Thus, because the court appointed counsel, counsel did not abandon Appellant at the PCRA level, and represented him at a hearing, the case law relied upon by Appellant is inapposite. The PCRA court, therefore, properly treated Appellant's petition as a serial petition subject to both the timeliness provisions and the miscarriage of justice standard.

Further, Appellant could not establish a miscarriage of justice, *i.e.*, that the result of the proceedings was one that no civilized society can tolerate. ***See Commonwealth v. Lawson***, 549 A.2d 107 (Pa. 1988). First, he does not claim or argue his actual innocence. ***See Commonwealth v. Beasley***, 967 A.2d 376 (Pa. 2009) (discussing differences between actual innocence and miscarriage of justice standards). Indeed, even if Appellant did not fire the fatal shot, the court correctly instructed the jury on accomplice liability relative to murder. Second, assuming that Appellant's own statement to police was inadmissible it was merely cumulative of the statement he provided to the girlfriend of one of his co-defendant's and he cannot establish prejudice. ***See Commonwealth v. DuPont***, 860 A.2d 525, 535 (Pa. Super. 2004). Accordingly, Appellant cannot demonstrate that his conviction was so unfair that no civilized society could tolerate it.

2. No Sixth Amendment or Due Process right to collateral review counsel exists and assuming Appellant's petition was timely filed he suffered no prejudice.

The Commonwealth disputes Appellant's claim that there is a constitutional right to collateral review counsel. In ***Pennsylvania v. Finley***, 481 U.S. 551 (1987), ***Murray v. Giarratano***, 492 U.S. 1 (1989), and ***Coleman v. Thompson***, 501 U.S. 722 (1991), the United States Supreme Court rejected a constitutional right to collateral review counsel. Appellant himself implicitly concedes that there is no Sixth Amendment right to a PCRA attorney and provides argument solely based on due process. This is because the Sixth Amendment by its plain terms applies to criminal prosecutions whereas the PCRA is considered civil and is not a prosecution. While Appellant asserts that the PCRA is the only means of challenging ineffective assistance of counsel and has become, in effect, an as-of-right direct appeal related to those claims, he is mistaken. Defendants still may raise ineffective assistance claims on direct review under ***Commonwealth v. Holmes***, 79 A.3d 562 (Pa. 2013).

Pursuant to ***Holmes***, as long as the defendant waives PCRA review and establishes good cause, ineffective assistance claims may be reviewed on direct appeal. Nonetheless, it is evident that defendants do have an avenue of raising ineffectiveness issues on direct appeal. Thus, the rationale that ***Commonwealth v. Grant***, 813 A.2d 726 (Pa. 2002), creates a constitutional right to collateral review counsel fails. Moreover, the Third Circuit Court of Appeals has concluded that even where state law provides a right to collateral review counsel, there is no federal due process constitutional right to effective counsel. ***Caswell v. Ryan***, 953 F.2d 853, 862 (3d Cir. 1992); *see also* ***Pursell v. Horn***, 187 F.Supp. 2d 260, 372-373 (W.D. Pa. 2002).

In addition, while the Commonwealth acknowledges that the Superior Court is without authority to disregard a Pennsylvania Supreme Court decision, for purposes of preserving the issue, it believes that ***Commonwealth v. Bennett***, 930 A.2d 1264 (Pa. 2007), was wrongly decided. Hence, Appellant's petition is untimely because the alleged newly-discovered fact, PCRA counsel's abandonment, does not pertain to the trial or direct appeal process. ***See generally Bennett, supra*** (Saylor, J., dissenting). However, both of these arguments are largely immaterial because even if Appellant's petition is timely, he cannot prove actual prejudice. Herein, as discussed previously, Appellant's confession was merely cumulative of a statement he gave to another witness. This latter testimony was admissible. Accordingly, the outcome of the proceedings was not likely to be different. Since trial counsel was not constitutionally ineffective, *ipso facto*, PCRA counsel cannot be held ineffective.

<u>Conclusion</u>

The PCRA court must be affirmed as Appellant cannot establish either that a miscarriage of justice occurred due to trial counsel's failure to suppress his statement to police or actual prejudice.

Sample *Turner/Finley* No-Merit Brief

IN THE SUPERIOR COURT
FOR THE WESTERN DISTRICT OF PENNSYLVANIA
No. --- WDA YEAR
COMMONWEALTH OF PENNSYLVANIA
v.
NAME OF APPELLANT
TURNER/FINLEY BRIEF

Turner/Finley brief filed regarding the order entered May 15, 2013, dismissing Appellant's PCRA petition without a hearing by the Honorable NAME of the _____ County Court of Common Pleas at CP-00-CR-NUMBER

Table of Contents

Table of Citations

Statement of Jurisdiction

Statement of Scope and Standard of Review

Order in Question

Statement of Questions Involved

Statement of Case

Summary of Argument

Argument

Conclusion

Proof of Service

Appendix A- Pa.R.A.P. 1925(a) opinion

Sample Turner/Finley No-Merit Brief

Appendix B- Final Order

Appendix C- Petition to Withdraw from Superior Court

Appendix D- *Turner/Finley* no-merit letter filed with PCRA Court

Statement of Jurisdiction

The Superior Court has jurisdiction over appeals from final orders in PCRA matters pursuant to 42 Pa.C.S. Section 742.

Statement of Scope and Standard of Review

The Superior Court reviews an order dismissing a PCRA petition in the light most favorable to the prevailing party at the PCRA level. ***Commonwealth v. Burkett***, 5 A.3d 1260 (Pa. Super. 2010). Its review is limited to the findings of the PCRA court and the evidence of record. *Id.* However, where the petitioner raises questions of law, the standard of review is *de novo* and scope of review plenary. *Id.*

Order in Question

This is an appeal from the May 15, 2013 order dismissing Appellant's PCRA petition without a hearing. A copy of the order is attached at Appendix B.

Statement of Questions Involved

1. Was trial counsel ineffective for not objecting to the prosecutor's questioning of Appellant's first character witness?

2. Whether trial counsel was ineffective for failing to object to the prosecutor's improper remark during closing statements that Appellant was a "thug."

Statement of the Case

Appellant was found guilty following a jury trial of attempted murder, aggravated assault, reckless endangerment of another person ("REAP"), carrying an unlicensed firearm, and simple assault and sentenced to a term of incarceration of twenty to forty years by the Honorable Judd Ge.

In the early morning hours of December 26, 2008, Appellant was involved in an altercation with three men: John Smith, Billy Baggins, and Dwight Baddin. Two of the men, Baggins and Baddin, were known by Appellant to be local drug dealers and he suspected that they were armed. The confrontation began after John Smith, the person unknown to Appellant, began to flirt with Appellant's girlfriend inside of a local establishment called Po' & Drunk. The two men were asked to leave after the confrontation turned physical with some brief shoving. Appellant, his girlfriend, and another couple exited the bar. John Smith also exited with Billy Baggins and Dwight Baddin. According to Appellant, Smith, Baggins and Baddin began to taunt him and his girlfriend as the three men walked toward him. Petitioner, believing Baggins and Baddin were armed, pulled out an unlicensed .40 caliber Glock handgun and told the men to stop moving. At this point, Petitioner alleges that Baddin and Baggins hands moved toward the back waist area of their body. Believing the men were going for guns, Petitioner fired four shots, wounding Smith three times and Baddin once. Baggins escaped unharmed.

At trial, Smith, Baggins and Baddin testified that as soon as they exited the bar, Appellant pulled a handgun on Smith and threatened them before firing three shots at Smith. Baggins and Baddin ran for cover and Appellant fired another round, hitting Baddin, before Appellant sped away in his vehicle. Trial counsel impeached these three men with prior *crimen falsi* convictions. Four other individuals in the parking lot testified to seeing Appellant exit the bar and immediately pull a gun. They each stated that some words were exchanged between Smith and Appellant before Appellant opened fire. The couple that exited with Appellant also testified against Appellant, stating that he fired the shots without warning. A videotape was also shown of the incident. The tape corroborated the testimony of the victims and the other Commonwealth witnesses.

Trial counsel's theory at trial was imperfect self defense. During Appellant's case-in-chief, Appellant and his girlfriend both took the stand and gave identical accounts of the altercation, averring that Smith threatened them inside the bar and Baggins and Baddin appeared to go for what they believed were their firearms once outside. Additionally, trial counsel for Appellant called three character witnesses that Appellant requested to be called on his behalf. These witnesses each testified that Appellant had a reputation in the community for being a peaceful and law-abiding citizen.

During the cross-examination of the first character witness, the prosecution improperly inquired with the witness if he knew Appellant had been arrested three times. Trial counsel objected, the trial judge sustained the objection, and called both counsel to side-bar and admonished the prosecutor that such questioning was inappropriate. Trial counsel requested a mistrial, but the court declined that motion and indicated that he would give a curative instruction if counsel wished. Counsel declined, stating that the instruction would only highlight the issue.

The jury returned a verdict of guilty on the charge of attempted murder-serious bodily injury and aggravated assault pertinent to John Smith. They also found Appellant guilty of aggravated assault, simple assault, and REAP of Dwight Baddin. Appellant was also convicted of carrying a firearm without a license. Thereafter, Appellant was sentenced to a term of imprisonment of twenty to forty years for attempted murder. The trial court imposed no further sentence. Appellant filed a timely post-sentence motion, raising weight and sufficiency claims, a discretionary sentencing claim that the sentence was excessive, as well as a challenge to the trial court's decision not to grant a mistrial. The trial judge denied the post-sentence motion without a hearing. Appellant filed a timely direct appeal raising weight and sufficiency of the evidence issues as well as the mistrial claim. The Superior Court affirmed the decision of the trial court and the Pennsylvania Supreme Court denied allowance of appeal. This PCRA petition followed.

Before reaching the merits of any claim under the PCRA, the petition must be timely. A petition which is untimely renders the court without jurisdiction to consider the merits of the claims, unless the petitioner can plead and prove that the claim falls within one of the PCRA timeliness exceptions. Instantly, Appellant was sentenced by the trial court on January 10, 2010. A post-sentence motion was filed on January 19, 2010, and denied without hearing on January 30, 2010. Appellant filed a timely direct appeal on February 8, 2010. The judgment of sentence was affirmed on May 10, 2011, and Appellant filed a timely petition for allowance of appeal. Appellant's petition for allowance of appeal was denied on June 21, 2011. Appellant had ninety days to seek review in the United States Supreme Court, but did not do so. Thus, the date of final judgment was on or about September 19, 2011. The underlying petition was filed August 14, 2012. Therefore, the petition was timely.

Appellant in his *pro se* petition raised the issues set forth previously in the statement of questions. Counsel filed a ***Turner/Finley*** no-merit letter and the court dismissed the petition. However, the PCRA court declined to affirmatively grant counsel's petition to withdraw in either its Pa.R.Crim.P. 907 notice of intent to dismiss or its final order. Accordingly, counsel now submits this ***Turner/Finley*** brief on appeal.

<u>Summary of Argument</u>

After careful review of the entire Podunk County, Pennsylvania record at case number _____, including the transcripts of both the trial and sentencing and Appellant's *pro se* PCRA petition, and correspondence and materials supplied by Appellant and prior counsel, counsel finds that the issues Appellant wishes to raise do not entitle him to PCRA relief and counsel has determined that no other meritorious issues exist. Counsel, therefore, requests that he be permitted to withdraw from representation for the reasons that will be outlined below and more fully in the argument portion of this *Turner/Finley* brief.

Appellant's first issue is whether trial counsel was ineffective for neglecting to object to the district attorney's improper questioning of a character witness regarding Appellant's prior arrests. Since trial counsel did object, stated on the record a reasonable basis for declining a curative instruction, and overwhelming evidence was introduced, this issue does not entitle Appellant to relief.

The second issue Appellant wishes to present is that trial counsel was ineffective in failing to object to the prosecutor's statement during his closing argument that Appellant was a "thug." As the Commonwealth's reference to the word thug occurred in the context of describing the victims and not Petitioner, the issue has no arguable merit. N.T., DATE, page number.

Argument

Ineffective assistance of trial counsel for not objecting to the prosecutor's questioning of Appellant's first character witness.

Appellant's first issue is whether trial counsel was ineffective for neglecting to object to the district attorney's improper questioning of a character witness regarding Appellant's prior arrests. Counsel is presumed effective and will only be deemed ineffective if the petitioner demonstrates that counsel's performance was deficient and he was prejudiced by the deficient performance. ***Commonwealth v. Steele***, 961 A.2d 786,

797 (Pa. 2008). Prejudice is established if there is a reasonable probability that but for counsel's errors the result of the proceeding would have been different. *Id*.

To properly plead ineffective assistance of counsel, a petitioner must plead and prove that the underlying issue has arguable merit; counsel's actions lacked an objective reasonable basis; and actual prejudice resulted from counsel's act or failure to act. ***Commonwealth v. Tedford***, 960 A.2d 1 (Pa. 2008) (citing ***Commonwealth v. Pierce***, 527 A.2d 973, 975 (Pa. 1987) adopting the U.S. Supreme Court's holding in ***Strickland v. Washington***, 466 U.S. 668 (1984)). If a petitioner fails to plead or meet any elements of the above cited test his claim must fail. ***Steele, supra***. The Pennsylvania Supreme Court has consistently deemed cross-examination of a character witness regarding the witness's knowledge of a defendant's prior arrests improper. *See* ***Commonwealth v. Morgan***, 739 A.2d 1033 (Pa. 1999); ***Commonwealth v. Scott***, 436 A.2d 607 (Pa. 1981); *see also* ***Commonwealth v. Yeager***, 461 A.2d 281 (Pa. Super. 1983). Moreover, Pa.R.E. 405(a) bars cross-examination of a witness with respect to allegations of criminal misconduct that did not result in a conviction. *See also **Commonwealth v. Doswell***, 621 A.2d 104 (Pa. 1993) (plurality).

However, counsel did object to the questioning, the court immediately halted the questioning, did not allow the witness to answer the inquiry, and told the jury to disregard the question. Counsel at side-bar requested a mistrial, which the court declined and instead offered to give a further curative instruction. Counsel declined, stating on the record that the instruction would merely highlight the improper question that had not yet been answered. Thus, counsel did object and the trial judge properly interrupted the prosecutor and told the jury to disregard the question immediately after the improper question. Additionally, besides the two victims, multiple other witnesses testified that Appellant began the altercation and pulled a firearm and fired the weapon numerous times. Furthermore, a video camera captured the incident on tape and demonstrated that Appellant was the clear aggressor. Because counsel did object, stated on the record a reasonable basis for declining a curative instruction, and overwhelming evidence was introduced, this issue does not entitle Appellant to relief.

<u>Ineffectiveness of trial counsel for failing to object to the prosecutor's improper remark during closing statements that Appellant was a "thug."</u>

Appellant's second issue is that trial counsel was ineffective in failing to object to the prosecutor's statement during his closing argument that Appellant was a "thug." Where the allegation is that the prosecutor committed misconduct during trial, and no objection was made, the claim must be argued as an ineffective assistance of counsel claim. The Pennsylvania Supreme Court in **Commonwealth v. Tedford**, 960 A.2d 1 (Pa. 2008), clearly outlined what a petitioner must prove to successfully raise an ineffectiveness claim for failure to object to a prosecutor's comments. The Court in **Tedford** stated, "ineffectiveness claims stemming from a failure to object to a prosecutor's conduct may succeed when the petitioner demonstrates that the prosecutor's actions violated a constitutionally or statutorily protected right, such as the Fifth Amendment privilege against compulsory self-incrimination or the Sixth Amendment right to a fair trial, or a constitutional interest such as due process." *Id.* at 29.

Additionally, the prosecutorial misconduct must be of sufficient significance to result in the denial of the defendant's right to a fair trial. A prosecutor's comments will only be reversible error when the comments effect is to unavoidably prejudice the jury, "forming in their minds a fixed bias and hostility toward the defendant such that they could not weigh the evidence objectively and render a fair verdict." *Id* at 33. If a prosecutor's comments "are based on the evidence or proper inferences therefrom, or represent mere oratorical flair," they are not objectionable. *Id.* Instantly, the Commonwealth's reference to the word thug occurred in the context of describing the victims and not Appellant; hence, the issue has no arguable merit. N.T., DATE, page number.

Conclusion

Counsel avers that he has carefully reviewed the record and found that the issues Appellant wishes to raise are without merit and counsel has determined that no other meritorious issues exist. Pursuant to *Turner/Finley*, and for the reasons outlined *supra*, counsel respectfully requests that he be permitted to withdraw from representation

Proof of Service

A copy of this brief has been served upon the following by certified mail/personal delivery, this DATE:

Name of DA/ADA

Address of District Attorney's Office

Appellant

Address of Appellant

Appendix

Attach relevant documents.

42 Pa.C.S. § 9541-9546--Post-Conviction Relief Act

Section 9541. Short title of subchapter

This subchapter shall be known and may be cited as the Post Conviction Relief Act.

CREDIT(S)

1982, May 13, P.L. 417, No. 122, § 2, imd. effective. Amended 1988, April 13, P.L. 336, No. 47, § 3, imd. effective.

HISTORICAL AND STATUTORY NOTES

2007 Main Volume

Act 1988-47 legislation

The 1988 amendment substituted "relief" for "hearing".

Section 6 of Act 1988, April 13, P.L. 336, No. 47, provides that the amendment to this section shall apply to all actions for collateral relief, whether statutory or common law, instituted on or after the effective date of this act, irrespective of the date of conviction or sentence.

Prior Laws:

1966, Jan. 25, P.L. (1965) 1580, No. 554, § 1 (19 P.S. § 1180-1).

Section 9542. Scope of subchapter

This subchapter provides for an action by which persons convicted of crimes they did not commit and persons serving illegal sentences may obtain collateral relief. The action established in this subchapter shall be the sole means of obtaining collateral relief and encompasses all other common law and statutory remedies for the same purpose that exist when this subchapter takes effect, including habeas corpus and coram nobis. This subchapter is not intended to limit the availability of remedies in the trial court or on direct appeal from the judgment of sentence, to provide a means for raising issues waived in prior proceedings or to provide relief from collateral consequences of a criminal conviction. Except as specifically provided otherwise, all provisions of this subchapter shall apply to capital and noncapital cases.

CREDIT(S)

1982, May 13, P.L. 417, No. 122, § 2, imd. effective. Amended 1988, April 13, P.L. 336, No. 47, § 3, imd. effective; 1995, Nov. 17, P.L. 1118, No. 32 (Spec. Sess. No. 1), § 1, effective in 60 days; 1997, June 25, P.L. 324, No. 33, § 2, imd. effective.

HISTORICAL AND STATUTORY NOTES

2007 Main Volume

Act 1988-47 legislation

Section 6 of Act 1988, April 13, P.L. 336, No. 47, provides that the amendment to this section shall apply to all actions for collateral relief, whether statutory or common law, instituted on or after the effective date of this act, irrespective of the date of conviction or sentence.

Act 1995-32 (SS1) legislation

Section 3(1) of Act 1995 (Spec. Sess. No. 1), Nov. 17, P.L. 1118, No. 32 provides that the amendment of 42 Pa.C.S. §§ 9542, 9543, 9544, 9545 and 9546 shall apply to petitions filed after the effective date of this act; however, a petitioner whose judgment has become final on or before the effective date of this act shall be deemed to have filed a timely petition under 42 Pa.C.S. Ch. 95 Subch. B if the petitioner's first petition is filed within one year of the effective date of this act.

Act 1997-33 legislation

The 1997 amendment, in the third sentence, deleted "nor is this subchapter intended" preceding "to provide", and added "or to provide relief from collateral consequences of a criminal conviction".

Prior Laws:

1966, Jan. 25, P.L. (1965) 1580, No. 554, § 2 (19 P.S. § 1180-2).

Section 9543. Eligibility for relief

(a) General rule.--To be eligible for relief under this subchapter, the petitioner must plead and prove by a preponderance of the evidence all of the following:

(1) That the petitioner has been convicted of a crime under the laws of this Commonwealth and is at the time relief is granted:

(i) currently serving a sentence of imprisonment, probation or parole for the crime;

(ii) awaiting execution of a sentence of death for the crime; or

(iii) serving a sentence which must expire before the person may commence serving the disputed sentence.

(2) That the conviction or sentence resulted from one or more of the following:

(i) A violation of the Constitution of this Commonwealth or the Constitution or laws of the United States which, in the circumstances of the particular case, so undermined the truth-determining process that no reliable adjudication of guilt or innocence could have taken place.

(ii) Ineffective assistance of counsel which, in the circumstances of the particular case, so undermined the truth-determining process that no reliable adjudication of guilt or innocence could have taken place.

42 Pa.C.S. § 9541-9546--Post-Conviction Relief Act

(iii) A plea of guilty unlawfully induced where the circumstances make it likely that the inducement caused the petitioner to plead guilty and the petitioner is innocent.

(iv) The improper obstruction by government officials of the petitioner's right of appeal where a meritorious appealable issue existed and was properly preserved in the trial court.

(v) Deleted.

(vi) The unavailability at the time of trial of exculpatory evidence that has subsequently become available and would have changed the outcome of the trial if it had been introduced.

(vii) The imposition of a sentence greater than the lawful maximum.

(viii) A proceeding in a tribunal without jurisdiction.

(3) That the allegation of error has not been previously litigated or waived.

<Subsec. (a)(4) is permanently suspended insofar as it references "unitary review" by Pennsylvania Supreme Court Order of Aug. 11, 1997, imd. effective.>

(4) That the failure to litigate the issue prior to or during trial, during unitary review or on direct appeal could not have been the result of any rational, strategic or tactical decision by counsel.

(b) Exception.--Even if the petitioner has met the requirements of subsection (a), the petition shall be dismissed if it appears at any time that, because of delay in filing the petition, the Commonwealth has been prejudiced either in its ability to respond to the petition or in its ability to re-try the petitioner. A petition may be dismissed due to delay in the filing by the petitioner only after a hearing upon a motion to dismiss. This subsection does not apply if the petitioner shows that the petition is based on grounds of which the petitioner could not have discovered by the exercise of reasonable diligence before the delay became prejudicial to the Commonwealth.

(c) Extradition.--If the petitioner's conviction and sentence resulted from a trial conducted in his absence and if the petitioner has fled to a foreign country that refuses to extradite him because a trial in absentia was employed, the petitioner shall be entitled to the grant of a new trial if the refusing country agrees by virtue of this provision to return him and if the petitioner upon such return to this jurisdiction so requests. This subsection shall apply, notwithstanding any other law or judgment to the contrary.

CREDIT(S)

1982, May 13, P.L. 417, No. 122, § 2, imd. effective. Amended 1988, April 13, P.L. 336, No. 47, Section 3, imd. effective; 1995, Nov. 17, P.L. 1118, No. 32 (Spec. Sess. No. 1), § 1, effective in 60 days; 1997, June 25, P.L. 324, No. 33, § 2, imd. effective; 1998, Jan. 27, P.L. 20, No. 3, § 2, imd. effective.

HISTORICAL AND STATUTORY NOTES

2007 Main Volume

Act 1988-47 legislation

Section 6 of Act 1988, April 13, P.L. 336, No. 47, provides that the amendment to this section shall apply to all actions for collateral relief, whether statutory or common law, instituted on or after the effective date of this act, irrespective of the date of conviction or sentence.

Act 1995-32 (SS1) legislation

Section 3(1) of Act 1995 (Spec. Sess. No. 1), Nov. 17, P.L. 1118, No. 32 provides that the amendment of 42 Pa.C.S. §§ 9542, 9543, 9544, 9545 and 9546 shall apply to petitions filed after the

42 Pa.C.S. § 9541-9546--Post-Conviction Relief Act

effective date of this act; however, a petitioner whose judgment has become final on or before the effective date of this act shall be deemed to have filed a timely petition under 42 Pa.C.S. Ch. 95 Subch. B if the petitioner's first petition is filed within one year of the effective date of this act.

Act 1997-33 legislation

The 1997 amendment, in subsec. (a), in the introductory language of paragraph (1), added ", at the time relief is granted".

Order of Aug. 11, 1997

Pennsylvania Supreme Court Order of Aug. 11, 1997, imd. effective, permanently suspended subsec. (a)(4) insofar as it references "unitary review". Said Order further provides that it shall apply retroactively to all cases in which the death penalty was imposed on or after January 1, 1996 and that appointments of counsel made pursuant to the Capital Unitary Review Act [42 Pa.C.S.A. §§ 9570 et seq.] shall remain in effect for purposes of challenges under the Post Conviction Relief Act (as amended in 1995 and by this Order), and under Pa. R.Crim.P. Chapter 1500 [now Pa.R.Crim.P. Rule 900 et seq.] (as amended by this Order).

Act 1998-3 legislation

The 1998 amendment added subsec. (c).

Section 3 of Act 1998, Jan. 27, No. 3 provides that the addition of subsec. (c) shall apply to all existing cases within its provisions.

Prior Laws:

1966, Jan. 25, P.L. (1965) 1580, No. 554, § 3 (19 P.S. § 1180-3).

Section 9543.1. Postconviction DNA testing

(a) Motion.--

42 Pa.C.S. § 9541-9546--Post-Conviction Relief Act

(1) An individual convicted of a criminal offense in a court of this Commonwealth and serving a term of imprisonment or awaiting execution because of a sentence of death may apply by making a written motion to the sentencing court for the performance of forensic DNA testing on specific evidence that is related to the investigation or prosecution that resulted in the judgment of conviction.

(2) The evidence may have been discovered either prior to or after the applicant's conviction. The evidence shall be available for testing as of the date of the motion. If the evidence was discovered prior to the applicant's conviction, the evidence shall not have been subject to the DNA testing requested because the technology for testing was not in existence at the time of the trial or the applicant's counsel did not seek testing at the time of the trial in a case where a verdict was rendered on or before January 1, 1995, or the applicant's counsel sought funds from the court to pay for the testing because his client was indigent and the court refused the request despite the client's indigency.

(b) Notice to the Commonwealth.--

(1) Upon receipt of a motion under subsection (a), the court shall notify the Commonwealth and shall afford the Commonwealth an opportunity to respond to the motion.

(2) Upon receipt of a motion under subsection (a) or notice of the motion, as applicable, the Commonwealth and the court shall take the steps reasonably necessary to ensure that any remaining biological material in the possession of the Commonwealth or the court is preserved pending the completion of the proceedings under this section.

(c) Requirements.--In any motion under subsection (a), under penalty of perjury, the applicant shall:

(1) (i) specify the evidence to be tested;

42 Pa.C.S. § 9541-9546--Post-Conviction Relief Act

(ii) state that the applicant consents to provide samples of bodily fluid for use in the DNA testing; and

(iii) acknowledge that the applicant understands that, if the motion is granted, any data obtained from any DNA samples or test results may be entered into law enforcement databases, may be used in the investigation of other crimes and may be used as evidence against the applicant in other cases.

(2) (i) assert the applicant's actual innocence of the offense for which the applicant was convicted; and

(ii) in a capital case:

(A) assert the applicant's actual innocence of the charged or uncharged conduct constituting an aggravating circumstance under section 9711(d) (relating to sentencing procedure for murder of the first degree) if the applicant's exoneration of the conduct would result in vacating a sentence of death; or

(B) assert that the outcome of the DNA testing would establish a mitigating circumstance under section 9711(e)(7) if that mitigating circumstance was presented to the sentencing judge or jury and facts as to that issue were in dispute at the sentencing hearing.

(3) present a prima facie case demonstrating that the:

(i) identity of or the participation in the crime by the perpetrator was at issue in the proceedings that resulted in the applicant's conviction and sentencing; and

(ii) DNA testing of the specific evidence, assuming exculpatory results, would establish:

(A) the applicant's actual innocence of the offense for which the applicant was convicted;

(B) in a capital case, the applicant's actual innocence of the charged or uncharged conduct constituting an aggravating circumstance under section 9711(d) if the applicant's exoneration of the conduct would result in vacating a sentence of death; or

(C) in a capital case, a mitigating circumstance under section 9711(e)(7) under the circumstances set forth in subsection (c)(1)(iv).

(d) Order.--

(1) Except as provided in paragraph (2), the court shall order the testing requested in a motion under subsection (a) under reasonable conditions designed to preserve the integrity of the evidence and the testing process upon a determination, after review of the record of the applicant's trial, that the:

(i) requirements of subsection (c) have been met;

(ii) evidence to be tested has been subject to a chain of custody sufficient to establish that it has not been altered in any material respect; and

(iii) motion is made in a timely manner and for the purpose of demonstrating the applicant's actual innocence and not to delay the execution of sentence or administration of justice.

(2) The court shall not order the testing requested in a motion under subsection (a) if, after review of the record of the applicant's trial, the court determines that there is no reasonable possibility that the testing would produce exculpatory evidence that:

(i) would establish the applicant's actual innocence of the offense for which the applicant was convicted;

(ii) in a capital case, would establish the applicant's actual innocence of the charged or uncharged conduct constituting an aggravating circumstance under section 9711(d) if the applicant's exoneration of the conduct would result in vacating a sentence of death; or

(iii) in a capital case, would establish a mitigating circumstance under section 9711(e)(7) under the circumstances set forth in subsection (c)(1)(iv).

(e) Testing procedures.--

(1) Any DNA testing ordered under this section shall be conducted by:

(i) a laboratory mutually selected by the Commonwealth and the applicant;

(ii) if the Commonwealth and the applicant are unable to agree on a laboratory, a laboratory selected by the court that ordered the testing; or

(iii) if the applicant is indigent, the testing shall be conducted by the Pennsylvania State Police or, at the Pennsylvania State Police's sole discretion, by a laboratory designated by the Pennsylvania State Police.

(2) The costs of any testing ordered under this section shall be paid:

(i) by the applicant; or

(ii) in the case of an applicant who is indigent, by the Commonwealth of Pennsylvania.

(3) Testing conducted by the Pennsylvania State Police shall be carried out in accordance with the protocols and procedures established by the Pennsylvania State Police.

(f) Posttesting procedures.--

(1) After the DNA testing conducted under this section has been completed, the applicant may, pursuant to section 9545(b)(2) (relating to jurisdiction and proceedings), during the 60-day period beginning on the date on which the applicant is notified of the test results, petition to the court for postconviction relief pursuant to section 9543(a)(2)(vi) (relating to eligibility for relief).

(2) Upon receipt of a petition filed under paragraph (1), the court shall consider the petition along with any answer filed by the Commonwealth and shall conduct a hearing thereon.

(3) In any hearing on a petition for postconviction relief filed under paragraph (1), the court shall determine whether the exculpatory evidence resulting from the DNA testing conducted under this section would have changed the outcome of the trial as required by section 9543(a)(2)(vi).

(g) Effect of motion.--The filing of a motion for forensic DNA testing pursuant to subsection (a) shall have the following effect:

(1) The filing of the motion shall constitute the applicant's consent to provide samples of bodily fluid for use in the DNA testing.

(2) The data from any DNA samples or test results obtained as a result of the motion may be entered into law enforcement databases, may be used in the investigation of other crimes and may be used as evidence against the applicant in other cases.

(h) Definitions.--As used in this section, the following words and phrases shall have the meanings given to them in this subsection:

"Applicant." The individual who files a motion under subsection (a).

"DNA." Deoxyribonucleic acid.

42 Pa.C.S. § 9541-9546--Post-Conviction Relief Act

CREDIT(S)

2002, July 10, P.L. 745, No. 109, § 1, effective in 60 days.

Section 9544. Previous litigation and waiver

(a) Previous litigation.--For purposes of this subchapter, an issue has been previously litigated if:

(1) Deleted.

(2) the highest appellate court in which the petitioner could have had review as a matter of right has ruled on the merits of the issue; or

(3) it has been raised and decided in a proceeding collaterally attacking the conviction or sentence.

<Subsec. (b) is permanently suspended insofar as it references "unitary review" by Pennsylvania Supreme Court Order of Aug. 11, 1997, imd. effective.>

(b) Issues waived.--For purposes of this subchapter, an issue is waived if the petitioner could have raised it but failed to do so before trial, at trial, during unitary review, on appeal or in a prior state postconviction proceeding.

CREDIT(S)

1982, May 13, P.L. 417, No. 122, § 2, imd. effective. Amended 1988, April 13, P.L. 336, No. 47, § 3, imd. effective; 1995, Nov. 17, P.L. 1118, No. 32 (Spec. Sess. No. 1), § 1, effective in 60 days.

HISTORICAL AND STATUTORY NOTES

2007 Main Volume

Act 1988-47 legislation

42 Pa.C.S. § 9541-9546--Post-Conviction Relief Act

Section 6 of Act 1988, April 13, P.L. 336, No. 47, provides that the amendment to this section shall apply to all actions for collateral relief, whether statutory or common law, instituted on or after the effective date of this act, irrespective of the date of conviction or sentence.

Act 1995-32 (SS1) legislation

The 1995 amendment rewrote this section, which formerly read:

"(a) Previous litigation.--For the purpose of this subchapter, an issue has been previously litigated if:

"(1) it has been raised in the trial court, the trial court has ruled on the merits of the issue and the petitioner did not appeal;

"(2) the highest appellate court in which the petitioner could have had review as a matter of right has ruled on the merits of the issue; or

"(3) it has been raised and decided in a proceeding collaterally attacking the conviction or sentence.

"(b) Issues waived.--For the purposes of this subchapter, an issue is waived if the petitioner failed to raise it and if it could have been raised before the trial, at the trial, on appeal, in a habeas corpus proceeding or other proceeding actually conducted or in a prior proceeding actually initiated under this subchapter."

Section 3(1) of Act 1995 (Spec. Sess. No. 1), Nov. 17, P.L. 1118, No. 32 provides that the amendment of 42 Pa.C.S. §§ 9542, 9543, 9544, 9545 and 9546 shall apply to petitions filed after the effective date of this act; however, a petitioner whose judgment has become final on or before the effective date of this act shall be deemed to have filed a timely petition under 42 Pa.C.S. Ch. 95 Subch. B if the petitioner's first petition is filed within one year of the effective date of this act.

42 Pa.C.S. § 9541-9546--Post-Conviction Relief Act

Order of Aug. 11, 1997

Pennsylvania Supreme Court Order of Aug. 11, 1997, imd. effective, permanently suspended subsec. (b) insofar as it references "unitary review". Said Order further provides that it shall apply retroactively to all cases in which the death penalty was imposed on or after January 1, 1996 and that appointments of counsel made pursuant to the Capital Unitary Review Act [42 Pa.C.S.A. § § 9570 et seq.] shall remain in effect for purposes of challenges under the Post Conviction Relief Act (as amended in 1995 and by this Order), and under Pa. R.Crim.P. Chapter 1500 [now Pa.R.Crim.P. Rule 900 et seq.] (as amended by this Order).

Prior Laws:

1966, Jan. 25, P.L. (1965) 1580, No 554, § 4 (19 P.S. § 1180-4)

Section 9545. Jurisdiction and proceedings

(a) Original jurisdiction.--Original jurisdiction over a proceeding under this subchapter shall be in the court of common pleas. No court shall have authority to entertain a request for any form of relief in anticipation of the filing of a petition under this subchapter.

(b) Time for filing petition.--

(1) Any petition under this subchapter, including a second or subsequent petition, shall be filed within one year of the date the judgment becomes final, unless the petition alleges and the petitioner proves that:

(i) the failure to raise the claim previously was the result of interference by government officials with the presentation of the claim in violation of the Constitution or laws of this Commonwealth or the Constitution or laws of the United States;

(ii) the facts upon which the claim is predicated were unknown to the petitioner and could not have been ascertained by the exercise of due diligence; or

(iii) the right asserted is a constitutional right that was recognized by the Supreme Court of the United States or the Supreme Court of Pennsylvania after the time period provided in this section and has been held by that court to apply retroactively.

(2) Any petition invoking an exception provided in paragraph (1) shall be filed within 60 days of the date the claim could have been presented.

(3) For purposes of this subchapter, a judgment becomes final at the conclusion of direct review, including discretionary review in the Supreme Court of the United States and the Supreme Court of Pennsylvania, or at the expiration of time for seeking the review.

(4) For purposes of this subchapter, "government officials" shall not include defense counsel, whether appointed or retained.

(c) Stay of execution.--

(1) No court shall have the authority to issue a stay of execution in any case except as allowed under this subchapter.

(2) Except for first petitions filed under this subchapter by defendants whose sentences have been affirmed on direct appeal by the Supreme Court of Pennsylvania between January 1, 1994, and January 1, 1996, no stay may be issued unless a petition for postconviction relief which meets all the requirements of this subchapter has been filed and is pending and the petitioner makes a strong showing of likelihood of success on the merits.

(3) Suspended by Pennsylvania Supreme Court Order of Aug. 11, 1997, imd. effective.

42 Pa.C.S. § 9541-9546--Post-Conviction Relief Act

(d) Evidentiary hearing.--

(1) Where a petitioner requests an evidentiary hearing, the petition shall include a signed certification as to each intended witness stating the witness's name, address, date of birth and substance of testimony and shall include any documents material to that witness's testimony. Failure to substantially comply with the requirements of this paragraph shall render the proposed witness's testimony inadmissible.

(2) Suspended by Pennsylvania Supreme Court Order of Aug. 11, 1997, imd. effective.

(3) When a claim for relief is based on an allegation of ineffective assistance of counsel as a ground for relief, any privilege concerning counsel's representation as to that issue shall be automatically terminated.

CREDIT(S)

1982, May 13, P.L. 417, No. 122, § 2, imd. effective. Amended 1988, April 13, P.L. 336, No. 47, § 3, imd. effective; 1995, Nov. 17, P.L. 1118, No. 32 (Spec. Sess. No. 1), § 1, effective in 60 days.

HISTORICAL AND STATUTORY NOTES

2007 Main Volume

Act 1988-47 legislation

Section 6 of Act 1988, April 13, P.L. 336, No. 47, provides that the amendment to this section shall apply to all actions for collateral relief, whether statutory or common law, instituted on or after the effective date of this act, irrespective of the date of conviction or sentence.

Act 1995-32 (SS1) legislation

The 1995 amendment rewrote this section, which formerly read:

42 Pa.C.S. § 9541-9546--Post-Conviction Relief Act

"(a) Original jurisdiction.--Original jurisdiction over a proceeding under this subchapter shall be in the court in which the conviction was obtained.

"(b) Rules governing proceedings.--The Supreme Court may, by general rule, prescribe procedures to implement the action established under this subchapter but shall not expand, contract or modify the grounds for relief set forth in this subchapter."

Section 3(1) of Act 1995 (Spec. Sess. No. 1), Nov. 17, P.L. 1118, No. 32 provides that the amendment of 42 Pa.C.S. §§ 9542, 9543, 9544, 9545 and 9546 shall apply to petitions filed after the effective date of this act; however, a petitioner whose judgment has become final on or before the effective date of this act shall be deemed to have filed a timely petition under 42 Pa.C.S. Ch. 95 Subch. B if the petitioner's first petition is filed within one year of the effective date of this act.

Order of Aug. 11, 1997

Pennsylvania Supreme Court Order of Aug. 11, 1997, imd. effective, permanently suspended

subsecs. (c)(3) and (d)(2). Said Order further provides that it shall apply retroactively to all cases in which the death penalty was imposed on or after January 1, 1996 and that appointments of counsel made pursuant to the Capital Unitary Review Act [42 Pa.C.S.A. § 9570 et seq.] shall remain in effect for purposes of challenges under the Post Conviction Relief Act (as amended in 1995 and by this Order), and under Pa. R.Crim.P. Chapter 1500 [now Pa.R.Crim.P. Rule 900 et seq.] (as amended by this Order). Prior to suspension, subsecs. (c)(3) and (d)(2) read:

"(c)(3) If a stay of execution is granted, all limitations periods set forth under sections 9574 (relating to answer to petition), 9575 (relating to disposition without evidentiary hearing) and

42 Pa.C.S. § 9541-9546--Post-Conviction Relief Act

9576 (relating to evidentiary hearing) shall apply to the litigation of the petition."

"(d)(2) No discovery, at any stage of proceedings under this subchapter, shall be permitted except upon leave of court with a showing of exceptional circumstances."

Prior Laws:

1966, Jan. 25, P.L. (1965) 1580, No. 554, § 5 (19 P.S. § 1180-5).

1970, Nov. 25, P.L. 759, No. 249, § 1.

Section 9546. Relief and order

(a) General rule.--If the court rules in favor of the petitioner, it shall order appropriate relief and issue supplementary orders as to rearraignment, retrial, custody, bail, discharge, correction of sentence or other matters that are necessary and proper.

(b) Deleted.

(c) Deleted.

(d) Review of order in death penalty cases.--A final court order under this subchapter in a case in which the death penalty has been imposed shall be directly appealable only to the Supreme Court pursuant to its rules.

CREDIT(S)

1982, May 13, P.L. 417, No. 122, § 2, imd. effective. Amended 1988, April 13, P.L. 336, No. 47, § 3, imd. effective; 1995, Nov. 17, P.L. 1118, No. 32 (Spec. Sess. No. 1), § 1, effective in 60 days; 1997, June 25, P.L. 324, No. 33, § 2, imd. effective.

HISTORICAL AND STATUTORY NOTES

2007 Main Volume

Act 1988-47 legislation

Section 6 of Act 1988, April 13, P.L. 336, No. 47, provides that the amendment to this section shall apply to all actions for collateral relief, whether statutory or common law, instituted on or after the effective date of this act, irrespective of the date of conviction or sentence.

Order of Aug. 11, 1997

Pennsylvania Supreme Court Order of Aug. 11, 1997, imd. effective, permanently suspended the 1995 and 1997 amendments to subsec. (d). Prior to suspension, subsec. (d) read:

"(d) Review of order in death penalty cases.--An order under this subchapter granting the petitioner final relief in a case in which the death penalty has been imposed shall be directly appealable by the Commonwealth to the Supreme Court pursuant to its rules. An order under this subchapter denying a petitioner final relief in a case in which the death penalty has been imposed shall not be reviewable in the Superior Court but shall be reviewable only by petition for allowance of appeal to the Supreme Court."

Said Order further provides that it shall apply retroactively to all cases in which the death penalty was imposed on or after January 1, 1996 and that appointments of counsel made pursuant to the Capital Unitary Review Act [42 Pa.C.S.A. §§ 9570 et seq.] shall remain in effect for purposes of challenges under the Post Conviction Relief Act (as amended in 1995 and by this Order), and under Pa. R.Crim.P. Chapter 1500 [now Pa.R.Crim.P. Rule 900 et seq.] (as amended by this Order).

Prior Laws:

1966, Jan. 25, P.L. (1965) 1580, No. 554, Section 6 (19 P.S. § 1180-6).

1967, Nov. 30, P.L. 639, § 1.

Capital Unitary Review Act suspended by August 11, 1997 order of the Pennsylvania Supreme Court

Section 9570. Short title of subchapter

This subchapter shall be known and may be cited as the Capital Unitary Review Act.

Section 9571. Scope of subchapter

"(a) Capital unitary review.--This subchapter establishes the sole means of challenging proceedings that resulted in a sentence of death. The unitary review proceeding provided by this subchapter shall replace postappeal collateral review of death penalty cases with preappeal collateral review.

(b) Appointment of collateral counsel.--Under the action provided in this subchapter, a person sentenced to death shall be immediately entitled to new counsel for purposes of collateral review. The collateral proceeding shall occur in the trial court after the imposition of sentence and before appeal. The petitioner may raise any claim that could not have been raised previously, including claims of ineffective assistance of counsel.

(c) Capital appeal.--Direct appeal shall occur after the trial court has concluded collateral review. Claims raised on direct appeal shall be limited to those claims that were preserved at trial and that may be resolved on the basis of the record created up to and including sentencing. Collateral appeal shall occur simultaneously with direct appeal. Claims raised on collateral appeal shall be limited to claims that were preserved in the collateral proceeding in the trial court and to any other claim that could not have been raised previously, including claims of ineffective assistance of counsel on direct appeal.

(d) Limitation on subsequent petitions.--No further review shall be available except as provided in this subchapter.

(e) Capital case in which death penalty not imposed.--This subchapter does not apply to capital cases in which the death penalty was not imposed.

Section 9572. Representation of counsel

(a) Collateral counsel.--Immediately after the formal imposition of sentence on all charges or within 30 days of the verdict of the death penalty, whichever occurs later, the court shall appoint new counsel for the purposes of collateral review, unless:

"(1) the petitioner has elected to proceed pro se and the court finds, after a colloquy on the record, that the petitioner's election is knowing, intelligent and voluntary; or

(2) the petitioner retains counsel for the unitary review proceeding.

(b) Prior attorney.--No petitioner may be represented on collateral review, either in the trial court or on appeal, by an attorney, whether retained or appointed, who has represented the petitioner at any other stage of the proceedings, including direct appeal, unless the court finds, after a colloquy on the record, that the petitioner has knowingly, intelligently and voluntarily waived his right to challenge the effectiveness of that attorney's representation.

(c) Standards for appointment of counsel.--The Supreme Court shall adopt standards for the appointment of counsel in capital cases. These standards shall apply for the appointment of trial counsel, collateral review counsel and appellate counsel. When adopting the standards, the Supreme Court shall consider, where practicable, the following criteria:

(1) Counsel is admitted to practice in Pennsylvania.

Capital Unitary Review Act

(2) Counsel is an experienced and active trial practitioner with at least five years' litigation experience in the field of criminal law.

"(3) Counsel has prior experience as counsel in a specified number of trials or other relevant proceedings.

(4) Counsel is familiar with the practice and procedure of the appropriate courts, including Federal courts of the jurisdiction.

(5) Counsel has demonstrated the necessary proficiency and commitment which exemplify the quality of representation appropriate to capital cases.

(6) Local practice for the appointment of counsel in capital cases.

Absent standards established under this subsection, the court may appoint such counsel as it deems qualified, in accordance with any local rules or practices. The existence or applicability of or failure to comply with such standards shall not provide a basis for relief.

Section 9573. Time for petition; contents of petition

(a) Filing date.--Any petition under this subchapter shall be filed within 120 days of the date the trial transcript is filed with the court. The court may, for good cause shown, grant extensions of time totaling no more than 90 days.

(b) Subsequent or untimely claims.--Any claim raised after the time specified in subsection (a) shall be dismissed unless it satisfies section 9578 (relating to subsequent petitions).

(c) Evidentiary hearing.--Where the petitioner requests an evidentiary hearing, the petition shall include a signed certification as to each intended witness stating the witness's name, address, date of birth and substance of testimony and shall include any documents material to that witness's testimony.

Failure to substantially comply with the requirements of this subsection shall render the proposed witness's testimony inadmissible.

(d) Discovery.--Discovery shall be permitted, and no reasonable discovery request of the petitioner shall be denied except upon demonstration of exceptional circumstances justifying denial of the discovery requests.

(e) Claim for relief.--When a claim for relief is based on an allegation of ineffective assistance of counsel as a ground for relief, any privilege concerning counsel's representation as to that issue shall be automatically terminated.

Section 9574. Answer to petition

The Commonwealth may file a written answer to the petition within 120 days of the filing and service of the petition. For good cause shown, the court may grant an extension of time of up to 90 days. Failure to file an answer shall not constitute an admission of any facts alleged in the petition.

Section 9575. Disposition without evidentiary hearing

(a) Evidentiary hearing.--No more than 20 days after the Commonwealth answers the petition or, if no answer is filed, 20 days after the deadline for answering, the court shall determine whether or not an evidentiary hearing is warranted. An evidentiary hearing shall not be warranted unless controverted, previously unresolved factual issues material to petitioner's conviction or sentence exist.

(b) Written order.--Failure of the court to issue a written order within the period prescribed under subsection (a) shall constitute a determination that an evidentiary hearing is warranted on any controverted, previously unresolved factual issues material to petitioner's conviction or sentence.

(c) Disposing of petition.--If the determination is made that no evidentiary hearing is warranted, the court shall, no later than 90 days from the date of that determination, dispose of the petition, after oral argument if requested, and any postsentence motions filed under the Pennsylvania Rules of Criminal Procedure.

Section 9576. Evidentiary hearing

(a) Order.--If the court determines that an evidentiary hearing is warranted, the court shall enter an order no more than 20 days after the Commonwealth answers the petition or, if no answer is filed, 20 days after the deadline for answering, setting a date for the hearing.

(b) Date.--The hearing shall be scheduled to occur not less than ten days and not more than 45 days from the date of the order setting the hearing. The court may, for good cause shown, grant leave to continue the hearing.

(c) Disposing of petition.--Not later than 90 days after the evidentiary hearing, the court shall dispose of the petition and any postsentence motions filed under the Pennsylvania Rules of Criminal Procedure.

Section 9577. Disposition and appeal

(a) Capital unitary review.--Review by the Supreme Court under section 9711(h) (relating to review of death sentence) shall comprise direct appeal and collateral appeal. The common pleas court order disposing of the petition under this subchapter shall constitute the final judgment for purposes of this review.

(b) Briefs for petitioner.--Unless the petitioner has waived the right to new counsel on collateral review, separate briefs shall be filed for direct appeal and collateral appeal. The time for filing the collateral appeal brief shall begin to run from service of the petitioner's brief on direct appeal.

(c) Brief for the Commonwealth.--The Commonwealth shall file a brief in response to the petitioner's direct and collateral appeal briefs. The time for filing the Commonwealth's brief shall begin to run from service of the petitioner's brief on collateral appeal.

Section 9578. Subsequent petitions

(a) Further review.--No further review shall be available unless a petition is filed under Subchapter B (relating to post conviction relief) alleging that:

(1) the failure to raise the claim previously was the result of interference by government officials with the presentation of the claim in violation of the Constitution of the United States or laws of the United States or the Constitution of Pennsylvania or laws of this Commonwealth;

(2) the facts upon which the claim is predicated were unknown to the petitioner and could not have been ascertained in the exercise of due diligence; or

(3) the right asserted is a constitutional right that was recognized by the Supreme Court of the United States or the Supreme Court of Pennsylvania after the time period provided in this section and has been held by that court to apply retroactively.

(b) Exception petition.--Any petition invoking an exception provided in subsection (a) shall be filed within 60 days of the date the claim could have been presented.

Section 9579. Certification

(a) General rule.--By presenting to the court, whether by signing, filing, submitting or later advocating, a pleading, written motion or other papers regarding a petition for collateral relief, an attorney or unrepresented party is certifying that, to the best of the person's knowledge, information and belief, formed after an inquiry reasonable under the circumstances, the following:

(1) it is not being presented for any improper purpose, such as to harass or to cause unnecessary delay or needless increase in the cost of litigation;

(2) the claims and other legal contentions in it are warranted by existing law or by a nonfrivolous argument for extension, modification or reversal of existing law or the establishment of new law; and

(3) the allegations and other factual contentions have evidentiary support or, if specifically so identified, are likely to have evidentiary support after a reasonable opportunity for further investigation.

(b) Sanctions.--If, after notice and a reasonable opportunity to respond, the court determines that this section has been violated, the court may impose an appropriate sanction on the attorneys, law firms or parties that have violated this section.

Post-Conviction Hearing Act (1966)

The General Assembly of the Commonwealth of Pennsylvania hereby enacts as follows:

Section 1. Short Title.—This act shall be known and may be cited as the "Post Conviction Hearing Act."

Section 2. Post Conviction Procedure.—This act establishes a post conviction procedure for providing relief from convictions obtained and sentences imposed without due process of law. The procedure hereby established shall encompass all common law and statutory procedures for the same purpose that exist when this statute takes effect, including habeas corpus and coram nobis. However, nothing in this act limits the availability of remedies in the trial court or on direct appeal.

Section 3. Eligibility for relief.—To be eligible for relief under this act, a person must initiate a proceeding by filing a petition under section 5 and must prove the following:

(a) That he has been convicted of a crime,

(b) That he is incarcerated in the Commonwealth of Pennsylvania under a sentence of death or imprisonment, or on parole or probation,

(c) That his conviction or sentence resulted from one or more of the following reasons:

(1) The introduction of evidence obtained pursuant to an unlawful arrest;

(2) The introduction of evidence obtained by an unconstitutional search and seizure;

(3) The introduction of a coerced confession into evidence;

(4) The introduction into evidence of a statement obtained in the absence of counsel at a time when representation is constitutionally required;

(5) The infringement of his privilege against self-incrimination under either Federal or State law;

(6) The denial of his constitutional right to representation by competent counsel;

(7) A plea of guilty unlawfully induced;

(8) The unconstitutional suppression of evidence by the State;

(9) The unconstitutional use by the State of perjured testimony;

(10) The obstruction by State officials of petitioner's right of appeal;

(11) His being twice placed in jeopardy;

(12) The abridgement in any other way of any right guaranteed by the constitution or laws of this State or the constitution or laws of the United States, including a right that was not recognized as existing at the time of the trial if the constitution requires retrospective application of that right; or

(13) The unavailability at the time of trial of exculpatory evidence that has subsequently become available and that would have affected the outcome of the trial if it had been introduced.

(d) That the error resulting in his conviction and sentence has not been finally litigated or waived.

Section 4. When an Issue is Finally Litigated or Waived.—(a) For the purpose of this act, an issue is finally litigated if:

(1) It has been raised in the trial court, the trial court has ruled on the merits of the issue, and the petitioner has knowingly and understandingly failed to appeal the trial court's ruling; or

Post-Conviction Hearing Act (1966)

(2) The Superior Court of the Commonwealth of Pennsylvania has ruled on the merits of the issue and the petitioner has knowingly and understandingly failed to avail himself of further appeals; or

(3) The Supreme Court of the Commonwealth of Pennsylvania has ruled on the merits of the issue.

(b) For the purposes of this act, an issue is waived if:

(1) The petitioner knowingly and understandingly failed to raise it and it could have been raised before the trial, at the trial, on appeal, in a habeas corpus proceeding or any other proceeding actually conducted, or in a prior proceeding actually initiated under this act; and

(2) The petitioner is unable to prove the existence of extraordinary circumstances to justify his failure to raise the issue.

(c) There is a rebuttable presumption that a failure to appeal a ruling or to raise an issue is a knowing and understanding failure.

Section 5. Petition.—Any person who desires to obtain relief under this act may initiate a post conviction proceeding by filing a petition (together with two copies thereof) verified by affidavit, with the clerk of the court in which he was convicted and sentenced which said court is hereby granted jurisdiction to hear and determine same. He may file a petition at any time. A petition shall be in the following forms:

(1) The petition must state that it is a post conviction procedure act petition and must include the name of the petitioner, his place of confinement, an identification of the proceedings in which the petitioner was convicted and the place of conviction, the date of the entry of judgment, the sentence imposed, all facts in support of the alleged error on which the petition is based, the

Post-Conviction Hearing Act (1966)

relief desired, and an identification of all previous proceedings that the petitioner has taken to secure relief from his conviction or sentence.

(2) The petition must either include affidavits, records, and other supporting evidence, or state why they are not included.

(3) The petition shall not include argument or citation and discussion of authorities.

(4) All facts within the personal knowledge of the petitioner must be set forth separately from other allegations of fact.

Section 6. Docketing.—Upon receipt of a petition seeking relief under this act, the clerk of the court in which the indictment upon which sentence was imposed shall immediately docket the petition to the same term and number as the original proceedings, and promptly notify the court and serve a copy upon the district attorney and the attorney general. In the event the petitioner's incarceration is by virtue of multiple indictments and sentences, the case shall be docketed to the same term and number as the indictment upon which the first unexpired sentence was imposed, but the court may take judicial notice of all proceedings had upon the multiple indictments.

Section 7. Amendment and Withdrawal of Petition.—The court may grant leave to amend or withdraw the petition at any time. Amendment shall be freely allowed in order to achieve substantial justice. No petition may be dismissed for want of particularity unless the petitioner is first given an opportunity to clarify his petition.

Section 8. Answer.—The district attorney shall respond by answer or motion within twenty days from the day the petition is served upon him, or within such time as the court orders. If the petition does not include records of the proceedings attached therein, the respondent shall file with his answer the records that are material to the questions raised in the petition.

Section 9. Hearings.—If a petition alleges facts that if proven would entitle the petitioner to relief, the court shall grant a hearing which may extend only to the issues raised in the petition or answer. However, the court may deny a hearing if the petitioner's claim is patently frivolous and is without a trace of support either in the record or from other evidence submitted by the petitioner. The court may also deny a hearing on a specific question of fact when a full and fair evidentiary hearing upon that question was held at the original trial or at any later proceeding. The petitioner shall have a full and fair hearing on his petition. The court shall receive all evidence, which shall be recorded, that is relevant and necessary to support the claims in the petition, including affidavits, depositions, oral testimony, certificate of the trial judge, and relevant and necessary portions of transcripts of prior proceedings. The petitioner has the right to appear in person at the hearing.

Section 10. Order of the Court and Final Disposition of the Petition. —If the court finds in favor of the petitioner, it shall order appropriate relief and issue any supplementary orders as to rearraignment, retrial, custody, bail, discharge, correction of sentence, or other matters that are necessary and proper. The order finally disposing of the petition shall state grounds on which the case was determined and whether a Federal or a State right was presented and decided. This order constitutes a final judgment for purposes of review.

Section 11. Appeal.—The party aggrieved by an order under section 10 of this act may, within thirty days from the day on which the order is issued, appeal to the court having appellate jurisdiction over the original conviction. An application for leave to appeal must be accompanied by a record which contains the petition, the district attorney's answer or motion, and the order and statement of the court. In addition, the appellate court, in its discretion or on motion by either party, may order a transcript of the post conviction hearing certified to it as a part of the record.

Section 12. Pauper Petitions.—If the petition alleges that the petitioner is unable to pay the costs of the proceeding, the court may order that the petitioner be permitted to proceed as a poor person and order a transcript of the proceedings delivered to the petitioner. If the petitioner is without counsel and alleges that he is without means to procure counsel, he shall state whether or not he wishes counsel to be appointed to represent him. If appointment of counsel is so requested, the court shall appoint counsel if satisfied that the petitioner has no means to procure counsel.

Section 13. 1 Repealer.—Those provisions of the act of May 15, 1951 (P. L. 415), entitled "An Act relating to habeas corpus; conferring jurisdiction upon the judges of the courts of common pleas; prescribing venue; defining procedure in all cases; authorizing service to be made upon persons anywhere in the Commonwealth; providing for the imposition of costs; allowing appeals; specifying the appellate court to which appeals may be taken; and repealing inconsistent legislation, including that conferring jurisdiction on courts of quarter sessions," which relate to prisoners under sentence are hereby repealed.

Section 14. 2 Effective Date.—This act shall take effect March 1, 1966.

APPROVED-The 25th day of January, A. D. 1966.

Law Review Articles and Other Publications

Thomas M. Place, Claim is cognizable but the petition is untimely: The Pennsylvania Supreme Court's recent collateral relief decisions, 10 Temp. Pol. & Civ. Rts. L. Rev. 49, (2000).

Thomas M. Place, Ineffectiveness of counsel and short-term sentences in Pennsylvania: A claim in search of a remedy, 17 Temp. Pol. & Civ. Rts. L. Rev. 109 (2007).

Thomas M. Place, Ineffective Assistance of Counsel Under the Pennsylvania Post-Conviction Relief Act, 69 Temp. L. Rev. 1389 (Winter 1996).

Thomas M. Place, Recent Post Conviction Developments, 81 PABAQ 110 (July 2010).

Donald Harris, Kim Nieves, Thomas M. Place, Dispatch and Delay: Post Conviction Relief Act Litigation in Non-Capital Cases, 41 Duquesne Law Review 467 (2003).

Kirk J. Henderson, The Right to Argue that Trial Counsel was Constitutionally Ineffective, 45 Duquesne Law Review 1 (2006).

Louis M. Natalie, Jr., New Bars in Pennsylvania Capital Post-Conviction Law and Their Implications in Federal Habeas Corpus Review, 73 Temp. L. Rev. 69 (Spring 2000).

Justice Thomas Saylor, Post-Conviction Relief in Pennsylvania, 69 PABAQ 1, (January 1998).

Quick Index/Case References

actual prejudice; *see also **Kimball, Commonwealth v.*** 724 A.2d 326 (Pa. 1999); ***Pierce, Commonwealth v.*** 527 A.2d 973 (Pa. 1987)--*pgs. 48, 55-61, 68, 75, 81, 84, 86-87, 90, 92-93, 95, 97-99, 109-111, 114, 118-119, 220, 222, 259, 296, 318-319, 355, 361, 370, 372-373, 377, 379, 380-381, 387-388*

Commonwealth ex rel. Washington v. Maroney, 235 A.2d 349 (Pa. 1967)

Commonwealth v. Rathfon, 899 A.2d 365 (Pa. Super. 2006)

Commonwealth v. Steele, 961 A.2d 786 (Pa. 2008)

Commonwealth v. Walker, 110 A.3d 1000 (Pa. Super. 2015)

***affidavits**—see also witness certifications*—*pgs. 174-175, 186-187, 281, 301, 310-311, 338-339, 419-421*

Commonwealth v. Brown, 767 A.2d 576 (Pa. Super. 2001)

Commonwealth v. Collins, 687 A.2d 1112 (Pa. 1996) (OAJC)

Commonwealth v. McLaurin, 45 A.3d 1131 (Pa. Super. 2012)

Commonwealth v. Pander, 100 A.3d 626 (Pa. Super. 2014) (*en banc*)

after-discovered evidence; § 9543(a)(2)(i)--*pgs. 41, 123-131, 143, 163-164*

Commonwealth v. Fiore, 780 A.2d 704 (Pa. Super. 2001)

Commonwealth v. Galloway, 640 A.2d 454 (Pa. Super. 1994)

Commonwealth v. Padillas, 997 A.2d 356 (Pa. Super. 2010)

Commonwealth v. Washington, 927 A.2d 586 (Pa. 2007)

alibi--*pgs. 94-95, 115, 307*

Commonwealth v. Dennis, 950 A.2d 945 (Pa. 2008)

Commonwealth v. Johnson, 139 A.3d 1257 (Pa. 2016)

Commonwealth v. Mikell, 729 A.2d 566 (Pa. 1999)

Commonwealth v. Rios, 920 A.2d 790 (Pa. 2007)

Commonwealth v. Stewart, 84 A.3d 701 (Pa. Super. 2013) (*en banc*)

Commonwealth v. McKendrick, 514 A.2d 144 (Pa. Super. 1986)

Commonwealth v. Olivencia, 402 A.2d 519 (Pa. Super. 1979)

Commonwealth v. Sileo, 32 A.3d 753 (Pa. Super. 2011) (*en banc*)

amended petition(s)--*pgs. 87-88, 103, 132-135, 160-161, 183-184,*

190-195, 205, 213, 215-217, 237, 242-249, 254, 259-260, 262-263, 267, 270-271, 273, 282, 286, 292-296, 298-304 sample—309-311, 326, 329-330, 332, 335-337, 347, 351, 358, 360-364, 369, 376-378
>Commonwealth v. Derrickson, 923 A.2d 466 (Pa. Super. 2007)
>Commonwealth v. Jerman, 762 A.2d 366 (Pa. Super. 2000)
>Commonwealth v. Jette, 947 A.2d 202 (Pa. Super. 2008)
>Commonwealth v. Kutnyak, 781 A.2d 1259 (Pa. Super. 2001)
>Commonwealth v. Flanagan, 854 A.2d 489 (Pa. 2004)
>Commonwealth v. Padden, 783 A.2d 299 (Pa. Super. 2001)
>Commonwealth v. Rykard, 55 A.3d 1177 (Pa. Super. 2012)

arguable merit—*pgs. 55, 75-76, 114, 117-119, 253, 290, 296-297, 318, 337, 352-353, 370-372, 387-388, 390*
>Commonwealth v. Jones, 876 A.2d 380, 385 (Pa. 2005)
>Commonwealth v. Stewart, 84 A.3d 701 (Pa. Super. 2013) (*en banc*)

attorney-client privilege—*pgs.* 153, 175, 406, 413
>Commonwealth v. Flor, 136 A.3d 150 (Pa. 2016)

bail—*pgs. 176, 408, 421*
>Commonwealth v. Bishop, 829 A.2d 1170 (Pa. Super. 2003)
>Commonwealth v. Bonaparte, 530 A.2d 1351 (Pa. Super. 1988)
>Commonwealth v. McMaster, 730 A.2d 524 (Pa. Super. 1999)

Batson claims—*pgs. 45, 105-108, 201, 295*
>Commonwealth v. Basemore, 744 A.2d 717 (Pa. 2000)
>Commonwealth v. Bond, 819 A.2d 33 (Pa. 2002)
>Commonwealth v. Clark, 961 A.2d 80 (Pa. 2008)
>Commonwealth v. Cook, 952 A.2d 594 (Pa. 2008)
>Commonwealth v. Hackett, 956 A.2d 978 (Pa. 2008)
>Commonwealth v. Hanible, 30 A.3d 426 (Pa. 2011)
>Commonwealth v. Jones, 951 A.2d 294 (Pa. 2008)
>Commonwealth v. Ligons, 971 A.2d 1125 (Pa. 2009)
>Commonwealth v. Perrin, 947 A.2d 1284 (Pa. Super. 2008)
>Commonwealth v. Reid, 99 A.3d 427 (Pa. 2014)
>Commonwealth v. Reid, 99 A.3d 470 (Pa. 2014)
>Commonwealth v. Smith, 17 A.3d 873 (Pa. 2011)
>Commonwealth v. Uderra, 862 A.2d 74 (Pa. 2004)
>Commonwealth v. Williams, 980 A.2d 510 (Pa. 2009)

Quick Index/Case References

boilerplate claims—pgs. *56, 147, 192, 247, 281, 311, 337, 352*
    Commonwealth v. Bond, 819 A.2d 33 (Pa. 2002)
    Commonwealth v. Steele, 961 A.2d 786 (Pa. 2008)

Brady claims—pgs. *51, 123-126, 162, 201, 231, 285*
    Commonwealth v. Appel, 689 A.2d 891 (Pa. 1997)
    Commonwealth v. Breakiron, 781 A.2d 94 (Pa. 2001)
    Commonwealth v. Burkett, 5 A.3d 1260 (Pa. Super. 2010)
    Commonwealth v. Busanet, 54 A.3d 35 (Pa. 2012)
    Commonwealth v. Galloway, 640 A.2d 454 (Pa. Super. 1994)
    Commonwealth v. Johnson, 815 A.2d 563 (Pa. 2002)
    Commonwealth v. Lambert, 884 A.2d 848 (Pa. 2005)
    Commonwealth v. Ly, 980 A.2d 61 (Pa. 2009)
    Commonwealth v. Miller, 987 A.2d 638 (Pa. 2009)
    Commonwealth v. Paddy, 15 A.3d 431 (Pa. 2011)
    Commonwealth v. Simmons, 804 A.2d 625 (Pa. 2001) (OAJC)
    Commonwealth v. Simpson, 66 A.3d 253 (Pa. 2013)
    Commonwealth v. Smith, 17 A.3d 873 (Pa. 2011)
    Commonwealth v. Stokes, 959 A.2d 306 (Pa. 2008)
    Commonwealth v. Williams, 732 A.2d 1167 (Pa. 1999)

Capital Unitary Review Act—pgs. *53, 70, 189, 226-227, 396, 404, 407, 409-416*

cognizability—pgs. *17, 19, 20-21, 29-30, 42-48, 51, 53, 74, 82, 85-86, 100-102, 123, 128, 153, 297, 331, 423*
    Commonwealth v. Beck, 848 A.2d 987 (Pa. Super. 2004)
    Commonwealth v. Burkett, 5 A.3d 1260 (Pa. Super. 2010)
    Commonwealth v. Chester, 733 A.2d 1242 (Pa. 1999)
    Commonwealth v. Deaner, 779 A.2d 578 (Pa. Super. 2001)
    Commonwealth v. Descardes, 136 A.3d 493 (Pa. 2016)
    Commonwealth v. Fahy, 737 A.2d 214 (Pa. 1999)
    Commonwealth ex rel. Dadario v. Goldberg, 773 A.2d 126 (Pa. 2001)
    Commonwealth v. Hackett, 956 A.2d 978 (Pa. 2008)
    Commonwealth v. Hall, 771 A.2d 1232 (Pa. 2001)
    Commonwealth v. Judge, 916 A.2d 511 (Pa. 2007)
    Commonwealth v. Masker, 34 A.3d 841 (Pa. Super. 2011) (*en banc*)
    Commonwealth v. Pagan, 864 A.2d 1231 (Pa. Super. 2004)
    Commonwealth v. Partee, 86 A.3d 245 (Pa. Super. 2014)

Commonwealth v. Stout, 978 A.2d 984 (Pa. Super. 2009)
Commonwealth v. West, 938 A.2d 1034 (Pa. 2007)

collateral consequences—pgs. 16, 21-35, 79, 100, 392-393
Commonwealth v. Abraham, 62 A.3d 343 (Pa. 2012)
Commonwealth v. Barndt, 74 A.3d 185 (Pa. Super. 2013)
Commonwealth v. Frometa, 555 A.2d 92 (Pa. 1989)
Commonwealth v. Lee, 820 A.2d 1285 (Pa. Super. 2003)
Commonwealth v. Masker, 34 A.3d 841 (Pa. Super. 2011) (*en banc*)
Padilla v. Kentucky, 130 S.Ct. 1473 (2010)

collateral order—pg. 201
Commonwealth v. Dennis, 859 A.2d 1270 (Pa. 2004)
Commonwealth v. Williams, 86 A.3d 771 (Pa. 2014)

colloquy, contradicting –pg. 95
Commonwealth v. Lawson, 762 A.2d 753 (Pa. Super. 2000)
Commonwealth v. Nieves, 746 A.2d 1102 (Pa. 2000)
Commonwealth Paddy, 800 A.2d 294 (Pa. 2002)
Commonwealth v. Peay, 806 A.2d 22 (Pa. Super. 2002)
Commonwealth v. Schultz, 707 A.2d 513 (Pa. Super. 1997)

colloquy, PCRA waiver—see also Holmes, Commonwealth v. 79 A.3d 562 (Pa. 2013)--*pgs. 71-73*
Commonwealth v. Baker, 72 A.3d 652 (Pa. Super. 2013)

colloquy, waiver of counsel—pgs. 179, 181, 208, 213, 216, 236, 262, 411
Commonwealth v. Grazier, 713 A.2d 81 (Pa. 1998)
Commonwealth v. Robinson, 970 A.2d 455 (Pa. Super. 2009) (*en banc*)
Commonwealth v. Stossel, 17 A.3d 1286 (Pa. Super. 2011)

competency—pgs. 150, 167-168
Commonwealth v. Cruz, 852 A.2d 287 (Pa. 2004)
Commonwealth v. Haag, 809 A.2d 271 (Pa. 2002)
Commonwealth v. Wiley, 966 A.2d 1153 (Pa. Super. 2009)
Commonwealth v. Zook, 887 A.2d 1218 (Pa. 2005)

conflict of interest—pg. 111
Commonwealth v. Collins, 957 A.2d 237 (Pa. 2008)
Commonwealth v. Small, 980 A.2d 549 (Pa. 2009)
Commonwealth v. Tedford, 960 A.2d 1 (Pa. 2008)
Commonwealth v. Townsend, 850 A.2d 741 (Pa. Super. 2004)

Quick Index/Case References

Commonwealth v. Williams, 980 A.2d 510 (Pa. 2009)

***constitutional claims**—pgs. 49-53, 74*
    Commonwealth v. Bretz, 830 A.2d 1273 (Pa. Super. 2003)
    Commonwealth v. Galloway, 640 A.2d 454 (Pa. Super. 1994)
    Commonwealth v. Grant, 992 A.2d 152 (Pa. Super. 2010)
    Commonwealth v. Robinson, 82 A.3d 998 (Pa. 2013)
    Commonwealth v. Simmons, 804 A.2d 625 (Pa. 2001) (OAJC)
    Commonwealth v. Smith, 717 A.2d 1032 (Pa. Super. 1998)

***coram nobis**—pgs. 16-20, 214, 291, 391-392, 417*
    Commonwealth v. Descardes, 136 A.3d 493 (Pa. 2016)
    Commonwealth v. Fiore, 665 A.2d 1185 (Pa. Super. 1995)
    Commonwealth v. Hayes, 596 A.2d 195 (Pa. Super. 1991) (*en banc*)
    Commonwealth v. Pagan, 864 A.2d 1231 (Pa. Super. 2004)
    Commonwealth v. Sheehan, 285 A.2d 465 (Pa. 1971)
    Commonwealth v. Turner, 80 A.3d 754 (Pa. 2013)

***credibility**—pgs. 116, 124, 126-127, 288, 296, 304*
    Commonwealth v. Clark, 961 A.2d 80 (Pa. 2008)
    Commonwealth v. Johnson, 966 A.2d 523 (Pa. 2009)
    Commonwealth v. Stewart, 84 A.3d 701 (Pa. Super. 2013) (*en banc*)

***cumulative claims**—pgs. 118-119*
    Commonwealth v. Johnson, 966 A.2d 523 (Pa. 2009)
    Commonwealth v. Spotz, 18 A.3d 244 (Pa. 2011)
    Commonwealth v. Washington, 927 A.2d 586 (Pa. 2007)

***deficient briefing**—pgs. 88, 216*
    Commonwealth v. Fink, 24 A.3d 426 (Pa. Super. 2011)
    Commonwealth v. Franklin, 823 A.2d 906 (Pa. Super. 2003)
    Commonwealth v. Johnson, 889 A.2d 620 (Pa. Super. 2005)
    Commonwealth v. Reed, 971 A.2d 1216 (Pa. 2009)

***delay, prejudicial**—pgs. 40-41, 66, 132-135, 256, 267-268, 297, 394-395*
    Commonwealth v. Markowitz, 32 A.3d 706 (Pa. Super. 2011)
    Commonwealth v. Renchenski, 52 A.3d 251 (Pa. 2012)
    Commonwealth v. Renchenski, 988 A.2d 699 (Pa. Super. 2010)
    Commonwealth v. Swartzfager, 59 A.3d 616 (Pa. Super. 2012)
    Commonwealth v. Weatherill, 24 A.3d 435 (Pa. Super. 2011)

Quick Index/Case References

Commonwealth v. Williams, 980 A.2d 510 (Pa. 2009)
deportation—see also Padilla v. Kentucky*, 130 S.Ct. 1473 (2010)--pgs. 19-27, 32-33, 79, 99-100*
    Commonwealth v. Escobar, 70 A.3d 838 (Pa. Super. 2013)
    Commonwealth v. Frometa, 555 A.2d 92 (Pa. 1989)
    Commonwealth v. Descardes, 136 A.3d 493 (Pa. 2016)
    Commonwealth v. McDermitt, 66 A.3d 810 (Pa. Super. 2013)
    Commonwealth v. Ghisoiu, 63 A.3d 1272 (Pa. Super. 2013)
    Commonwealth v. Wah, 42 A.3d 335 (Pa. Super. 2012)
diminished capacity*—pgs. 110-111, 333, 335*
    Commonwealth v. Hutchinson, 25 A.3d 277 (Pa. 2011)
    Commonwealth v. Johnson, 815 A.2d 563 (Pa. 2002)
    Commonwealth v. Smith, 17 A.3d 873 (Pa. 2011)
direct appeal, failure to file*—pgs. 46, 67, 81-84, 86, 88, 148, 163*
    Commonwealth v. Donaghy, 33 A.3d 12 (Pa Super. 2011)
    Commonwealth v. Harmon, 738 A.2d 1023 (Pa. Super. 1999)
    Commonwealth v. Markowitz, 32 A.3d 706 (Pa. Super. 2011)
    Commonwealth v. Touw, 781 A.2d 1250 (Pa. Super. 2001)
    Roe v. Flores-Ortega, 528 U.S. 470 (2000)
direct appeal, raising ineffectiveness—see also Holmes, Commonwealth v. *79 A.3d 562 (Pa. 2013)--pgs. 62, 64-73, 76-78, 82, 228, 289, 365, 380*
    Commonwealth v. Bomar, 826 A.2d 831 (Pa. 2003)
    Commonwealth v. Fitzgerald, 877 A.2d 1273 (Pa. Super. 2003)
    Commonwealth v. Marts, 889 A.2d 608 (Pa. Super. 2005)
    Commonwealth v. Moore, 978 A.2d 988 (Pa. Super. 2009)
    Commonwealth v. O'Berg, 880 A.2d 597 (Pa. 2005)
    Commonwealth v. Wright, 961 A.2d 119 (Pa. 2008)
discontinuing appeal*—pg. 154*
    Commonwealth v. Conway, 706 A.2d 1243 (Pa. Super. 1997)
discovery*—pgs. 106, 124, 153, 182, 184-190, 200-202, 269, 311, 408, 413*
    Commonwealth v. Abu-Jamal, 720 A.2d 79 (Pa. 1998)
    Commonwealth v. Dennis, 859 A.2d 1270 (Pa. 2004)
    Commonwealth v. Hanible, 30 A.3d 426 (Pa. 2011)
    Commonwealth v. Ly, 980 A.2d 61 (Pa. 2009)
    Commonwealth v. Martin, 705 A.2d 1337 (Pa. Super. 1998)

Commonwealth v. Miller, 987 A.2d 638 (Pa. 2009)
Commonwealth v. Tilley, 780 A.2d 649 (Pa. 2001)
Commonwealth v. Williams, 732 A.2d 1167 (Pa. 1999)
Commonwealth v. Williams, 86 A.3d 771 (Pa. 2014)
***discretionary sentencing**—pgs. 74, 87, 100-103, 214, 317, 385*
Commonwealth v. Hernandez, 755 A.2d 1 (Pa. Super. 2000)
Commonwealth v. Jones, 942 A.2d 903 (Pa. Super. 2008)
Commonwealth v. Lawrence, 960 A.2d 473 (Pa. Super. 2008)
Commonwealth v. Rigg, 84 A.3d 1080 (Pa. Super. 2014)
Commonwealth v. Scassera, 965 A.2d 247 (Pa. Super. 2009)
Commonwealth v. Watson, 835 A.2d 786 (Pa. Super. 2003)
Commonwealth v. Wrecks, 934 A.2d 1287 (Pa. Super. 2007)
***DNA**—pgs. 136-144, 286, 292, 396-401*
Commonwealth v. Baker, 828 A.2d 1146 (Pa. Super. 2003)
Commonwealth v. Brooks, 875 A.2d 1141 (Pa. Super. 2005)
Commonwealth v. Conway, 14 A.3d 101 (Pa. Super. 2011)
Commonwealth v. Edmiston, 65 A.3d 339 (Pa. 2013)
Commonwealth v. Gacobano, 65 A.3d 416 (Pa. Super. 2013)
Commonwealth v. Heilman, 867 A.2d 542 (Pa. Super. 2005)
Commonwealth v. McLaughlin, 835 A.2d 747 (Pa. Super. 2003)
Commonwealth v. Perry, 959 A.2d 932 (Pa. Super. 2008)
Commonwealth v. Scarborough, 64 A.3d 602 (Pa. 2013)
Commonwealth v. Walsh, 125 A.3d 1248 (Pa. Super. 2015)
Commonwealth v. Weeks, 831 A.2d 1194 (Pa. Super. 2003)
Commonwealth v. Williams, 899 A.2d 1060 (Pa. 2006)
Commonwealth v. Wright, 14 A.3d 798 (Pa. 2011)
Commonwealth v. Young, 873 A.2d 720 (Pa. Super. 2005)
In re Payne, 129 A.3d 546 (Pa. Super. 2015) (*en banc*)
Williams v. Erie County District Attorney's Office, 848 A.2d 967 (Pa. Super. 2004)
***eligibility**—pgs. 19-20, 39-48, 54, 73, 140, 393, 401, 417*
Commonwealth v. Ahlborn, 699 A.2d 718 (Pa. 1997)
Commonwealth v. Auchmuty, 799 A.2d 823 (Pa. Super. 2002)
Commonwealth v. Camps, 772 A.2d 70 (Pa. Super. 2001)
Commonwealth v. Fisher, 703 A.2d 714 (Pa. Super. 1997)
Commonwealth v. James, 771 A.2d 33 (Pa. Super. 2001)
Commonwealth v. Matin, 832 A.2d 1141 (Pa. Super. 2003)

Quick Index/Case References

Commonwealth v. Pagan, 864 A.2d 1231 (Pa. Super. 2004)
Commonwealth v. Turner, 80 A.3d 754 (Pa. 2013)
Commonwealth v. Williams, 977 A.2d 1174 (Pa. Super. 2009)

***expert witnesses; testimony**—pgs. 93-94, 116, 307*
Commonwealth v. Balodis, 747 A.2d 341 (Pa. 2000)
Commonwealth v. Begley, 780 A.2d 605 (Pa. 2001)
Commonwealth v. Chmiel, 30 A.3d 1111 (Pa. 2011)
Commonwealth v. Collins, 957 A.2d 237 (Pa. 2008)
Commonwealth v. Cox, 983 A.2d 666 (Pa. 2009)
Commonwealth v. Jarosz, __ A.3d __ (Pa. Super. 2016) (filed December 13, 2016)
Commonwealth v. Johnson, 815 A.2d 563 (Pa. 2002)
Commonwealth v. Lowery, 784 A.2d 795 (Pa. Super. 2001)
Commonwealth v. Williams, 640 A.2d 1251 (Pa. 1994)
Commonwealth v. Wright, 961 A.2d 119 (Pa. 2008)

***evidentiary hearings**—pgs. 52, 57, 85-86, 88, 93, 100-101, 108, 116, 127, 132-133, 153, 173-175, 186, 196-197, 207, 210, 217, 235-236, 255-261, 263-269, 270-271, 273, 275-278, 282, 286, 288, 290-291, 294-300, 303, 309, 320, 325, 327, 330, 342, 347, 373-374, 401-403, 407-409, 411, 416*
Commonwealth v. Albrecht, 994 A.2d 1091 (Pa. 2010)
Commonwealth v. Clark, 961 A.2d 80 (Pa. 2008)
Commonwealth v. Collins, 957 A.2d 237 (Pa. 2008)
Commonwealth v. Derrickson, 923 A.2d 466 (Pa. Super. 2007)
Commonwealth v. Khalifah, 852 A.2d 1238 (Pa. Super. 2004)
Commonwealth v. King, 999 A.2d 598 (Pa. Super. 2010)
Commonwealth v. Morris, 684 A.2d 1037 (Pa. 1996)
Commonwealth v. Payne, 794 A.2d 902 (Pa. Super. 2002)
Commonwealth v. Rush, 838 A.2d 651 (Pa. 2003)
Commonwealth v. Walls, 993 A.2d 289 (Pa. Super. 2010)
Commonwealth v. Williams, 980 A.2d 510 (Pa. 2009)

***final order**—pgs. 117, 130, 177, 195, 254, 261-263, 266, 268, 274, 278, 283-286, 293, 295-296, 299, 335-336, 348*
Commonwealth v. Bryant, 780 A.2d 646 (Pa. 2001)
Commonwealth v. Gaines, 127 A.3d 15 (Pa. Super. 2015) (*en banc*)
Commonwealth v. Morris, 771 A.2d 721 (Pa. 2001)

Quick Index/Case References

    Commonwealth v. Porter, 35 A.3d 4 (Pa. 2012)
    Commonwealth v. Rompilla, 983 A.2d 1207 (Pa. 2009)
    Commonwealth v. Scarborough, 64 A.3d 602 (Pa. 2013)
    Commonwealth v. Swartzfager, 59 A.3d 616 (Pa. Super. 2012)
governmental interference; § 9543(a)(2)(iv)—*pgs. 120-122, 163*
    Commonwealth v. Hanes, 579 A.2d 920 (Pa. Super. 1990)
governmental interference; timeliness—*pgs. 162-163, 246*
    Commonwealth v. Barrett, 761 A.2d 145 (Pa. Super. 2000)
    Commonwealth v. Blackwell, 936 A.2d 497 (Pa. Super. 2007)
    Commonwealth v. Crider, 735 A.2d 730 (Pa. Super. 1999)
    Commonwealth v. Howard, 788 A.2d 351 (Pa. 2002)
Grant, Commonwealth v. 813 A.2d 726 (Pa. 2002)--*pgs. 15, 23, 29-30, 33, 37-38, 43, 47, 62-69, 72-81, 90-91, 148, 160, 220-223, 225-229, 238, 289, 365-368, 380*
guilty plea—*pgs. 22, 24, 27-28, 32-33, 35, 41-42, 62, 82, 98-100, 109, 120-121, 334-335, 337, 339*
    Commonwealth v. Barbosa, 819 A.2d 81 (Pa. Super. 2003)
    Commonwealth v. Barndt, 74 A.3d 185 (Pa. Super. 2013)
    Commonwealth v. Bedell, 954 A.2d 1209 (Pa. Super. 2008)
    Commonwealth v. D'Collanfield, 805 A.2d 1244 (Pa. Super. 2002)
    Commonwealth v. Fluharty, 632 A.2d 312 (Pa. Super. 1993)
    Commonwealth v. Hickman, 799 A.2d 136 (Pa. Super. 2002)
    Commonwealth v. Laszczynski, 715 A.2d 1185 (Pa. Super. 1998)
    Commonwealth v. Lawson, 762 A.2d 753 (Pa. Super. 2000)
    Commonwealth v. Lynch, 820 A.2d 728 (Pa. Super. 2003)
    Commonwealth v. McDermitt, 66 A.3d 810 (Pa. Super. 2013)
    Commonwealth v. Melendez-Negron, 123 A.3d 1087 (Pa. Super. 2015)
    Commonwealth v. Pollard, 832 A.2d 517 (Pa. Super. 2003)
    Commonwealth v. Rathfon, 899 A.2d 365 (Pa. Super. 2006)
    Commonwealth v. Turetsky, 925 A.2d 876 (Pa. Super. 2007)
    Hill v. Lockhart, 474 U.S. 52 (1985)
habeas corpus—*pgs. 12, 14, 16-17, 20-21, 30-31, 44, 66, 113, 119, 142, 146, 157, 170, 214, 223, 227, 230-231, 233, 263, 283, 291, 330-331, 336, 366, 378, 391, 398, 403, 417, 419, 422*
    Commonwealth v. Ahlborn, 699 A.2d 718 (Pa. 1997)

Quick Index/Case References

>*Commonwealth v. Beck*, 848 A.2d 987 (Pa. Super. 2004)
>*Commonwealth v. Breakiron*, 781 A.2d 94 (Pa. 2001)
>*Commonwealth v. Chester*, 733 A.2d 1242 (Pa. 1999)
>*Commonwealth v. Fahy*, 737 A.2d 214 (Pa. 1999)
>*Commonwealth v. Judge*, 916 A.2d 511 (Pa. 2007)
>*Commonwealth v. Peterkin*, 722 A.2d 638 (Pa. 1998)
>*Commonwealth v. Stout*, 978 A.2d 984 (Pa. Super. 2009)
>*Commonwealth v. Taylor*, 65 A.3d 462 (Pa. Super. 2013)
>*Commonwealth v. West*, 938 A.2d 1034 (Pa. 2007)
>*Commonwealth v. Whitney*, 817 A.2d 473 (Pa. 2003)
>*Joseph v. Glunt*, 96 A.3d 365 (Pa. Super. 2014)

***harmless error**—pgs. 58-59, 213, 257, 294*
>*Commonwealth v. Howard*, 645 A.2d 1300 (Pa. 1994)
>*Commonwealth v. Barnett*, 121 A.3d 534 (Pa. Super. 2015)

Holmes, Commonwealth v. 79 A.3d 562 (Pa. 2013)--*pgs. 37, 64, 66-, 73, 77-78, 80-81, 232, 237-238, 380*

Hubbard, Commonwealth v. 372 A.2d 687 (Pa. 1977)--*pgs. 63, 65, 70, 78, 226, 289-290*

***hybrid representation**—pgs. 192, 222-223, 225, 234, 238-240, 271, 299*
>*Commonwealth v. Jette*, 23 A.3d 1032 (Pa. 2011)
>*Commonwealth v. Pursell*, 724 A.2d 293 (Pa. 1999)

***illegal sentencing**—pgs. 15-16, 36-37, 45, 50-53, 127-128, 148-149, 157, 199, 391*
>*Commonwealth v. Berry*, 877 A.2d 479 (Pa. Super. 2005 (*en banc*)
>*Commonwealth v. Fahy*, 737 A.2d 214, 223 (Pa. 1999)
>*Commonwealth v. Fowler*, 930 A.2d 586 (Pa. Super. 2007)
>*Commonwealth v. Hockenberry*, 689 A.2d 283 (Pa. Super. 1997) (*en banc*)
>*Commonwealth v. Jackson*, 30 A.3d 516 (Pa. Super. 2011)
>*Commonwealth v. Jones*, 932 A.2d 179 (Pa. Super. 2007)
>*Commonwealth v. Ousley*, 21 A.3d 1238 (Pa. Super. 2011)
>*Commonwealth v. Rivera*, 10 A.3d 1276 (Pa. Super. 2010)
>*Commonwealth v. Robinson*, 931 A.2d 15 (Pa. Super. 2007) (*en banc*)
>*Commonwealth v. Roach*, 453 A.2d 1001 (Pa. Super. 1983)
>*Commonwealth v. Springer*, 961 A.2d 1262 (Pa. Super. 2008)

Quick Index/Case References

Commonwealth v. Staples, 471 A.2d 847 (Pa. Super. 1984)
Commonwealth v. Stultz, 114 A.3d 865 (Pa. Super. 2015)
ineffective assistance; generally—*pgs. 54-119*
insanity—*pg. 111*
  Commonwealth v. Smith, 17 A.3d 873 (Pa. 2011)
jurisdiction—*pgs. 14-15, 40-41, 62-63, 73, 82-83, 87, 117, 123, 129-130, 132, 140, 143, 150-177, 180-181, 189, 201, 222, 233, 243, 258, 263, 271, 275, 286, 290, 292, 295, 299, 310, 317, 336, 340, 357, 361, 364, 375, 378, 383, 386, 394-395, 401, 404, 407, 412, 419, 421*
  Commonwealth v. Albrecht, 994 A.2d 1091 (Pa. 2010)
  Commonwealth v. Anderson, 788 A.2d 1019 (Pa. Super. 2001)
  Commonwealth v. Cappello, 823 A.2d 936 (Pa. Super. 2003)
  Commonwealth v. Fahy, 737 A.2d 214 (Pa. 1999)
  Commonwealth v. Fairiror, 809 A.2d 396 (Pa. Super. 2002)
  Commonwealth v. McKeever, 947 A.2d 782 (Pa. Super. 2008)
  Commonwealth v. Meehan, 628 A.2d 1151 (Pa. Super. 1993) (not related to timeliness of petition)
  Commonwealth v. Peterkin, 722 A.2d 638 (Pa. 1998)
  Commonwealth v. Yarris, 731 A.2d 581 (Pa. 1999)
jury instructions—*pgs. 112-116, 118, 146, 285*
  Commonwealth v. Bennett, 57 A.3d 1185 (Pa. 2012)
  Commonwealth v. Billa, 555 A.2d 835 (Pa. 1989)
  Commonwealth v. Brady, 741 A.2d 758 (Pa. Super. 1999)
  Commonwealth v. Collins, 687 A.2d 1112 (Pa. 1996) (OAJC)
  Commonwealth v. Cook, 952 A.2d 594 (Pa. 2008)
  Commonwealth v. Daniels, 963 A.2d 409 (Pa. 2009)
  Commonwealth v. Howard, 645 A.2d 1300 (Pa. 1994)
  Commonwealth v. Hutchinson, 25 A.3d 277 (Pa. 2011)
  Commonwealth v. Johnson, 815 A.2d 563 (Pa. 2002)
  Commonwealth v. Miller, 746 A.2d 592 (Pa. 2000)
  Commonwealth v. Perez, 103 A.3d 344 (Pa. Super. 2014)
  Commonwealth v. Reyes-Rodriguez, 111 A.3d 775 (Pa. Super. 2015) (*en banc*)
  Commonwealth v. Rios, 920 A.2d 790 (Pa. 2007)
  Commonwealth v. Uderra, 862 A.2d 74 (Pa. 2004)
  Commonwealth v. Williams, 980 A.2d 510 (Pa. 2009)
jury trial waiver—*pg. 90*
  Commonwealth v. Mallory, 941 A.2d 686 (Pa. 2008)

Quick Index/Case References

juveniles—pgs. 18, 168, 173, 289-291
    In re A.J., 829 A.2d 312 (Pa. Super. 2003)
    In re B.S., 831 A.2d 151 (Pa. Super. 2003)
    In re K.A.T., 69 A.3d 691 (Pa. Super. 2013)
    Matter of Smith, 573 A.2d 1077 (Pa. Super. 1990) (*en banc*)
Kimball, Commonwealth v. 724 A.2d 326 (Pa. 1999)--*pgs. 59-62*
layered claims—*pgs. 63-64, 67, 69-70, 75-76, 90-93, 116, 217-218, 337, 369-370*
    Commonwealth v. Birdsong, 24 A.3d 319 (Pa. 2011)
    Commonwealth v. Chmiel, 30 A.3d 1111 (Pa. 2011)
    Commonwealth v. Daniels, 963 A.2d 409 (Pa. 2009)
    Commonwealth v. Gonzalez, 858 A.2d 1219 (Pa. Super. 2004)
    Commonwealth v. Hall, 872 A.2d 1177 (Pa. 2005)
    Commonwealth v. Hutchinson, 25 A.3d 277 (Pa. 2011)
    Commonwealth v. Keaton, 45 A.3d 1050 (Pa. 2012)
    Commonwealth v. McGill, 832 A.2d 1014 (Pa. 2003)
    Commonwealth v. Reyes, 870 A.2d 888 (Pa. 2005)
    Commonwealth v. Robinson, 82 A.3d 998 (Pa. 2013)
    Commonwealth v. Rush, 838 A.2d 651 (Pa. 2003)
    Commonwealth v. Sileo, 32 A.3d 753 (Pa. Super. 2011) (*en banc*)
    Commonwealth v. Walker, 36 A.3d 1 (Pa. 2011)
    Commonwealth v. Williams, 980 A.2d 510 (Pa. 2009)
legality of sentence; *see illegal sentencing*
life qualifying—*pg. 90*
    Commonwealth v. Carson, 913 A.2d 220 (Pa. 2006)
    Commonwealth v. Lark, 698 A.2d 43 (Pa. 1997)
Mills claim—*pgs. 112-113, 285*
    Commonwealth v. Breakiron, 729 A.2d 1088 (Pa. 1999)
    Commonwealth v. Cox, 863 A.2d 536 (Pa. 2004)
    Commonwealth v. Cross, 726 A.2d 333 (Pa. 1999)
    Commonwealth v. Duffey, 889 A.2d 56 (Pa. 2005)
    Commonwealth v. Ly, 980 A.2d 61 (Pa. 2009)
    Commonwealth v. Steele, 961 A.2d 786 (Pa. 2008)
miscarriage of justice—*pgs. 84, 144, 161, 190, 240, 255-256, 375-377, 379, 381*
    Commonwealth v. Allen, 732 A.2d 582 (Pa. 1999)
    Commonwealth v. Beasley, 967 A.2d 376 (Pa. 2009)

Quick Index/Case References

    Commonwealth v. Lawson, 549 A.2d 107 (Pa. 1988)
    Commonwealth v. Morales, 701 A.2d 516 (Pa. 1997)
    Commonwealth v. Szuchon, 633 A.2d 1098 (Pa. 1993)
mitigation—*pgs. 46, 103-105, 174*
    Commonwealth v. Basemore, 744 A.2d 717 (Pa. 2000)
    Commonwealth v. Gorby, 909 A.2d 775 (Pa. 2006)
    Commonwealth v. Gribble, 863 A.2d 455 (Pa. 2004)
    Commonwealth v. Hall, 701 A.2d 190 (Pa. 1997)
    Commonwealth v. Lesko, 15 A.3d 345 (Pa. 2011)
    Commonwealth v. Malloy, 856 A.2d 767 (Pa. 2004)
    Commonwealth v. Martin, 5 A.3d 177 (Pa. 2010)
    Commonwealth v. Miller, 746 A.2d 592 (Pa. 2000)
    Commonwealth v. Rollins, 738 A.2d 435 (Pa. 1999)
    Commonwealth v. Small, 980 A.2d 549 (Pa. 2009)
    Commonwealth v. Sneed, 899 A.2d 1067 (Pa. 2006)
    Commonwealth v. Tharp, __ A.3d __ (Pa. 2014)
    Commonwealth v. Williams, 950 A.2d 294 (Pa. 2008)
    Commonwealth v. Williams, 732 A.2d 1167 (Pa. 1999)
    Commonwealth v. Zook, 887 A.2d 1218 (Pa. 2005)
new constitutional right—*see retroactivity*
newly-discovered facts—*pgs. 85, 88, 127, 143, 163-168, 231, 339, 358, 362, 364, 381*
    Commonwealth v. Bennett, 930 A.2d 1264 (Pa. 2007)
    Commonwealth v. Blackwell, 936 A.2d 497 (Pa. Super. 2007)
    Commonwealth v. Brandon, 51 A.3d 231 (Pa. Super. 2012)
    Commonwealth v. Edmiston, 65 A.3d 339 (Pa. 2013)
    Commonwealth v. Carr, 768 A.2d 1164 (Pa. Super. 2001)
    Commonwealth v. Chester, 895 A.2d 520 (Pa. 2006)
    Commonwealth v. Cintora, 69 A.3d 759 (Pa. Super. 2013)
    Commonwealth v. Cruz, 852 A.2d 287 (Pa. 2004)
    Commonwealth v. Fahy, 959 A.2d 312 (Pa. 2008)
    Commonwealth v. Gamboa-Taylor, 753 A.2d 780 (Pa. 2000)
    Commonwealth v. Howard, 788 A.2d 351 (Pa. 2002)
    Commonwealth v. Lambert, 884 A.2d 848 (Pa. 2005)
    Commonwealth v. Lark, 746 A.2d 585 (Pa. 2000)
    Commonwealth v. Marshall, 947 A.2d 714 (Pa. 2008)
    Commonwealth v. Monaco, 996 A.2d 1076 (Pa. Super. 2010)
    Commonwealth v. Pursell, 749 A.2d 911 (Pa. 2000)

Quick Index/Case References

Commonwealth v. Robinson, 12 A.3d 477 (Pa. Super. 2011)
Commonwealth v. Stokes, 959 A.2d 306 (Pa. 2008)
Commonwealth v. Vega, 754 A.2d 714 (Pa. Super. 2000)
Commonwealth v. Watts, 23 A.3d 980 (Pa. 2011)
Commonwealth v. Whitney, 817 A.2d 473 (Pa. 2003)
***no-merit letter**; see Turner/Finley*
***notice of intent to dismiss**; **notice of dismissal**—pgs. 83, 131, 160, 193, 196, 224-225, 235-237, 245-246, 257-266, 278, 286, 292-295, 300, 304, samples 328-347, 370, 386*
Commonwealth v. Albrecht, 720 A.2d 693 (Pa. 1998)
Commonwealth v. Anderson, 801 A.2d 1264 (Pa. Super. 2002)
Commonwealth v. Barbosa, 819 A.2d 81 (Pa. Super. 2003)
Commonwealth v. Boyd, 923 A.2d 513 (Pa. Super. 2007)
Commonwealth v. Brown, 830 A.2d 536 (Pa. 2003)
Commonwealth v. Carson, 913 A.2d 220 (Pa. 2006)
Commonwealth v. Blackwell, 936 A.2d 497 (Pa. Super. 2007)
Commonwealth v. Feighery, 661 A.2d 437 (Pa. Super. 1995)
Commonwealth v. Guthrie, 749 A.2d 502 (Pa. Super. 2000)
Commonwealth v. Hopfer, 965 A.2d 270 (Pa. Super. 2009)
Commonwealth v. Lark, 698 A.2d 43 (Pa. 1997)
Commonwealth v. Morris, 684 A.2d 1037 (Pa. 1996)
Commonwealth v. Paddy, 15 A.3d 431 (Pa. 2011)
Commonwealth v. Pitts, 981 A.2d 875 (Pa. 2009)
Commonwealth v. Porter, 728 A.2d 890 (Pa. 1999)
Commonwealth v. Pursell, 749 A.2d 911 (Pa. 2000)
Commonwealth v. Rush, 838 A.2d 651 (Pa. 2003)
Commonwealth v. Rykard, 55 A.3d 1177 (Pa. Super. 2012)
Commonwealth v. Swartzfager, 59 A.3d 616 (Pa. Super. 2012)
Commonwealth v. Williams, 782 A.2d 517 (Pa. 2001)
Commonwealth v. Williams, 732 A.2d 1167 (Pa. 1999)
***nunc pro tunc appeals**—pgs. 67, 81-85, 155, 256, 268, 276, 279, 283, 298, 331*
Commonwealth v. Bronaugh, 670 A.2d 147 (Pa. Super. 1995)
Commonwealth v. Callahan, 101 A.3d 118 (Pa. Super. 2014)
Commonwealth v. Eller, 807 A.2d 838 (Pa. 2002)
Commonwealth v. Geer, 936 A.2d 1075 (Pa. Super. 2007)
Commonwealth v. Glacken, 32 A.3d 750 (Pa. Super. 2011)
Commonwealth v. Harris, 114 A.3d 1 (Pa. Super. 2015)

Quick Index/Case References

    Commonwealth v. Hoyman, 561 A.2d 756 (Pa. Super. 1989)
    Commonwealth v. Kubis, 808 A.2d 196 (Pa. Super. 2002)
    Commonwealth v. Lane, 81 A.3d 974 (Pa. Super. 2013)
    Commonwealth v. Mikell, 968 A.2d 779 (Pa. Super. 2009)
    Commonwealth v. Pulanco, 954 A.2d 639 (Pa. Super. 2008)
    Commonwealth v. Robinson, 837 A.2d 1157 (Pa. 2003)
    Commonwealth v. Walter, 119 A.3d 255 (Pa. 2015)
***opinion, inadequate**—pgs. 264-265*
    Commonwealth v. Beasley, 967 A.2d 376 (Pa. 2009)
    Commonwealth v. Brown, 830 A.2d 536 (Pa. 2003)
    Commonwealth v. Daniels, 963 A.2d 409 (Pa. 2009)
    Commonwealth v. Glover, 738 A.2d 460 (Pa. Super. 1999)
    Commonwealth v. Smith, 17 A.3d 873 (Pa. 2011)
    Commonwealth v. Williams, 732 A.2d 1167 (Pa. 1999)
***Padilla v. Kentucky**, 130 S.Ct. 1473 (2010)--pgs. 19, 21-29, 32-33, 79, 99, 171*
***pending appeals**—pgs. 83, 158-159, 164*
    Commonwealth v. Leslie, 757 A.2d 984 (Pa. Super. 2000)
    Commonwealth v. O'Neil, 573 A.2d 1112 (Pa. Super. 1990)
    Commonwealth v. Seay, 814 A.2d 1240 (Pa. Super. 2003)
    Commonwealth v. Lark, 746 A.2d 585 (Pa. 2000)
***per se ineffectiveness**—pgs. 68, 81-90, 94, 217, 351, 364*
    Commonwealth v. Brooks, 839 A.2d 245 (Pa. 2003)
    Commonwealth v. Brown, 18 A.3d 1147 (Pa. Super. 2011)
    Commonwealth v. Burton, 973 A.2d 428 (Pa. Super. 2009)
    Commonwealth v. Fink, 24 A.3d 426 (Pa. Super. 2011)
    Commonwealth v. Grant, 992 A.2d 152 (Pa. Super. 2010)
    Commonwealth v. Halley, 870 A.2d 795 (Pa. 2005)
    Commonwealth v. Hopfer, 965 A.2d 270 (Pa. Super. 2009)
    Commonwealth v. Lantzy, 736 A.2d 564 (Pa. 1999)
    Commonwealth v. Liebel, 825 A.2d 630 (Pa. 2003)
    Commonwealth v. Poindexter, 646 A.2d 1211 (Pa. Super. 1994)
    Commonwealth v. Porter, 728 A.2d 890 (Pa. 1999)
    Commonwealth v. Reaves, 923 A.2d 1119 (Pa. 2007)
    Commonwealth v. Rigg, 84 A.3d 1080 (Pa. Super. 2014)
    United States v. Cronic, 466 U.S. 648 (1984)
***petition for allowance of appeal, failure to file**—pgs. 46, 82, 85-87,*

Quick Index/Case References

210, 308
    Commonwealth v. Bath, 907 A.2d 619 (Pa. Super. 2006)
    Commonwealth v. Cooke, 852 A.2d 340 (Pa. Super. 2004)
    Commonwealth v. Ellison, 851 A.2d 977 (Pa. Super. 2004)
    Commonwealth v. Gadsden, 832 A.2d 1082 (Pa. Super. 2003)
    Commonwealth v. Liebel, 825 A.2d 630 (Pa. 2003)
    Commonwealth v. Rigg, 84 A.3d 1080 (Pa. Super. 2014)
plea bargaining—*pgs. 46, 98-100, 170*
    Commonwealth v. Anderson, 995 A.2d 1184 (Pa. Super. 2010)
    Commonwealth v. Copeland, 554 A.2d 54 (Pa. Super. 1988)
    Commonwealth v. Korb, 617 A.2d 715 (Pa. Super. 1992)
    Lafler v. Cooper, 132 S.Ct. 1376 (2012)
    Missouri v. Frye, 132 S.Ct. 1399 (2012)
Pierce, Commonwealth v. 527 A.2d 973 (Pa. 1987)--*pgs. 54-60, 90, 319, 370, 388*
prejudice, see actual prejudice; ***Kimball, Commonwealth v.*** 724 A.2d 326 (Pa. 1999); ***Pierce, Commonwealth v.*** 527 A.2d 973 (Pa. 1987)
prejudicial delay—*see delay, prejudicial*
preliminary hearing—*pgs. 46, 116, 307*
    Commonwealth v. Lassen, 659 A.2d 999 (Pa. Super. 1995)
    Commonwealth v. Lyons, 568 A.2d 1266 (Pa. Super. 1989)
    Commonwealth v. Stultz, 114 A.3d 865 (Pa. Super. 2015)
previous litigation—*pgs. 40, 42-44, 69, 71, 146, 148, 189, 192-193, 246-247, 259, 310, 330-332, 337, 352-353, 360-362, 369-370, 372, 394*
    Commonwealth v. Allen, 732 A.2d 582 (Pa. 1999)
    Commonwealth v. Bond, 819 A.2d 33 (Pa. 2002)
    Commonwealth v. Collins, 888 A.2d 564 (Pa. 2005)
    Commonwealth v. Fahy, 737 A.2d 214 (Pa. 1999)
    Commonwealth v. Faulkner, 735 A.2d 67 (Pa. 1999)
    Commonwealth v. Jones, 932 A.2d 179 (Pa. Super. 2007)
    Commonwealth v. Marshall, 812 A.2d 539 (Pa. 2002)
    Commonwealth v. Miller, 987 A.2d 638 (Pa. 2009)
    Commonwealth v. Reyes, 870 A.2d 888 (Pa. 2005)
    Commonwealth v. Smith, 17 A.3d 873 (Pa. 2011)
prisoner mailbox rule—*pg. 158*
    Commonwealth v. Castro, 766 A.2d 1283 (Pa. Super. 2001)
    Commonwealth v. Jerman, 762 A.2d 366 (Pa. Super. 2000)

Quick Index/Case References

Commonwealth v. Little, 716 A.2d 1287 (Pa. Super. 1998)

***prosecutorial misconduct; see also Brady claims**—pgs. 63, 96-98, 123-126, 162, 201, 285, 319-320, 336-338, 389*

Commonwealth v. Morales, 701 A.2d 516 (Pa. 1997)
Commonwealth v. Tedford, 960 A.2d 1 (Pa. 2008)
Commonwealth v. Rollins, 738 A.2d 435 (Pa. 1999)
Commonwealth v. Travaglia, 661 A.2d 352 (Pa. 1995)

***reasonable basis**—pgs. 24, 55-58, 75, 92, 96, 109, 116, 174, 318-319, 370, 372, 387, 388-389*

Commonwealth v. Colavita, 993 A.2d 874 (Pa. 2010)
Commonwealth v. Miller, 987 A.2d 638 (Pa. 2009)
Commonwealth v. Reyes-Rodriguez, 111 A.3d 775 (Pa. Super. 2015) (*en banc*)
Commonwealth v. Stewart, 84 A.3d 701 (Pa. Super. 2013) (*en banc*)
Commonwealth v. Williams, 899 A.2d 1060 (Pa. 2006)

***recantation**—pgs. 127, 229, 338-340*

Commonwealth v. Birdsong, 24 A.3d 319 (Pa. 2011)
Commonwealth v. Bond, 819 A.2d 33 (Pa. 2002)
Commonwealth v. Washington, 927 A.2d 586 (Pa. 2007)

***recusal**—pgs. 205-206*

Commonwealth v. Birdsong, 24 A.3d 319 (Pa. 2011)
Commonwealth v. Hutchinson, 25 A.3d 277 (Pa. 2011)
Commonwealth v. Travaglia, 661 A.2d 352 (Pa. 1995)

***reinstatement of appellate rights**—pgs. 36, 68, 81-89, 134, 155, 161, 246, 266, 279*

Commonwealth v. Bronaugh, 670 A.2d 147 (Pa. Super. 1995)
Commonwealth v. Donaghy, 33 A.3d 12 (Pa Super. 2011)
Commonwealth v. Geer, 936 A.2d 1075 (Pa. Super. 2007)
Commonwealth v. Fairiror, 809 A.2d 396 (Pa. Super. 2002)
Commonwealth v. Harmon, 738 A.2d 1023 (Pa. Super. 1999)
Commonwealth v. Hoyman, 561 A.2d 756 (Pa. Super. 1989)
Commonwealth v. Karanicolas, 836 A.2d 940 (Pa. Super. 2003)
Commonwealth v. Markowitz, 32 A.3d 706 (Pa. Super. 2011)
Commonwealth v. Mikell, 968 A.2d 779 (Pa. Super. 2009)
Commonwealth v. Robinson, 837 A.2d 1157 (Pa. 2003)
Commonwealth v. Touw, 781 A.2d 1250 (Pa. Super. 2001)

Quick Index/Case References

    Roe v. Flores-Ortega, 528 U.S. 470 (2000)
    Commonwealth v. Walter, 119 A.3d 255 (Pa. 2015)
reinstatement of post-sentence motion rights—*pg. 85*
    Commonwealth v. Corley, 31 A.3d 293 (Pa. Super. 2011)
    Commonwealth v. Fransen, 986 A.2d 154 (Pa. Super. 2009)
    Commonwealth v. Liston, 977 A.2d 1089 (Pa. 2009)
relaxed waiver—*pgs. 113, 147*
    Commonwealth v. Albrecht, 720 A.2d 693 (Pa. 1998)
    Commonwealth v. Smith, 17 A.3d 873 (Pa. 2011)
retroactivity—new constitutional rule—*pgs. 18-19, 21, 24-26, 50, 53, 112-114, 152, 162, 168-173, 405, 415*
    Chaidez v. United States, 133 S.Ct. 1103 (2013)
    Commonwealth v. Abdul-Salaam, 812 A.2d 497 (Pa. 2002)
    Commonwealth v. Bracey, 986 A.2d 128 (Pa. 2009)
    Commonwealth v. Brooks, 875 A.2d 1141 (Pa. Super. 2005)
    Commonwealth v. Blystone, 725 A.2d 1197 (Pa. 1999)
    Commonwealth v. Chambers, 35 A.3d 34 (Pa. Super. 2011)
    Commonwealth v. Cintora, 69 A.3d 759 (Pa. Super. 2013)
    Commonwealth v. Copenhefer, 941 A.2d 646 (Pa. 2007)
    Commonwealth v. Cunningham, 81 A.3d 1 (Pa. 2013)
    Commonwealth v. Feliciano, 69 A.3d 1270 (Pa. Super. 2013)
    Commonwealth v. Garcia, 23 A.3d 1059 (Pa. Super. 2011)
    Commonwealth v. Ghisoiu, 63 A.3d 1272 (Pa. Super. 2013)
    Commonwealth v. Hughes, 865 A.2d 761 (Pa. 2004)
    Commonwealth v. Miller, 102 A.3d 988 (Pa. Super. 2014)
    Commonwealth v. Moss, 871 A.2d 853 (Pa. Super. 2005)
    Commonwealth v. Riggle, 119 A.3d 1058 (Pa. Super. 2015)
    Commonwealth v. Secreti, 134 A.3d 77 (Pa. Super. 2016)
    Commonwealth v. Sneed, 899 A.2d 1067 (Pa. 2006)
    Commonwealth v. Spotz, 896 A.2d 1191 (Pa. 2006)
    Commonwealth v. Washington, 142 A.3d 810 (Pa. 2016)
    Commonwealth v. Wojtaszek, 951 A.2d 1169 (Pa. Super. 2008)
    Danforth v. Minnesota, 552 U.S. 264 (2008)
    Schriro v. Summerlin, 542 U.S. 348, 351 (2004)
    Teague v. Lane, 489 U.S. 288 (1989)
right to PCRA counsel—*pgs. 195-197, 213-214, 219-240, 248, 256, 362, 364-365, 369, 377*
    Coleman v. Thompson, 501 U.S. 722 (1991)

Quick Index/Case References

    Commonwealth v. Albert, 561 A.2d 736 (Pa. 1989)
    Commonwealth v. Albrecht, 720 A.2d 693 (Pa. 1998)
    Commonwealth v. Auchmuty, 799 A.2d 823 (Pa. Super. 2002)
    Commonwealth v. Brooks, 875 A.2d 1141 (Pa. Super. 2005)
    Commonwealth v. Christy, 656 A.2d 877 (Pa. 1995)
    Commonwealth v. Colavita, 993 A.2d 874 (Pa. 2010)
    Commonwealth v. Duffey, 713 A.2d 63 (Pa. 1998)
    Commonwealth v. Davis, 526 A.2d 440 (Pa. Super. 1987)
    Commonwealth v. Ferguson, 722 A.2d 177 (Pa. Super. 1998)
    Commonwealth v. Figueroa, 29 A.3d 1177 (Pa. Super. 2011)
    Commonwealth v. Ford, 44 A.3d 1190 (Pa. Super. 2012)
    Commonwealth v. Hampton, 718 A.2d 1250 (Pa. Super. 1998)
    Commonwealth v. Irons, 385 A.2d 1004 (Pa. Super. 1978)
    Commonwealth v. Jackson, 965 A.2d 280 (Pa. Super. 2009)
    Commonwealth v. Jette, 23 A.3d 1032 (Pa. 2011)
    Commonwealth v. Kutnyak, 781 A.2d 1259 (Pa. Super. 2001)
    Commonwealth v. Lasky, 934 A.2d 120 (Pa. Super. 2007)
    Commonwealth v. Ligons, 971 A.2d 1125 (Pa. 2009)
    Commonwealth v. Malone, 823 A.2d 931 (Pa. Super. 2003)
    Commonwealth v. Perez, 799 A.2d 848 (Pa. Super. 2002)
    Commonwealth v. Pitts, 981 A.2d 875 (Pa. 2009)
    Commonwealth v. Powell, 787 A.2d 1017 (Pa. Super. 2001)
    Commonwealth v. Priovolos, 715 A.2d 420 (Pa. 1998)
    Commonwealth v. Quail, 729 A.2d 571 (Pa. Super. 1999)
    Commonwealth v. Ramos, 14 A.3d 894 (Pa. Super. 2011)
    Commonwealth v. Smith, 818 A.2d 494 (Pa. 2003)
    Commonwealth v. Staton, 120 A.3d 277 (Pa. 2015)
    Commonwealth v. Stossel, 17 A.3d 1286 (Pa. Super. 2011)
    Commonwealth v. Tedford, 781 A.2d 1167 (Pa. 2001)
    Commonwealth v. Wiley, 966 A.2d 1153 (Pa. Super. 2009)
    Commonwealth v. Williams, 950 A.2d 294 (Pa. 2008)
    Martinez v. Ryan, 132 S.Ct. 1309 (2012)
    Murray v. Giarratano, 492 U.S. 1 (1989)
    Pennsylvania v. Finley, 481 U.S. 551 (1987)

Rule 600—*pgs. 46, 130, 297*
    Commonwealth v. Anderson, 995 A.2d 1184 (Pa. Super. 2010)
    Commonwealth v. Prout, 814 A.2d 693 (Pa. Super. 2003)

scope of the PCRA—*pgs. 16-38, 62, 66, 78, 391*

Quick Index/Case References

>Commonwealth v. Descardes, 101 A.3d 105 (Pa. Super. 2014) (*en banc*), *reversed at*, 136 A.3d 493 (Bowes, J., concurring and dissenting)
>Commonwealth v. Haun, 32 A.3d 697 (Pa. 2011)
>Commonwealth v. Haun, 984 A.2d 557 (Pa. Super. 2009)
>Commonwealth v. Heredia, 97 A.3d 392 (Pa. Super. 2014)
>Joseph v. Glunt, 96 A.3d 365 (Pa. Super. 2014)

second or subsequent petitions; *serial petitions*—pgs. 72, 144, 151, 155, 159-161, 165, 190, 207, 209, 215, 217, 240, 247-248, 251-252, 255, 259, 257, 275, 278, 285, 292, 298, 362, 364, 376, 379

>Commonwealth v. Figueroa, 29 A.3d 1177 (Pa. Super. 2011)
>Commonwealth v. Fowler, 930 A.2d 586 (Pa. Super. 2007)
>Commonwealth v. Kubis, 808 A.2d 196 (Pa. Super. 2002)
>Commonwealth v. Lawson, 549 A.2d 107 (Pa. 1988)
>Commonwealth v. O'Bidos, 849 A.2d 243 (Pa. Super. 2004)
>Commonwealth v. Porter, 35 A.3d 4 (Pa. 2012)
>Commonwealth v. Rienzi, 827 A.2d 369 (Pa. 2003)
>Commonwealth v. Szuchon, 633 A.2d 1098 (Pa. 1993)
>Commonwealth v. Tedford, 781 A.2d 1167 (Pa. 2001)
>Commonwealth v. Williams, 828 A.2d 981 (Pa. 2003)

self representation; *alleging own ineffectiveness*—pgs. 62, 216, 235-236, 289-90

>Commonwealth v. Appel, 689 A.2d 891 (Pa. 1997)
>Commonwealth v. Blakeney, 108 A.3d 739 (Pa. 2014)
>Commonwealth v. Fletcher, 986 A.2d 759 (Pa. 2009)
>Commonwealth v. Green, 709 A.2d 382 (Pa. 1998)
>Commonwealth v. Marts, 889 A.2d 608 (Pa. Super. 2005)
>In re B.S., 831 A.2d 151 (Pa. Super. 2003)

Simmons instruction—pg. 114

>Commonwealth v. Lesko, 15 A.3d 345 (Pa. 2011)
>Commonwealth v. Ly, 980 A.2d 61 (Pa. 2009)
>Commonwealth v. Paddy, 15 A.3d 431 (Pa. 2011)
>Commonwealth v. Rollins, 738 A.2d 435 (Pa. 1999)
>Commonwealth v. Watkins, 108 A.3d 692 (Pa. 2014)
>Commonwealth v. Williams, 732 A.2d 1167 (Pa. 1999)

spousal privilege—pg. 117

>Commonwealth v. Hancharik, 633 A.2d 1074 (Pa. 1993)
>Commonwealth v. Savage, 695 A.2d 820 (Pa. Super. 1997)

Quick Index/Case References

standard of review—pgs. 287-288, 357, 383
 Commonwealth v. *Baumhammers*, 92 A.3d 708 (Pa. 2014)
 Commonwealth v. *Colavita*, 993 A.2d 874 (Pa. 2010)
 Commonwealth v. *Fahy*, 959 A.2d 312 (Pa. 2008)
 Commonwealth v. *Reaves*, 923 A.2d 1119 (Pa. 2007)
Strickland v. Washington, 466 U.S. 668 (1984)--*pgs. 25-26, 54-61, 89, 171, 246, 296, 319, 388*
subject matter jurisdiction—pgs. 40-41, 73, 117, 123, 129-130, 151, 157
 Commonwealth v. *Butler*, 566 A.2d 1209 (Pa. Super. 1989)
 Commonwealth v. *Martorano*, 89 A.3d 301 (Pa. Super. 2014)
 Commonwealth v. *Quinlan*, 639 A.2d 1235 (Pa. Super. 1994)
 Commonwealth v. *Stultz*, 114 A.3d 865 (Pa. Super. 2015)
suppression—pgs. 108-110, 307, 359-363, 369, 372, 418
 Commonwealth v. *Arch*, 654 A.2d 1141 (Pa. Super. 1995)
 Commonwealth v. *Boyer*, 962 A.2d 1213 (Pa. Super. 2008)
 Commonwealth v. *Davido*, 106 A.3d 611 (Pa. 2014)
 Commonwealth v. *Franklin*, 990 A.2d 795 (Pa. Super. 2010)
 Commonwealth v. *Harris*, 972 A.2d 1196 (Pa. Super. 2009)
 Commonwealth v. *Hill*, 104 A.3d 1220 (Pa. 2014)
 Commonwealth v. *Kilgore*, 719 A.2d 754 (Pa. Super. 1998)
 Commonwealth v. *Nelson*, 574 A.2d 1107 (Pa. Super. 1990)
 Commonwealth v. *Vealey*, 581 A.2d 217 (Pa. Super. 1990)
timeliness—pgs. 17, 20-21, 24-25, 53, 70-71, 82-83, 85, 88, 121, 143-144, 154-173, 201, 212-213, 215, 221-223, 227, 246-247, 287, 292-294, 297, 299, 300, 301, 310, 361-364, 369, 376-379, 381, 386, 392, 396, 403, 407, 412
 Commonwealth v. *Anderson*, 788 A.2d 1019 (Pa. Super. 2001)
 Commonwealth v. *Baldwin*, 789 A.2d 728 (Pa. Super. 2001)
 Commonwealth v. *Baroni*, 827 A.2d 419 (Pa. 2003)
 Commonwealth v. *Beasley*, 741 A.2d 1258 (Pa. 1999)
 Commonwealth v. *Bennett*, 930 A.2d 1264 (Pa. 2007)
 Commonwealth v. *Berry*, 877 A.2d 479 (Pa. Super. 2005 (*en banc*)
 Commonwealth v. *Breakiron*, 781 A.2d 94 (Pa. 2001)
 Commonwealth v. *Brown*, 943 A.2d 264 (Pa. 2008)

Quick Index/Case References

Commonwealth v. Burton, 121 A.3d 1063 (Pa. Super. 2015) (*en banc*), *allowance of appeal granted*, 134 A.3d 446 (Pa. 2016).
Commonwealth v. Callahan, 101 A.3d 118 (Pa. Super. 2014)
Commonwealth v. Cappello, 823 A.2d 936 (Pa. Super. 2003)
Commonwealth v. Crawley, 739 A.2d 108 (Pa. 1999)
Commonwealth v. Crider, 735 A.2d 730 (Pa. Super. 1999)
Commonwealth v. Davis, 816 A.2d 1129 (Pa. Super. 2003)
Commonwealth v. Fahy, 959 A.2d 312 (Pa. 2008)
Commonwealth v. Fahy, 737 A.2d 214 (Pa. 1999)
Commonwealth v. Fairiror, 809 A.2d 396 (Pa. Super. 2002)
Commonwealth v. Fowler, 930 A.2d 586 (Pa. Super. 2007)
Commonwealth v. Garcia, 23 A.3d 1059 (Pa. Super. 2011)
Commonwealth v. Harris, 972 A.2d 1196 (Pa. Super. 2009)
Commonwealth v. Hutchins, 760 A.2d 50 (Pa. Super. 2000)
Commonwealth v. Jackson, 30 A.3d 516 (Pa. Super. 2011)
Commonwealth v. Kubis, 808 A.2d 196 (Pa. Super. 2002)
Commonwealth v. Lambert, 884 A.2d 848 (Pa. 2005)
Commonwealth v. Lesko, 15 A.3d 345 (Pa. 2011)
Commonwealth v. Owens, 718 A.2d 330 (Pa. Super. 1998)
Commonwealth v. Perrin, 947 A.2d 1284 (Pa. Super. 2008)
Commonwealth v. Pursell, 749 A.2d 911 (Pa. 2000)
Commonwealth v. Robinson, 837 A.2d 1157 (Pa. 2003)
Commonwealth v. Saunders, 60 A.3d 162 (Pa. Super. 2013)
Commonwealth v. Stokes, 959 A.2d 306 (Pa. 2008)
Commonwealth v. Stout, 978 A.2d 984 (Pa. Super. 2009)
Commonwealth v. Taylor, 65 A.3d 462 (Pa. Super. 2013)
Commonwealth v. Taylor, 933 A.2d 1035 (Pa. Super. 2007)
Commonwealth v. Thomas, 718 A.2d 326 (Pa. Super. 1998) (*en banc*)
Commonwealth v. Wilson, 824 A.2d 331 (Pa. Super. 2003)
Commonwealth v. Yarris, 731 A.2d 581 (Pa. 1999)

Turner/Finley—*pgs. 83, 103, 192, 194-200, 213, 215-217, 229, 238-239, 246, 257-259, 261-264, 293-294, 298-302, samples—pgs 315-325, 328-329, 362, 382-390*

Commonwealth v. Bond, 630 A.2d 1281 (Pa. Super. 1993)
Commonwealth v. Dukeman, 605 A.2d 418 (Pa. Super. 1992)
Commonwealth v. Doty, 48 A.3d 451 (Pa. Super. 2012)

Quick Index/Case References

Commonwealth v. Finley, 550 A.2d 213 (Pa. Super. 1988) (*en banc*)
Commonwealth v. Friend, 896 A.2d 607 (Pa. Super. 2006)
Commonwealth v. Glover, 738 A.2d 460 (Pa. Super. 1999)
Commonwealth v. Hampton, 718 A.2d 1250 (Pa. Super. 1998)
Commonwealth v. Jones, 932 A.2d 179 (Pa. Super. 2007)
Commonwealth v. Karanicolas, 836 A.2d 940 (Pa. Super. 2003)
Commonwealth v. Liebensperger, 904 A.2d 40 (Pa. Super. 2008)
Commonwealth v. Maple, 559 A.2d 953 (Pa. Super. 1989)
Commonwealth v. Pitts, 981 A.2d 875 (Pa. 2009)
Commonwealth v. Porter, 728 A.2d 890 (Pa. 1999)
Commonwealth v. Rykard, 55 A.3d 1177 (Pa. Super. 2012)
Commonwealth v. Schultz, 707 A.2d 513 (Pa. Super. 1997)
Commonwealth v. Turner, 544 A.2d 927 (Pa. 1988)
Commonwealth v. Widgins, 29 A.3d 816 (Pa. Super. 2011)
Commonwealth v. Willis, 29 A.3d 393 (Pa. Super. 2011)
Pennsylvania v. Finley, 481 U.S. 551 (1987)
untimely post-sentence motion—*pgs. 100, 102, 214*
Commonwealth v. Evans, 866 A.2d 442 (Pa. Super. 2005)
Commonwealth v. Guthrie, 749 A.2d 502 (Pa. Super. 2000)
Commonwealth v. Hockenberry, 689 A.2d 283 (Pa. Super. 1997) (*en banc*)
Commonwealth v. Wrecks, 934 A.2d 1287 (Pa. Super. 2007)
voluntary intoxication; *see diminished capacity*
waiver—*pgs. 42, 66, 70-71, 73, 75, 78-79, 89, 103, 113, 145-150, 205, 217, 220, 223, 245, 290, 294-295, 402*
Commonwealth v. Allen, 732 A.2d 582 (Pa. 1999)
Commonwealth v. Berry, 877 A.2d 479 (Pa. Super. 2005 (*en banc*)
Commonwealth v. Blakeney, 108 A.3d 739 (Pa. 2014)
Commonwealth v. Brown, 872 A.2d 1139 (Pa. 2005)
Commonwealth v. Butler, 756 A.2d 55 (Pa. Super. 2000)
Commonwealth v. Fahy, 737 A.2d 214 (Pa. 1999)
Commonwealth v. Hanyon, 772 A.2d 1033 (Pa. Super. 2001)
Commonwealth v. Hill, 16 A.3d 484 (Pa. 2011)
Commonwealth v. Judge, 779 A.2d 250 (Pa. 2002)

Quick Index/Case References

Commonwealth v. Kenney, 732 A.2d 1161 (Pa. 1999)
Commonwealth v. Kindler, 722 A.2d 143 (Pa. 1998)
Commonwealth v. Morales, 701 A.2d 516 (Pa. 1997)
Commonwealth v. Ousley, 21 A.3d 1238 (Pa. Super. 2011)
Commonwealth v. Quaranibal, 763 A.2d 941 (Pa. Super. 2000)
Commonwealth v. Reyes, 870 A.2d 888 (Pa. 2005)
Commonwealth v. Simpson, 66 A.3d 253 (Pa. 2013)
Commonwealth v. Wallace, 724 A.2d 916 (Pa. 1999)
Commonwealth v. Walls, 993 A.2d 289 (Pa. Super. 2010)

witness certifications—pgs. 153, 174-175, 186, 247, 299, 302, 311-314

Commonwealth v. Brown, 767 A.2d 576 (Pa. Super. 2001)
Commonwealth v. McLaurin, 45 A.3d 1131 (Pa. Super. 2012)
Commonwealth v. Pander, 100 A.3d 626 (Pa. Super. 2014) (*en banc*)

witnesses, failure to call and interview—pgs. 93-96

Commonwealth v. Carbone, 707 A.2d 1145 (Pa. Super. 1998)
Commonwealth v. Dennis, 950 A.2d 945 (Pa. 2008)
Commonwealth v. Hall, 872 A.2d 1177 (Pa. 2005)
Commonwealth v. Hall, 701 A.2d 190 (Pa. 1997)
Commonwealth v. Hull, 982 A.2d 1020 (Pa. Super. 2009)
Commonwealth v. Johnson, 815 A.2d 563 (Pa. 2002)
Commonwealth v. Mabie, 359 A.2d 369 (Pa. 1976)
Commonwealth v. Matias, 63 A.3d 807 (Pa. Super. 2013) (*en banc*)
Commonwealth v. Morales, 701 A.2d 516 (Pa. 1997)
Commonwealth v. Perry, 644 A.2d 705 (Pa. 1994)
Commonwealth v. Stewart, 84 A.3d 701 (Pa. Super. 2013) (*en banc*)
Commonwealth v. Weiss, 606 A.2d 439 (Pa. 1992)

withdrawing petition—pgs. 159, 181

Commonwealth v. Bronshtein, 729 A.2d 1102 (Pa. 1999)
Commonwealth v. Rienzi, 827 A.2d 369 (Pa. 2003)
Commonwealth v. Wright, 78 A.3d 1070 (Pa. 2013)

P

Wednesday
↳

VA LLCs
↳ Grayson is no longer used

Dis